THE BATTLE OF LEYTE GULF

Twentieth-Century Battles

Spencer C. Tucker, Editor

THE
BATTLE
OF
LEYTE GULF
The Last Fleet Action

H. P. WILLMOTT

INDIANA UNIVERSITY PRESS

BLOOMINGTON AND INDIANAPOLIS

This book is a publication of

Indiana University Press
601 North Morton Street
Bloomington, IN 47404-3797 USA

http://iupress.indiana.edu

Telephone orders	800-842-6796
Fax orders	812-855-7931
Orders by e-mail	iuporder@indiana.edu

The paper used in this publication meets the minimum
requirements of American National Standard for Information
Sciences—Permanence of Paper for Printed Library Materials, ANSI
Z39.48-1984.

Manufactured in the United States of America

· Library of Congress Cataloging-in-Publication Data

Willmott, H. P.
The battle of Leyte Gulf : the last fleet action / H.P. Willmott.
p. cm. — (Twentieth-century battles)
Includes bibliographical references and index.
ISBN 0-253-34528-6 (cloth : alk. paper)
1. Leyte Gulf, Battle of, Philippines, 1944. I. Title. II. Series.
D774.P5W56 2005
940.54'25995—dc22
2005000730

1 2 3 4 5 10 09 08 07 06 05

Dedicated to FY1645
and
in Praise of
Dissent, Uncertainty, and Tolerance

The
chance
to
bloom
as
Flowers of Death

CONTENTS

MAPS

TABLES

DIAGRAMS

ACKNOWLEDGMENTS

IN THE PREPARATION of this book acknowledgment must be made to those who, over many years and whether in the form of conferences, letters, or general conversation, provided me with the basis of knowledge and critical facility that made this work possible. To attempt to list these people is impossible, but they have the satisfaction of knowing that without them this book could never have been written and also that they are not responsible for the various errors, the sins of omission and commission, that litter its pages.

Nonetheless, specific acknowledgment needs to be made to individuals who spent many hours helping me try to settle a host of difficulties that arose in the course of this book's writing. I would specifically acknowledge and offer my sincere and unreserved gratitude for the help I received from Dr. Robert M. Browning, historian, U.S. Coast Guard headquarters, Washington, D.C.; Dr. Robert J. Cressman and Dr. Randy Papadopolous, Naval Historical Center, Washington, D.C.; Gary A. LaValley, archivist at the Nimitz Library, U.S. Naval Academy; Brett Mitchell of the Naval History Section in the Australian Department of Defence; and Barry L. Zerby of the National Archives, Washington, D.C., for all the help they afforded in the completion of the Allied order of battle, and to Kobayashi Go and Shindo Hiroyuki of the Military History Department, National Institute for Defence Studies, for all the help they afforded in the completion of the Japanese order of battle. I would wish to acknowledge the advice and assistance I received from Michael Coles, Professor Ken Hagen, Commander John Kuehn, USN, Captain Gerard Roncolato, USN, Professor John Sweetman, and Steven Weingartner in putting together and then testing various matters that together went into one of the appendixes. I would specifically wish to acknowledge all the help and personal kindnesses afforded me by

Captain William Spencer and Andrea Johnson, Professor Spencer C. and Beverly Tucker, and Professor Tohmatsu Haruo, Tamagawa University; they always seemed to be with me in the writing, and without hesitation offered and provided help far beyond the call of friendship.

I would note, however, that acknowledgment has to be made to other professional colleagues and friends who provided me with support and encouragement at a time of personal and professional disaster, and without whose comfort and support what were truly difficult times would have been nearly impossible. Among those I would acknowledge are Tim Bean, Patrick Birks, Tony Clayton, Nigel and Martine de Lee, Christopher Duffy, Paul Harris and Cliff Krieger, Jim Mattis, George Raach, John Votaw, and John Andreas and Tine Olsen. I would not wish to thank one more than another; to these especially, but to all who have helped me, I owe a special debt that I will attempt to discharge in due course. And with these I would add, not as an afterthought but deliberately, Professor Sarah Palmer of Greenwich Maritime Institute and my present colleagues at The Citadel for the confidence they have shown in me by virtue of my present employment. Their faith, commitment, and loyalty I appreciate beyond my poor power to acknowledge in these lines.

I also wish to acknowledge my debt to those without whose patience, tact, and ability this book would probably have gone the way of many of the ships cited in these pages. Specifically I would wish to acknowledge my debts to Robert Sloan, Jane Quinet, Jane Lyle, Drew Bryan, and Keith Chaffer, and I trust they will accept this acknowledgment of their support and efforts. I trust they will not try to amend this poor acknowledgment of their efforts.

There remains one group that always appears in my acknowledgments section and for one reason: they have been the means of ensuring sanity. I would acknowledge my debts to and my love for my dogs, Everton, Sherry, Kondor, Jamie, and Suki; I trust they are at peace. I would acknowledge my present debt to and love for Lancaster, Mishka, and Cassie and for Junior and Yanya; I trust much time will pass before they join their predecessors and chase together across the celestial fields.

H. P. Willmott

Mark W. Clark Chair   Visiting Lecturer
Department of History   Greenwich Maritime Institute
The Citadel   University of Greenwich
Charleston, South Carolina   London SE
25 October 2004

THE BATTLE OF LEYTE GULF

THE BATTLE OF LEYTE GULF

CHAPTER ONE

THE NATURE OF WAR
AND OF VICTORY

ONE IS TEMPTED to suggest that there are only two problems in the study of naval history: naval historians and naval officers. The study of naval power and naval history is the prerogative of those who lack either or both. Those with naval power are never to be found in the ranks of theorists and commentators since their only concern is its use. And, with a few honorable exceptions, naval officers hold views and opinions in inverse relationship to knowledge. They hold to ignorance and lack of learning with such certainty of conviction that they have achieved what would seem to be the impossible: they make army officers appear both liberal and well-educated.

Alfred Thayer Mahan meets the least demanding of all these criteria with much to spare, and it is difficult to overstate the pernicious, anachronistic influence of this naval officer's writings in terms of the understanding of twentieth-century warfare. Mahan wrote of naval power that for the most part, though not always, he identified with battle formations, and he wrote of the primacy of battle and exercise of command of the sea as a result of victory in battle. To Mahan the various elements flowed from one to another, and critically he wrote at a time of massive certainties. He identified British victory at sea as the product of national characteristics, the nature of the state and government institutions, and, inevitably, in terms of the deeds of great men, as befitted a product of the Carlyle school. There was in Mahan's writings no recognition that British victories were the product of British supremacy at sea in terms of warship numbers, geographical position, and the British state's financial strength, and there was no appreciation, amid the certainty that "history is about chaps," of the reality and significance of systemic warfare.

The battle of Leyte Gulf was an extremely unusual battle. It was unusual on five separate counts that are so obvious that they are usually missed. It was unusual in that it was a series of actions, not a single battle. It was unusual as a naval battle in that it was fought over five days; historically, naval battles have seldom spread themselves over more than one or two days. It was unusual in terms of its name. This battle involved a series of related actions subsequently grouped together under the name of just one of these engagements, but in fact none of the actions were fought inside Leyte Gulf. This name was different from the name given to these actions at the time. Its contemporaneous name was "The Battle of the Philippines, 24–25 October 1944." Perhaps it should have been "The Naval Battle for the Philippines," and the dates may be disputed, but nonetheless this was a more accurate title and definition of the actions than the name or names that have been handed down over subsequent decades and with which we are presently familiar.

More importantly, it was unusual in that it was a full-scale fleet action fought after the issue of victory and defeat at sea had been decided, and it was unusual in that it resulted in clear, overwhelming victory and defeat. So much of naval accounting concerns itself with the day of battle, but the nature and extent of the American naval victory in October 1944 was twofold, a double set of sinkings, those that took place in the course of the various actions that together form this battle and those that followed in the next month as American forces secured command of the skies over and the seas that washed the Philippines. In this second period the Americans sank more Japanese warships in theater than they had sunk in the battle itself, while Japanese service and merchant shipping, bereft of cover and support, incurred losses that were more than three times those sustained during the period of the battle. Herein one touches upon a reality of war that confounds easy analysis and presentation. If one looks, for example, at Japanese shipping losses in the last full month of war, in July 1945, one notes that all but three of Japan's 123 service and merchant shipping losses were incurred in home waters or the East China Sea. Such losses, and where they were incurred, most definitely indicate that Japan had lost all semblance of strategic mobility by this stage of proceedings, but more seriously these losses pose the question of whether they were the cause or the result of defeat. The answer, of course, is both, and for the good reason that the route between victory and defeat is a two-way, not a one-way, street. The Japanese losses of July 1945 were most definitely the result of a defeat that had already taken shape, but they contributed to and hastened the final form of that defeat. The Japanese losses at Leyte Gulf and in the month after the battle seemingly must be the cause of defeat because of its distance in time from the final act of August 1945, but in reality the losses incurred in these battles for the Philippines in October 1944 by the *Nippon Teikoku Kaigun*, the Imperial Japanese Navy, were the product of defeat; the decision of the war had been passed by this time.

It is possible to argue that the decision of the war had been reached, if not with the Japanese attack on the U.S. Pacific Fleet at its Pearl Harbor base on 7 December 1941, then sometime before November 1943, the month which witnessed the start of the American offensive across the central Pacific. In this offensive the Americans moved with a strength that ensured that the objective could be isolated and overwhelmed before it could be supported by either Japanese land-based aircraft or *Kaigun* fleet formations. Thereafter, the American offensives across the central and southwest Pacific and thence to the approaches of the Philippines represented no more than applied, and improved, technique. The questions that remained to be answered after this time, given the *Kaigun's* inability to offer effective resistance to American offensives, was the exact nature and timing of Japan's various defeats and the cost that would be exacted in the process; the outcome of operations was never in question. In these matters acknowledgment of one matter is crucial to any understanding of Japan's defeat in the Second World War. The *Kaigun* was defeated in this war, and national defeat thereby ensured, not because the *Kaigun* was defeated by an American navy, but by two American navies. The Imperial Japanese Navy was checked and fought to a standstill, to a point of mutual exhaustion, by the pre-war U.S. Navy, but it was another U.S. Navy, a wartime navy largely built after December 1941, that took the war to the Japanese home islands.

Lest these points seem somewhat obtuse, clarification can be sought by reference to one set of statistics relating to the battle and its outcome, of the relationship between supremacy and victory. Historical attention

naturally has tended to focus upon the carrier and battle groups in this battle, but on the American side there were no fewer than nineteen major task
groups employed in the various actions that go under the collective name
of Leyte Gulf, and these formations between them numbered nine fleet,
eight light fleet, and twenty-nine escort carriers, twelve battleships, twelve
heavy and sixteen light cruisers, 178 destroyers, forty destroyer escorts, and
ten frigates. The link between supremacy and victory lies in the fact that
the Americans had more destroyers than the Japanese had carrier aircraft.
The basic point can be repeated by references to operations throughout the
last year of the Pacific war—in the great raid over the Inland Sea on 24–25
July 1945 Allied carriers employed 1,747 aircraft and flew combat air patrol
over Japanese airfields on Honshu—but really to no greater effect. The
point, once made, does not really improve with the retelling. It is sufficient
to note the obvious, namely that the relationship between supremacy and
victory cannot be gainsaid, but that supremacy does not alter the fact that
victories nonetheless have to be fought for and won.

Thus in our initial consideration of this battle its important aspects
have been cited: that the battle was fought after the issue of victory and
defeat at sea had been decided, that it resulted in clear, overwhelming victory and defeat, and that its outcome must be considered in terms of initial
and overwhelming American advantage. One would suggest that these
definitions sit ill alongside the standard representations of the battle, which
do not afford it such consideration, but one would also suggest that these
matters form only the starting point for our consideration of this battle, and
that there are other matters relating to the battle that deserve attention.

The first such matter is perhaps quixotic, but the battle of Leyte Gulf
included within itself one action, fought in the Surigao Strait, that represented the *dénouement* of the dreadnought battleship. This was one of
only two actions in the Pacific war, and one of only half a dozen actions
in the whole of the Second World War, when capital ships sought to fulfill
their *raison d'être* in battle with their opposite numbers. The battleship
remained in service in various navies into the fifties but thereafter only the
United States, at prohibitive cost in money and manpower, returned battleships to service before the last to be stricken, the *Missouri*, tied up for the
last time at Pearl Harbor on 16 June 1998. Yet in any examination of the
battle of Leyte Gulf few would note the appropriateness of the historical
finality of the Surigao Strait action: this action represents the counterpoint
to the battle of Manila Bay, fought on 1 May 1898. In that action, in which
battleships were not involved, one can see the origins of the dreadnought

battleship, but lest this point is not obvious, even less obvious is that this battle represented the last battle in the Age of Sail. It was an action fought on the one side by five American cruisers and two gunboats and on the other by four Spanish cruisers, three gunboats, and three other vessels. The Spanish warships, inferior in gun power and of dubious seaworthiness, were anchored under the cover of guns in the fortified base of Cavite. The battle resulted in the annihilation of the Spanish force though it was a victory that could not be exploited for two months because it was not until 30 June that American military formations arrived in the Philippines. In terms of other battles and the comparison and contrast that may be thus drawn, the obvious counters are Navarino (20 October 1827) and Sinope (30 November 1853), but these are too easy and simplistic. Why this action, the battle of Manila Bay, should be considered the last battle of the Age of Sail is on account of the nature of the action. It was fought without reference to mines, torpedoes, and submarines, and it was fought without reference to airships and aircraft. It was a battle fought with flags since there was no radio. All those elements with which we associate naval battle in the twentieth century, which were to figure so prominently in war at sea in the last century, were not present at Manila Bay in May 1898. This was a battle fought in line ahead with no centrally controlled firing systems and no means of firing individual guns other than by eye. It was an action that should immediately invoke thoughts of Quiberon Bay (1759), the Nile (1798), first and second Copenhagen (1801 and 1807) in terms of pedigree. Even though all the warships in Manila Bay in May 1898 were steam-powered, the battle they fought properly belonged to a previous age.

The portrayal of the dreadnought era, a representation of events by nature rather than exact dates, is perhaps a little perverse, but then mendacity, the arrangement of evidence to support a pre-conceived conclusion, is the necessary hallmark of a historian, evidence of the fact that anyone who wants to change history has to become a historian. But in any objective consideration of the battle of Leyte Gulf one would note that the battle of Leyte Gulf was the greatest naval battle in modern history, and indeed was one of the greatest naval battles of all time. Of course, as Shelby Foote noted about another episode, the portrayal of this battle thus in terms of the whole of history would be peculiarly American. But the normal criterion by which such definitions are made, numbers, is not particularly helpful in terms of the understanding of events and context. Much ink has been spilled in seeking to set out the claims of Leyte Gulf in this respect, but whether or not there were three or four more units giving battle in

October 1944 than there were at Jutland (31 May–1 June 1916) is of little real consequence. Moreover, there may well have been more ships in the waters that washed the Philippines in this fourth week of October 1944 than at either Lepanto (7 October 1571) or Salamis, which was fought more than twenty-four centuries before in September 480 B.C. In fact, there were probably fewer ships than there were galleys in these two Mediterranean battles, and in one respect Leyte Gulf does not begin to compare to two battles that really do represent *fin de siècle* in terms of Persian and Ottoman imperial aspirations and dreams of conquest. After the battle of Leyte Gulf, the Americans came into possession of no advantage that they had lacked before the battle, and in that respect it was not unlike Jutland and quite different from Salamis and Lepanto. Most certainly one would admit that numbers are important, that numbers do provide a guide to the significance of events, but numbers alone seldom provide the definitive statement of significance. It is numbers in association with some other aspect of events wherein true worth may be identified, and in the case of Leyte Gulf the true worth is to be found across area.

Naval battles, like air battles but unlike battles fought on land, are demarcated in terms of latitude, longitude, and time, and Leyte Gulf in effect saw a redefinition of such terms of reference. In 1898 the American area of deployment for the battle of Manila Bay was the line-ahead formation along the 628 miles between Hong Kong and Manila. The area of operations was perhaps ten and certainly no more than twenty square miles. At Leyte Gulf, the area of deployment covered an area of about 450,000 square miles, an area greater than France, Belgium, Luxembourg, the Netherlands, Germany, Switzerland, and Austria combined, or in American terms an area greater than Utah, Colorado, Arizona, and New Mexico together, while the area of operations, the area across which battle was joined, covered 115,000 square miles, an area slightly smaller than the British Isles or slightly larger than Nevada. And herein one touches upon a subject seldom addressed directly in the relevant histories: how battle on such a scale can be conducted. It is not individual commanders that are important in this matter but staffs, standard operating procedures, and coordination of efforts of different services and commands. Those histories that have sought to minimize Admiral William F. Halsey's responsibility for the situation whereby the route through the Visayans was left undefended on the night of 24–25 October 1944 have done little good for the cause of understanding, and for obvious reason. What was important was neither command nor areas of responsibility and interest that were not fully reconciled, but role and function. Halsey's responsibility for covering the San Bernardino Strait was not to be wished away by virtue of the fact that it was within South West Pacific Command's area of responsibility. With the carrier and battle forces under his command, Halsey was responsible for providing the support forces with cover. Yet he was faced with problems of distance and time that had been transformed since the Age of Sail but was physically no better served than commanders in the nineteenth century. Halsey and his staff could receive reconnaissance and contact reports from land-based aircraft, carrier- or ship-based aircraft, submarines, escort forces, perhaps even friendly forces ashore, and by radio from superior commands thousands of miles distant, yet the physical space and command facilities within a flagship were scarcely better than those of Nelson in the *Victory* in 1805.

In a real sense the battle of Leyte Gulf represented *fin de siècle* in terms of naval warfare as it had come to be represented over thousands of years—fought in a single dimension on the surface of the sea and within line of sight. By the dawn of the twentieth century the mine and torpedo, along with the submarine, served notice that such simplicity was passing, and within four years there had taken place the first controlled flight by a heavier-than-air flying machine. Within another four decades the opposed assault landing had presented itself as the fourth dimension of naval warfare, an eventuality that had never been needed in previous times that lacked mass armies and road and rail communications. In one obvious sense, Leyte Gulf presents itself as the point where these various elements came together, a sort of state that corresponds to perfection on the point of obsolescence, because within another generation the terms of reference of naval power were to be rewritten in the form of nuclear-powered submarines that had the role of assured second strike as the U.S. Navy assumed the role of mainstay of strategic deterrence. Less than twenty more years were to pass before space was to provide a hitherto untapped dimension of war. American carrier and other forces were involved in the Korean and Vietnamese wars and in a host of other episodes, of which the most obvious was the Cuban crisis of October 1962. In these wars and crises the United States employed ships that dated from the Second World War, many of which indeed were present at the battle of Leyte Gulf. But this action in a real sense forms one part of the series of offensives that in ending the Second World War spelled the end of the Age of Mass; it merely took another thirty years for this to become apparent.

In this respect it was not alone. It took a long time for the extent of the victory at Leyte Gulf to become apparent, and one wonders whether the real extent of the victory that had been won was ever fully and properly grasped by the American high command during the war itself. In this matter, Leyte Gulf was similar to the battle of the Philippine Sea, 19–20 June 1944, which, with thirteen fleet and eleven light fleet carriers on the two sides, was second only to Leyte Gulf as the greatest carrier battle in history, though the losses incurred were less than those off Midway Islands two years earlier (one American carrier and one destroyer and four Japanese carriers and one heavy cruiser). Nonetheless, it is with this battle in the Philippine Sea that this book necessarily starts because it was the American victory in this battle in June 1944 that bared the approaches to the Philippines and began the process whereby the various aspects of Japanese defeat began to come together.

The Japanese defeat in the Second World War was total and comprehensive. It possessed political and diplomatic dimensions, economic and industrial failure, and defeat in the air, at sea and on the islands of the Pacific and Southeast Asia, and on the Asian mainland in northeast India and Burma, southern China, and Manchuria and northern China. The Japanese failure was one that ultimately left her without allies to face the world's most populous power, China, the world's greatest empire, Britain, the world's foremost industrial, naval, and air power, the United States, and the world's greatest military power, the Soviet Union. It was a defeat that left Japan without any real friends and supporters in any of the conquered territories, in which there were people who were associated with Japan but no more; their power and importance was minimal, their relevance even less. From what time and occasion one can date Japan's defeat, the moment when one can identify the inevitability of Japan's final defeat, is very much a matter of individual choice. There is certainly a strong argument that this should be identified with the Pearl Harbor attack, that the entire Pacific war was for the Japanese something closely akin to a national *kamikaze* effort. In an obvious sense, there is little that can be said to contradict such a view; on the date that will live in infamy, the Japanese attacked the only state in the world that had the measure of their country and which could ensure her defeat. In an easily identifiable way the events that followed can be seen as the process whereby, amid initial defeats and then victories, massively superior American power was brought to bear upon a Japan that was dragged down to national defeat by the weight of industrial resources and military power mobilized against her.

Such a perspective seems possessed of some academic antiseptic, almost detached from war's fundamental characteristic, its dimension involving people collectively and as individuals. Wars are not resolved in so neat and painless a manner whereby sides might together look at a situation and decide what will be the outcome and thence move on. Victories have to be won, since they can never be commanded, and hence battles have to be fought. Herein the Japanese war, even if, with all the advantages of hindsight, its outcome could be predicted before, on, or at some time after 7 December 1941, conforms to the reality that campaigns and individual battles nonetheless had to be fought and won. Herein one can identify June 1944 as crucial in terms of the nature and conduct of the Pacific war. It was the month that saw the start of the American bombing of the Japanese home islands from bases in India and southern China, and June 1944 was the month when American forces came ashore on Saipan and provoked the *Kaigun* into giving battle in the Philippine Sea. This was the battle the Japanese lost in a triple sense. First, their carrier air groups were ripped to pieces in the course of this battle and were never reconstituted in the course of what remained of the Pacific war. Second, three Japanese fleet carriers were sunk, though only one, the *Hiyo*, was sunk by carrier aircraft. The other two, the *Shokaku* and *Taiho*, were sunk by the submarines *Cavalla* and *Albacore* respectively, outside, as it were, the terms of reference of the carrier battle *per se*. Third, the defeat produced both political and strategic crises for Japan, the political crisis in that it precipitated the fall of the Tojo government that had led Japan into war, and the strategic crisis in that in the aftermath of the battle the two complementary parts of Japan's defeat at sea came together.

These two aspects of Japan's defeat at sea were naval and maritime. The first necessarily involved main forces, the *raison d'être* of which was battle. This was an aspect of defeat that had seen American forces move to overwhelm Japanese forces in the Gilberts and Marshalls, land on Saipan in the central Pacific, secure various bases that resulted in the isolation of Rabaul, and undertake landings in northern New Guinea that reached almost to the Vogelkop. The process of advance involved landings and the construction of airfield and base facilities from which the next phase of advance could be supported, but in the course of these offensives the second aspect of Japan's defeat assumed a serious dimension. This was the mounting destruction of Japanese shipping, a matter imperfectly understood in most Western accounts of the Japanese war. For the most part these accounts note one matter, the formation of the General Escort

Command in November 1943, as crucial in the story of the Allied attack on Japanese shipping. In such accounts the Japanese attempt to institute convoy for shipping without adequate number of escorts, without escorts equipped with adequate means of detecting and attacking submarines, and, critically, without any real understanding of how and why convoys worked and the relationship between numbers of escorts and merchantmen in individual convoys, has been deemed crucial in exposing Japanese shipping to losses that quickly became overwhelming.

Between the outbreak of war and 31 October 1943 and in addition to 199 warships of 626,893 tons, Japan lost to all causes 149 naval auxiliary ships of 790,088 tons, 177 army transports of 725,120 tons, and 214 merchantmen of 792,804 tons; these totals indicate overall shipping losses of 2,308,012 tons and an average monthly loss of 25.93 ships of 101,451 tons. What is so notable about these losses was the negligible contribution of carrier aircraft to the process of destruction of shipping, but this changed in the next phase of the war between November 1943 and June 1944. In this eight-month phase, Japanese losses more or less equaled what had been lost over the previous two years. Totals of 196 warships of 335,046 tons, 225.5 naval auxiliaries of 1,115,389 tons, 174 army transports of 667,333 tons, and 154.5 merchantmen of 519,187 tons were lost to all causes. In other words, in this single period when the Americans broke into the outer layer of Japanese defenses in the central Pacific and bypassed Rabaul, the Japanese lost 554 ships of 2,301,909 tons, or an average of 69.25 ships of 287,739 tons per month.

The real increase in losses was not so much among the merchantmen, though their rate of losses more or less doubled, as among service shipping obliged to operate in waters directly controlled by American carrier aircraft and infested by submarines deployed in support of specific landing operations. In this phase of the war submarines accounted for 225 service ships of 1,099,451 tons and 89 merchantmen of 367,823 tons, while carrier aircraft, most notably in the great raid on Truk in February 1944, accounted for 76.5 service ships of 420,337 tons but only three merchantmen of just 4,375 tons. Shore-based aircraft, so often the Cinderella at this particular ball, accounted for 71 service ships of 202,349 and 23 merchantmen of 56,970 tons.

The significance of these losses is that in this period, between November 1943 and June 1944, losses in the southern resources area assumed genuinely serious levels for the first time, and for the first time the Americans, after their victory in the Philippine Sea, were in a position to move directly against Japanese holdings throughout this area. Prior to November 1943 Japan's losses in the region from which she drew so much of the raw materials vital to her war effort amounted to 35 merchantmen of 134,613 tons, less than two merchantmen a month, still less than five a month with service losses added to the scales. Japan lost only one ship every six days in theater. Losses in this second phase, that ended with the battle in the Philippine Sea, increased fourfold, but losses in theater were not particularly heavy in either May or June 1944 as submarine activity was curtailed in readiness for the landings in the Marianas, or in July, when the effect of previous deployment still lingered. Now, however, the Americans were poised to move on the Philippines and thence astride Japan's lines of communication between the home islands and the southern resources area. Japan's shipping would be obliged to negotiate these waters if the nation was to continue to wage war.

Even without any appearance of the carriers, both Japanese service ship and merchantmen losses in this theater separately rose to more than 100,000 tons in August 1944, and in the following month carrier aircraft alone accounted for almost 200,000 tons of shipping, while all losses in theater reached nearly 350,000 tons. The significance of these figures is that pre-war Japanese calculations, or miscalculations, indicated that Japan could not afford shipping losses of more than 75,000 tons a month, but in fact Japanese yards barely exceeded half that much output in 1942 and 1943. In 1944, it is true, Japanese yards nearly doubled output of service and merchant shipping, but by this stage the Japanese shipping position was beyond recall. The losses incurred already were too great to be replaced, and Japanese imports were already in a decline that was to assume disastrous proportions in 1945.

In 1941 Japanese imports reached the scales at 48,720,000 tons, declining to 39,840,000 tons in 1942, falling slightly to 36,400,000 tons in 1943 before plummeting to 21,780,000 tons in 1944. In the seven and a half months of war in 1945, Japanese imports totaled just 7,710,000 tons, and this collapse, by over two-fifths in 1944 and by almost two-thirds in a shortened 1945, represents the starting point for our examination of events, since it was the promise and the threat that the Americans would move into the Philippines, and thence against Japanese shipping lines to the southern resources area, that provides the terms of reference for the situation that existed in the aftermath of the battle of the Philippine Sea.

CHAPTER TWO

THE OPTION OF DIFFICULTIES

The American Situation in the Aftermath
of the Victory in the Philippine Sea

WAR LENDS ITSELF to the sound bite as instant wisdom, but amid the cli-
chés and the wisdom that single sentences allegedly impart to proceedings,
two perhaps have relevance to the situation that confronted the United
States in the wake of her navy's victory in the Philippine Sea in June 1944.
The first, taken from Wavell's writings of some eighty years ago, is that war
is an option of difficulties. The most obvious and immediate difficulties
exist at the point of contact with the enemy, but the argument that Wavell
made was that the option of difficulties exists at each and every level of war.
The second, source unknown, is one that has been handed down to us,
and it is quite simply that wars never solve problems. Wars might transpose
problems or might alter problems, but wars never produce solutions.

In examining these truisms one is struck by the variety of difficulties.
These could be physical or abstract, man-made or natural, yet whether
one's first attention is fixed upon the operational or tactical, the historical
account necessarily must fix its first consideration upon the strategic or,
to use the term that was applied in the first half of the twentieth century,
the grand strategic, level of war. Herein, any child of Clausewitz must
encounter problems because his trinity necessarily involves rationalism,
reason, yet any examination of the framing of national policy, and even
more obviously alliance policy, immediately brings to the fore those considerations and calculations that are not rational. In waging war one thinks
instinctively that reason will apply at the grand strategic level and that this

is the one area of struggle that can be examined in relative ease in terms of the identification of objectives, the ordering of priorities, and the allocation of resources. But, of course, if this were the case then Wavell would have been wrong.

The American victory in the Philippine Sea in June 1944 is notable on two counts at the grand strategic level. It was the month that saw the United States come of age, when the irresponsibility of post-1918 adolescence was superseded by entry into the national inheritance as the world's greatest and only truly global power. June 1944 saw American forces enter Rome and other American forces, along with those of Britain, Canada, and other allies, establish themselves ashore in northwest Europe. It was a month that saw the strength of the 8th Air Force reach 2,000 heavy bombers, and it was a month that saw other American heavy bombers strike for the first time against the Japanese home islands from bases in China. June 1944 saw a second American amphibious endeavor, half a world away from Normandy, and it was this effort that led to the battle of the Philippine Sea, which was the greatest naval battle fought to date in the Pacific and indeed in terms of carrier, battleship, and cruiser numbers was the greatest naval battle of all time.[1] June 1944 was one of those moments in history when Time itself waited upon events that all involved knew possessed fundamental, overwhelming importance. It was the month that ensured that Germany and Japan could not avoid utter and total defeat, the month that ensured the eclipse of Europe. It was the month of arrival in the American century. For the second count, June 1944 saw the coming together of all the problems that confronted the American high command in its ordering of national affairs with regard to the Japanese war. Both in terms of mainland China and the western Pacific, the month that more than any other moment of time marked the emergence of American national power on the international stage saw difficulties compounded, the affliction of complexities, in the wake of a national victory which might have been expected to simplify such matters.

Even at a distance of almost sixty years, almost a lifetime, it is difficult to set out an order of both importance and significance to the three problems that the American national leadership faced at this juncture in the prosecution of the war against Japan. In terms of final destination, June 1944 saw the American high command, specifically the Joint Chiefs of Staff, decide that future planning for the war against Japan was to be based upon the assumed need for an invasion of the home islands rather than on the basis that an invasion might prove necessary; in the first week of July this decision was passed to London.[2] The second matter that June 1944 brought to the fore was the basic question of the nature of the American relationship with the nationalist government of China, headed by Generalissimo Chiang Kai-shek, in the aftermath of the first Japanese moves throughout central and southern China against the airfields from which the Americans had intended to take the tide of war to the home islands.

The third matter was the definition of the next American objectives in the western Pacific. This was the most immediate of the American high command's problems because clearly the gathering pace of the drives across the western Pacific could not long wait upon the definition of priorities in theater. The point, however, was most complicated and beset with difficulties, and for one simple reason which it shared with the other two problems: all three involved definition of national priorities that carried with them major implications for the American armed services relative to one another. The change for the basis of planning for the final stages of a Pacific war necessarily involved a definition of command arrangements in the western Pacific and called into question both the existing definition of priorities—a drive across the Pacific to link with Chinese nationalist forces on the mainland before the invasion of the Japanese home islands—and the alternative naval view that the war might be won by blockade and bombardment and without the necessity of landings in the home islands. But the China question, or more accurately the China quagmire, necessarily called into question two matters, the view that Japan's national defeat had to involve a mainland dimension and American aid had to be directed to Kuomintang forces which had to bring about the defeat of the *Nippon Teikoku Rikugun*, the Imperial Japanese Army, in China, and the alternative to a major American undertaking on the mainland, namely a strategic bombing offensive against the Japanese home islands conducted from airfields in China. The latter, of course, had its own rationale but it involved the extreme claim that Japan could be brought to defeat by a strategic bombing campaign waged by 200 heavy bombers from airfields in China. Such absurdity was challenged within the American military establishment by such individuals as Lieutenant General Joseph W. Stilwell and by leading members of the State Department, who feared too close an American association with the hopelessly corrupt, incompetent, and militarily useless Kuomintang regime. But these questions necessarily went hand in hand with another, more immediate, question: whether American attention should be turned to the recovery of the Philippines, lost under disgraceful circumstances in the opening months of the war. This, however, sat alongside yet another matter, the struggle between the U.S. Army and Navy for supremacy in the western Pacific in terms of command appointments and the direction of the future conduct of operations.

Much of the difficulty attending this latter question stemmed from the personality of one man, General Douglas MacArthur, supreme Allied commander in the southwest Pacific theater of operations. MacArthur was an individual who in his lifetime provoked extreme reactions, adulation and loathing in roughly equal measure, and most certainly the historical treatment of man and soldier has largely followed the wartime divide. What needs be stated with reference to the situation that had emerged in June 1944, however, is simple, though simplicity will not make it any more attractive to those who believe that MacArthur long ago entered the pantheon of American heroes and as such remains beyond reproach. In real terms the contribution of the U.S. Army to the Pacific war to this time was minimal, other than losing the Philippines; prior to Saipan no part of an Allied offensive across the Pacific witnessed a corps commitment on the ground. The most important contributions of the U.S. Army to the war against Japan took the form of the Army Air Force and the American signals intelligence effort that provided American forces with a margin of superiority over the Japanese that literally was beyond price. In terms of operational commitment to date, the U.S. Army played only a *minor inter pares* role even in the southwest Pacific theater, and the role of MacArthur at best had been dubious, both in terms of results and personal integrity. MacArthur's incompetent defense of the Philippines, his blatant self-advertisement and deceit, and his procurement of a fortune from the commonwealth government when on Corregidor should have resulted at least in dismissal from the army, but he had emerged with the United States' highest award for bravery and was appointed Allied commander in the southwest Pacific in spring 1942. The army chief of staff, George C. Marshall, had attempted to have MacArthur appointed as commander of a single Pacific theater but was defeated as a result of the U.S. Navy's refusal to be subordinated to an army commander.[3] The Pacific, in effect, was divided between the two services.

MacArthur's antics when in the southwest Pacific theater, his attempts to dictate policy to the American high command, and his sickening self-conceit again should have led to dismissal at any one of several times in 1942. Perhaps the most amazing claim, made in May 1942 in an effort to ensure that his command would receive the public attention he so craved, was that South West Pacific Command be furnished with the means to secure Rabaul, which would be the national effort best guaranteed to provide support for the Soviet Union in facing the German offensive of that summer.[4] Nonetheless MacArthur was not recalled at this or any other time, and it needed a president and a high command, and a different war, to bring about the his dismissal when once more he sought to establish himself as arbiter of national policy. That matter remained for the future; suffice it to note that from January 1944 the various parts of the American strategic jigsaw began to come together with the realization, for the first time, that with B-29 Superfortress air groups the American bombing effort could be staged from the Marianas. Prior to this time the basis of American strategic thinking was that Japan's defeat had to be total, comprehensive, and one that embraced an Asian mainland dimension. This necessarily involved China, both for her airfields from which American bombers could take the war to the home islands and for an army which, suitably and properly supplied and armed by the Americans, was to bring about the defeat of the *Rikugun* in China. This fundamental premise of American strategic policy was the basis of the American insistence that British forces clear Burma in order to ensure the overland supply of the nationalist regime in China and also the definition of Formosa as an American priority in the western Pacific. The American high command saw a juncture of American sea power and Chinese armies, somewhere in coastal China, as the necessary prerequisite for the final closing upon Japan, and it saw these various efforts as complementary. For example, American heavy bombers working from Chinese airfields would be able to support the move against Formosa, and obviously once on Formosa there could be moves into Chinese coastal areas across an extended front.

Such was the basic strategic framework devised by the American high command in 1942–1943 that governed the national conduct of the Japanese war, but also the national agenda in dealing with Britain and China, neither of which were prepared to undertake the roles ascribed to them. The British had no real interest in a campaign designed to clear Burma and thereby ensure the restoration of overland communications with Chungking, and on two counts: they did not share the American belief that China could or would play the role allotted and most certainly lacked both the inclination and the means to undertake the reconquest of Burma. The nationalist government in China was more than willing to be the recipient of American military and civil aid programs, but, while it sought Japan's defeat, Chungking was quite prepared to let other powers bring about that defeat. China did not have to undertake an effort that could only result in the devastation of vast tracts of national territory. In any case, the nationalists sought to preserve their strength in order to fight their real enemy, the communists, in the civil war that was certain to follow in the wake of Japan's defeat.

The worst of the problems that these priorities represented for the American high command was that of heavy bomber forces operating from Chinese airfields against the Japanese home islands. This was because so much of the means whereby American heavy bombers were to be maintained and supplied had to be undertaken in India, which had obvious inter-alliance implications. From bases in India and China American bombers could undertake operations not just against the home islands but in areas covered by the Pacific and Southeast Asia commands, again with obvious inter-alliance ramifications. Within China itself the position was to become ever more difficult, partly because of Stilwell's abrasiveness in his dealings with Chiang Kai-shek but mainly because, beginning in April 1944, the Japanese, knowing they could not meet the American challenge in the air with any real hope of success, undertook a series of offensives aimed at capturing the airfields from which American bombers were operating. By late May 1944 the Japanese had secured Loyang and the Chengchow-Hakow line and were preparing for offensives in Kwangsi, Hunan, and Kiangsi that were to result in their briefly establishing continuous overland communications from Korea to Johore. The American problem herein was simple. Stilwell and others in Washington had predicted a Japanese move against the airfields and the patent inability of Chiang Kai-shek's forces, despite the aid they had received, to resist any Japanese offensives. So it proved, apart from the spirited resistance offered in defense of Hengyang, but that city was lost because of Chiang Kai-shek's refusal to provide any means of support for a garrison that was commanded by individuals who were not part of his coterie. Hengyang was to be lost on 8 August, by which time Washington was caught in a deepening crisis in its dealings with Chungking. In an attempt to breathe new life into nationalist military forces, Washington insisted that Stilwell assume command of all Chungking's forces. In making this demand Washington overplayed its hand. No nationalist government could agree to such a demand, but with the Roosevelt administration not having thought through its policy and not

having secured a potential replacement for Chiang, the Chungking clique
had the better of Washington. The combination of the China lobby and
the air power lobbies was enough to confound a Roosevelt administration
that was frightened to either end aid to China or seek to discard Chiang lest
either result in the one thing it was trying to avoid, the collapse of China.
The reality was that the Americans could not have their way in China in
summer 1944 unless Chiang Kai-shek actively assisted in his being placed
in the political wilderness: Chiang knew that if the Americans threatened
to choke him to death all he had to do was threaten to die and the Roosevelt administration would have no alternative but to desist. Washington
simply could not deal with such egotistical calculation, and when Chiang
rejected American demands, castigated Stilwell as the cause of China's
present problems, and demanded his recall, Washington had no option
but to comply and try to gloss over what was a disastrous turn for American
diplomacy. Thereafter Washington found itself the prisoner, for the best
part of three decades, of the nationalist regime.[5]

Such was the essential background to the American high command's
deliberations in mid-year that sought to settle national priorities. The
China crisis, though long in the making, assumed serious proportions in
June 1944 and broke on 25 September when Chiang Kai-shek delivered a
response to American demands that indicated he would accept an American officer as chief of staff as long as it was not Stilwell. On 11 October
Chiang made his demand for Stilwell's recall and on 18 October Franklin
Delano Roosevelt acquiesced in this demand. The timing of this crisis, a
massive American diplomatic defeat at a time of unprecedented military
success, formed the prelude to Leyte Gulf. The overture, however, was
somewhat different.

The overture, in the aftermath of the battle of the Philippine Sea, consisted of the question of whether the next American moves in the western
Pacific should be directed against or bypass the Philippines. South West
Pacific Command's entire attention was directed to the Philippines and
specifically on political grounds, namely that the liberation of the islands
represented an obligation that the United States could not forgo. Within
the American high command in Washington and specifically within the
navy, however, no imperative attached itself to the islands. As American power, and the tempo of the American advances across the Pacific,
increased, the Philippines, and specifically Luzon, assumed importance

primarily for what they might be able to offer compared to other islands, particularly Formosa. As far as the American high command considered the Philippines separately, the islands were examined in terms of what a campaign might entail. The Formosa option was strongly favored by Admiral Ernest J. King, chief of naval operations, and hence by the navy as a whole, and the basic rationale embraced three points: possession of Formosa would facilitate the move to the Chinese mainland and thus be in accord with defined national objectives; Formosa would provide port and airfield facilities essential to the future conduct of the war; and Formosa would place American forces astride Japanese seaborne lines of communication with the southern resources area.[6] In early March 1944 the Joint Chiefs of Staff set a date for the invasion of Formosa, 15 February 1945, but with the provision that Luzon would not be subject to invasion on this date in the event of its being decided that Luzon had to be secured before Formosa was invaded. At this stage of proceedings, the Joint Chiefs of Staff did not treat Formosa and Luzon as alternatives to one another, and there was no question at this time of a decision between the two.

In the aftermath of the Hollandia-Aitape operation in April 1944, the American planners considered the conflicting claims of Formosa and Luzon, and in light of the subsequent dispute, their conclusion—that Formosa promised to be less daunting than had initially been believed but that the Philippines were likely to be more difficult given the recent Japanese strengthening of their defenses in the Halmahera islands and on Mindanao—was most interesting. Formosa, therefore, beckoned as a clear alternative to the Philippines because of the obvious danger of becoming trapped in a protracted campaign in the southern islands. At this point events in China served to strip the Formosa option of at least some of its attractiveness, but in an attempt to gather all relevant material prior to a decision in early June, the Joint Chiefs of Staff sought from Admiral Chester W. Nimitz's Pacific Ocean Area and MacArthur's South West Pacific Command their projected timetables. MacArthur had already submitted one program that set out landings on the northern Vogelkop for 1 August, in the Halmahera Islands on 15 September, and on Mindanao on 15 November. In the aftermath of the Philippine Sea victory, MacArthur's command revised and extended this program to provide for landings at Sarangani on Mindanao on 25 October and on Leyte on 15 November, and after various preparatory landings on Luzon and Mindoro in January and February 1945, the main effort would be made at Lingayen Gulf on 1 April 1945.[7] The least that could be said about this timetable was its slowness—which meant that it was quite unacceptable to all the planners in Washington, and not just those of the navy—and its singular lack of imagination.

In these circumstances Nimitz's proposal that a part of MacArthur's forces be committed to Mindanao in order to establish airfields from which Japanese air power in the Visayans and Luzon could be neutralized and that the main part of MacArthur's force be used, along with forces from the central Pacific, to secure Formosa caused no real problems in Washington, but MacArthur demanded he be allowed to return to Washington to place on record his objections to such a course of action. This proved unnecessary because Roosevelt, then in the middle of what he described as one of the dirtiest presidential election campaigns in history, had decided that after the party convention (in Chicago) he would go to Hawaii with a view to resolving what was clearly a political issue with obvious implications for the two Allied commands in the Pacific and the two services within the U.S. military establishment. Before he was able to do so, however, King visited Nimitz and the islands of Eniwetok and Saipan, between 13 and 22 July. In the course of their various conversations Formosa emerged as the preferred option, though the chief of staff of the 3rd Fleet, Rear Admiral Robert B. Carney, dared oppose King and argued that Luzon should be the object of American attention. Vice Admiral Raymond A. Spruance, who had commanded the 5th Fleet at the Philippine Sea and attracted much ill-informed criticism, stated his preference for a move against Okinawa.[8] Nimitz was less than fully convinced by Formosa's military claims over those of Luzon. He was in the process of considering the reduction of the Palau commitment in favor of landings on Angaur and Peleliu, and also moving against Yap and Ulithi. But with the detail of a Formosa commitment suggesting that indeed "it is easy to conquer but hard to occupy," the naval argument was showing signs of wear and tear even before the celebrated meetings of Roosevelt, Nimitz, and MacArthur of 26–29 July at Pearl Harbor. MacArthur emerged from these meetings convinced that Roosevelt had been won over and that Luzon would be afforded precedence over Formosa, but the fact was that though the Luzon argument seemed to have fared better than its rival, Roosevelt had no intention of imposing one or other alternative on the Joint Chiefs of Staff.

Throughout August there was minimal progress, and indeed it was not until the 29 September–1 October conference in San Francisco attended by Nimitz, Spruance, and Rear Admiral Forrest P. Sherman (Nimitz's head planner) that King, confronted by army estimates that the Formosa operation could involve as many as nine American divisions and perhaps 50,000 casualties, finally gave way. By that time, however, the Formosa option had really begun to unravel not because such individuals as Spruance suggested moving against the Bonin Islands and securing Iwo Jima and Okinawa as the bases from which to take the war, finally, to the home islands, but because of the success of Task Force 38 (Vice Admiral Marc A. Mitscher) in its raids over the Philippines on 12 September. The lack of opposition encountered over the Philippines led the 3rd Fleet commander, Halsey, to recommend the cancellation of all preliminary operations on the approaches to the Philippines and that the landings on Leyte be brought forward and executed as soon as possible. Halsey proposed that the carrier force take responsibility for covering the landings and airfields established on Leyte until such time that the latter could be brought into service. This recommendation was passed to the Joint Chiefs of Staff, then to a meeting with their British opposite numbers at the OCTAGON conference in Quebec, Canada, with the result that apart from those landings that were scheduled for 15 September and which could not be cancelled at so late a stage, the revised Leyte schedule, now fixed for 20 October, was approved after just ninety minutes of discussion. There was no decision on the outstanding Formosa-Luzon issue at this time, but in effect the acceleration of the move into the Philippines, when combined with the naval hesitations about Formosa, meant that Luzon emerged as the front runner as a result of the 12 September decision. The San Francisco conference buried the Formosa option, and the Joint Chiefs of Staff issued the appropriate directive, ordering a landing on Luzon and the bypassing of Formosa, on 3 October. For good measure, this directive set out the Luzon schedule for 20 December, the original Leyte date, and incorporated Nimitz's proposal that Luzon be followed by landings on Iwo Jima in January 1945 and Okinawa in March.[9]

Such was the process that was to lead the Americans to Leyte, but before the military events that were to lead to this decision are examined, two matters demand attention. The first is the obvious one, the claims that military personnel made about Formosa and particularly the disparaging comparisons made with Luzon. The nine divisions and 50,000 casualties estimate went alongside the fact that three senior officers on the army planning staff in Washington had gone to Brisbane for discussions with MacArthur and that he had no confidence . . . that the air forces of the Southwest Pacific Area from Leyte or Mindanao could neutralize enemy air power based on Luzon. He had spoken of the seizure of Formosa as "a massive operation, extremely costly in men and shipping, logistically precarious and time consuming." Luzon, he thought would have to be taken in any case, but Formosa could be bypassed if Luzon were seized first. General MacArthur was willing to predict that his losses in a Luzon campaign would be "inconsequential." He sent General Marshall "his personal guarantee" that the Luzon campaign could be completed in a maximum of six weeks, and that he was confident it would be completed in less than thirty days after the landing at Lingayen.[10]

It is hard to resist the idea that this must represent a most scathing indictment of MacArthur's generalship, or its conspicuous absence. Thirteen American divisions were committed to operations in the Philippines, and the Japanese army was still in the field in northern Luzon at the time of the national surrender in August 1945. The landings in Lingayen Gulf were conducted on 9 January 1945, which was slightly more than thirty days, or even six weeks, before the end of the Pacific war. No less interesting is that the Americans sustained 10,380 killed and 36,550 wounded, plus 93,410 non-battle casualties, in the course of the fighting in the Philippines, the campaigns on Leyte and Samar excluded.[11] It is most difficult to believe that events showed King to have been wrong.

The second matter, no less obvious, is the question whether King was wrong and Spruance was the one that was correct all along. Of course, the Spruance suggestions that the American efforts should be made first against Okinawa and then against Iwo Jima have all the attractiveness of their never having been attempted at the time designated; by the time these two islands were assaulted the Japanese had been afforded months in which to ready their defenses and had prepared themselves for protracted struggle for control of these islands. Nonetheless, the Americans secured both islands with relatively light casualties,[12] and the interesting question is whether these islands could have been secured, at much less cost, in the third quarter of 1944. The case in favor of the easy acquisition of Iwo Jima, *en passant* as it were, would seem to be strong given that the carrier formations could ensure the isolation of the Bonin Islands from outside supply and support. It is difficult to resist the notion that nothing more than a most modest force need have been committed to have ensured Iwo Jima's capture in the third or fourth quarters of 1944, and that the difficulties that surrounded its invasion and conquest in 1945 stemmed from the fact that eight months separated the battle of the Philippine Sea and the landings on the island.

The Okinawa argument would seem to be more finely balanced. To Spruance the problem that dogged the suggestion was the lack of any means for the transfer of ammunition to the carriers while at sea, and without any means whereby the carrier formations could remain on station over a protracted period, the initiative, in terms of getting men and material into Okinawa, would have been in Japanese hands. As it turned out, a more serious problem would probably have been the *kamikaze* threat. In a perverse sense, the Philippines experience after 25 October 1944 provided the U.S. Navy with the experience and technique that enabled it to survive the four-month campaign off Okinawa. Put the other way around, the Japanese expended some 7,000 aircraft in the course of the Philippines campaign, and if such numbers had been committed against an American fleet off Okinawa in the second half of 1944, American warship losses would almost certainly have been more grievous than was the case. Nonetheless, if the Okinawa option had been taken up and put through successfully, the Americans would have stood astride Japanese lines of communication with the southern resources area perhaps three or four months, and perhaps even six months, earlier than was the case, the last ships reaching the home islands from the south in late March 1945. Again, much of the difficulties that surrounded the invasion and conquest of Okinawa in 1945 stemmed from the fact that more than nine months separated the battle of the Philippine Sea and the landings on Okinawa, though one is left to wonder on one other matter, perhaps a corrective to this speculation. If the Americans had moved against Okinawa in September or October 1944 and had provoked the Imperial Navy into trying to fight one more "decisive battle," then there is every likelihood that their carrier and battle formations would have faced surface and air forces attacking from both the south and the north, from the Philippines and the home islands. As it happened, with the threat from the Philippines having been eliminated, the Okinawa campaign saw the Japanese effort directed from just the home islands, and perhaps it was this fact that ensured it was contained.

The counterpoint to the deliberations that ultimately gave rise to the revised Leyte plan was the series of military operations that unfolded between the end of the battle of the Philippine Sea and early October 1944. This series of operations in effect divided into two, those operations that were already in hand in the second half of June and those that were implemented in September and which, at least in part, stood outside the terms of reference supplied by these approved operations. The latter represented the series of carrier operations that began when Task Force 38 sailed from Eniwetok on 28 August. Its immediate responsibility was to conduct a series of raids in readiness for the landings on Morotai and in the Palau Islands, but these operations reached the Bonins and throughout the Philippines and were the operations that led to the revision of the Philippines schedule and its approval at Quebec.

The other operations were far more wide-ranging and extensive than might first be considered. The obvious operation in hand was the conquest of Saipan, which was declared secure on 9 July, and Maniagassa, a small island just off Saipan, which was secured on the thirteenth. Marines came ashore on Guam on 21 July and on Tinian three days later, Japanese resistance on the latter coming to an end on 1 August; Guam was declared on 10 August though the last Japanese did not come out of the jungle until 1972. On the Vogelkop, units from the 6th Infantry Division came ashore on Amsterdam and at Middleburg, east of Cape Sansapor, on 30 July, and then at Cape Sansapor itself on the following day, when the first rehearsals for the landings in the Palau Island were conducted in the Hawaiian islands.

At the same time these operations were conducted, two other sets of operations were in hand. Although and because the tide of war had swept along the northern coast of New Guinea and sidestepped the main centers of Japanese resistance in the process, Japanese forces opposite Aitape and Hollandia remained intact and in the last days of July and first days of August mounted a series of determined attacks around Aitape. By 4 August these attacks had been broken. The extent of the Japanese failure in this area can be gauged by the fact that after 10 August there was never an American air raid in the Aitape area. In an obvious sense, what the Americans had been doing was using aircraft to economize on troops in the course of a bypass strategy that had been put in effect along the northern coast of New Guinea, with medium bombers and fighter aircraft being used to frustrate Japanese attempts to concentrate against various individual beachheads which the Americans abandoned as the tide of war moved on. Japanese forces were left in this area, and many American holdings were turned over to Australian forces, which were ungraciously discarded by South West Pacific Command as more American formations became available. But the more immediate point, the military as opposed to the political point, was that the pattern of operations by American land-based aircraft was beginning to change around this time. In the second half of July 1944 American aircraft were operating over the New Guinea rear areas but also reaching forward, to the Vogelkop and to points beyond. B-24 Liberators were operating against such targets as Yap and Woleai (in the Carolines) while others, including B-25 Mitchells and P-38 Lightnings, were taking the tide of war into the Moluccas and to Halmahera and, of course, Morotai and the Palaus. More targets were being attacked by more bombers and fighter-bombers as the number of American aircraft in theater increased and the pace of operations quickened, but of course the major change came at the end of August when the carrier force, under the command of Halsey, sailed from Eniwetok on what proved to be a fateful mission.

Prior to that the carrier force, constituted as Task Force 58 under Spruance's command, had been involved in supporting the landings on Guam and in softening up Iwo Jima and Chichi Jima for good measure. These operations occupied various carrier task groups between 23 June and 5 July with two groups then systematically working over Guam and Rota between 6 and 13 July. All four groups were gathered together thereafter for a series of raids throughout the Marianas before they were joined on 18 July by bombardment and support formations. In the time it took American forces to secure Guam and Tinian, the carrier forces stood off the islands in an attempt to ensure the isolation of their garrisons from outside support, the only major departure being the move of three carrier groups against the Palaus. This mission also involved a major photographic reconnaissance effort, with a number of anchorages—including Yap and Ulithi—scouted with a view to securing a forward base for the fleet in advance of operations in the Philippines. This particular foray ended with a renewed attack on Iwo Jima, Chichi Jima, and Haha Jima on 4–5 August, an operation that was notable for the fact that the carriers caught a Japanese convoy leaving the islands and destroyed every freighter and their solitary escort.[13]

When Task Force 38 sailed from Eniwetok, it mustered Task Group 38.1 with two fleet and two light carriers, three heavy and one light cruisers, and fifteen destroyers, Task Group 38.2 with three fleet and two light carriers, two battleships, four light cruisers, and eighteen destroyers, Task Group 38.3 with two fleet and two light carriers, four battleships, four light cruisers, and fourteen destroyers, and Task Group 38.4 with two fleet and two light carriers, one heavy cruiser, one light cruiser, and eleven destroyers. Its task was threefold. It was to strike at the two major targets that were to be subjected to amphibious assault—Morotai and the Palaus—during September as part of the normal softening-up process. It was to try to write down Japanese air strength throughout the Philippines and in forward areas, and it was to conduct a series of operations designed to deceive the Japanese with reference to the allotted role of Morotai and the Palaus. To realize these aims, Task Force 38 was to operate with unprecedented strength, with more carriers than had fought in the Philippine Sea, and it had 1,077 aircraft—to which totals had to be added the aircraft from six escort carriers from the 7th Fleet that were assigned to support the landings on Morotai and from the eleven escort carriers tasked to support the landings in the Palaus. In the company of the escort carrier formations committed to these operations were five battleships, five heavy and three light cruisers, and fourteen destroyers.

Task Force 38 cleared Eniwetok on 28 August (see Table 2.1) and immediately divided, with Task Group 38.4 detached to carry out attacks on Iwo Jima and Chichi Jima on 31 August, 1 September, and 2 September; the 298-ton auxiliary minesweeper *Toshi Maru No. 8* was sunk on the first day of operations. Also detached was the light carrier *Monterey*, which provided support for the bombardment of Wake by the heavy cruisers *Chester*, *Pensacola* and the *Salt Lake City* and destroyers *Dunlap*, *Fanning* and the *Reid* of Task Group 12.5 on 3 September. Two days later aircraft from the *Monterey* struck at Japanese positions on the island.

Moving westward, Task Group 38.4 struck Yap on 6 September, which was the first of three successive days in which carriers from the other three task groups attacked the Palaus. With Task Group 38.4 refueling on the ninth, the other groups moved to attack airfields on Mindanao, specifically in the Sarangani Bay area, on 9 and 10 September. Meeting little resistance, further attacks on targets on Mindanao were abandoned and the carrier air groups were directed into the Visayans on 12, 13, and 14 September, with various targets on Mindanao added to the repertoire of Task Group 38.1 on the last of these three days. In these strikes the American carriers flew a total of 2,400 offensive missions and claimed to have destroyed some 200 Japanese aircraft. For the first time since the attacks on the Palaus at the end of March, the American carrier aircraft encountered shipping and on 12 September accounted for two minesweepers, two gunboats, three submarine chasers, and one netlayer, plus seven naval support ships of 17,350 tons, two army transports of 4,934 tons, and five small merchantmen of 5,888 tons, all of which were sunk off or in the immediate vicinity of Cebu City. Two days later, aircraft from Task Group 38.1 accounted for one transport in Davao Gulf.

The concentration of American carrier formations against targets in the Philippines at this stage was clearly a major factor in the Japanese failure to anticipate the moves against Morotai and against Angaur and Peleliu, in the Palaus, on 15 September. On Morotai, the landings by the three regiments of the 31st Infantry Division were unopposed and the American formations were able to secure the airfield at Pitoe and the Gila peninsula, the island's most southerly point. Task Group 38.1 provided support for the various amphibious formations involved in this operation on the day of the landing before being withdrawn, the escort carriers remaining on station until 4 October when the airfield was brought into service with the arrival of its first army fighters.[14] In the Palaus, however, the situation was very different. The landings were staged on Peleliu by the 1st Marine Division on 15 September and on Angaur by the 8th Infantry Division two days later. Angaur was more or less secured by 21 October, but the fighting on Peleliu, or perhaps more accurately the fighting on the Umurbrogol Ridge on Peleliu, continued until 27 November, and the last defenders were not killed until Christmas Day. Though both islands lacked depth, the Japanese defense had abandoned any attempt to prevent land-ings or to counterattack on beaches and had sited defensive positions in caves, in dug-out positions that were well-camouflaged, provided in depth, and which were mutually supporting. The result was as nasty and vicious a campaign for these islands as had been endured on Tarawa, though it is probably accurate to argue that most American objectives, including the securing of the airfield on Peleliu, the neutralization of the main Japanese garrison on Babeldaob, and the clearing of the Kossol Passage anchorage in the north part of the group, had been registered if not by the end of the first week of fighting then by the end of September. The American dif-ficulty on these islands was probably that both efforts were underinvested and single divisions on each island could win but could not win quickly and decisively. As a result, in Marine Corps lore Peleliu assumed a place alongside Tarawa and Iwo Jima. As it was, the Palau commitment did not prevent American forces from occupying Ulithi on 23 September, while Task Group 38.4, which had supported the ten escort carriers used during the assault phase in the Palaus, left on the eighteenth in order to resupply itself at Manus while the other formations resumed operations over the Philippines.[15]

These operations were directed against Luzon on 21 and 22 September and the Visayans on 24 September. Again the primary targets were Japanese aircraft and airfields, but while the success of the previous strikes was repeated, American success against shipping was even more extensive than on 12 September. On 21 September, American carrier aircraft accounted for three warships of 2,465 tons, two naval support ships of 20,094 tons, eight army transports of 37,144 tons, and eight merchantmen of 43,788 tons, all but two or three units being caught within Manila Bay, while on the following day a couple of submarine chasers and a tiny gunboat (collectively 749 tons of warship), three army transports of 13,710 tons, and five merchantmen of 6,028 tons were sunk, mostly off northwest Luzon. On 24 September, four warships of 3,055 tons, three naval support ships (including a seaplane tender) of 18,536 tons, five army transports of 23,621 tons, and one merchantman of 4,658 tons were sunk, and if the cause of certain of these Japanese losses may be disputed then overall in this month it would seem that carrier aircraft accounted for nineteen warships of 10,887 tons and fifty-three service support and civilian merchant ships of 199,854 tons, and they probably had some share in the eight warships of 2,705 tons and five service support ships and merchantmen of 10,718 tons that were lost on dates and to causes that remain unknown but which were lost in the Philippines theater of operations during September.[16] Be that as it may, the operations of 24 September were the last in this phase, the carrier task groups thereafter dispersing, with Task Group 38.3 reaching the safety of the Kossol Passage on 27 September, Task Group 38.2 reaching Saipan on 28 September, and Task Group 38.1 attaining the safety afforded Seeadler harbor, Manus, on 29 September.

One would suggest that these operations invite four comments. The first is the obvious one, made previously but which bears repeating because of its significance. On 13 September, because of the lack of any real opposition over the Philippines from Japanese land-based aircraft over the previous four days, Halsey made his recommendation that the American operational schedule be accelerated, with the proposed landings on Morotai and in the Palau Islands abandoned and the Leyte landings brought forward to 20 October. There is little doubt that Halsey was correct in his assessment of Japanese weakness though a certain care needs be noted because the monsoon was a factor in the inadequacy of the Japanese response to the American challenge over the Philippines. This caveat notwithstanding, the fact was that the American foray caught the Japanese on the wrong foot and ensured that they remained thus because it imposed upon the Japanese either "the wrong battle" or the right battle which they nevertheless managed to fight wrongly. The American raids of September 1944 led the Japanese to commit their forces piecemeal to the battle, with the result that these forces were defeated in detail and the prerequisite of any successful defensive battle, the concentration of air forces, was lost. In the first attacks, the Americans destroyed Japanese air formations in the southern and central Philippines, then in the second series of attacks destroyed Japanese air formations in the central and northern Philippines. The number of Japanese aircraft the Americans were able to destroy in the course of these operations is generally reckoned to be around the four-figure mark,[17] and there can be little real doubt that the inroads made into Japanese air strength in the Philippines was one of the critical factors that made for American success in the air battles of October 1944, which in turn was one of the most important single factors in deciding the battle of Leyte Gulf in the Americans' favor. In terms of the individual, it is difficult to resist the idea that these operations, and the sudden insight into Japanese weakness, represented Halsey's finest moment. In terms of Halsey's own professional reputation, both Leyte Gulf and his subsequent conduct of operations do have question marks placed against them, if indeed errors and typhoons can be thus reduced to question marks, but here in September 1944, just as in the rampage that led American carrier aircraft to the waters of Indo-China in January 1945, was a conduct of operations and strategic perception that were critically important in that the Japanese were forced to react to events and were kept off-balance.

The second point is one that travels hand-in-hand with the first and represents another compliment for Halsey in that he was undoubtedly correct in recommending that the Palaus be bypassed. This was the one part of the Halsey proposal of 13 September that was not taken up, the view of superior command being that it was too late to cancel this operation and that it had to proceed as planned. It was one of the admirals at Leyte Gulf, Rear Admiral Jesse B. Oldendorf of the battle line and Surigao Strait fame, who noted that

If military leaders (including naval) were gifted with the same accuracy of foresight that they are with hindsight, undoubtedly the assault and capture of the Palaus would never have been attempted.[18]

and there can be little doubt that the general comment in the work in which this comment appeared was correct. The Palaus operation was planned in early 1944 when the bypass policy was still young, when the Palaus appeared to be a major obstacle to any move into and beyond the Philippines, and when the islands, in American hands, would provide useful airfields and a potentially valuable base. Certainly by September 1944 the gains that had been made and the future direction of American advances, particularly the options opened by the reduction of the Marianas, meant that the Palaus had lost most of what value it had possessed, at least in the minds of American planners. That the airfields had not been returned fully into service after the raids of March 1944 and the Japanese defeat in the Philippine Sea pointed to the fact that the enemy was unlikely to have the means to make the Palaus a barrier to forces moving against the Philippines. The capture of Angaur and Peleliu was not worth the effort expended, and the only redeeming feature of the effort in terms of the planning and conduct of the war was that the main island, Babeldaob, was not subjected to attack, as had been foreshadowed when planning first started. With the main part of the Japanese garrison in the Palaus on the main island, the result would almost certainly have been unfortunate for the Americans' timing and effort.

As it was, the strategic value of the Palaus was demeaned by the one American gain made *en passant*, Ulithi. The importance of this gain can be gauged by the fact that prior to the invasion of Okinawa, no fewer than 617 ships lay inside the atoll. At different times before Operation ICEBERG, first Task Force 58 and then the British Pacific Fleet were gathered there, and for obvious reason: beginning in October 1944 the Americans began moving their various administrative support squadrons to Ulithi from such bases as Kwajalein, Majuro, and Eniwetok. Ulithi was some 1,400 miles nearer to the Philippines than was Eniwetok, and if such distance meant longer voyages and slower turnaround times for ships bearing the where-withal of war than had previously been the case, more than adequate compensation was to be found in the deployment of a reserve of oilers to Ulithi as well as vessels that would operate all repair and salvage ships in the forward zone and other ships that would provide routine maintenance. At Ulithi, the Americans, now benefiting from the massive building programs that had been effected in the first thirty months of the war, were able to gather formations of escort carriers and oilers, and later ammunition and stores, that enabled the carrier formations to be maintained at sea by successive replenishment operations. The vastness of these undertakings has served to conceal the immense strategic change that these measures represented. In history there are but very few examples of a state, or a polity, having been overwhelmed from the sea. Leaving aside city-states, only two examples other than the Spanish conquests in the New World—the Eastern Empire's conquest of the Vandal kingdom and the Norman conquest of Anglo-Saxon England—are obvious examples of such a phenomenon. Very seldom in history has sea power proved the critical strategic dimension, and even less frequently has sea power, deployed on an oceanic scale, possessed singular significance. But here, in 1944, was an example of sea power and the overwhelming of an enemy state—like a *tsunami* breaching the enemy's defenses. But if such matters are obvious, even if they have been seldom identified in such terms, then there is an additional third point that confounds a basic military definition, the Clausewitzian concept of the diminishing force of the offensive. The Japanese anticipated that the farther the Americans advanced across the Pacific the more their difficulties would mount, but the combination of support shipping becoming available on a lavish scale plus the acquisition of advanced bases such as Ulithi meant that the pace of offensive action quickened. Two of Task Force 38's carrier groups sailed from Ulithi for a second round of operations over and off the Philippines on 6 October, and the first group to return to Ulithi did so on 23 November. Task Force 38 sailed again on 11 December, but after encountering a typhoon which meant that planned attacks on Luzon had to be abandoned, it returned to Ulithi on the 22nd. It sailed again on 30 December and returned on 25 January after its aircraft had conducted a massacre of shipping in the Luzon Strait, off the Ryukyu Islands and Formosa, and finally in the South China Sea, and then, on 10 February 1945, it sailed to attack Tokyo. The American fleet by this time may have earned its unofficial title of "the fleet that came to stay," but such a record of constancy on station added a new dimension to war at sea, a dimension that had been lost with the passing of the Age of Sail.

The fourth and last point is to note the number of Japanese ships sunk by American carrier aircraft, not simply in the Philippines in September but afterward. If, for example, one looks at the January 1945 returns, it can be seen that these amounted to no fewer than twenty-six warships of 31,278 tons, ten naval auxiliaries and support ships (and another shared with a submarine) of 40,096 tons, six army transports of 36,830 tons, and no fewer than forty-four merchantmen of 146,977 tons, and perhaps one small warship, and an equally small merchantman listed in the "unknown" total properly belong to the toll exacted by carrier aircraft. The significance of these months in terms of the shipping losses inflicted on the Japanese is hard to overstate, but two comments may be made. The first is that the shipping losses inflicted in September 1944 were virtually without precedent, and most certainly were without precedent in terms of merchant as opposed to service shipping. Admittedly the losses incurred at Truk on 17–18 February, when Japanese losses amounted to six fleet units and escorts of 24,077 tons and four other units of 9,770 tons, twenty-six naval auxiliaries and support ships of 169,787 tons, four army transports of 19,679 tons, and two merchantmen of 7,075 tons, for a total of thirty-two ships of 196,541 tons, were heavier and were notable in two respects: they were inflicted in a day rather than in a month, and they were inflicted by a force that consisted of five fleet and four light fleet carriers. The losses inflicted by the Americans at Truk in February 1944 were extraordinary by any standard, but the losses of September 1944, more than a hundred service and merchant ships of more than 400,000 tons, were without parallel and were a sign of what was to come.

The second comment is that such losses would prove unavoidable in the future, and for a nation that had gone to war in the belief that its replacement capacity was some 75,000 tons per month, the implications were obvious: the losses of September 1944 represented almost six months of construction. In fact Japan's yards were able to produce more than 75,000 tons of shipping in a month, but only at the price of cutting back on refits and overhauls of existing ships. This matter notwithstanding, the fact was that the campaign against Japanese shipping in September 1944 entered a new phase when carrier-based aircraft could move directly against shipping in waters that the latter had to cross.[19] With losses in the three-month period that opened in September 1944 representing almost eighteen months of production, the Japanese at this time were about to add an entirely new dimension to national defeat.

Table 2.1. Japanese Warship and Shipping Losses, September 1944 to March 1945 (ships: tonnage)	Warships		Naval shipping		Army shipping		Civilian shipping		Monthly shipping totals	
September 1944	50	50,337	29	105,309	37	153,971	56	155,390	122	414,670
October 1944	63	347,222	27	139,028	28	105,274	63	234,187	118	478,489
November 1944	64	224,429	29	126,790	25	117,445	43	165,006	97	409,241
December 1944	35	61,520	6	15,519	12	50,834	27	111,324	45	177,677
January 1945	51	52,904	18	68,038	16	65,227	72	229,313	106	362,578
February 1945	31	21,092	3	17,962	5	14,588	32	85,522	40	118,072
March 1945	53	34,144	21	69,933	21	56,768	46	92,825	88	219,526
TOTAL	347	791,648	133	542,579	144	564,107	339	1,073,567	616	2,180,253

Table 2.2. Japanese Warship and Shipping Losses to Carrier-Based Aircraft, December 1941–August 1944

	Warships		Naval shipping		Army shipping		Merchantmen	
December 1941–30 April 1942	8	21,407	1	6,567	1	6,143	-	-
1 May 1942–28 February 1943	11.75	158,664	-	-	1	6,788	-	-
1 March–31 October 1943	-	-	-	-	-	-	-	-
1 November 1943–30 June 1944	43	65,399	64.50	381,991	12	38,346	3	4,375
1 July–31 August 1944	16.50	13,024	8	22,266	2	9,736	-	-
Total	79.25	258,494	73.50	410,824	16	61,013	3	4,375

CHAPTER THREE

THE SEARCH FOR SOLUTIONS

The Japanese Situation in the Aftermath of Defeat in the Philippine Sea

WHAT DOES A NATION and its navy do after "the decisive battle," which the navy had gone to war and sought to fight and win and on which the security and well-being of the nation was dependent, has been fought and lost? In an obvious sense, the only sensible thing that Japan could have done was to have sought an end to the war which she had initiated, that somehow she might avoid at the conference table the total defeat that was taking shape in the Pacific.[1] States, however, seldom act so rationally and responsibly in such situations, and indeed if Japan in 1941 had been inclined to adopt so rational an approach to proceedings she might well have sought a solution to her problems that did not lead the way of Pearl Harbor. Be that as it may, the basic point that confronted the Japanese national leadership in the wake of the *Kaigun*'s defeat in the Philippine Sea in June 1944, and the annihilation of the carrier air groups that had been readied for "the decisive battle," was that the home islands and conquered areas of Southeast Asia lay exposed to an enemy with the full power of choice of when, where, and in what strength the next moves would be made.

The latter point, that the home islands and conquered areas of the southern resources area lay open to the enemy, was the crucial fact in providing the Japanese military leadership with focus and purpose in the wake of this disastrous defeat. In the immediate aftermath of this devastating failure,

Imperial General Headquarters (and hence the Naval General Staff) and the Combined Fleet "were both at a loss as to what to do."[2] Such is the nature of military staffs and planning, however, that nothing so minor as a defeat, however disastrous, can long frustrate ill intent; within a month the basis of future resistance had been determined.

Without knowing where the Americans might make their next effort, the Japanese high command was obliged to plan for four separate contingencies against landings anywhere between the southern Philippines and the Kuriles. The critical calculation, however, involved the Philippines, and for two obvious reasons. The first, simply, was that these islands clearly beckoned the enemy in the sense that both American drives across the Pacific, along the northern coast of New Guinea and through the Carolines, pointed in the general direction of this archipelago. The second, and all-important, point for the Japanese high command was the simple fact that the Philippines lay astride Japan's communications with the southern resources area, and, in strategic terms, the loss of the island group would represent a defeat virtually indistinguishable from an invasion and conquest of the home islands.[3] The importance of the Philippines to Japan in terms of national ability to wage war was critical: the Americans had to be denied the positional advantage that would result in their severing Japan's seaborne lines of communication with the south.

This basic consideration was one of three matters that shaped Japanese strategic thinking in the month following the defeat in the Philippine Sea. The second and third matters must await their turn to come to center stage, but suffice it to note that this fundamental calculation, involving the strategic geography of Japan and her conquests, was immediately tied to two contradictory caveats. After 20 June and defeat in the Philippine Sea, the bulk of the Japanese fleet had withdrawn to the Nansei Shoto (i.e., Okinawa and the Ryukyu Islands) and thence to home waters. But even in 1942, at its peak strength and capability, the greater part of the Japanese fleet was deployed in the south primarily because Japan lacked the number of tankers to sustain the nation and a navy in home waters. Put at its simplest, and with scarcely any exaggeration, Japan went to war in December 1941 in order to secure control of certain resources, most obviously oil, without which she could not ensure national survival, but even in the period of her greatest success, and before defeats made their appearance, Japan could supply the nation with oil or it could supply a navy in home waters with oil, but not both and not at the same time. Japan was able to negotiate 1942 and 1943 precisely because the greater part of the *Kaigun* was stationed in the south, and in these years the fleet took more oil directly from source than from the homeland. But by the third quarter of 1944, as Japanese merchant shipping—and particularly tanker—losses mounted, the simple fact was that after having been defeated in the Philippine Sea and withdrawn to home waters, the greater part of the *Kaigun* had to go to the south to be near oil supplies.[4]

Allied to this point was the contradiction which seems an inevitable part of any Japanese decision: consideration of tanker numbers might dictate the movement of most of the fleet to the south, but at least one part of the fleet had to remain in home waters. The defeat in the Philippine Sea was severe in terms of the loss of the fleet carriers *Taiho*, *Shokaku* and the *Hiyo*, but the real disaster, if it can be properly separated from the carrier losses, was the annihilation of the carrier air groups. In the immediate aftermath of the battle, Japan proclaimed her victory in the Philippine Sea, claiming to have sunk or damaged nine aircraft carriers and five battleships, but even as this claim was made and then further exaggerated, there was the admission, but not to the Japanese people, that Japan would need at least a year to make good her losses.[5] At the Philippine Sea, the Imperial Navy lost its third intake of carrier air groups since the start of the Pacific war. The first had been lost in the battles in the Coral Sea, off Midway atoll, and over the lower Solomon Islands. The second was destroyed during and after November 1943 in the battles that resulted in American neutralization of Rabaul. In summer 1944 American carrier formations in the Philippine Sea gave battle in defense of their carriers, and in so doing annihilated Japanese carrier air groups that were outclassed in terms of the quality of aircraft, aircrew, organization, and effectiveness of individual formations. Moreover, the American carrier formations also registered another victory. Their aircraft, used *en masse*, shattered Japanese land-based air formations in the Mariana and Bonin Islands before the landings on Saipan and the battle of the Philippine Sea, and after the battle they continued to attack Japanese airfields in these islands and any aircraft fed into these bases in the meantime. In so doing the Americans confirmed a pattern of operations that had been established in November 1943 during the invasion of the Gilbert and Ellice Islands and then repeated in the descent on the Marshall Islands in January–February 1944. American carrier groups operated in such numbers as to be able to both overwhelm any individual Japanese air base and ensure its isolation from outside support. The problem the Japanese faced in the aftermath of the Philippine Sea was that they needed five months to make good the losses that had been incurred, and while the Japanese staffs calculated that American landings in the Philippines could come as soon as August or September,[6] the immediate problem for the *Kaigun* was that its training facilities were in the home islands. The greater part of the fleet might have to make its way south to be near the oilfields and local refineries, but if the Imperial Navy was to try to reconstitute its air groups then the majority of its carriers had to be retained in home waters. Leaving aside the obvious point, that no training program initiated at this stage of proceedings by the *Kaigun* was ever going to reverse the advantages that the Americans had established in terms of numbers and quality of aircraft, aircrew, and air groups, the simple fact was that after June 1944 the Combined Fleet was in effect divided into three, the escort forces held with the General Escort Command, which formed no part of this story, a force held in home waters, and a force at Singapore in a position to secure oil from Sumatra and Borneo.

Thus any Japanese attempt to respond to an American assault on the Philippines threatened to labor under a threefold handicap. The land-based air formations, and specifically the *Kaigun's* land-based air formations, were certain to face an enemy that had a double advantage in terms of aircraft numbers and quality as well as a clear advantage in quality of personnel and formations. The *Kaigun* faced exactly the same situation in terms of surface and submarine forces, and it faced the added problems created by the need to coordinate operations over thousands of miles. Singapore and Tokyo are separated by 3,490 nautical or 4,019 statute miles, and clearly, given Japan's lack of tanker numbers, such distances represented major problems in what was in any event certain to be a very difficult task for the Japanese high command. To meet any American move into the Philippines, the Japanese would have to use two formations, each of which was inferior to the enemy they separately faced, and they would have to ensure their timely and effective coordination of effort across a thousand miles of ocean and at the very limits of operational effectiveness. If one wished to be churlish one could note that even at its peak, when it possessed clear advantages in terms of numbers and quality, the *Kaigun* had not been able to secure victory for itself, as events in the Coral Sea in May 1942 and off Midway in the following month had demonstrated only too well. How it was to conjure up victory when the enemy possessed clear advantages in all aspects of the conduct of operations did imply a faith in victory that somehow stood outside the normal criteria by which military effectiveness was measured.

✳   ✳   ✳

Of course, throughout the Pacific war, and not simply at this stage of proceedings, the Japanese did possess a faith in victory and a set of military standards that did not accord with normal (i.e., Western) criteria. These, however, form the third and final matter that shaped Japanese strategic thinking in the month following the defeat in the Philippine Sea, and to which reference has been made, and it is the second that now demands consideration. This refers to Japanese weakness to which *en passant* reference has been made, that in effect any Japanese response to an American move into the Philippines had to see various efforts complement one another, to somehow produce a synergistic response to a losing strategic situation whereby all aspects of Japan's efforts covered individual weaknesses. The second matter is the definition of these weaknesses, and in one sense this can be done simply by one aspect of Japanese weakness. Most Western accounts of the battle of Leyte Gulf note Japanese numerical weakness, and the disparity between American and Japanese numbers is striking. If one wishes to see the relationship between superiority and victory, the crucial matter where victory is the product of superiority, then one need look no further than the battle of Leyte Gulf. What is seldom appreciated, however, is that the number of warships that the Japanese committed to this battle more or less represented the sum of the fleet units available to Japan and the Imperial Navy at this stage of the war.

The extent of Japanese weakness at this time is generally not recognized in specific form. It may be noted in a general sense, but it is seldom put into tangible form. The observation that "almost all of the sixty-three remaining vessels in the Japanese Navy were participating in (this) operation" is most unusual.[7] In fact this total may be disputed, but by only one or two units, and there can be no disputing that the basic point is well-made: the warships that were committed to action on the Japanese side at Leyte Gulf represented virtually the sum of the strength that remained in the Imperial Navy. In the course of the Second World War in the Far East, between December 1941 and September 1945, the United States commissioned into service eighteen fleet, nine light fleet, and 77 escort carriers, eight battleships and two battlecruisers, thirteen heavy and 33 light cruisers, 349 destroyers and 420 destroyer escorts, 73 other escorts, and 203 submarines,[8] and these totals exclude the number of ships that were commissioned but turned over to allies. Such is the context of "the sixty-three remaining vessels in the Japanese Navy" that saw service at Leyte Gulf.

Whatever date one selects in setting out tables of establishment, orders of battle, and just mere numbers is certain to be condemned as inherently flawed or simply misguided. Suffice it to note that the date of 1 October has been selected simply because of chronological neatness. It may be that a date when the planners were at their most earnest might be considered more appropriate, but this date has the redeeming feature of representing, more or less, what the Japanese had ready for battle. In terms of carriers the *Kaigun* mustered the fleet carriers *Zuikaku* and *Junyo*, though the latter, a converted NYK liner, was no longer fit for frontline service. In addition the Imperial Navy completed the *Amagi* and *Unryu* in August and the *Katsuragi* in October 1944, but even discounting the fact that they had no air groups, all three units were too new to be considered for immediate operations. The *Kaigun* also had the light carriers *Hosho, Ryuho, Zuiho, Chitose* and the *Chiyoda*, but the old *Hosho*, which was held for training duties, and the *Ryuho*, a converted submarine support ship with virtually no armor and wretchedly inadequate internal subdivision, were no longer fit for first-line operations, if indeed they had ever been worthy of such description.

In terms of battleship numbers, having lost the *Hiei* and *Kirishima* in November 1942 and the *Mutsu* in June 1943, the *Kaigun* retained the *Haruna* and *Kongo*, the *Fuso* and *Yamashiro*, the *Hyuga* and *Ise*, the *Nagato*, and the *Yamato* and *Musashi*. With respect to cruisers, by 1 October 1944 the *Kaigun* had lost just four heavy cruisers—the *Mikuma* and, lost in 1942 in the course of the campaign in the lower Solomon Islands, the *Kako, Furutaka* and the *Kinugasa*—which left it with fourteen heavy cruisers in service, namely the *Aoba*, the *Ashigara, Haguro, Myoko* and the *Nachi*, the *Atago, Chokai, Maya* and the *Takao*, the *Kumano, Mogami* and the *Suzuya*, plus the scout-cruisers *Chikuma* and *Tone*. The *Kaigun* to date had lost thirteen light cruisers, namely the *Yura* and *Tenryu* in 1942, the *Jintsu* and *Sendai* in 1943, and the *Kuma* in January 1944, the *Agano, Katori* and the *Naka* at Truk on 17 February 1944, the *Tatsuta, Yubari* and the *Oi* in March, April, and July 1944 respectively, and then the *Nagara* and *Natori* in August 1944. Such losses meant that the Imperial Navy retained just nine light cruisers—the *Tama* and *Kiso*, the *Abukuma, Kinu* and the *Isuzu*, the *Noshiro, Yahagi* and the *Sakawa*, and the *Oyodo*—three units being discounted from consideration; the *Kitakami* was in dockyard being rebuilt as a result of massive damage incurred in February 1944, and the *Kashima* and *Kashii*, built as training cruisers, had been assigned to escort duties in mid-1944.[9]

Destroyer numbers are much more difficult to state with certainty because of two considerations, the relegation to secondary duties of a number of older units and a degree of uncertainty surrounding the status of sister ships, plus the fact that the last class of destroyers built during the war, the *Akizuki* class, straddled the dividing line between large destroyers and light cruisers and could be listed under the latter classification. With reference to the older units, which for the sake of convenience can be considered to be all those destroyers constructed before such units were built with the 24-in. torpedo armament, plus the first such class since its members had been reclassified as fast transports in 1941–1942, prior to 30 September 1944 the *Kaigun* had lost six of eleven units of the *Minekaze* class, none of three remaining *Momi*-class units, four of the six *Wakatake*-class warships, six of nine *Kamikaze*-class ships, and ten of the twelve *Mutsuki*-class destroyer-transports. This represented a total of twenty-six units lost from a total of forty-one warships, and it left the *Kaigun* by 1 October 1944 with just fifteen of these older destroyers, and of these the *Namikaze* had been torpedoed in the Sea of Okhotsk on 8 September 1944 and was under repair at the time; she was never returned to service as a destroyer. As it was, none of these older ships were involved in the October 1944 battles but for one of the oldest of their number; the *Akikaze*, from the 1919 program, served as escort to oilers with the carrier force.[10]

At the outbreak of the Pacific war, and excluding the units of the *Mutsuki* class from consideration, the destroyers in service or being built around the 24-in. torpedo armament totaled just eighty-seven. This total consisted of nineteen destroyers of the *Fubuki* class (the *Miyuki* having been lost as a result of a collision in June 1934), four from the *Akatsuki* and six from the *Hatsuhara* classes, ten from each of the *Shiratsuyu* and *Asashio* classes, eighteen from the *Kagero* class, and twenty from the *Yugumo* class. To this total must be added the solitary *Shimakaze*, built under the 1939 provisions but not laid down until August 1941 and not completed until May 1943. As a lone ship, with no sisters from the same class, she defies easy classification but may be included in this total, necessarily adjusted to eighty-eight. To this total, but considered separately, could be added another eight units from the twelve-strong *Akizuki* class, four of which were completed after October 1944.

Of this total of eighty-eight destroyers, just twenty-nine remained to the *Kaigun* at the end of September 1944. It is possible to argue that such numbers remained only because the destroyers from the later classes had not been in service long enough to have been sunk. The *Fubuki* class had three in service at this time, the *Akatsuki* and *Shiratsuyu* classes each had just one solitary survivor, while the *Hatsuhara* and *Asashio* classes contributed three and four units respectively to the September 1944 list. Seven members of the *Kagero* class and nine of the *Yugumo* class, plus the *Shimakaze*, remained in service. Along with the six units of the *Akizuki* class, the number of destroyers available for fleet operations was thirty-five, plus the fourteen older destroyers that were nominally available.[11]

Such is the detail of a matter seldom afforded the attention it merits in accounts of these events. The problem of what to do after the decisive battle has been fought and lost is, at least in relative terms, easily identifiable, but the real point was that it was accompanied by the complementary question: with what forces? Accounts of these events, and specifically the battle of Leyte Gulf, seldom acknowledge one fact: the forces committed by the *Kaigun* to this battle represented nearly the whole of the fleet strength available to Japan at this stage of proceedings. Excluding submarines and escorts, the total fleet strength available to the *Kaigun* on 1 October 1944 was just eighty-one units, while the total number of units committed to battle this month was sixty-five.

The extent of Japanese weakness is part and parcel of the history, and indeed an understanding, of the Pacific war. In terms of the *Kaigun*'s preparations, after the battle of the Philippine Sea, the Imperial Navy could muster only about sixty fleet units to fight the second, deferred, "decisive battle." Put another way, at the start of the proceedings that ultimately went under the collective name of the battle of Leyte Gulf, two American carrier groups, Task Groups 38.1 and 38.2, between them mustered more destroyers than were available to the *Kaigun* as a service, and to Japan as a nation, in October 1944. In fact, the situation was even more catastrophic than the mere "head count" might suggest because the balance of ship types had been destroyed to the extent that one could question whether, in "the decisive battle" that the *Kaigun* intended to fight, the battleships, carriers, and cruisers were supposed to escort the destroyers. The critical element herein, of course, was the light cruisers, which for the most part had been built to serve as destroyer leaders. But on a simple count by type at the battle of Leyte Gulf, the Imperial Navy deployed four carriers, nine capital ships, and fourteen heavy cruisers and just seven light cruisers and thirty-one destroyers, and these were gathered into formations separated by more than three thousand miles of ocean.

✳   ✳   ✳

Table 3.1. The Number of Japanese Ships Retained and in Service,
1 October 1944

	(1)	(2)	(3)	(4)
Fleet carriers	4	2	1	The *Junyo:* see Note A
Light carriers	5	4	3	The *Ryuho:* see Note B
Capital ships	9	9	9	-
Heavy cruisers	14	14	14	-
Light cruisers	8	8	7	The *Kiso*
Fleet destroyers	35	35	31	The *Hibiki, Amatsukaze, Suzutsuki* and the *Fuyutsuki:* see Note C
TOTAL	75	72	65	See Note D
Old destroyers	15	12	1	

Key: (1) Nominally available 1 October 1944. (2) In real terms the number available 1 October 1944. (3) The number committed to operations. (4) The names of those units not used in these operations.

Notes:

A. These totals do not include the fleet carriers *Unryu* and *Amagi*, which had been completed but were not in service on 1 October 1944.
B. These totals do not include the light carrier *Hosho*, which was assigned training duties.
C. The *Hibiki, Suzutsuki* and the *Fuyutsuki* were not available for operations. The *Hibiki* was torpedoed by the submarine *Hake* on 6 September, the *Fuyutsuki* by the *Trepang* on 12 October and the *Suzutsuki* by the *Besugo* on 16 October.[1]
D. The total of sixty-five warships does not include the four destroyer escorts with the 31st Destroyer Squadron, and nor does it include the *Akikaze* and the six corvettes with the oiler formation.

Source: James A. Field, Jr., *The Japanese at Leyte Gulf: The Sho Operation*, pp. 36–37, fn. 8. Rohwer, pp. 301, 307. *Dictionary of American Naval Fighting Ships*, Volume I, p. 121, has no reference for the *Besugo* ref. the *Suzuksuki* though Theodore Roscoe, *United States Submarine Operations in World War II*, p. 390, makes a passing reference to an incident, Japanese ship (claimed as a cruiser) unnamed. See *DANFS*, III, p. 205 for the *Hake* ref. her torpedoing and damaging an unnamed destroyer, date and whereabouts unspecified, and VII, p. 269, for the *Trepang* and the claims to have damaged a *Yamashiro*-class battleship and sunk a destroyer. The entry states that neither claim could be verified.

The question of numbers was but one of the problems the Japanese high command had to address in the aftermath of the battle of the Philippine Sea, and the most obvious of the other problems, and one that went hand-in-hand with fleet unit numbers, was air strength. Herein were a multitude of individual problems that together bordered on the insoluble, and for one simple reason: any defensive plan, designed to forestall the next American moves, necessarily involved fully trained and balanced formations operating from intact and well-defended bases across an area that reached from the Kuriles to the Philippines. With the Americans possessed of choice of when, where, and in what strength to make their opening moves in the next phase of operations, unless the Japanese had timely notice of enemy intentions there was a real prospect of overwhelming disaster, and for obvious reason. American ability to overwhelm a local defense has been noted, but the Japanese need for time for the training and re-equipment of its air forces, and also the need to disperse aircraft in an attempt to ensure some degree of security against attack, necessarily militated against the need for concentration for offensive operations.

In fact the Japanese problem in terms of air power was much more serious than even this bare statement would suggest. The Japanese problem was that the *Kaigun* began the war with two air fleets, the 1st Air Fleet, which had provided air groups for the carriers, and the 11th Air Fleet, which had formed the land-based complementary establishment. The process of conquest in 1941–1942 had seen new commands established, but these, and the two original formations, were always beset by three basic problems: an inadequate number of aircraft, a declining quality of aircraft as new aircraft entered enemy ranks without Japan being able to match these newcomers, and a simple lack of numbers in terms of pilots and aircrew. The Japanese needed strength in depth across a vast front, they needed to be able to bring this strength into a concentrated mass before or in the immediate hours after a landing, and they needed both the numbers and levels of professional skill that would enable them to do battle with a U.S. Navy that ended the war in 1945 with something like 40,000 aircraft and 60,000 trained pilots.

The American achievement in the Second World War in terms of building and the training of highly specialist naval and air personnel was massively impressive, even by the most exacting of standards. Various accounts of this achievement have set out the detail, but suffice it to note just two matters relating to air power. At their peak, in March 1944, American factories produced one aircraft every 295 seconds, and in the course of the Pacific war the United States outproduced Japan in aircraft 279,813 to 64,800, in aircraft engines 728,467 to 104,446, and in tons of airframe 1,029,911 to 126,339.[12] Even allowing for a division of American strength on account of the European conflict, the simple fact of the matter was that American aircraft were roughly four times more numerous and twice the size of their Japanese counterparts. In terms of defensive qualities there was no comparison between American and Japanese aircraft, and whatever advantages the Japanese had enjoyed in terms of numbers, concentration, and aircraft quality at the start of the war in the Pacific had long since passed.

The problems Japan faced in these matters were indeed without solution, but in the aftermath of the defeat in the Philippine Sea the Japanese high command determined upon three sets of measures to provide itself with an offensive capability that had been notable by its failure in the Marianas. The first was the raising of a new formation, the 2nd Air Fleet, which, along with a reconstituted 1st Air Fleet, was to be based in the Philippines, while the defense of the southern and central home islands was to be entrusted to the 3rd Air Fleet, with the 12th Air Fleet remaining in Hokkaido and the Kuriles. The second was the preparation of a system of dispersed feeder airfields both in the Philippines and between these islands and Japan, to be completed in the home islands by October and in the Philippines by September. Ultimately some seventy airfields and strips were prepared and brought into service in the Philippines within easy flying time of the landing beaches on Leyte, the Japanese intention being to present the Americans with so large and diverse a defensive infrastructure that it could not be neutralized as had happened in the Mariana and Bonin Islands during the Saipan campaign.[13] The third was that in preparing to meet the next American move in the western Pacific, the *Kaigun* was afforded an unprecedented degree of cooperation by its sister service.

The lack of cooperation between the two Japanese services—Japanese admirals and generals addressed one another as "excellency," which was the form of address reserved for ambassadors of foreign powers—was notorious and is so well-known and documented as to need no elaboration, but suffice it to note two matters. First, thus far in the war the conduct of operations in the Pacific had been largely a *Kaigun* preserve, but with the next phase of operations clearly set for the home islands and the western Pacific, the *Rikugun* naturally had to be involved on an equal basis with its sister service. Second, there was within the army sections of Imperial General Headquarters a basic awareness, articulated for the first time, that what was taking shape was not simply defeat in a campaign or related campaigns, but defeat in the war. As noted by one Japanese officer at this time,

> Japan's national power . . . will gradually decrease, no matter how much effort Japan may exert, and, although she may be able to engage in a decisive battle before the end of this year, it will hardly be possible for her to counter any powerful attack during, and after, next year. The only way out is to check the enemy's advance.[14]

Herein was the basis of the logic behind the *Rikugun*'s moves to ensure the closest possible cooperation between the services, even to the extent that army air formations—three air regiments—were placed under the operational command of the naval air service. The American advance into the western Pacific had to be halted, and thus a full effort had to be made in defense of the Philippines.[15] In fact the logic was flawed in that Japan could have sought to extricate herself from the situation by seeking a negotiated end to the war, and, indeed, it was this argument that ensured the dismissal of General Tojo Hideki as prime minister on 18 July. The problem therein was the obvious one. The dismissal of a prime minister who had taken Japan into the Pacific war and who identified with the hard-line element in the Japanese army and high command was one thing; how to take the next step and try to end the war in the face of entrenched opposition, an opposition that would have no compunction about killing its opponents, was quite another matter.[16]

Such were the main features of the Japanese high command's deliberations once the ill-considered proposal to try to fight a reinforcement expedition through to Saipan—which, incredible though it may seem, was seriously entertained and indeed proposed by the Naval General Staff in Tokyo— was abandoned.[17] But the critical point about these factors was the manner in which they hung together and to what purpose, or to put the matter in military terms, how the various parts would be fought and to what end. Herein the waters, already somewhat murky, quickly become opaque.

The essential feature of Japanese intent was that the land-based air and naval efforts had to complement one another. Expressed another way, they had to make good one another's weaknesses, and in particular land-based air power had to cover the limitations of the fleet. Herein was the crucial aspect of Japanese intent because as days passed and the Japanese high command and the *Kaigun* began to examine in detail what this intention entailed, one matter became clear. The Imperial Navy, as noted elsewhere, had long since committed itself to fighting "the decisive battle." In fact, this idea was central to its very existence, its *raison d'être*, and it was a concept it had tried to implement, with disastrous results, in the Philippine Sea and which the *Kaigun* assumed it would try to fight for a second time in the event of American landings in the Philippines. The basic Japanese position and intent were laid down in two Imperial General Headquarters directives, the first (No. 431) issued on 21 July and the second (No. 435) on 25 July. These set out the basic SHO GO/VICTORY OPERATION formula with SHO 1/SHO-ICHI-GO applying to meeting an American landing in the Philippines, SHO 2/SHO-NI-GO on Formosa or the Ryukyu Islands, SHO 3/SHO-SAN-GO on Kyushu, Shokaku, and Honshu, and the last, SHO 4/SHO-YON-GO, on Hokkaido and the Kuriles.[18] The main provision was the formation of a central reserve of aircraft that could be directed to the appropriate theater of operations once the Americans showed their hand. At the same time, the fleet at Lingga, the base 130 miles south of Singapore next to the Palembang oilfields, "will be moved up to the Philippines or temporarily to the Nansei Shoto" while fleet formations in home waters "will engage in mobile tactics as expedient. . . . co-ordinating actions with base air forces to crush the enemy fleet and advancing forces."[19] The *Kaigun*'s reading of this intent was summarized in a Combined Fleet operational order (No. 83), issued on 1 August, which stated that the aim of naval forces, operating in cooperation with *Rikugun* aircraft, was "to intercept and destroy the invading enemy at sea in a decisive battle."[20] But the simple fact of the matter was that if the Combined Fleet could not fight and win "the decisive battle" when it had nine carriers and nine complete air groups in the Philippine Sea in June 1944, then it was in no position to fight a second battle in the Philippines in or after September 1944 when it had just one fleet carrier fit for operations and, in effect, at most one or two carrier air groups.[21] If the *Kaigun* wanted to fight its "decisive battle," it could do so, but not with the fleet. Thus land-based air power, despite its abject failure in the Philippine Sea, moved to center stage because it alone might be able to inflict telling loss on the enemy. As it did so, the fleet inevitably assumed secondary importance, and its offensive role came to be seen as operating against American amphibious and support shipping while land-based air formations operated against American carrier forces.

Such an ordering of affairs invites so many observations, none exactly favorable, that it is difficult to know where to start. The obvious point relates to the provisions made for land-based air formations, specifically those allocated to the Philippines and those that were expected to make their way to the archipelago in the event of an American move in this theater. The 1st and 2nd Air Fleets were supposed to be established at 350 and 510 aircraft respectively, while the 3rd Air Fleet, in the home islands, was assigned 300 aircraft. The *Rikugun* was to contribute 600 aircraft among the 4th Air Army in the Philippines, the Formosa Army, and the various training establishments in the home islands. These, along with aircraft from the 12th Air Fleet and the 13th Air Fleet in Malaya and the Indies, were earmarked for commitment in support of the 1st and 2nd Air Fleets as circumstances dictated.[22] The least that can be said about such arrangements was that they were somewhat optimistic. At the very best, these various formations were about one-third under establishment, and serviceability rates were low, as indeed was quality of aircrew both at individual and unit levels. The formations that were available were certainly no better than those that had failed so abysmally in the Mariana and Bonin Islands, yet these were the formations that were expected to deal with American carrier forces before turning and cooperating with the naval surface forces to overwhelm American amphibious and transport shipping. The premise simply did not make any sense, but what caused immediate problems within the naval establishment was that this plan of campaign denied the Imperial Navy the right to fight "the decisive battle."

It was small wonder, therefore, that as the basic SHO GO concept was circulated among staffs and officers in general, there emerged opposition to the idea on the grounds that the Imperial Navy's warships would be misused, that their proper target had to be enemy warships, and that really it was beneath the dignity of the *Kaigun* and individual formations and ships to be thus employed. Such ideas found their natural supporters in the battle and cruiser formations that were earmarked for this operation. The Combined Fleet's chief of staff, Rear Admiral Kusaka Ryunosuke, was more than a little sympathetic to such sentiments, but there were two wider dimensions to this particular aspect of Japanese planning. On the first score, the idea that a carrier force, properly supported with battleship and cruiser formations, could play a full part in inflicting loss upon American carrier formations died at this time. This belated realism was the result of the carrier commander, Vice Admiral Ozawa Jisaburo, coming to the realization that his formation could not expect to do battle with its counterparts. Ozawa suggested that land-based air support for battle and cruiser formations committed against a beachhead was unlikely to materialize, and therefore he suggested that his carriers should be attached to the battle and cruiser force in order that its air groups provide whatever overhead cover they could. But what was more relevant was that Ozawa saw that the battle and cruiser forces assigned to his command could not be expected to provide an adequate screen for his carriers, and he also saw his command's role as primarily diversionary. Therefore he suggested stripping his command of all but the minimum number of warships necessary to discharge this role.[23] Thus Ozawa parted company with his cruiser force and with the battle formation, which he was prepared to pass to the formations in the south.

Such realism overlapped the idea of the "decisive battle" and turned the idea on its head. In dealing with the opposition generated by the plan of campaign among his subordinate officers, most obviously on the part of the captain of the *Musashi*, the commander of the main battle force, Vice Admiral Kurita Takeo, argued that the *Kaigun* was not strong enough to fight a decisive battle and therefore had no choice but to seek to overwhelm enemy amphibious, support, and supply formations in a surprise attack.[24] In any other circumstances than those that prevailed at this time, Kurita's answer might well have provoked more questions than it attempted to answer, but Kurita's response to the critics of the SHO GO proposal was not to deal with their criticism but to silence them by making the question one of authority. After a series of detailed discussions over ten days, the SHO GO package was formally presented at an Imperial General Headquarters session on 18 August and approved in formal session on the following day.[25] The involvement of the emperor in these meetings ensured a curbing of dissent within the ranks of the *Kaigun*'s officers.

On the second score, however, the situation was very different because, quite clearly, many senior planners and fleet officers realized that any attempt to fall upon American amphibious, support, and transport formations was likely to end in the annihilation of the Japanese forces thus committed to the offensive. Moreover, it is clear that many Japanese officers, including admirals involved in subsequent operations, were of similar persuasion, and indeed would welcome their own deaths, and the annihilation of their forces, in some last desperate battle that somehow would atone for previous failures and ensure that most elusive aspect of the *Kaigun*'s existence, its honor.[26] At the Imperial General Headquarters liaison meeting of 18 October, when the military members urged its opposite numbers to reconsider the whole of the SHO-ICHI-GO formula, the head of the naval operations section asked that the fleet, and with it the *Kaigun* as a whole, be afforded "a fitting place to die" and "the chance to bloom as flowers of death. This is the Navy's earnest request."[27] Such language, and such a request, do not sit easily alongside the previous representation of what the fleet was supposed to achieve, but there was another dimension to this "earnest request": the Imperial Navy would not meet the same fate that had befallen the Imperial German Navy in November 1918 and the Royal Italian Navy in September 1943. The realization that the war was probably lost, a conclusion that was difficult for senior planners to resist in the aftermath of the battle of the Philippine Sea and the loss of Saipan, which together brought the home islands within the range of heavy bombers based in the Marianas, paradoxically strengthened the argument that forces had to be used even if the odds were stacked massively against them. At the very best, as the commander of the Combined Fleet, Admiral Toyoda Soemu, noted in post-war interrogation:

> Since without the participation of our Combined Fleet there was no possibility of the land-based air forces in the Philippines having any chance against (American) forces at all, it was decided to send the whole fleet, taking the gamble. If things went well, we might obtain unexpectedly good results: but if the worst should happen there was a chance that we might lose the entire fleet. I felt that chance had to be taken.[28]

Here was the same recognition of the possibility of overwhelming defeat, but the point was that under the terms of the SHO GO proposal, land-based air power was supposed to open the way for the surface force. But here, according to the Combined Fleet commander, the role of the surface force was to augment the chances of land-based aircraft registering significant results against American carrier forces. Either way, there were many high-ranking naval officers who feared that the fleet might be destroyed in a battle for the Philippines and others who quite willingly accepted the likelihood that this would prove the case.

*   *   *

The least that can be said about these different shades of emphasis, if they can be thus termed, is that they possess a certain incoherence. There was clearly on one side of the naval table those who believed that the *Kaigun* could not be allowed to survive national defeat and who embraced the logic that justified the dispatch of the battleship *Yamato,* a warship that bore the ancient name of Japan, to the Ryukyu Islands in April 1945 in the sure and certain knowledge that she would be destroyed.[29] But there was also present, in the various arguments that characterized the delibera- tions of the naval staff, the Combined Fleet staff, and the command staffs, a rationalist and realistic view that clearly sought to establish the means by which battle could be sought in the face of potentially overwhelming American superiority.[30] The problem herein, however, was the context, and whatever arrangements were sought there was no escaping one basic reality which the Japanese high command almost certainly did not know at the time and which History has not really defined over the past sixty years. This was the fact that, American submarine losses being discounted from the reckoning, between 24 November 1943, when the escort carrier *Liscome Bay* was torpedoed off the Gilberts by the submarine I. 175, and 24 October 1944, when the *Princeton* was lost off the northern Philippines as a result of attack by a land-based aircraft, Japanese shells, torpedoes, and bombs failed to account for a single U.S. Navy fleet unit other than the *Fletcher*-class destroyer *Brownson,* which was lost on 26 December 1943 off Cape Gloucester, New Britain, to air attack. In other words, the whole of the American effort that resulted in the breaking of the outer perimeter defense in the central Pacific, the carrier rampages into the western Pacific that resulted in the shipping massacres at Truk (17–18 February) and Koror (30–31 March), the landings at Hollandia and Aitape, which took the war from one end of New Guinea to the other in two months and which finally led to overwhelming victory in the Philippine Sea (19–20 June), cost the United States just one destroyer, plus the destroyer escort *Shelton,* which was sunk off Morotai on 3 October by the submarine Ro. 41.[31] It has been noted elsewhere that the Pacific war ended, in terms of decision, if not on 7 December 1941 then in November 1943 when the Americans moved against the Gilbert and Ellice Islands in such strength that the outcome was assured. Thereafter, the Pacific war witnessed the application of tech- nique, and the only questions that remained to be answered after this time were when and how the war would be ended and the cost that would be exacted in the process. But if one had recognized the point of decision in terms of possession of advantages, of choice, of superiority of numbers, and of technique, that ensured American victory, one had never realized the extent to which these advantages more or less guaranteed the U.S. Navy against loss.

The problem with this particular argument, however, is what the Japanese at the time believed to be the balance of losses in the various offensive efforts by the Americans in the central and southwest Pacific in the first nine months of 1944. Throughout the war the Japanese high command claimed to have inflicted losses on a scale and at a rate which even American shipyards could never have matched, and indeed Japanese claims were, by the least exacting of standards, fantastical. Thus the loss of the battleship *Hiei* off Guadalcanal (12–13 November 1942) could be portrayed as the price to be paid for a victory that had resulted in the sinking of five heavy cruisers, two anti-aircraft cruisers, eight destroyers, and one PT boat, with another two heavy cruisers heavily damaged and one destroyer moderately damaged.[32] Likewise the Japanese claim that in the November 1943 air battles over Rabaul and the upper Solomons they sank ten aircraft carriers, five battleships, nineteen cruisers, seven destroyers, and nine transports prompts not simply incredulity that they were even entertained, still less given credence for a minute, but the thought of what in retrospect is so obvious: Japanese claims seem almost deliberately to have been inversely related to reality.[33] The passing of time merely confirmed this trend to absurdity. On 16 October Tokyo announced that ten American carriers, two battleships, three cruisers, and one destroyer had been sunk, and three carriers, one battleship, four cruisers, and eleven other units had been damaged, over the previous four days. Just ninety minutes after this radio announcement, the totals were amended with the addition of one more carrier sunk and three more carriers plus either a battleship or cruiser damaged east of Luzon that day. On the following day, the final score was stated to have been eleven carriers, two battleships, three cruisers, and one cruiser or destroyer sunk, and eight carriers, two battleships, four cruisers, one cruiser or destroyer, and thirteen unidentified warships damaged, all since 12 October.[34] As noted elsewhere, only the heavy cruiser *Canberra* and light cruiser *Houston* were as much as damaged in the initial October 1944 exchanges off Formosa and the northern Philippines. By way of comparison with reference to previous Japanese claims, the Americans lost no warships in the actions off Rabaul and in the upper Solomons in November 1943, and in the first naval battle of Guadalcanal in November 1942 just one American light cruiser and two destroyers were sunk in battle, though two more destroyers sank afterward; another three American cruisers and two destroyers were badly damaged.

The Japanese naval air force was most certainly not alone among air services in consistently overstating its successes,[35] but it seems alone in terms of the Second World War in the sheer scale and consistency of overstatement, not simply in terms of overestimation of whatever success it commanded but in turning abject failure into massive, overwhelming victory. Indeed, Japanese representation of the events of 12–18 October 1944 has been called "a campaign of mendacity unprecedented since Napoleon proclaimed the destruction of Nelson's fleet at Trafalgar."[36] What seems truly extraordinary about the Japanese situation in this respect, however, is what seems to be the usually uncritical acceptance of the most preposterous of claims on the part of higher authority, almost as if individual aircrew could not survive battle and report back to their superiors without having accounted for an enemy and their superiors being morally bound to believe them. While various individual commanders seem to have entertained personal reservations which led them to discount the most extravagant claims but nonetheless still vastly overestimate the losses that had been inflicted on the Americans,[37] two points would seem to be relevant. The first, simply, was that there was no possible basis whereby land-based air power could inflict upon American carrier formations defeat on a scale that might be deemed significant. The second, which is an extension of the first, is that the Japanese recourse to "special attack tactics," *kamikaze* attack, actually makes sense in terms of reality, though not when set against Japanese perception at the time. *Kamikaze* attack did not merely offer the Japanese their best chance of registering success against American carrier, amphibious, and support formations: *kamikaze* attack offered the Japanese their only chance of inflicting loss on the enemy. *Kamikaze* attack could hardly do worse than register one sinking in eleven months.

This matter, the whole question of air power and its role and its relationship to surface forces, was but one of three matters of critical importance as the Japanese faced up to the prospect of the next American move or moves in the western Pacific. These three matters, one would suggest, were more or less of equal importance at this stage of proceedings. The second was the organization of surface forces and the tasks they would be given, and the third was Japanese expectation of enemy intent. On this latter point, one item of business would seem to be worthy of more than passing interest. Japan has not been afforded kind consideration in intelligence matters in the course of the Pacific war and, admittedly, the fact that her hand was shown at virtually every stage of proceedings because the security of her naval signals had been compromised accounts in large measure for such a state of affairs. But in the aftermath of the Philippine Sea, the SHO GO proposals were prepared on the basis of likely American moves rather than on the basis of a specific date, the first time Japanese planning had been so directed,[38] and certain highly placed officers correctly predicted American moves both in terms of theater and timing, though in one matter the Japanese were caught flat-footed: the American moves against Morotai and Peleliu, and the attendant carrier foray against the Philippines, which clearly foreshadowed a move into the Philippines, had not been anticipated by the Japanese.[39] At the planning meeting in Manila on 10 August between chiefs of staff and operations officers from the Naval General Staff, Combined Fleet, Southwest Area Fleet, and associated commands, the Naval General Staff estimate was that the next major offensive would be in the Philippines in late October, while one month later Ozawa predicted that the next American move would be made in the Philippines, and the Imperial General Headquarters directive (No. 462) of 21 September directed the *Kaigun* to complete its defensive arrangements on the basis of an enemy landing in the Philippines "in or after the last part of October."[40] With this as the starting point for subsequent planning, the weeks that followed the defeat in the Philippine Sea and the loss of the Marianas saw the various planning staffs try to bring together two very different forces. Air power was given the task of early warning, with reconnaissance conducted to a depth of 700 miles. This was considered extremely important because if the enemy's amphibious and support forces were to be caught, Japanese warships would have to be in the beachhead area in short order, within forty-eight hours of the initial landings according to the Japanese initial calculation.[41] If the enemy was able to establish himself ashore then the *Rikugun* was entrusted with the task of ensuring his destruction, though somehow this was not to intrude upon the general instruction that the army was to preserve its strength for "the decisive battle." As it turned out, the veteran 16th Infantry Division, which Japanese intelligence thought was involved with three American divisions on Leyte, was expected to contain American landings on Leyte and thereby allow reinforcements to be brought to the island.[42]

The most immediate of the *Kaigun*'s problems arose from the need to coordinate its naval effort with land-based air power, to be able to get to the prescribed battle areas in the shortest possible time despite their distance from the bases used by Japanese warships, and from the exact composition of Japanese naval formations. The second and third of these presented real difficulty. American landings in the Philippines would be well beyond the range of any naval force in terms of "immediate reaction time." Leyte was separated by twenty degrees of longitude from Lingga Roads and by twenty degrees of latitude from the Inland Sea. Such distances meant that battle and cruiser forces, whether based in the south or in home waters, would have to be refueled at least once before going into battle, and this meant that these formations would have to move to Brunei or to oilers sent to Coron Bay, which is the stretch of water that separates the two main islands in the Calamian Group. Given the slenderness of Japanese resources in terms of the number of oilers that remained in service at this stage of proceedings, such arrangements meant that any Japanese movement of major forces into the Philippines had to represent something close to the very limit of *Kaigun* administrative capability, not least because—and this is seldom properly appreciated—Japanese losses of oilers and crews had been so heavy that there was no longer any question of Japanese warships indulging in underway replenishment. Refueling had to be undertaken in bays, and any operation in the Philippines meant that with the few oilers still available, two months would be needed to ready the fleet for a second operation.[43]

More immediate, however, remained the questions of organization and the type of battle that was to be fought. Certainly in August there were arguments that the Imperial Navy should conduct normal operations with the intention of wearing down the enemy, though the wisdom of trying to conduct an attritional battle against an enemy with massive numerical superiority was seemingly elusive for such individuals as Vice Admiral Ugaki Matome, commander of the battle division containing the *Yamato*, *Musashi* and the *Nagato*; his short-lived championing of "naval guerrilla warfare," which seems to have been undefined, seems thoroughly in keeping with his very strong grip on lack of realism.[44] Admittedly in the course of the war games played in September it was agreed that surface forces, even if tasked to seek out amphibious and transport formations, could do battle with any carrier force they encountered *en route*, but apart from Ozawa this whole process of games and evaluation seems to have produced very little of note. As a result of Ozawa's continuous prodding, however, his carrier force shed first a cruiser detachment (which consisted of two heavy cruisers, one light cruiser, and seven destroyers under the command of Vice Admiral Shima Kiyohide), then a battle formation (with two battleships, one heavy cruiser, and four destroyers).[45] Originally the latter formation (commanded by Vice Admiral Nishimura Shoji) was to join the main battle force, under the overall command of Kurita. The exact role of Shima's force was initially not properly defined, but it was eventually ordered to proceed to Leyte Gulf via the Surigao Strait. Such employment, with its enormously long approach to contact, was then complemented at the last moment when Kurita's force was at Brunei and was given orders to enter Leyte Gulf on the morning of 25 October, when Nishimura's formation was detached from Kurita's command and instructed to proceed separately to Leyte Gulf via the Surigao Strait. With Ozawa having argued that his deception force could not coordinate its efforts with Kurita's force and that the latter would have to come under the direct command of the Combined Fleet,[46] there was no attempt either by the Combined Fleet or Kurita's command to synchronize the movements of Kurita's and Nishimura's forces, and also no attempt to ensure proper cooperation, even the concentration, of these two formations.[47] Moreover, and to anticipate one further matter, the precise orders that Kurita's force should negotiate the San Bernardino Strait and enter Leyte Gulf on the morning of Wednesday, 25 October, set at naught one of the basic assumptions that had governed the battle formation's preparation and training of recent weeks. The latter had been geared to fighting a night action, but the move against American carrier or amphibious formations would be in daylight.

Such developments were rather strange, especially after weeks of such careful attention to detail and planning, but the fact was that for all the planners' efforts in so many areas, by this time (20–21 October) the thread had already been lost for a number of reasons, of which one was obvious. The American carrier operations that began on 10 October lasted one week and ranged over the Ryukyus, Formosa, and the Philippines, and on the morning of the first day Combined Fleet headquarters ordered the implementation of SHO 2/SHO-NI-GO. This particular effort, as noted elsewhere, achieved little but resulted in something closely akin to the destruction of the entire land-based air part of Japanese intent. In one week the Japanese committed 1,425 aircraft to these battles, drawing from the northern home islands, China, and, much more seriously in light of future intent, even Ozawa's carrier air groups.[48] In all, the Japanese flew 761 offensive missions against the American carrier formations, with the Japanese losing 321 aircraft in the first three days of operations. By 17 October the 1st Air Fleet had been reduced to just ninety-eight aircraft and three days later had just forty in service, its one strike mission of the day consisting of two dive-bombers and three fighter-bombers. The disparity between the two sides was never more obvious than on 18 October when the 1st Air Fleet committed seventeen aircraft to attacks on American forces at Leyte Gulf while the American carriers used 685 aircraft in strike operations, close support missions over Leyte and combat air patrol excluded; by 21 October the 1st Air Fleet had been reduced to eight aircraft.[49] The two parts of SHO GO had been pulled apart days before the American landing forces had approached the 700-mile range set down as the limit of Japanese reconnaissance, while in terms of naval formations assigned to operations, by the time the various changes in the Japanese order of battle had resolved themselves, there were three fleets, each in effect under independent command. Kurita's fleet was divided into two fleets, which were to be separated by hundreds of miles, while Shima's formation was to duplicate the effort of Nishimura's force without knowing its plans, intention, and timetable, and liaison between naval forces and land-based air power, whether naval or army, was at best highly problematical.[50] By this stage, however, the Japanese commanders were left to wonder how the Americans could continue to put up so many aircraft after having lost so many carriers,[51] but the real point was that the Japanese had no option but to continue with the SHO-ICHI-GO option even though it had been wrecked beyond recall. Here were the circumstances that provided the context of the Imperial General Headquarters liaison meeting of 18 October, when the head of the naval operations section asked that the fleet be afforded "a fitting place to die," "the chance to bloom as flowers of death." That chance was now at hand, despite all the efforts of the previous four months.

CHAPTER FOUR

PRELIMINARIES
6–18 October 1944

ON THE AFTERNOON of Friday, 6 October 1944, Task Groups 38.2 (Rear Admiral Gerald F. Bogan) and 38.3 (Rear Admiral Frederick C. Sherman) sailed from Ulithi. Task Group 38.1 (Vice Admiral John S. McCain) had sailed from Seeadler harbor, at Manus, on 4 October, and Task Group 38.4 (Rear Admiral Ralph E. Davison) had sailed from Manus on 24 September and then operated off the Palaus until 5 October, when it discontinued operations in readiness for the concentration of Task Force 38's four groups two days later, just before dark, some 375 miles west of the Marianas.[1] During this time other elements of conflict manifested themselves. On 6 October the Japanese corvette C.D. 21 and the 10,241-ton merchantman *Akane Maru* were sunk off northwest Luzon by the submarines *Seahorse* and *Whale* respectively, while the submarine *Cabrilla* accounted for the 5,154-ton *Yamamizu Maru No. 2* west of the Luzon Strait. Off Penang, the British submarine *Tally-ho* sank a small auxiliary submarine chaser. On the following day P-47 Thunderbolts from the 10th Air Force and P-51 Mustangs and P-40 Kittyhawks from the 14th Air Force attacked a variety of targets in China and Indo-China, and B-24 Liberators from the Far East Air Force struck at Zamboanga, on the western tip of Mindanao, while fighter escorts attacked various targets of opportunity there and offshore. B-25 Mitchell medium bombers attacked Langoan, Tompaso, and Tondegesang, all of these targets being on Celebes, and also various installations on western Amboina as well as the Japanese airfield at Babo, in western

New Guinea, and positions on Doom Island. Other aircraft from the Far East Air Force attacked Kaoe, in northern Halmahera, and the oil storage tanks at Boela, in eastern Ceram, while Liberators from the 7th Air Force, operating from Saipan, attacked various targets on and shipping off Marcus Island, but to no discernible effect.[2] Marcus itself was subjected to bombardment by a task group consisting of three heavy cruisers and six destroyers on 9 October. On the previous day nine oilers replenished the carriers in 18°00'North 138°00'East in readiness for the start of operations.[3]

All these activities, spread over just four days and supplemented by other bombing activities and the sinking of Japanese warships, naval auxiliaries, and other ships, were evidence of a totality of war that was indeed the hallmark of the First and Second World Wars. Yet if one were to provide a single example of the totality of war across the globe, one would not cite any of these—though one would be tempted to cite the bombing of inoffensive Tondegesang for the first and only time during the war—but rather an event, actually two incidents, seldom afforded much attention in histories of the Second World War. On 5 October, on which day Task Group 38.4 came off station and Task Group 38.1 was making its way to the combat zone, the German submarine U-168, which was leaving for home after the German navy had decided to close down its base at Penang and end its operations in the Indian Ocean, was sunk in 06°20'South 111°28'East, north of Java. Two days later the 2,330-ton Japanese minelayer *Itsukushima* was sunk in 05°26'South 113°48'East, southeast of Bawaen Island in the central Java Sea. Both, the one the representative of the nation that occupied the homeland and the other of the nation that occupied the empire, were torpedoed and sunk by the Dutch submarine *Zwaardvisch*, operating from an Australian base under American orders. There is always something especially poignant about the operations of those ships or submarines, air force squadrons, and military formations from the conquered states of Europe that, rather than surrender, fought and so often died without homeland, in the cause of freedom and honor, but these two small episodes, and more obviously a Dutch submarine sinking a German submarine in the middle of the Java Sea, do represent the global dimension of total war as it came to be fought in the first half of the twentieth century.

After the concentration of its carrier formations, which for the first time meant that an American carrier force had more than a thousand aircraft embarked, Task Force 38 moved to the northwest, and passed the Douglas Reef (now called Parece Vela) in order to attack its first targets in the Ryukyu Islands. The attention of the air groups was divided, with aircraft from one group attacking targets in and off the Sakishima Gunto, from two groups—which were operating off Okino Daito Shima (or, more splendidly named, the Borodino Islands)—on and off Okinawa, and from the remaining group in and off Amami-o-shima. On this single day American carriers flew a total of 1,396 sorties and, in addition to sinking a number of warships, service auxiliaries, and merchantmen, claimed to have destroyed more than a hundred Japanese aircraft.[4] On the afternoon of the following day, 11 October, while the carriers from the other two groups refueled from twelve oilers, some sixty-one aircraft drawn from Task Groups 38.1 and 38.4 attacked the airfield and neighboring targets at Aparri in northern Luzon. With the Americans claiming fifteen enemy aircraft destroyed on the ground for the loss of seven of their own aircraft, and the carriers' combat air patrol accounting for just three Japanese aircraft during the day, little of any consequence was registered in these attacks, and it is generally conceded that the efforts of this day represented effort wasted; the main targets were on Formosa and these were afforded one day's respite. Admittedly some sixty-one replacement aircraft were flown into the carriers from the escort carriers of Task Group 30.8, but the basic point was that this was a day of preparation. After 1748, when refueling was completed, Task Force 38 steered north-northwest at a speed of twenty-four knots in order to reach its flying-off position off Formosa in readiness for arguably the most important phase of strike operations before the main effort unfolded in the fourth week of the month.

The American operations against Formosa were conducted with a total of 1,378 sorties on 12 October, 974 sorties on 13 October, and 146 fighter and a hundred bomber sorties by the carriers of Task Group 38.1 on the morning of 14 October, the latter effort being supplemented by the 20th Air Force with no fewer than 115 B-29 Superfortresses based at Chengtu. The main part of this second effort was directed against the aircraft factory in Okayama (Kang-Shan) some twenty miles north of Takao (Kaohsiung) in southwest Formosa, with Takao harbor being an alternate target for a number of Superfortresses. This was the first occasion when a raid by Superfortresses was numbered in three figures, and it was also the first occasion when American air power based in China cooperated directly with American naval power in the western Pacific.[5] The attack of 10 October was the first time since the Doolittle Raid of April 1942 that aircraft from American carriers had operated against the home islands. The carrier *Enterprise* and destroyer *Grayson* were the only ships from the original force employed here in October 1944 though two other warships in company, the light cruiser *Vincennes* and destroyer *Benham*, were slightly more than shadows of their former selves.

On 12 October the American operations missed aircraft that had left Okinawa for Formosa but nonetheless accounted for eighty-three aircraft, something like sixty being destroyed on the ground. The cost to the Americans was twenty-one aircraft, all but nine of the aircrew being rescued. On 13 October the offensive effort, which was concentrated in the morning, seems to have registered few successes in terms of Japanese aircraft destroyed and airfields neutralized. In fact, on this day the Americans found that there were at least fifteen airfields and airstrips in an area where they had expected to find only four. Moreover, late on this day, during twilight, the carrier *Franklin* narrowly avoided two aerial torpedoes delivered by an attack formation of four Betty bombers that managed to get under the radar cover, but she was hit by one of the Japanese aircraft, which careered across the flight deck doing little damage before it slid into the sea off the carrier's starboard beam.[6] At roughly the same time, the heavy cruiser *Canberra* was struck below her armor belt by a torpedo, causing damage that admitted some 4,500 tons of seawater that flooded the engine and boiler rooms and brought the ship to a halt. The *Canberra* nonetheless was saved from sinking and was taken in tow by first the heavy cruiser *Wichita* and then the tug *Munsee*.[7] On the following day (14 October) the light cruiser *Houston*, from this same task group, was damaged in almost the same circumstances as the *Canberra*: she was struck below the armor belt by a torpedo that wrought serious damage, flooding the engine room and causing a loss of power. She had to be taken in tow by the heavy cruiser *Boston*, but after the fleet tug *Pawnee* assumed the tow she was again hit by a Japanese aerial torpedo, this time in the stern, late on the afternoon of 16 October.[8]

American offensive operations, which on the afternoon of 14 October saw fighters from Task Group 38.4 attack the Aparri and Laoag airfields in northern Luzon,[9] produced meager returns, most certainly on the second and third days of operations. But these three days of operations brought the Americans success on a scale that could not have been expected because it prompted a Japanese reaction that brought about a defeat in the air that ensured the overall failure of the SHO GO endeavor. The reason was to be found in the very range of options the Japanese had prepared in readiness for the next American moves in the western Pacific. The SHO GO variants covered all likely targets, and the American move against Formosa thus presented the Japanese high command with the immediate question of whether to respond immediately to the challenge presented by the

American carrier force even though its own intelligence sources clearly pointed to the main American effort being made in the Philippines.

As early as 2 October radio traffic analysis had reported that American carrier forces in the Marianas were moving, and American signals intelligence in its turn recovered two Japanese assessments that the American moves would be directed against either the northern Philippines or Formosa or the entire Philippines. Even before these events, in the second half of September, the general consensus within the naval staff in Tokyo was that the next American offensive would be directed into the Philippines "in or after the last part of October,"[10] and with the beginning of that month the various national and regional commands still held to the belief that there would be a landing in the Philippines.[11] Such assessment went more or less alongside the 11 October Japanese intelligence assessment, which stated that Task Force 38 consisted of four task groups, each with two fleet and two light fleet carriers, plus one additional fleet carrier, and was supported by formations that numbered between them eight to ten battleships, fourteen to eighteen cruisers, and sixty destroyers plus escort carrier formations.[12] These were not the only estimates, and, inevitably, their accuracy has to be set against the errors of other estimates. In one matter the Japanese did have considerable difficulty, and that was their failure, if such it was, to anticipate that the Americans had chosen to move directly against the Visayans; to the Japanese the Americans' bringing airfields on Morotai and Angaur into service pointed clearly to a move against the southern Philippines, and probably not until November.

In large measure the Japanese defeat in the Philippines had assumed substance, indeed was an accomplished fact, prior to the landing operations of 17 and 20 October. This was the case because of the nature and extent of the victory won by American carrier air groups in the course of their operations after 10 October, but in effect these matters, the nature and extent of the American victory, and the reasons why the Americans prevailed have not been well understood, still less explained, until recent times. In large measure the reason for this lay with official accounts, specifically Morison's account of proceedings, which was more concerned with a most pretentious rendition of the ordeal of the *Canberra* and *Houston* and with Halsey's famous signal of 17 October than with an explanation of events.[13]

An explanation, as opposed to a description, of the Japanese defeat after 10 October is that in large measure the defeat was the result of piecemeal commitment of formations over a number of days rather than the concentrated use of air power that alone might have provided the Japanese with some chance of registering real success. With the first American attack, throughout the Ryukyus on the tenth, came the need for a Japanese decision regarding the response, if there would be any, but with the SHO options in place there was no realistic prospect of a Japanese finesse, letting the Americans strike at more or less empty airfields along what had never been considered a future battlefield but which had been prepared as a feeder route between the home islands and the Philippines and points south. With Toyoda, the Combined Fleet commander, on Formosa and hence in no position to make a decision, Kusaka, his chief of staff, made the decision to implement the air parts of SHO 1 or 2 at 0925.[14]

This decision proved disastrous, and on two counts. First, Kusaka ordered that the carrier air groups that were being trained at the Oita naval air base in Kyushu in readiness for fleet operations should be committed to this offensive. It was a decision that was immediately questioned by Ozawa and the senior staff officer of the carrier force, Captain Ohmae Toshikazu, but despite Ohmae's personally proceeding to Combined Fleet headquarters at Hiyoshi to question this order, the instruction stood and the carrier groups were committed, and suffered disastrous losses, after 12 October. With the air groups thus ravaged, the rationale for Ozawa's Mobile Fleet in the forthcoming battle was destroyed. It could not be expected to undertake offensive operations in its own right and it could not be put in the company of the battle force in an attempt to provide it with some semblance of air cover. At very best it could only play the decoy role, and it did not need all the units that had been allocated to it in order to do this. As a result, in the aftermath of the air battle the formation commanded by Shima was to be detached from the Mobile Fleet and ordered southward.

The second disastrous aspect of Kusaka's decision, and indeed the reason why this decision proved so disastrous for Japanese hopes, in part arose from the inevitable dispersal of force to which Japanese air power was subjected throughout the home islands, the Ryukyus and Formosa, and the Philippines. None of the various formations in these islands were at full strength, at best they were perhaps at two-thirds establishment,[15] but it was the combination of their dispersal, their vulnerability to a numerically superior enemy, and the fragmented nature of their commitment as they arrived in the Ryukyus or on Formosa that left them at a hopeless disadvantage despite what in the end amounted to a considerable superiority of overall numbers. As noted earlier, on 10 October the American carriers flew a total of 1,396 sorties[16] and on 12 October, which was the first day of the Japanese main effort, another 1,378.[17] Against such strength the numbers gathered by the Japanese on any single day after 11 October were wholly inadequate for the task in hand. The SHO 2 option was authorized by Kusaka at 1030 on the morning of 12 October,[18] but even by the time this decision was reached, the effort he had ordered was falling to pieces precisely because no single force, whether in the Ryukyus, on Formosa, or in the Philippines, could gather together the numbers needed to give battle on the basis of mere equality. On 14 October, for example, the Japanese committed about 400 aircraft against Task Force 38 and another 170 aircraft on the following day,[19] and overall, with 31 aircraft drawn from China, 250 from northern Japan, 172 from the Mobile Fleet, and about 200 army aircraft from Formosa, some 761 offensive sorties were flown against the American carrier force.[20] Nevertheless, the fact was that the 1,425 aircraft committed to the battle in one week was a force, both overall and by individual efforts on the days concerned, greater than any the U.S. Navy had faced at any stage over the previous thirty-four months; it was greater than anything that had been encountered in the course of the Solomons campaign and it was three times the size of the carrier air formations which had fought and lost the battle of the Philippine Sea. The point, however, was that the Americans savaged the formations committed piecemeal to battle with contemptuous ease. American losses amounted to seventy-six aircraft lost in combat and another thirteen operationally,[21] and these losses were incurred in the course of operations that accounted for 321 Japanese aircraft—which was the cost exacted from the Japanese for torpedoing just two cruisers.

The disparity of losses, and the outcome of these individual battles, owed themselves to a number of matters, the superior quality of American aircrew and aircraft being two of the most obvious and important. But certainly no less important were factors identified in the Naval War College analysis, namely

> the failure of the Japanese to realize (a) the excellence of Allied radar, (b) the Allied capability of long-range interceptions, and (c) the method of conducting such long-range interceptions.[22]

It was this combination, and specifically the American ability to hold strong fighter formations a hundred miles in front of carrier formations and then break the greater part of any Japanese effort without the Japanese

being able to sight—still less attack—the American carriers, that was crucial. This had been the lesson that the battle in the Philippine Sea could
have taught the Japanese, but the very nature of that defeat served to hide
its reasons and causes from the Japanese, with the result that there was a
curiously similar pattern to the air battles fought in the Philippine Sea and
prior to the landings in the Philippines in terms of the Japanese conduct
of operations, American effectiveness in defense, and what was almost
a complete immunity of American carriers from attack. It was not until
the aftermath of these battles in October 1944 that the Japanese came to
appreciate the reality and extent of their technological and operational
inferiority to the Americans in the air.

The crucial point about the air battles over the Ryukyus, Formosa,
and Luzon, however, was that in effect the SHO plan died. The critical
aspect of the SHO intention was for Japanese air and naval formations to
operate together, that they each contribute efforts that would complement
one another, but the destruction of Japanese air power between 10 and
15 October meant that if the fleet was to be committed it would not have
any real support from land-based air formations. And, as noted elsewhere,
Ozawa's carrier force most certainly would not be able to play any offensive
role and would be confined simply to a decoy and deception task because
the air groups of the carriers had been committed to the Formosa battle on
10 October. But scarcely less important were two other matters. First, the
Japanese claims of victory were pressed upon a nation that over the previous
two years had sustained a series of reverses, and while post-war interrogation of Japanese naval officers suggested that few were convinced of the
genuineness of their claims in the second week of October, the events of
the time strongly suggest otherwise. On the basis of the claims presented to
him by *Kaigun* representatives, claims that included the sinking of sixteen
carriers and overall more than half a million tons of American warships
in six days,[23] the emperor issued a victory rescript and there were celebrations throughout Japan and victory celebrations in *Rikugun* headquarters
throughout the Philippines. Indeed, and second, such was the confidence
in the victory that the Imperial Navy claimed it had won that its sister
service started to plan a "radical modification of Operation SHO-GO,"[24]
and there appears to have been a general confidence within the Japanese
services that if the Americans persisted with any offensive operation itself
in the Philippines despite their recent catastrophic losses, the opportunity
to administer the *coup de grâce* would present itself. It appears, on the
basis of such calculations, that the *Kaigun* was not prepared to use its

submarines to harass American shipping *en route* to its landing areas, though it seems that it had only sixteen of its total of fifty-eight boats available for such operations.[25] It was also not prepared to use its land-based air power offensively—not that it had any to use at this critical juncture. With the Japanese intent on bringing more air formations into the Philippines after the initial exchanges, their main consideration appears to have been to avoid a premature commitment of these air formations lest the Americans prove able to defeat them and thus leave the naval formations without air cover.[26] This latter consideration would seem to be a belated dose of objectivity, an objectivity that had been needed as never before over the previous ten days, but how these various pieces of Japanese calculations, planning, and public statements fit together defies understanding as, indeed, does the *Kaigun*'s capacity and willingness to lie to and deceive not just itself and the Japanese people but even the Sacred Crane.[27]

In this opening phase there are two episodes which most accounts of this battle cite and to which due acknowledgment must be made. The first concerned Vice Admiral Fukudome Shigeru, the commander of naval air forces first in the Philippines and then on Formosa, and the post-war story he told against himself. On 12 October,

> As I watched from my command post, a terrific aerial combat began directly above my head. Our interceptors swooped down in great force at the invading enemy planes. Our planes appeared to do so well that I thought I could desire no better performance. In a matter of moments, one after another, planes were seen falling down, enveloped in flames. "Well done! Well done! A tremendous success!" I clapped my hands. Alas! to my sudden disappointment, a closer look revealed that all those shot down were *our* fighters, and all those proudly circling above our heads were enemy planes! Our fighters were nothing but so many eggs thrown at the stone wall of the indomitable enemy formation. In a brief one-sided encounter, the combat terminated in our total defeat.[28]

One is not exactly sure how "a closer look" could have distinguished so clearly between two sets of aircraft, and one is less than convinced that it was either a sudden or an immediate discernment, not least because this episode infringed upon the second. This was the American attempt to lure Japanese fleet units to destruction by using the *Canberra* and *Houston* as bait.

The two parts came together when Toyoda, on the basis of reports from returning Japanese pilots, ordered Fukudome on the afternoon of

14 October to use his formations to annihilate what he described as the "remnants" of the American carrier formations.[29] Fukudome's "closer look" does not appear to have imparted much in the way of sober reality to the reports reaching Combined Fleet headquarters, nor does it seem to have imparted caution in complying with instructions from superior authority,[30] but the following morning Fukudome's command received a report that indicated the presence of a carrier task group some 240 miles from Manila. This formation was Task Group 38.4, then in the process of working over Luzon's airfields, but the first indication that the Americans might retain a greater strength than Japanese pilots were prepared to admit did not prevent Fukudome from ordering three strikes on the fifteenth. The first, by aircraft operating from Shinchiku airfield on Formosa, failed to find the group with the two crippled American ships, but the second ran into aircraft from Task Group 38.1 and was badly mauled for its troubles. The third strike was called off, and the formation returned to its bases after the flight commander's aircraft developed engine trouble. Two other attacks were entertained this day, the first resulting in minor damage to the carrier *Franklin*,[31] the other, involving some ninety aircraft from Luzon, failing to get anywhere near Task Group 38.4 because of the effectiveness of the combat air patrol, but this did not prevent claims being made about American carriers being hit.[32] On the following day there was one major air attack, involving more than a hundred aircraft, which resulted in the second torpedo hit on the *Houston* to which reference has already been made, but what was more significant was that Shima's command was ordered to sea in order to deal with what little remained of the Americans after the successful attacks by Japanese aircraft over the last few days.[33] What a force with two heavy cruisers and a destroyer screen was supposed to achieve even if all that had been claimed had been sunk is hard to discern, and evidently Shima was similarly persuaded and indeed seems not to have been fully convinced by the various claims in the first place. After refueling off Okinawa on the morning of 16 October, Shima led his force back to home waters.[34] That afternoon he received a signal informing him that an American force, with a minimum of six carriers, was operating east of Formosa.[35] At least in this case belated realism saved one Japanese force from pointless destruction, but amid all the claims of victory five matters are worthy of note. The first, simply, was that two American cruisers were torpedoed and heavily damaged within 150 miles of Formosa, but the Americans were able to recover these ships and get them back safely to Ulithi on 27 October.[36] It was not quite the epic of the *Franklin* of 19 March 1945 but it was nonetheless an

impressive feat, a *coup de théâtre*, and herein through coincidence was the second matter: the signal from Halsey to Nimitz that enabled the latter to release a press communiqué that read:

> Admiral Nimitz has received from Admiral Halsey the comforting assurance that he is now retiring toward the enemy following the salvage of all the Third Fleet ships recently reported sunk by Radio Tokyo.[37]

It was a statement that placed in proper perspective all Japanese claims of victory, specifically the official Japanese communiqué of 16 October,[38] and it was a statement that naturally entered the national archives. The third matter was simple: on this same day, 17 October, the first American landings took place in the Philippines.

The American plan of campaign, as outlined in the first command directive of 31 August 1944, set out the capture of "objectives in the Mindanao, Leyte and Samar areas in order to establish air, naval and logistic bases to cover subsequent operations to complete the re-occupation of the Philippines." At this stage of proceedings, the timetable for such operations were landings in southern Mindanao on 15 November 1944, in northwest Mindanao on 7 December 1944, and on Leyte and in the area of the Surigao Strait on 20 December.[39] The simplicity of this program and timetable belies the complexity of arguments and decisions at presidential and chiefs-of-staff levels, though three points may be noted *en passant*. It is interesting that MacArthur's directive should have referred to "the re-occupation of the Philippines" and not the liberation of the island archipelago, and it is equally interesting, though perhaps inevitable, that there was no reference to objectives beyond the Philippines and to the small matter of the prosecution of the war against Japan *per se*. No less significantly, the three operations stated had no provision for Allied land forces, even though the commander of land forces in South West Pacific Area was an Australian; now that the war had reached into the western Pacific the Australians and New Zealanders were to be consigned to secondary backwaters.[40]

In September 1944, a change of plans meant that the proposed landings in the southern Philippines were abandoned in favor of an assault on Leyte on 20 October. The American intention basically was to clear Leyte and southern Samar, primarily to serve as a springboard for further operations into the Philippines by ground and air forces and to clear the various straits that washed Leyte in order to facilitate naval movement into the Visayans. The military effort was to be undertaken by the 6th U.S. Army, which had under command the X and XXIV Corps. The X Corps had under command the 1st Cavalry and 24th Infantry Divisions, and under XXIV Corps were the 7th and 96th Infantry Divisions. Two more formations, the 32nd and 77th Infantry Divisions, constituted the reserve. Approximately 174,000 troops were available for the initial landings on Leyte, while the total number of ground troops assigned to operations on Leyte was about 202,500. In the initial assault the two corps each were to contribute about 52,000 men, with the balance of forces, especially in the initial landing phase, consisting of specialist assault and service troops. This phase was to open with landings by the 6th Army's two corps on northeast Leyte, XXIV Corps landing north of the Marabang River around Dulag and X Corps landing some fifteen miles to the north, between Palo and San Ricardo, just below Tacloban and the San Juanico Strait and San Pedro Bay. In addition, a reinforced regiment, drawn from the 24th Infantry Division, was to land in southern Leyte and on Panaon Island. The second phase of operations was to see the main American effort made, by X Corps, through the Leyte valley to Carigara and its bay. This valley was to be the main air and logistics base for further operations in the direction of Luzon. The final phase of operations envisaged the securing of Abuyog, on Leyte Gulf, the whole of southern Leyte, and Baybay and Ormoc on Leyte's west coast, and also Wright in southwest Samar, the beachhead at La Paz having been secured during second-phase operations.

The preliminary operations, designed to facilitate the landings inside Leyte Gulf, were to begin at dawn on 17 October when units from the 6th Ranger Infantry Battalion were to secure Homonhon Island and the northern tip of Dinagat Island, encouragingly known as Desolation Point. The aim of these efforts was to establish harbor lights on Homonhon Island and Desolation Point to facilitate the passage of the main invasion formations. The belief, or perhaps the hope, that the lighthouse on Suluan might yield charts showing the position of minefields meant that this island was added to the list. It was the American intention to pass minesweepers and Seals teams into Leyte Gulf once these outposts had been secured and thereby provide two days in which offshore defenses might be neutralized. Major bombardment of beach areas was to be undertaken on 19 October preparatory to main force landings the following day.

This plan of campaign dictated two immediate matters, the anchorages from which the main forces would sail and the timings of their departure.

Basically there were only two harbors, Humboldt Bay (Hollandia, present-day Jayapura), in Dutch New Guinea, and Seeadler harbor, Manus, in the Admiralties, that were large enough to gather together and then dispatch the various assault formations, while speed of available ships meant that the first force to make its way forward—the minesweepers and hydrographic ships bound for the islands and point guarding Leyte Gulf—cleared Manus on 10 October. Thus the opening of the American carrier offensive against Okinawa and the Ryukyus on 10 October took place at the same time as the first ships bound for Leyte sailed from Manus, though in fact certain units, because of the relatively slow speed of LSTs and the fact that they were embarked near Cape Cretin, more or less opposite Cape Gloucester in western New Britain, had to set out four days earlier on 6 October.[41] These forces being the exception, on 11 October the LST component of the XXIV Corps assault force sailed from Manus, and on the following day, 12 October, the greater part of the Northern Transport Group, plus the troops bound for Desolation Point, sailed from Hollandia while the close support and cover formations, including the escort carriers of Task Group 77.4 (Rear Admiral Thomas L. Sprague) and a number of transports bound for the northern beaches, sailed from Manus. On 13 October the balance of X Corps' assault formations, plus their close support forces, cleared Hollandia, while on 14 October the Southern Transport Group sailed from Manus. The *Wasatch*, the flagship of fleet commander Vice Admiral Thomas C. Kinkaid, with Lieutenant General Walter Krueger, the commander of the 6th Army, also embarked, sailed from Humboldt Bay at 0622 on 15 October, and did so in the company of most of the units of Task Force 77. The light cruiser *Nashville*, with MacArthur aboard, and her escorts joined company three days later.[42]

The Americans possessed such potential advantage in terms of numbers and qualitative superiority that they stood in no need to heed that fundamental Clausewitzian element of war—chance—though by the very nature of things this commodity impressed itself upon events to further American benefit. On 16 October, as the massive convoys headed for Leyte Gulf, the barometer fell and seas began to rise, and the greater part of the voyage was completed in storm conditions, with the carrier force, caught in the typhoon belt, unable to conduct offensive operations over the Visayans until the morning of 18 October.[43] This, however, was of small account when set against the twin facts that by this time the Japanese had few aircraft in this area and, having conducted reconnaissance missions over Ulithi and Hollandia–Humboldt Bay after they had been emptied of their guests, had no sighting of the invasion formations and no inkling of landings in Leyte Gulf until American troops, backed by fire from the light cruiser *Denver*, landed on Suluan on the morning of 17 October.[44]

Of course, American intentions had been discerned, and the American target of Leyte had been identified, by certain Japanese intelligence sources, but the critical point at this time was that the days when the various task groups were making their way toward Leyte were the same days that saw Japanese intoxication, a return of victory disease, as a result of the victories that had been won over the American carrier formations. The realization that the various claims were false may have dawned on certain individuals, but not upon the mass of Japanese army and navy formations in the Philippines. To such individuals, belated reports of sightings of American ships were immediately taken to mean that the last storm-lashed remnants of defeated carrier formations were trying to make their way to safety[45] or, if the Americans were so foolish as to try to undertake an offensive into the Philippines after the losses they had suffered, there seemed to be at hand an opportunity to administer the *coup de grâce*. Whichever way the cards lay, the Japanese, who had not used submarines to conduct reconnaissance of American anchorages or as picket lines which the Americans might cross and hence provide notice of intention,[46] were caught by surprise, both strategically and tactically, and their cause was not helped by events on 17 October. The lighthouse and position on Suluan was home to a detachment of thirty-two Japanese troops which, when attacked, sent a signal informing superior headquarters of their being attacked by a force that included two battleships, two carriers, and six destroyers. Exaggeration, it seems, was endemic in the Japanese forces, for here were just two light cruisers, four destroyers, and eight destroyer-transports.[47] Not altogether surprisingly, a reconnaissance mission over the Gulf flown in response to this message found no trace of a battleship, and in the stormy conditions failed to find a trace of any American force.[48] It was an unfortunate start to proceedings which at this stage many senior *Rikugun* personnel still thought might lead to "the decisive battle" that might overturn the reverses of the last two years.

Some pages ago there was reference to the fact that amid the various Japanese claims of victory "five matters are worthy of note." In fact, however, only three were then considered, hence the need to draw this chapter to a close by reference to the remaining two—this being quite deliberate and not a case of belated improvisation as a result of a sudden awareness of unintended negligence.

The fourth point, simply stated, was that it was on 17 October that Ozawa proposed changes to the SHO plan to take account of the losses incurred by the carrier groups, and in so doing set in train a series of changes that determined the final form of Japanese plans. The basis of this proposal was the fact, noted elsewhere, that the air groups from the 3rd and 4th Carrier Divisions, i.e., those belonging respectively to the *Zuikaku, Chitose, Chiyoda* and the *Zuiho* (the 3rd) and to the *Junyo* and *Ryuho* and the hybrid battleship-carriers *Hyuga* and *Ise* (the 4th), between them had lost about half of the 300 aircraft that had been committed to the previous week's battles and no longer had enough aircraft to fully equip even the units of the 3rd Carrier Division. Moreover, the units in the 4th Carrier Division were quite unfit for frontline operations, and from this time ceased to count in terms of their operating air groups. The *Junyo* was under repair between June and September 1944 as a result of damage sustained at the battle of the Philippine Sea, while the *Ryuho*, on account of her small flight deck, was allocated training duties in home waters for most of her service career, though she did serve at the battle of the Philippine Sea in June. As a consequence, these two carriers were to be used in a familiar transport role; the *Ryuho* sailed from Sasebo on 25 October with aircraft for Formosa while on 30 October the *Junyo* sailed from Singapore via Brunei Bay for Manila.[49] The *Hyuga* and *Ise* had for some time ceased to be considered seriously in terms of operating aircraft, and in any event there could never be any question of their having groups while carriers were under establishment. The two hybrids, therefore, were assigned the supporting role for Ozawa's carriers.

On 17 October, as a result of various discussions, the four operational carriers plus the *Hyuga* and *Ise* refueled at Tokuyama, on the Inland Sea, then sailed for the Oita air base. There the carriers were loaded with their aircraft for the simple reason that the pilots were not considered good enough to fly aboard, a conclusion that clearly left question marks against the carriers' collective ability to fly more than a single mission. This process was completed on 20 October, by which time fifty-two fighters, twenty-eight fighter-bombers, twenty-nine torpedo-bombers, and seven dive-bombers had been embarked, this total of 116 aircraft being complemented by the two seaplanes, apparently E15K Norms, with the light cruiser *Oyodo*.[50]

Table 4.1. The Japanese Carriers Assigned to Operations
in the Philippines and the Size of Their Air Groups, 18 October 1944

	Type 00 A6M Zeke fighters	Type 00 A6M5 Zeke dive-bombers	Type 2 D4Y1 Judy dive-bombers	Type 2 B6N2 Jill torpedo-bombers	Type 97 B5N2 Kate torpedo-bombers	Total
Zuikaku	28	16	7	14	-	65
Chitose	8	4	-	6	-	18
Chiyoda	8	4	-	-	4	16
Zuiho	8	4	-	5	-	17
Total	52	28	7	25	4	116

The extent to which the carrier force was under capacity can readily be understood. The *Zuikaku* was capable of embarking seventy-two aircraft and the *Zuiho* twenty-seven, while the other two carriers could be home to thirty-strong air groups. With the *Zuikaku* and *Zuiho* respectively able to carry twelve and three aircraft as spares, the total capacity of the four carriers was 174 aircraft, with an operational strength of 159.[51] The carrier force was roughly one-quarter under capacity, with the light carriers at not much more than half strength.

This disastrous state of affairs meant that Ozawa insisted on 17 October that the naval plan of campaign be recast in three significant ways. First, the original Japanese plan had envisaged the use of a decoy force operating from the home islands that would lure American carrier formations away from the Philippines, and hopefully into a position of vulnerability in which they might be attacked by air groups from the Japanese carriers. Clearly, after air group losses that precluded the carrier force playing its allotted role, there was little point in retaining battle and cruiser forces in the north. Ozawa, therefore, in proposing that the carrier force play a decoy and sacrificial role, set out the suggestion that formations not essential to this role be released for service with the other formations in the south. In effect, since it was decided that the *Hyuga* and *Ise*—which throughout the war had always been regarded as second-string units—should be retained with Ozawa's force, this meant that Shima's force, which consisted at this stage of three heavy and two light cruisers plus supporting destroyers, was ordered southward. The fact that there was no attempt to coordinate its operation with the other formation with which it was supposed to work in concert was quite another matter.

Second, the recasting of the carrier role meant that the battle force, which would be committed to moving through the Visayans in order to strike at American formations off Leyte and Samar, would not be afforded overhead cover by a carrier force operating either directly or in close association with it. In one immediate sense this decision had one result: it brought to an end the struggle to try to coordinate the operations of two forces that would begin their operations separated by something like 4,000 miles. What was involved in such a plan of campaign beggars the imagination, but, too easy to miss, the implication of this change was simply that the battle force would have to rely on land-based air power for cover during the approach-to-contact phase. Herein, of course, the events of the previous week told their own story. On 18 October Combined Fleet headquarters finally ordered the implementation of SHO 1/SHO-ICHI-GO,[52] this time in full and not just one of its parts, but by the time it did so there was no land-based air component. On the previous day, 17 October, the 1st Air Fleet had just ninety-eight aircraft in the Philippines, and three days later, on 20 October, it had a serviceable strength of no more than forty.[53] In effect, therefore, the battle force would not have any air support whatsoever, but in light of subsequent events, and specifically the signals sent as the battle force moved through the Visayans, it is doubtful that Kurita's command was ever thus informed.

The last matter relating to this sequence of events whereby various changes determined the form that the Japanese effort at Leyte was to take stemmed directly from what amounted to the destruction of Japanese land- and carrier-based air power. After the defeat in the Philippine Sea, a movement developed within the Imperial Navy to abandon conventional attacks in favor of "special attack" tactics. The first deliberate use of such tactics occurred on the afternoon of 15 October when Rear Admiral Arima Masafumi led such an attack, apparently in response to the realization that American carrier formations were more or less intact despite all the losses that had been sustained by Japanese air formations over the previous five days. Needless to report, this attack was supposed to have accounted for an aircraft carrier which "blew up and sank in thirty seconds"; in reality Japanese aircraft were unable to get past the American combat air patrol.[54]

Recourse to *kamikaze* tactics seems to have been a deliberate Japanese decision based on the realization that to date the conventional response to the challenge presented by the Americans was a failing one, but in truth the Japanese commanders simply could never have grasped the hopelessness of their position. The disparity of strengths was so great—on 18 October the Japanese formations in the Philippines flew seventeen sorties against ships in Leyte Gulf whereas the Americans committed 685 aircraft to strike operations alone[55]—that there was no real alternative to the use of *kamikaze* tactics, but this was of small account when set alongside a totally ineffective Japanese performance over the previous year that was wholly unsuspected by the Japanese high command at the time and which has been afforded very little consideration in the six decades that have elapsed since the end of the Second World War. Between 27 October 1942 and 23 October 1944 Japanese aircraft, whether land- or carrier-based, accounted for just the heavy cruiser *Chicago* in the central Solomons on 30 January 1943, the destroyer *De Haven* off Cape Esperance two days later, the destroyer *Aaron Ward* off Guadalcanal on 7 April 1943, and the destroyer *Brownson* off Cape Gloucester, New Britain, on 26 December 1943. Even if the sinking of the attack transport *McCawley* is credited to Japanese air power, this record is, by the least exacting standard, wretchedly inadequate, indeed quite pathetic: one cruiser and three destroyers sunk by Japanese aircraft in nearly two years, and this at a time when the Americans had broken into and through the main defensive zone.[56] What made the Japanese situation so disastrous was that the record of warships and submarines in the same period really represented no improvement over the aircraft. Japanese warships accounted for the heavy cruiser *Northampton* at the battle of Tassafaronga on 1 December 1942, the destroyer *Strong*, the light cruiser *Helena*, and the destroyer *Gwin* in a series of actions in the central Solomons in the first half of July 1943, and finally the destroyer *Chevalier* off Vella Lavella on 7 October 1943. If the Japanese, with some cause, could feel aggrieved not to have accounted for more than the *Northampton* in December 1942, the fact was that this was the sum of their sinkings by warships after the two naval battles of Guadalcanal had been lost in mid-November 1942. Japanese warships failed to account for a single enemy warship for more than a year after the *Chevalier* was sunk, and basically the same was the case for Japanese submarines. In the whole of the war Japanese submarines accounted for just four American destroyers, and apart from the escort carrier *Liscome Bay*, sunk off the Gilberts in November 1943, and the heavy cruiser *Indianapolis*, sunk in the Philippine Sea on 29 July 1945, Japanese submarines failed to account for a single enemy fleet unit after 26 October 1943. What is so striking about American losses is their slenderness, how cheaply victory was won, especially when the European war provides an example of the cost incurred in continental warfare. But that point notwithstanding, the fact was that by October 1944 the Japanese, even if they did not fully understand the position they were in, had no real means of offering resistance unless it was by recourse to *kamikaze* attack. As noted elsewhere, it was not a case of "special attack" tactics providing the best means of inflicting losses on the enemy but the only means whereby losses might be caused.

The fifth and final point that bears recounting at this stage concerns the nature of the American effort, and here one's starting point is the size of the forces that the Americans deployed for this operation. Gathered in various anchorages, but primarily at Hollandia, Dutch New Guinea, and Manus, in the Admiralties, were the units of three task forces. Most of the 183 ships of Task Force 77 were warships, while Task Force 78, the Northern Task Force, and Task Force 79, the Southern Task Force, numbered 518 oceangoing vessels. There were six old battleships, five heavy and six light cruisers, eighteen escort carriers, 86 destroyers, 25 destroyer escorts, and eleven frigates, a total of 157 warships, and 420 transport vessels, a total that included five headquarters ships, 40 attack transports and eighteen high-speed transports (converted destroyers), ten LSDs, and 151 LSTs, plus 79 LCIs and 221 LCTs. The balance consisted of patrol craft, minesweepers, and hydrographic and service ships. These formations and totals, obviously, did not include the ships of Halsey's carrier fleet, and perhaps the most notable feature of the ships gathered for the American return to the Philippines was that very few of these vessels had existed when the Philippines had been lost.[57]

The number of warships, which was to be exceeded both at Lingayen Gulf in January 1945 and at Okinawa in the following April, compares with the numbers employed at Normandy, and, of course, they had to operate over much greater distances and were dependent upon carrier air power in a manner which the forces employed in Operation NEPTUNE in June 1944 were not. But the real points of significance, which reached beyond mere numbers, are twofold. The first, directly related to the fact that so few of the vessels employed in October 1944 had been in existence in 1941, would repeat the point made in the opening chapter: the Japanese, through their basic error in underestimating their enemy, had to face not one enemy fleet but two. They had to face an inter-war and a wartime enemy. In a sense that is obvious but easily overlooked, the Imperial Navy fought the inter-war enemy, and itself, to exhaustion; it was then that American strength in depth—industrial and financial strength and stamina—provided the force that simply overwhelmed the *Kaigun*. It was possession of two fleets, one that fought for and won the initiative and another that then used it to ever-more telling advantage, that provided the basis of American victory.

But what is no less significant is that the victories that were won in the week prior to the landings on the islands off Leyte were very different from the ones that had been won during previous offensive operations in the central and southwest Pacific. In the Gilbert and Ellice Islands and then in the Marshalls, and throughout the central and upper Solomons, around Rabaul and then eastern New Guinea, the Americans had faced individual air bases, which were simply isolated from outside support and overwhelmed by carrier air power, then secured by amphibious assault. In fighting, or trying to fight, this battle, the weakness of the Japanese position was that there was no fleet at permanent readiness to come to the support of garrisons and air bases under attack, and each individual air base, by the very nature of things, was massively inferior in numbers to the force brought against it. Each Japanese base could be isolated from outside support, and it was this ability to pick off individual bases that made for American success to the extent that losses conformed to, and indeed perhaps gave rise to, "the-more-you-use-the-less-you-lose" dictum. But the attack on the Philippines was very different. Here there were many air bases and feeder strips and, of course, there were the fields in the Ryukyus and on Formosa that, in effect if not in geographical terms, presented the Americans with an enemy land-based air power that was essentially conti-nental in character. Obviously these islands did not present a contiguous land mass, but in strategic terms this was precisely what the Americans faced, and by any standard definition of the time they should have been defeated. The basic calculation of the inter-war period, and indeed the first three years of the European war, was that carrier air power simply could not match land-based air power in terms of numbers and quality of individual aircraft. The initial Japanese offensive in 1941–1942 had nailed the second of these points, but by October 1944 the balance had changed not in terms of aircraft but in terms of ownership. It was now American, not Japanese, carrier-based aircraft that were clearly superior in quality to their land-based opposite numbers, and this, of course, left aside the whole question of numbers and relative command and control facilities. What the American offensive after 10 October represented was something that was without precedent: naval air power took on and defeated an enemy with potential advantages of depth and dispersal, but advantages which proved to be obstacles to timely concentration for offensive operations. This was a state of affairs that might have been glimpsed by the most exceptional of the inter-war air power enthusiasts, but these must have been few in number because, one would suggest, there could have been few who could have foreseen such a development even in 1942. One would also suggest that the near-immunity of the U.S. Navy to operational loss simply could not have been anticipated since it ran directly counter to the main air power argument, which was the effectiveness of air power and the vulnerability of the attacker to losses. Be that as it may, the basic point was by the end of the third week of October events had unfolded in such a way as to ensure potentially overwhelming American advantage of position and numbers and a dispersal, and novelty, of Japan's response.

CHAPTER FIVE

ADVANCE AND CONTACT

18–24 October 1944

AFTER TWO DAYS of initial sweeping, clearance, and fire upon Japanese positions ashore in the course of which one LCI was lost and one seaplane tender and two destroyers were damaged,[1] American troops were put ashore on northeast Leyte on 20 October. On the day of the assault landings the American formations put ashore were not able to register inland advances of much more than a mile even though it was not until the third day ashore that real resistance was encountered. Nonetheless, on this first day, and at a cost of just forty-nine dead,[2] American formations were able to secure the Tacloban airfield and link the various beachheads across a front of some seventeen miles. Tacloban itself and the Dulag airfield were secured the next day, and American formations thereafter advanced in two separate directions, after coming south to Abuyog, to secure Baybay on 1 November and across Leyte to reach and take Carigara on the following day. Thereafter, even though on 29 October the 77th Infantry Division was transferred by MacArthur to reserve because it seemed it would not be needed, the Leyte campaign really began.[3]

Nonetheless, the landings on the offshore islands had been enough to set in train the Japanese naval effort that resulted in the battle of Leyte Gulf, and indeed the main Japanese formation, Kurita's battle force, sailed from the Lingga Roads at 0100 on 18 October.[4] With the Americans on 20 October deciphering a Japanese naval signal of the previous day that ordered two tankers then being held off Hainan to make their way to Coron

Bay to fuel Kurita's force,[5] the Americans had fair warning of Japanese intent, and, having refueled all four of the carrier task groups between 16 and 19 October, were able to deploy their full strength in support of the landings on the 20th. Two formations, Task Groups 38.1 and 38.4, were held covering Leyte and in a position to move against Japanese airfields and units in the Visayans. The other formations were held in the general area 15°30'North 128°00'East, south of Okinawa and east of Luzon. After a series of operations by carrier formations against Luzon after 17 October, the Americans held such massive superiority of numbers in theater that on 20 October Japanese air formations on Luzon managed just two attacks on American formations, one with two aircraft and the other with three.[6]

In looking at the Japanese services and subordinate formations one is reminded of the dictum that the weaker the formations the greater their number. The Japanese ultimately had six separate naval task groups committed to battle in the Philippines, plus a minimum of three air formations employed in or off the Philippines between 12 and 25 October. The complexity of Japanese arrangements can be gauged by the fact that when the SHO GO option was implemented it was afforded a date of 25 October, which meant that air reinforcements bound for the Philippines had to be on station at least one day previously in order to make their maximum effort at the same time as the surface formations. For the 4th Air Army, which in reality was a reinforced 2nd Air Division, this meant the concentration of heavy and light bombers on Clark Field and Lippa, both on Luzon, and of shorter-ranged fighters, fighter-bombers, and reconnaissance aircraft at bases around Bacolod in northern Negros. What this meant in practical terms was that various fighter formations from Luzon, plus other units from Formosa, Celebes, and northern Borneo, were directed to Bacolod, which rapidly became a quagmire. While fighters from the Japanese home islands and from China made their way to Clark Field, bombers from Formosa and Celebes were directed to Lippa, while heavy bombers from as far afield as Malaya and Formosa were sent to Clark Field. At the same time naval aircraft from the 2nd Air Fleet moved into the Philippines. The end result was the gathering of some 400 army and navy aircraft in the Philippines by the evening of 23 October, a remarkable achievement in light of the defeats of the previous two weeks.[7] But even with this effort the Japanese in the Philippines were no better provided than at any time in the previous seven weeks. Whatever formations were gathered would be outnumbered by the carrier groups that could be brought against them, and they faced a defeat as comprehensive as those that had overwhelmed Japanese formations in the Philippines in September and throughout the Ryukyus, Formosa, and the Philippines in the second ten days of October.

These movements reflected the fact that by the time American forces came ashore on Leyte, the Imperial Army had decided that its "decisive battle" would be fought on Leyte rather than on Luzon, as had been generally presumed until that time. That the Imperial Navy intended to fight its "decisive battle," plus the extent of the deployment of air formations to the Philippines as part of this effort, really left the *Rikugun* with very little option, but the fact that these decisions flowed from one another has served to obscure one fact: by the *Kaigun's* own calculations, it could not fight such a battle off Leyte. The basis of this statement is that the *Kaigun's* line of reasoning was that if the battle force was to be committed against the enemy amphibious, support, and covering formations off the beachheads then it had to do so within two days of the enemy landings, i.e. by or on, but not later than, 22 October. Two days was the maximum length of time the *Kaigun* estimated the American formations would need to unload and clear the beachhead area.[8] To take the story forward, this calculation was correct. At 1600 on 24 October the command post for the 6th U.S. Army was established ashore, a sure indication that the amphibious phase of operations was over, and by 2359 on 24 October the Americans had just three flagships, one attack transport, twenty-three LSTs, two LSMs, and twenty-eight Liberty Ships in Leyte Gulf; destroying these could hardly be part of the "decisive battle."[9] Now this basic calculation presented problems aplenty, and for obvious reason: there was no potential landing area in the Philippines within two days' sailing of the main Japanese formations.

This inability to bring forces against an enemy beachhead within the time that the *Kaigun* itself represented as the single period in which strategically significant results might be registered was the result of one simple fact, namely, the dispersal of forces across thousands of miles against an enemy possessed of decisive advantage of power of decision as to where, when, and in what force to mount successive operations. Japanese forces, shorn of the initiative and necessarily defensively dispersed, simply could not be concentrated across thirty-five degrees of latitude and forty degrees of longitude in time and in such strength as to present any real threat to American intent, wherever it might manifest itself. But if this was an unalterable fact of life, one that the Japanese could not have reversed under any circumstances, then there was another matter that exacerbated Japanese weakness at the time. This was a lessening of the *Kaigun's* strategic mobility in terms of the range and speed of fleet operations, which was directly related to a national weakness in oil supplies and oilers and a declining *Kaigun* replenishment at sea (RAS) capability.

For the *Kaigun*, RAS represented an ability acquired only late in 1941—the units of the formation that attacked the U.S. Pacific Fleet at Pearl Harbor undertook their first RAS exercises in the three weeks before they sailed from Etorofu in the Kuriles—but was never generally acquired throughout the various fleets and had been more or less lost by autumn 1944. Such a state of affairs appears to have been the result of four sets of circumstances coming together by this stage of the war. First, Japan was always short in numbers of oilers. The number of oilers that were available could not meet both national and service requirements, and the numbers available to the *Kaigun* were insufficient to meet the conflicting claims of training, transport, and operational requirements. Second, as naval oiler losses mounted the *Kaigun* was obliged to take up civilian oilers, and these, having been built before 1941, were not fitted to provide underway replenishment and were beset by declining standards of seamanship; manpower losses, not just in numbers but in quality, simply could not be made good. Third, the extent of *Kaigun* losses by this time meant that it lacked the number of destroyers needed to provide effective screens for major units and most certainly lacked the number of destroyers to provide effective screens for major units when undertaking RAS—as events off the Marianas on 19 June had indicated only too well. Fourth, the increasing reach of American air power, whether land-based or carrier-borne, meant that the Japanese could not afford to commit oilers in the forward battle areas. Knowledge and experience of RAS procedures could not be wholly lost, but as losses rose throughout the spring and summer of 1944, so the formations that remained to the *Kaigun* began to shed strategic mobility. In May 1944 it lost two large oilers, in the following month two large and four smaller oilers. In July one large oiler and one small one were lost, and in both August and September four oilers were lost; the August losses included two of the largest tankers in service.[10] The loss of eighteen oilers of 167,976 tons was prohibitive, and the significance of such losses can be gauged by the fact that Japan began the war with just fifty-nine oilers of 2,000 tons or above while the *Kaigun* had just twelve purpose-built service oilers, a total that excludes those requisitioned from civilian sources. The losses of spring and summer 1944 clearly pointed to a drastic lessening of the *Kaigun*'s RAS capacity, though it needs to be noted that Kurita's formations were scheduled to undertake a series of RAS exercises during the second half of October.[11] Obviously this represented an attempt to recover some degree of strategic mobility in anticipation of "the decisive battle."

With carrier formations based in home waters and the battle force held in Lingga Roads, just south of Singapore, any American movement against the Philippines presented what was, in essence, an insoluble problem for the Japanese high command. For the battle force, the approach to Mindoro would involve steaming nearly 1,600 miles, and even if a force was refueled, whether under way or in a suitable bay such as Brunei Bay on northern Borneo, Ulugan Bay on the northern coast of central Palawan, or Coron Bay in the Calamian group between northeast Palawan and Mindoro,[12] the fuel problem was certain to be acute once battle was joined, speed increased, and fuel consumption increased considerably. The problem was not so much the battleships and heavy cruisers, which carried enough oil to undertake high-speed action even after protracted steaming at economical speed, but the light cruisers and destroyers. But with no real RAS capability the battle force would be obliged to refuel in one of the bays with an obvious loss of time it simply could not afford.

For the forthcoming battle the Japanese naval high command made six oilers available to Kurita's formation. These were the *Itsukushima Maru*, *Nichiei Maru*, *Omurosan Maru*, *Ryoei Maru*, *Banei Maru* and the *Yuho Maru*. Belatedly, it appears that the *Kaigun* also acquired two tankers, the *Hakko Maru* and *Nippo Maru*; these had been army tankers and were transferred after heated exchanges between the staffs. With the exception of the *Nichiei Maru*, which was at Hainan, and *Ryoei Maru*, which was *en route* to Makou in the Pescadores off Formosa, all these oilers were at Singapore when Kurita's formation was ordered to proceed to sea. Accordingly, at 1125 on 17 October Kurita ordered two oilers, the *Hakko Maru* and *Yuho Maru*, to proceed to Brunei Bay in order to replenish his force, and he detached the destroyers *Michishio* and *Nowaki* in order to provide these two oilers with escorts.[13] Subsequently he ordered the *Banei Maru* and *Itsukushima Maru*, in the company of the escorts *Chiburi* and C.D. 19, and the *Omurusan Maru* and *Nippo Maru*, escorted by the minelayer *Yurijima* and the escort C.D. 27, to proceed to Brunei Bay. With the first group leaving on 19 October and the second group on the following day, their movement could only have been intended as the means of ensuring the refueling of Kurita's force after battle; both groups arrived at Brunei Bay on 22 October but after Kurita's force had sailed.[14] At this same time Combined Fleet headquarters ordered the *Nichiei Maru*, escorted by the

Kurahashi and C.D. 25, to proceed to Coron Bay. This group of ships sailed
at 1830 on 18 October, but was advised by the local escort commander to
make for Ulugan Bay, on the northern coast of central Palawan, because
the anchorage in Coron Bay was within the range of American land-based
aircraft. This advice was heeded, and the *Nichiei Maru* and her consorts
arrived in Ulugan Bay on 22 October, but two days later the *Nichiei Maru*
sailed for Coron Bay, where she remained between 25 and 28 October.
Thereafter she proceeded to Manila, where she remained for a day before
returning to Singapore.[15]

The deployment and whereabouts of the oilers were obviously crucial
to Japanese operations, and the whole issue of refueling was one of the
two principal activities undertaken by Kurita's formations and units once
they had arrived in Brunei Bay. Western accounts of these proceedings
have been confused and confusing, but the basic story can be told simply.
Kurita's force arrived off Brunei Bay on the morning of 20 October and
Kurita gave orders at 0918 for units to proceed independently to anchorages
in the bay; all units were secured between 1100 and 1230. With the *Hakko
Maru* and *Yuho Maru* and their escorts not having arrived, Kurita gave
orders for the heavy cruisers to refuel the destroyers and the battleships to
refuel the heavy cruisers. With Kurita's force needing some 16,000 tons of
oil and the battleships passing between 500 and 600 tons of oil to individual
cruisers and the latter supplying about 200 tons to the individual destroyers,
the arrival of the oilers saw the *Hakko Maru* refuel first the *Musashi* and
then the *Mogami* while the *Yuho Maru* refueled the *Yamato* and *Tone* in
turn. The process of refueling the entire force was completed by 0500 on
22 October, some three hours before the Japanese formations were to sail.[16]
When set against the relative smoothness of this development, plus the fact
that all the Japanese units were fully supplied with oil, the codicil is easy
to miss. The distance from Brunei Bay to Leyte, via the San Bernardino
Strait, is some 1,400 miles, and if that was well within the range of *Yugumo*-
class destroyers with an endurance of about 5,000 miles at eighteen knots,
in real terms, when the requirements of high-speed steaming in the face
of air attack or contact with enemy surface forces are taken into consideration, Leyte and Samar represented the very limits of endurance. Kurita,
in a signal to Combined Fleet, noted that his force could arrive off Leyte
on the evening of 24 October if it made sixteen knots during its passage,
and would have three-fifths of its oil remaining, but that it could arrive on
the morning of that same day if it made twenty knots. If it did so, however,
it would have used half its fuel and would need to be refueled, presumably

in Coron Bay or Ulugun Bay, on its return.[17] There were oilers available for this task but the basic point was that Kurita's formations had virtually no capacity for extended high-speed operations off Samar and Leyte.

These matters have commanded little attention in histories of this campaign and battle; oilers, refueling at Brunei, and related matters invariably are given scant consideration. What has commanded the greater attention has been two other matters that manifested themselves at Brunei Bay—the reorganization of Japanese formations and the final orders for the whole SHO offensive, and the meeting of Kurita with senior officers on the evening before the Japanese formations sailed.

With reference to the framing of the final orders for this offensive and the attendant changes in the Japanese order of battle, there were three main provisions. First, the timing of the operation was set, with the morning of 25 October selected for the arrival of Japanese battle formations off Samar and Leyte.[18] Second, Kurita's force was divided between two formations. He retained the 1st and 2nd Task Groups, but Nishimura's 3rd Task Group, the weakest of the three formations with just two battleships, one heavy cruiser, and three destroyers, was detached and formed into a separate command. It was to proceed to Leyte via the Surigao Strait while Kurita's force sailed through the northern Visayans and via the San Bernardino Strait.[19] Third, with Ozawa's carrier force beset by losses among its air groups which precluded its playing anything other than the role of decoy, Shima's cruiser force was formally detached and ordered south where, under the command of Southwest Area Fleet, it was to proceed to the battle area via the Surigao Strait.[20]

The meeting of Kurita with senior officers took place in the *Atago* between 1700 and 2000 on 21 October. This was the last fleet briefing prior to the operation,[21] when the final orders were issued, and it was a session notable for the fact that by the time it was held there was open dissent within the ranks of senior naval officers on three separate counts. There was disbelief that the battle fleet, which had been training assiduously for a night action, was to be committed to an unprecedented daylight attack, and there was a belief among some *Kaigun* officers that if this operation really was as important as was claimed then Toyoda, the fleet commander, should have been personally in command.[22] More substantially, there was widespread disenchantment with a plan of campaign that indicated that the Japanese would seek to get among the transport and amphibious forces off Leyte; this was held to be demeaning to the *Kaigun* and that its proper role, and any hope of fighting a decisive battle, had to involve battle with enemy main forces, i.e., carrier and battle formations. Kurita answered the latter concerns in a speech noted in all accounts of this battle:

> I know that many of you are strongly opposed to this assignment. But the war situation is far more critical than any of you can possibly know. Would it not be shameful to have the fleet remain intact while our nation perishes? I believe that the Imperial General Headquarters is giving us a glorious opportunity. Because I realize how very serious the war situation actually is, I am willing to accept even this ultimate assignment to storm into Leyte Gulf.
>
> You must all remember that there are such things as miracles. What man can say that there is no chance for our fleet to turn the tide of war in a decisive battle? We shall have a chance to meet our enemies. We shall engage his task forces. I hope you will not carry your responsibilities lightly. I know that you will act faithfully and well.[23]

This was a speech that silenced doubts, that was greeted by standing applause and shouts of "Banzai!" and which has been afforded generous historical treatment. In an obvious sense it is not difficult to see why this was so, though it is quite possible that in Kurita's audience there were individuals who could say that there was no chance of the Japanese fleet turning the tide of war in one decisive battle. The fact was that the *Kaigun*, very likely the best in the world in 1941 in terms of carrier and battleship operations, was a one-shot force, and by 1944 there was nothing that it could have done to reverse the verdict of arms. The Americans, possessed of a strength in depth that was denied the Japanese, held such overwhelming superiority of numbers and qualitative advantage that even a major Japanese success was unlikely to have any significant or lasting impact upon the unfolding of events.

Kurita's speech and reorganization of Japanese forces have tended to obscure a number of pertinent points. The first concerns the change in the balance of Japanese forces. On 14 October the deployment of Japanese forces was as shown in Table 5.1.

Table 5.1. Japanese Formations and Assigned Units, 14 October 1944							
	Carriers		Battle-ships	Cruisers		Destroyers	
	Fleet	Light		Heavy	Light	Fleet	Escort
Ozawa's force	1	3	-	-	2	4	4
Shima's force	-	-	-	2	1	3	-
Northern formations	1	3	2	3	4	12	4
1st Task Group	-	-	3	6	1	9	-
2nd Task Group	-	-	2	4	1	5	-
3rd Task Group	-	-	2	1	-	3	-
Southern formations	-	-	7	11	2	17	-
Detached units	-	-	-	-	-	2	-
OVERALL TOTAL	1	3	9	14	6	31	4

By 17 October, and allowing for some inconsistencies as intentions changed, the Japanese deployment of force was as shown in Table 5.2.

Table 5.2. Japanese Formations and Assigned Units, 17 October 1944							
	Carriers		Battle-ships	Cruisers		Destroyers	
	Fleet	Light		Heavy	Light	Fleet	Escort
Ozawa's force	1	3	-	-	2	4	4
Shima's force	-	-	-	2	1	7	-
Northern formations	1	3	2	2	3	11	4
1st Task Group	-	-	3	6	1	9	-
2nd Task Group	-	-	2	4	1	5	-
3rd Task Group	-	-	2	1	-	3	-
In company				1	1	1	-
Southern formations	-	-	7	12	3	18	-
Detached units	-	-	-	-	-	2	-
OVERALL TOTAL	1	3	9	14	6	31	4

By 22 October, however, with the *Oyodo* having joined Ozawa's force, Shima's force was now committed to the south and had shed three destroyers for local duties. Kurita's force had been divided into two separate formations, but with the two destroyers that had escorted oilers to Brunei having rejoined their parent formations, the Japanese order of battle reflected the change of emphasis in favor of the south, as shown in Table 5.3.

The reason for the recasting of formations was a final plan of attack that envisaged a double envelopment on the part of two separate formations converging on Leyte Gulf, one via the San Bernardino Strait and the other, after an advance through the southern Visayans, via the Surigao Strait. Such deployment, with the attendant division of forces thus, has been—*mutatis mutandis*—a feature of war throughout the ages, but these Japanese arrangements prompt the immediate and obvious thought: Nishimura's command was so small that it is difficult to see what it might have achieved even under the most favorable of circumstances, which were unlikely given that its approach to contact necessarily involved crossing the Sulu Sea in full view of extensive American reconnaissance by land-based aircraft. Moreover, the division of Kurita's original command seems to have had very little administrative and tactical justification. The formation of a separate command might have been sensible in terms of dividing the battleships *Fuso* and *Yamashiro* from formations otherwise slowed by their

Table 5.3. Japanese Formations and Assigned Units, 22 October 1944							
	Carriers		Battleships	Cruisers		Destroyers	
	Fleet	Light		Heavy	Light	Fleet	Escort
Ozawa's force	1	3	2	-	3	4	4
1st Task Group	-	-	3	6	1	9	-
2nd Task Group	-	-	2	4	1	6	-
Central formations	-	-	5	10	2	15	-
Detached units	-	-	-	-	-	3	-
3rd Task Group	-	-	2	1	-	4	-
Shima's force	-	-	-	2	1	4	-
Southern formations	-	-	2	3	1	8	-
Detached units	-	-	-	1	1	1	-
OVERALL TOTAL	1	3	9	14	7	31	4

presence, but such an argument fails in light of the retention of the *Nagato* with Kurita's force. Unless Nishimura's formation was detached from the main force because its battleships, having been assigned to training duties since 1942, were the least prepared for fleet operations,[24] it is difficult to see what logic underpinned these arrangements, though it is equally difficult to discern what might have transpired had Kurita's force been maintained intact. Nishimura's force attracted upon itself no more attention and forces than were already there in the first place, while there seems no possible basis for a view that suggests that the heavy cruiser and destroyers with Nishimura might have provided an extra measure of security against submarine and air attack during the approach to contact and against American forces off Leyte Gulf. The same point could be made about the deployment of the 16th Cruiser Division, which consisted of the heavy cruiser *Aoba*, the light cruiser *Kinu,* and the destroyer *Uranami.* These three units had been part of the Southwest Area Fleet but were in the company of Kurita's fleet when it sailed from Lingga Roads on 18 October, on which date Combined Fleet headquarters ordered these ships to provide close support for army transports that were to make their way forward to Leyte. The *Aoba* was eventually hit by one of six torpedoes aimed at her by the American submarine *Bream* outside Manila on 24 October, and her two consorts were separately sunk by carrier aircraft on 26 October, the *Kinu* off Masbate and the *Uranami* off Panay.[25] In light of their collective and individual loss it could be argued that they would have been better lost had they remained with Kurita's force rather than expended during what was a secondary or tertiary operation, albeit one with obvious importance to inter-service relations.

More seriously, the same basic points can also be made about Shima's command. If Nishimura's force was assigned a diversionary role, to attract and hold American attention as Kurita's forces moved through the Sibuyan Sea into the San Bernardino Strait, then it hardly needed a second force, complete with what was by Japanese standards at this stage of the war a fair number of destroyers, in this same area of operations. The failure to ensure any measure of coordination between Nishimura's and Shima's formations has largely been explained in terms of personal antipathy and an unwillingness to gather the two formations together lest Nishimura be placed under Shima's command. But the force under Shima's command could hardly add much to any victory won by Nishimura's task group, while it could not hope to reverse any check or defeat that Nishimura's formation encountered.

But the lack of any coordination of the two formations detailed to break into Leyte Gulf through the Surigao Strait was matched by another: Kurita and Nishimura, who were old friends, made no attempt to relate their separate endeavors. The timing for arrival off Leyte was given for the morning of 25 October and there seems to have been no other arrangement. This lack of coordination between the three forces that were to fight in Philippine waters seems extraordinary, and it has been the subject of much historical comment. But what seemingly has never been the subject of critical consideration is another matter: if the Japanese intention was to put the battle forces off Samar and Leyte, and it was known from the pattern of American air operations that the U.S. carrier forces were gathered off Luzon, then there was little point in committing the main force to the route through the Sibuyan Sea and San Bernardino Strait while the secondary or diversionary force came through the Sulu Sea. It would seem, *prima facie*, that a case could be made for either of two arguments, namely that Japanese interest and intent would have been best served by a reversal of the deployment that was put into effect or, perhaps more interestingly, Kurita's original force should not have been divided but, with Shima's cruisers and escorts attached, should have instead been directed to the Surigao Strait. The attractiveness of this latter argument is obvious, but no less obvious is its weakness: such a course of action could not have produced a situation more promising than the one that unfolded on the morning of 25 October for Kurita's force when it arrived off Samar after passing through the San Bernardino Strait. But a clash between the six old battleships of the American battle line, complete with advantages of position and radar, and seven of Japan's remaining nine battleships—including the *Yamato* and *Musashi*—in the Surigao Strait during the night of 24–25 October would have been most interesting.

The Japanese deployment and intention largely shaped the course of subsequent events, albeit not to *Kaigun* advantage, yet at this same time, when Kurita's force sailed from Lingga Roads to Brunei and refueled and Shima's force began its journey south, there were two matters on the American side that were scarcely less important in the shaping of events. The first of these can be defined simply: a reconnaissance aircraft found Kurita's force as it approached Brunei, but its incomplete sighting report was disregarded and the American high command remained unaware of the whereabouts of the Japanese battle force for the moment. The second is more difficult to define and is a matter which appears to have been passed over without comment in all accounts of this battle.

The sighting report, and its being ignored, are somewhat surprising, and for obvious reason. U.S. naval intelligence agencies did not know the whereabouts of the Japanese battle force, but they knew that after March 1944 it had been based at Singapore, and 7th Fleet intelligence did its sums and worked out that any force coming from Singapore would have to be refueled en route to the Philippines. Accordingly, when American ability to read Japanese signals provided crucial information that indicated that Japanese warships were to be refueled off Formosa, in Coron Bay, and at Brunei, the latter was subjected to special reconnaissance by American aircraft. On the morning of 20 October, as Kurita's force arrived off Brunei, it was found and reported. The Japanese overheard no fewer than nine sighting reports and the report being relayed by radio stations on Oahu and the Admiralties, and they assumed that their presence had been compromised. In fact, because the main report referred to a battleship, three light cruisers, three destroyers, and six other warships, the report was discounted,[26] and there seems to have been no attempt to work out what might have been seen and no other reconnaissance flight ordered. In fact, the section and individuals within 7th Fleet intelligence concerned with the ordering of reconnaissance over Brunei Bay were never informed of the sighting report which, even if wrong in numbers and composition, nonetheless placed a force with a battleship exactly where such a force was expected to be at or about this time.

The significance of this error is easily overstated. The Americans found Kurita's force on 23 October and both on this and the following day inflicted significant losses upon it. In effect, Halsey and Kinkaid were afforded two days' warning of Japanese deployment, and in one obvious sense the loss of two or three days in warning time, prior to 23 October, was neither here nor there; the time that was made available was sufficient to allow the Americans to inflict significant losses upon the enemy and to undertake basic precautionary measures which should have confounded Japanese intent. But herein one touches upon the second matter, previously noted but not defined. Accounts of the battle of Leyte Gulf invariably focus upon two matters—Halsey's failure to maintain a force covering the San Bernardino Strait on the night of 24–25 October and Kurita's turnaway off Samar when in contact with enemy carrier formations on the morning of 25 October. Accounts of this battle invariably pass over the question of why Halsey, at the very time when Kurita was in Brunei Bay, should have

ordered two of his four carrier formations back to Ulithi for rest and replenishment. Lest the point be missed, Halsey did so on 21 October at a time
when intelligence for the first time suggested that the Japanese, contrary
to previous expectation, were likely to give battle in the Philippines[27] and
when Halsey was unaware of the whereabouts of any Japanese naval forces,
whether to the north or to the west. Even if this point is overdrawn, at the
very least Halsey should have retained all his formations on station until
definitive intelligence indicated that the Japanese fleet would not contest
the Leyte landings.[28]

A certain care needs be exercised in making this point. Any criticism of
Halsey for detaching two of his task groups before he was aware that the
Japanese were on the move invites an obvious answer: if formations were to
be detached then the only time they could be so ordered would be before
the whereabouts of the Japanese force was established. Criticism, or at least
the questioning of decisions, needs be measured, but this decision, and the
treatment of it in histories of this battle, does seem rather perverse.

   This decision followed the Formosa air battle (11–16 October), the air
operations in support of the preliminary landings in the Visayans preparatory to the main landings on Leyte (17–20 October), and the operations
that attended those landings. In the course of second-phase operations, by
which time the American hope of precipitating a fleet action by the bait
supplied by the *Canberra* and *Houston* had largely dissipated, and at a time
when the escort carrier *Sangamon*, the heavy cruiser *Australia*, and the
light cruiser *Honolulu* were hit off the beachheads,[29] the four carrier formations of Task Force 38 refueled and carried out offensive operations more
or less in succession, their main effort being concentrated against northern
Luzon. The American intention was to have all four formations on station
during and immediately after the landings on Leyte on 20 October.[30] In
the course of these operations, however, Halsey declined to commit the
carriers of Task Force 38 to sustained operations over southern Luzon and
the Visayans on 18–19 October. Halsey held his formations northeast of
Luzon and thus ensured that the task of neutralizing Japanese air power
in and over the Visayans was left to the escort carriers of Task Force
77, the proper task of which was providing air cover and support for the
amphibious forces during their approach to Leyte and during the assault
phase.[31] Once the landings were conducted and American forces securely
established ashore, Halsey ordered Task Groups 38.1 and 38.4 to refuel,

the former being ordered to proceed to Ulithi on 22 October and Task Group 38.4 to follow the next day.[32] At the same time, on 22 October, the fleet carrier *Hancock* was transferred from Task Group 38.2 to Task Group 38.1,[33] while on the following day the *Bunker Hill* was detached from Task Group 38.2 in order to take on more fighters from Ulithi.[34] With the light carriers *Cowpens* and *Cabot* having left on 20 October in order to return to Task Groups 38.1 and 38.2, respectively, Task Group 30.3 finally arrived at Ulithi on 27 October, after which time the *Canberra* and *Houston* were sent to Manus.[35] What this meant was that Halsey intended to have on station two carrier formations. One, Task Group 38.3, was to have the fleet carriers *Essex* and *Lexington* and light carriers *Langley* and *Princeton*, and the other, Task Group 38.2, which had been the strongest single formation in Task Force 38, was to be reduced to just the fleet carrier *Intrepid* and light carrier *Independence.* However, the *Cabot* was to be recalled and was to play a full part in the events of 24 October.

Amid the various changes of the order of battle and alternative refueling and strikes, it is easy to lose sight of one salient point. As a result of Halsey's orders, a task force that at the time of its first offensive operation mustered nine fleet and eight light fleet carriers, and a total of 1,077 aircraft, was to have been reduced to a total of just three fleet and four light fleet carriers, with just 400 aircraft. Even if allowance is made for the return of Task Group 38.4 to the fray, the totals are raised to five fleet and five light fleet carriers, and a total of about 600 aircraft. The overall reduction in number of aircraft would have been in the order of two-fifths of original establishment, and the most powerful single formation available to Task Force 38 was to be absent in the crucial phase of the battle (Table 5.4).

Such a situation—half of the American carriers being ordered to clear the Philippines before the Japanese battle force had been encountered and reported on the morning of 23 October—would seem to justify the description of the somewhat unusual. The orders would not seem to have been justified in terms of real need. The carriers of Task Groups 38.1 and 38.4 were able to play a full part in operations when they rejoined the fray, and American losses to that date had been decidedly modest. The six days of the Formosa battle had cost the fast carriers seventy-six aircraft in combat and another three operationally, while losses between 17 and 23 October from all causes numbered just thirty-six, of which twenty-five were incurred on 17 and 18 October.[36] Such overall losses, divided between two formations and nine fleet and eight light fleet carriers, hardly suggest that one or two formations had to return to Ulithi for more aircraft. But the absence

Table 5.4. Task Force 38 and Assigned Units
with Its Task Groups, 9 and 24 October 1944

	CV	CVL	BB	CA	CL	DD
At 0001 9 October 1944						
Task Group 38.1	2	2	-	4	-	14
Task Group 38.2	3	2	2	-	3	18
Task Group 38.3	2	2	4	-	4	14
Task Group 38.4	2	2	-	1	1	11
Total	9	8	6	5	8	57
At 0001 25 October 1944						
Task Group 38.2	1	2	2	-	4	18
Task Group 38.3	2	1	2	2	3	11
Task Group 38.4	2	2	2	2	-	12
Total	5	5	6	4	7	41

Key:
CV Fleet Carriers   BB Battleships   CL Light Cruisers
CVL Light Carriers   CA Heavy Cruisers   DD Destroyers

of Task Group 38.1 from the American order of battle on 24 October may well have been crucial in shaping events in one of two respects. First, and leaving aside the point that the two groups ordered back to Ulithi would not have been so directed if the report of 20 October had been properly processed and then been the basis of subsequent decisions, if all four carrier formations had been on station on 24–25 October then Halsey could have run to the north in the search for Ozawa's carrier force and at the same time left a force covering the San Bernardino Strait. Second, one wonders what might have happened if Task Force 38 had had all four of its carrier formations available on 24 October for the attacks on Kurita's force when it was crossing the Sibuyan Sea prior to its negotiating the San Bernardino Strait.

The second of these considerations is probably the more relevant, and for an obvious reason: the principle of concentration of force. Unreasoning obedience to this principle of war probably means that if Halsey had had all four carrier formations with him on 24–25 October then he would have gone north with all four rather than three. But in terms of what might have been, the first consideration presents real difficulty of interpretation. The battle of the Sibuyan Sea is generally regarded as having been resolved to considerable American advantage, albeit not the advantage claimed by American carrier aircrew on the day. Only one Japanese battleship, admittedly the *Musashi*, was sunk in this action, but perhaps the point of note is that the three carrier groups may have had about three-fifths the number of aircraft that had been available to all four groups at the start of operations, but in terms of attack aircraft they possessed little more than half of their original strength—148 Helldivers and 144 Avengers from original establishments of 274 and 234 respectively. The smallest of the three task groups (with single fleet and light carriers plus the night carrier *Independence*) that were available on 24 October was the one that was closest to the San Bernardino Strait, and another formation, Task Group 38.4, was involved with operations over the Visayans and not against Kurita's force. In terms of both numbers and position, Halsey's decision to detach two task groups before contact with Japanese formations had been made had unfortunate consequences, both in terms of what might have been achieved had American carrier formations been concentrated at the point of contact, but also in terms of historical attention.[37]

Kurita's force sailed from Brunei Bay at 0805 on 22 October,[38] and Nishimura's formation sailed some seven hours later, at 1500. But by the time they did, two of the other formations had already put to sea and the air battle over the Philippines had been renewed, lost, and was poised to assume a very different dimension. Ozawa's force sailed on the evening of 20 October. Having gathered from various ports in the Inland Sea, the force was led by the light cruiser *Isuzu* and four destroyer escorts through the eastern channel of the Bungo Strait,[39] and it sailed with instructions that are probably unique in naval history:

> In co-operation with friendly forces, the [carrier force] . . . was to . . . risk its own destruction in a spirit of self-sacrifice in order to divert and draw enemy carrier task forces from the waters east of Luzon to the north and northwest, thereby ensuring the successful penetration of the enemy landing area by the 1st and 2nd Task Groups.[40]

The formation once at sea was beset almost immediately by a series of false sighting reports of enemy submarines, but chance was such that the patrol line off the Strait, which had consisted of the submarines *Besugo, Gabilan* and the *Ronquil*—which had detected previous movements during the Formosa battle when the *Besugo* torpedoed the destroyer *Suzutsuki*[41]—had been dispersed. The *Besugo* and *Ronquil* had been ordered westward while the *Gabilan* was sent to patrol the Kii Strait to the east. In addition, the scouting role was exchanged for general attacks on Japanese shipping. The change left the eastern channel of the Bungo Strait unattended, with the result that Ozawa's force fortunately escaped immediate detection and thus was freed to proceed to the south in order to play its sacrificial role.[42] In its first three days at sea its aircraft activities were minimal while radio silence was observed; its main air efforts, in both senses, were to begin on 23 October.[43]

To the south on 20 October, at Makou, was Shima's grandiloquently named 5th Fleet. The end of its brief foray during the Formosa battle meant that it was at Amami-o-Shima, in the northern Ryukyus, when American forces landed on Suluan Island on 17 October.[44] It was ordered forward to Makou, where, after arriving on 20 October, the force took on fuel from the *Ryoei Maru*, which had arrived at the harbor at 0930.[45] While here Shima was ordered to give up one destroyer formation so that these units, namely the *Wakaba, Hatsuharu* and the *Hatsushimo*, could transport air personnel, ground crews, and equipment from Formosa to the Philippines.[46] At this stage of proceedings the role allotted the remainder of this formation was unclear. Shima personally wanted to return to home waters and to Ozawa's carrier force, but, though ordered by Combined Fleet headquarters to effect a rendezvous with Kurita's force bound for the San Bernardino Strait, opinion within the Fleet staff was hardening in favor of Shima's force being ordered to try to reach Leyte Gulf via the Surigao Strait. At this time there was no question of any other force, i.e. Nishimura's battle force, being ordered to proceed to Leyte Gulf by the southern route, and just what Shima's formation was supposed to achieve,[47] given its decidedly modest size and composition, is hard to discern, not least because intelligence information indicated that the Americans had two battleships, five or six cruisers, and ten or more destroyers in the Strait.[48] Shima's force sailed at 1600 on 21 October, but by the afternoon of 23 October when Shima's force arrived in Coron Bay, Nishimura's force had been detached from Kurita's command and assigned to this route.[49] With the *Nichiei Maru* at Ulugan Bay, the lack of an oiler in the Calamians meant that Shima's cruisers topped up the destroyers before the force sailed at 0200 on 24

October.[50] Lack of knowledge of Nishimura's plan of operations meant that it sailed more or less as an independent formation.

The cruiser formation, once part of Shima's command, then assigned to Kurita but never part of his force, and finally detailed to provide close escort for forces being shipped to Leyte, sailed from Makou during the afternoon of 21 October.[51] As noted previously, Kurita's two task groups sailed on the morning of 22 October and were then followed, in mid-afternoon, by Nishimura's battle force. The latter, rounding northern Borneo, would use the Balabac Strait to reach the Sulu Sea. The reefs, banks, and shoals of the Dangerous Ground, the shallows in the South China Sea that are home to the Spratly Islands, dictated that the two forces bound for the north should use the Palawan Passage. These two forces were to share a common but separate experience. The cruiser formation was to lose one heavy cruiser, disabled but not sunk, to submarine attack, while Kurita's force lost two heavy cruisers sunk and a third badly damaged and forced to withdraw, under escort, to Singapore, again to submarine attack. All these losses took place in the early hours of 23 October.

Kurita's sailing has elicited a host of comment, little of it favorably disposed to the Japanese admiral. The basis of most of the critical comments made about Kurita's conduct of operations has been a disposition of units that was questionable, the dispatch of seaplanes for reconnaissance duties off Samar which meant there were no anti-submarine patrols mounted for the defense of the formations during the approach to contact, and a general lack of provision against submarine attack.[52] The latter is a most difficult matter on which to pronounce with any certainty. In the weeks and months before this time all Japanese fleet units had been fitted with radar, some with search radar, but one suspects that the real Japanese weakness lay not so much with equipment as with training and experience; suffice it to note that the *Bream* closed on the heavy cruiser *Aoba* on the surface to a range of 800 yards without being detected, while the *Dace* and *Darter*, operating on the surface, were in contact with Kurita's force for seven minutes short of five hours before submerging, again without being detected.[53] Clearly, Japanese defensive measures and anti-submarine capability were not all they might have been.

These matters, however, have not attracted much historical attention, which has tended to concentrate on the related matters of cruising disposition, lack of even the most basic precaution in cruising, and Kurita himself. On the first of these, there is no disputing the basic criticism that the cruiser formation adopted by Kurita was questionable.[54]

The presence of no fewer than five of the formation's fifteen destroyers not around the perimeter but between the cruiser and battleship lines, and the lack of any destroyers leading the formations, present cause for hesitation. There was a genuine Japanese problem of a chronic shortage of destroyers, and probably, by British standards, Kurita's two battle forces between them needed another ten destroyers to be properly protected. What is most striking is the balance of numbers, between battleships and heavy cruisers on the one hand and destroyers on the other. But scarcely less striking was the fact that Kurita's flagship was the *Atago*, which was in the van of the formation.

The employment of the fleet flagship in a lead position was questionable at best, but perhaps the real question that should be asked about such an arrangement concerned the fact that Kurita's flagship was a heavy cruiser. Herein there is an obvious problem: Kurita's playing for effect. Kurita was a "cruiser admiral" and therefore he had to be in a cruiser for this action—the role and man coming together. With Ugaki flying the flag of the 1st Battleship Division in the *Yamato*, the logical choice as flagship for the fleet was either the *Musashi* or the *Nagato*. The latter had been the Combined Fleet flagship until 1942 and most certainly could have accommodated Kurita, his staff, and, critically, the fleet signals establishment. Likewise the *Musashi*, as sister ship to the *Yamato*, would have been able to play the role of fleet flagship. Of course in one obvious sense it was fortunate that Kurita did not choose the *Musashi* as fleet flagship, but the matter of his choice, and various related matters, should raise certain other considerations that return to the whole question of Kurita's turnaway off Samar when in contact with enemy carrier formations on the morning of 25 October and the treatment of this episode by history.

One word is invariably used in descriptions of Kurita: taciturn.[55] Moreover, historical accounts of this battle consistently note Kurita's post-war refusal to provide any reasoned or reasonable account of his conduct of battle off Samar. One would suggest that it was not so much that Kurita was taciturn as that he had nothing much to say. Indeed, it is hard to resist the impression that Kurita was the only person in the Pacific war able to make Halsey appear intellectually gifted. What is decidedly odd about the historical treatment afforded Kurita is that his turnaway on 25 October 1944 is never set alongside two other, not dissimilar, episodes. Kurita had

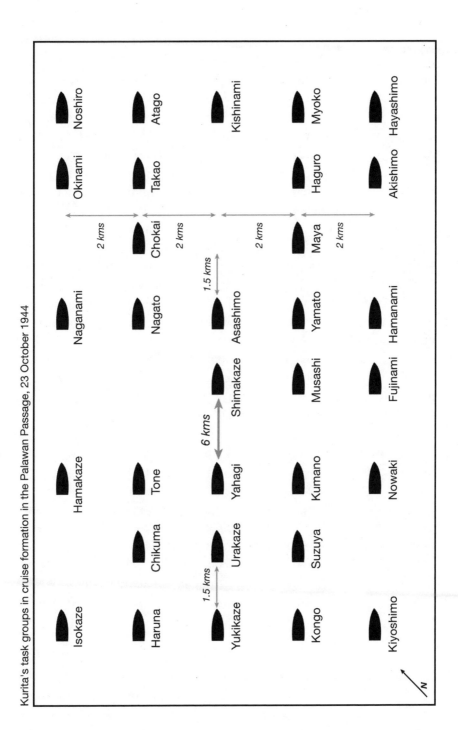

Kurita's task groups in cruise formation in the Palawan Passage, 23 October 1944

been overall commander and cover force commander of the Japanese forces deployed in the west during the Battle of the Java Sea, 27–28 February 1942, in which capacity Kurita can hardly be said to have covered his force and himself in glory. There certainly appears to have been a disinclination to make for "the sound of the guns" on the part of Kurita and his force, and both seem to have been notably absent in the exchanges that pass under the name of the Battle of the Sunda Strait (28 February–1 March 1942). Moreover, off Midway in June 1942 Kurita could be said, not altogether unfairly, to have literally abandoned two heavy cruisers that had been damaged, exerting minimal effort to save them or remove their crews. Admittedly there is no basis for any serious questioning of Kurita's role at Guadalcanal in October–November 1942 and at Rabaul one year later; the elements of defeat were there and cannot be attributed in any way to errors of omission or commission on the part of Kurita. But the fact that Kurita continued to command major formations at sea, and to do so at a time when the *Kaigun* was in sharp decline and when such able but outspoken commanders as Rear Admiral Tanaka Raizo were sidelined, poses a number of obvious questions and invites a number of equally obvious, and unflattering, answers. The latter, indeed, may be connected to the fact that in the six months before the start of the Pacific war, the *Kaigun*, like the *Rikugun*, undertook a purge of officers deemed less than enthusiastic about the prospect of a war with the United States. Many officers were retired or shunted into dead-end posts, and it may very well be that by 1944 the qualitative decline of naval personnel and training was related to this development, which is known to have resulted in the navy's shedding some of its most able middle-ranking officers. It needs to be noted, however, that in setting out these points perhaps one has been somewhat unfair to Kurita. The action off Java can be portrayed differently, that as force commander he displayed a proper caution and was unfortunate in how events unfolded, and off Midway he had no real choice; if he had tried to help the two stricken heavy cruisers, one of which improbably survived, he might easily have lost all four in his formation. One is not convinced by such arguments, but they need to be noted nonetheless.[56]

In terms of the events of 22–23 October, however, proceedings opened at 0325 with the torpedoing of the heavy cruiser *Aoba* by the *Bream* in 14°05'North 119°43'East, a dozen miles south of Cape Calavite, northwest Mindoro. The initial contact was believed by the American captain of the

Bream to be with two heavy cruisers led by one light cruiser, and aiming at the second ship in line the American submarine hit the *Aoba* in the No. 2 engine room with one torpedo. The *Aoba* was towed to Cavite by the light cruiser *Kinu,* and there she was subjected to running repairs that enabled her, despite the American control of Philippine waters after the battle, to return to Kure, where she arrived on 12 December. She was never repaired. Reduced to the reserve, the *Aoba* was subsequently rated as an anti-aircraft unit, in which role she was subjected to increasing damage in successive American raids before being finally wrecked in the great carrier raid of 28 July 1945.[57]

The contact between the *Bream* and the Japanese cruiser formation was not the first contact between American and Japanese forces, and, of course, this was not a contact that was to play any direct part of the battle of Leyte Gulf. Prior to 21 October the contacts the Americans had with Japanese ships primarily related to small craft movements off the western coast of Leyte, from which it was deduced that the Japanese were in the process of reinforcing their division on the island. Various sightings on 21 and 22 October were fragmented and inconclusive, and on the American side certain reports referred to Japanese movements that were seemingly related to the retirement of Shima's force from the Formosa battle. The contact with Kurita's force obtained by the submarines *Darter* and *Dace,* which placed the Japanese force in 08°20'North 116°20'East at 0116 on 23 October,[58] was the first contact with any major Japanese force that clearly indicated that a Japanese response to the landings on Leyte was in hand. The initial contact, with a Japanese force that was thought to include three battleships and which was reported to be on a course of 040 degrees, placed the Japanese force at the entrance to the Palawan Passage. The two submarines immediately sought to place themselves ahead of the Japanese force, which initially was estimated to be making twenty-two knots, their intention being to attack in the half-light of dawn when it would be possible to see and identify the enemy warships. The *Darter* was to attack ships in the port column and the *Dace,* which was ahead of the *Darter,* was to attack ships in the starboard column. A second report placed the Japanese force in 08°47'North 116°37'East and making fifteen knots, and it was this relative slowness that enabled the two American submarines to place themselves in the Japanese path by 0525. At 0609 the *Darter* and·*Dace* submerged, and at 0632, with the Japanese formation beginning to zigzag with the dawn's light and having just begun a turn to port, the *Darter* emptied her six bow tubes at a range of 980 yards at Kurita's flagship, the *Atago*, then turned to train her stern tubes on the *Takao*. At 0633 the *Atago* was hit by four torpedoes, and within a couple of minutes was beginning to settle by the bow. Such was the massive initial damage that the cruiser was allegedly listing at twenty-five degrees even before the last torpedo hit her in the generator room. At 0634 the *Takao* was hit by two torpedoes which sheered off her rudder and two of her four propellers and flooded three of her boiler rooms.[59] Then, with Japanese destroyers moving for the first time to positions from which to counterattack the American submarine with depth charges, the *Dace* fired four torpedoes at what was believed to be a *Kongo*-class battleship but which was the *Maya*. The heavy cruiser was hit by all four torpedoes at 0657[60] and according to Ugaki literally disintegrated. She exploded, and "nothing was left after the smoke and spray subsided" other than a torpedo track some 1,500 meters ahead of where she had been. Other sources suggest that she took between four and ten minutes to sink, and the fact that the destroyers *Akishimo* and *Shimakaze* came alongside and rescued 769 officers and men does suggest that Ugaki was guilty of overstatement. Nonetheless, with the *Maya* being hit, chaos engulfed the Japanese force that increased speed to twenty-four knots in order to get clear of the immediate danger area.[61]

The historical treatment of this episode necessarily has concentrated upon two matters. The first was the loss of the *Atago*, which sank in about twenty minutes,[62] and the immersion of Kurita, though the latter has been the subject of some dispute.[63] The fact was that the destroyer *Kishinami* tried to come alongside the *Atago*, but with the cruiser *in extremis* she was forced to stand off some 300 meters from the flagship. She and the *Asashimo* then picked up survivors, including Kurita and members of his staff, who were forced to swim from the stricken heavy cruiser. A total of 359 personnel were lost but the two destroyers picked up 710 officers and men. Kurita's flag was raised in the *Kishinami* at 0700, but while Kurita and his immediate staff were gathered in the *Kishinami*, about half the fleet signals personnel were killed and the *Asashimo* recovered most of those who survived.[64] With the *Asashimo*, along with the *Naganami*, detailed to stand by the *Takao* and to escort the stricken heavy cruiser to Brunei and beyond,[65] the separation of Kurita and staff from a communications staff has been cited as one of the contributing factors in what was something closely akin to a lack of command and control on the part of Kurita during the action off Samar.[66] But while this may indeed have been the case, the fleet and squadron signals organizations, or perhaps it was the formation staffs, do not appear to have been working effectively during the hours before these attacks. It appears that in the *Yamato* a report of a nearby submarine transmitting a special signal was submitted to Ugaki at 0250,[67] but this report does not seem to have made its way to Kurita. Even allowing for the alleged limited capacity for evasive action in the Palawan Passage and the fact that the Japanese force may well have been unable to act upon this report, such a state of affairs seems somewhat surprising.[68]

The second matter to exercise historical consideration has been the subsequent loss of the *Darter*. After going deep in order to avoid depth-charge attack, the two American submarines sought to close on the stricken *Takao*, but without enough torpedoes to go after both the destroyers and the cruiser, the decision was made to wait until night when attacks by both submarines might prove sufficient to overwhelm the Japanese. After surfacing at about 2015, the *Darter*, after submitting her first full report of what had happened that morning, ran on the surface to a position ahead of the Japanese ships. Her first attempt to attack miscarried, but in seeking to work herself around to the starboard quarter, and on her own estimate about an hour from carrying out a second attack, she ran herself onto the Bombay Shoal. Making some seventeen knots when she hit the reef, she had ridden up to a height of nine feet forward, and she was so firmly grounded that all efforts to lighten her failed. The *Dace* sought to tow her off the reef, but once this effort proved unavailing it was decided to abandon the *Darter*. It took more than two hours to transfer all the *Darter*'s crew, a task made difficult by a current that caused the *Dace* to use half her battery capacity in maintaining her position. Obstinate to the end, the *Darter* proved all but immune first to self-inflicted scuttling charges, then to four torpedoes and thirty 5-in. rounds from the *Dace*, and finally the assorted attention of Japanese aircraft and warships when they happened upon the wrecked submarine the next morning.[69] Such matters are well-known; less well-known are that the submarines *Rock* and *Nautilus* were directed to complete the *Darter*'s destruction, effected 31 October, and that the crew of the *Darter*, once they were returned to Fremantle by the *Dace*, were not dispersed but assigned directly to the submarine *Menhaden*. Under construction and the last boat built at Manitowoc, Wisconsin, she was commissioned into service on 22 June 1945 and sailed for Pearl Harbor on 1 September.[70]

The loss of the *Darter* in a high-speed chase into the Dangerous Ground was accepted as one of the hazards of war, an unfortunate chance rather than the consequence of unwise or injudicious calculation. This aspect of operations was treated as being of little consequence when set against the very real achievements of the *Dace* and *Darter*, which in this single action in effect removed three heavy cruisers and two destroyers from a force that had numbered five battleships, ten heavy and two light cruisers, and fifteen destroyers. This was indeed no mean achievement, and no less important was that at 0620 on 23 October, Halsey, in the *New Jersey*, received the initial sighting report and thus knew from this time that a major Japanese force was moving into the Visayans.[71] But there were two other matters relating to these events which seem to have attracted little in the way of judicious examination. First, if the mission on which the Japanese were embarked was so overwhelmingly important, it is unclear why two destroyers should have been detached in order to escort a badly damaged heavy cruiser to safety. It was not as though Kurita's formations had destroyers to spare—as indeed the *Dace* and *Darter* had demonstrated only too well. The provision of escort for a stricken ship may well have been standard procedure, and commendable under normal circumstances, but given the terms of reference of this operation it does seem somewhat curious. The destroyers had not proved numerous enough or effective in shielding the battleships and cruisers from costly attack, and so were reduced before the main action—when they would be most needed—was joined.[72] Second, certainly the *Darter*, and it seems also the *Dace*, were under instruction to keep the Balabac Strait under surveillance,[73] and in chasing Kurita's formation the two American submarines abandoned this task and allowed Nishimura's force unobserved access to Balabac Strait. This proved of small account; Nishimura's force was detected crossing the Sulu Sea by land-based aircraft the next day and in sufficient time to allow Kinkaid's force to prepare the appropriate reception, but the failure to discharge the primary task oddly duplicated what had happened off the Bungo Strait. In both areas local command, not fleet command, had followed a course which was tantamount to a blatant disregard of the reconnaissance role at the very time when battle, if it was to come, would be in the offing. These matters may be of small account when set against other matters or events that were unfolding at this time, and in any case any comment about the uncovering of the Balabac Strait needs be balanced against the fact that after dark on 23 October first the submarine *Angler* and then the submarine *Guitarro* made contact with and reported Kurita's force as it left the passage and entered the Mindoro Strait.[74] But these two matters relating to events on 23 October in the Palawan Passage, the submarines moving off station and the dispatch of destroyers to stand by the *Takao*, form a neat if somewhat unusual juxtaposition.[75]

It was thus not until 23 October that the American naval high command became aware that Japanese forces were at sea. Indeed at this stage there were no fewer than six Japanese forces at sea and only two had been detected, and both in the early hours of the day. Such a state of affairs was perhaps somewhat surprising,[76] not least because as early as 21 October, the day immediately after the landings on Leyte but with forces already securely established ashore, American carrier groups were reaching across the whole width of the Philippines for Japanese forces. Task Group 38.3, for example, was some 100 miles northeast of the San Bernardino Strait while its aircraft sought targets on Mindoro and Coron Bay. The next day this formation refueled in 14°00'North 130°00'East in readiness for its searching for Japanese formations.

This pattern of searching and attacking targets across Luzon and the Visayans and alternating refueling characterized the operations of the four task groups of Task Force 38. After supporting the landings on 17 October, McCain's Task Group 38.1 and Davison's Task Group 38.4 refueled on the 21st and on the following day set course for Ulithi in order to provision and rearm. As soon as the first rumblings of trouble became audible on the 23rd, Halsey summoned Davison's group back to Leyte but let Task Group 38.1 continue on its way until the next day when, at a distance of some 625 miles east of Samar, it too was recalled. By dawn on 24 October, the three groups remaining on station were roughly aligned with about 125 miles between groups. Task Group 38.3 was in the north opposite central Luzon and roughly sixty miles off Polillo Island, Task Group 38.2 was in the center opposite the San Bernardino Strait, and Task Group 38.4 was off Samar.[77]

Throughout the night of 23–24 October, the northern formation, Task Group 38.3, was shadowed by a number of Japanese aircraft; at one time the *Essex* was able to track on her radar no fewer than five enemy aircraft shadowing the formation. The Japanese reconnaissance aircraft failed to detect any American formation until 0700,[78] however, and thereafter the Japanese aircraft mounted three concerted attacks against this formation, which was the nearest formation to Luzon, rather than against Task Group 38.2, which was the formation in the position directly in the line of Kurita's advance. These attacks coincided with American carrier aircraft finding both Kurita's and Nishimura's formations, and the subsequent American attacks, directed primarily against Kurita's force coming through the central Philippines, occupied much of the remaining hours of daylight. Only late in the afternoon of 24 October did American carrier aircraft locate Ozawa's carriers to the northeast, and thereafter came Halsey's decision to concentrate against this formation that was to be one of the two decisions and actions that came to dominate the history of this battle.

The reports from the *Angler* and *Guitarro* during the night, coming after the action involving the *Dace* and *Darter* on the previous night,[79] convinced Halsey that the Japanese were intent on battle, and accordingly he ordered his three carrier groups to mount extensive reconnaissance patrols at dawn on 24 October. These were conducted by teams of one Helldiver and two Hellcat fighters to a range of 300 miles and was intended to cover all the channels through the Philippines. Other fighters were stationed at 100-mile intervals to ensure that reports of sightings could be relayed. With search teams assigned ten-degree sectors and the areas of search assigned to the three carrier groups overlapping, aircraft from Task Group 38.3 were to cover the area from Lingayen Gulf to the Mindoro Strait while aircraft from 38.2 were to search between northern Mindoro and southern Panay. Aircraft from Task Group 38.2 were to search the area between northern Panay and southern Negros. At the same time the search aircraft were dispatched shortly after 0600, the *Essex* (Task Group 38.3) launched a sweep by twenty fighters directed against airfields around Manila.[80]

The American searches resulted in a number of contacts with Japanese units, of which two were of primary importance. The first, made at 0746 by a Helldiver from the *Intrepid* that was searching the third sector, was a radar contact obtained at a range of twenty-five miles with a number of warships south of Mindoro island.[81] Turning south, the three American aircraft at a height of 9,000 feet made out wakes before closing, and once in visual contact with the ships were able to report the presence of two formations some eight miles off the southern tip of Mindoro, on a course of 050 degrees and making ten to twelve knots. There were to be a number of reports with slight differences of numbers and type, but the initial signal, with a clear indication that no transports were in company, was sent at 0810 and received by Bogan and Halsey at 0822.[82] It was on the basis of this report that at 0827 Halsey, bypassing Mitscher, issued orders directly to the three carrier groups for the start of strike operations against Kurita's formation. At the same time Task Groups 38.3 and 38.4 were ordered to close Task

Group 38.2 while Task Group 38.1 was recalled. As it happened, however, Task Group 38.3 was not in a position to comply with its orders. It was in the process of being attacked and all its fighters were needed for defense, the result being that the American attack on Kurita's formation was staggered and only began after the initial Japanese attacks on Sherman's carrier group.[83] The second American contact at this time, by aircraft from the *Enterprise*, was made at 0820 at extreme 325-mile range with Nishimura's force. Once the contact was made and reported, all the scouts and fighters were gathered, a total of twenty-six aircraft in all, and they carried out an attack in the face of what was described as heavy and accurate anti-aircraft fire.[84] The battleship *Fuso* was hit on her fantail and her catapults and seaplanes were destroyed, but apart from a fire that obstinately refused to be doused for an hour she was neither damaged nor seriously inconvenienced. The destroyer *Shigure* was hit by a bomb that penetrated her foremost turret, killing five and wounding six of the gun crew, but her seaworthiness was not impaired and the formation continued on its course, its speed unreduced.[85] There were two other contacts obtained at this time. The first was about 0745 when aircraft from the *Intrepid* found the light cruiser *Kinu* and the destroyer *Uranami* off Corregidor just as they were leaving Manila Bay for Cagayan in northern Mindanao. Both were bombed and incurred moderate damage, the *Kinu* suffering forty-seven killed and wounded and the *Uranami* twenty-five.[86] The second was at 0800 when aircraft from the *Franklin* were in contact with three destroyers off Panay and conducted an attack which accounted for the *Wakaba*, the sinking of which was seen by search aircraft from the *Intrepid* that were returning to their carrier.[87] Though strictly she and her associates were not part of the battle then taking shape, the *Wakaba* was the first ship of either side to be sunk in the time span generally associated with the battle of Leyte Gulf.[88]

The main operations on the morning of 24 October thus opened with the Japanese attacks on Task Group 38.3, and the historical treatment of this phase of the battle has focused primarily upon two episodes, namely the events that involved Commander David McCampbell, the air group commander from the *Essex*, and the loss of the light carrier *Princeton*. The Japanese attacks materialized because on the previous day most of the 2nd Air Fleet's total of 450 aircraft were flown from Formosa to the Philippines. The commander of the 1st Air Fleet in the Philippines, Vice Admiral Onishi Takijiro, conferred overnight with Fukudome, the 2nd Air Fleet's commander, and specifically sought to commit the newly arrived aircraft to *kamikaze* attacks,[89] but this proposal was resisted by Fukudome. The result was that on the morning of 24 October his aircraft mounted three successive attacks, each involving some fifty to sixty aircraft, and all committed to conventional bombing attacks on the American carrier formations. Their target was Task Group 38.3, the northernmost carrier group and the one closest to the main airfields around Manila.[90]

The three Japanese attacks were met and comprehensively defeated by fighters from Task Group 38.3 and with one codicil: the attacks had been mounted on the basis of minimal information from the 1st Air Fleet and with little held in reserve, and with very little to show in return the Japanese really had no further offensive capability. That it was the episode that resulted in McCampbell's winning the Congressional Medal of Honor was evidence of a hopeless Japanese inferiority in quality of both aircraft and aircrew that foreshadowed the adoption of *kamikaze* tactics within another two days. McCampbell and his wingman were respectively credited with the destruction of nine and six Japanese fighters, apparently as many as forty Japanese fighters forming themselves initially into a Lufberry circle to provide themselves with maximum mutual protection at least for a time, but once these aircraft broke formation they were singly and separately destroyed. Fighters from the *Essex* were credited with the destruction of twenty-four Japanese aircraft, the *Lexington*'s fighters with the destruction of a further thirteen for the loss of just one of their number.[91] The first Japanese attacks began around 0833, a matter of a couple of minutes or so after the last fighters were flown off the carriers of Task Group 38.3, and were over in an hour. The attacks were singularly ineffective with not a single Allied warship, transport, or oiler attacked or in any way damaged in the course of these three attacks.[92] But at 0938 in the subsequent lull when the *Princeton* (with ten aircraft in the air) had recovered ten Hellcats and was refueling them preparatory to landing another two fighters, one Judy dive-bomber, which apparently had hugged the clouds in the hope that an opportunity to attack would present itself,[93] dived on the *Princeton* and planted a 250 kg/550-lb. semi-armor-piercing bomb on the flight deck some seventy-five feet forward of the rear elevator. The damage at first appeared slight and from the bridge the initial reaction was that flying operations would not be subject to much disruption—"slapping on a patch in a hurry and resuming operations"—but in fact the bomb penetrated the flight deck and hangar and exploded in the ship's bakery, the back-blast reaching into the hangar to engulf six Avengers that had been rearmed and refueled and had full auxiliary tanks.[94] The resultant explosions of these aircraft and torpedoes threw first the rear elevator onto the flight deck and then the forward elevator mast high into the air before it fell back into its pit. It also wrecked the pressure system, which meant that not all the sprinklers and hoses were able to work. Flames quickly reached along the *Princeton* from island to stern, and at 1010, after an explosion that tore up the flight deck between the elevators, the order was given that the ship should be abandoned by all the crew other than damage control and firefighting personnel; at 1020 the former were also ordered to leave the ship.[95]

As fires spread and ammunition in the various locker rooms exploded, the *Princeton* lost way, taking a position across the wind and drifting leeward. As she staggered from formation, she was attended by the light cruiser *Reno* and destroyers *Irwin* and *Morrison*, and as she was racked by explosions the formation commander, Sherman, ordered the light cruiser *Birmingham* to stand by the crippled carrier.[96] The problem confronting these ships, other than the men in the water,[97] was different rates of drift that rendered it all but impossible to keep a ship alongside the *Princeton* without suffering extensive damage from the carrier's projecting gun positions. In addition, the initial attempts at fighting fires from the escorts was largely ineffective since they were used from upwind and it was at this stage blowing hard, and it was impossible for the destroyers to come alongside to leeward because of the intense heat and thick smoke.[98] With the *Birmingham* alongside at 1100, firefighting became more ordered with the start of a systematic attempt to fight the fires from the forward end of the carrier to the stern.[99] Volunteers from the *Birmingham* boarded the *Princeton*, but after some four hours, in which time the *Morrison* had become trapped by the *Princeton's* stacks and the escorts had to scatter because of a Japanese attack that proved ineffectual, it was decided to try to tow the carrier to Ulithi. The problem was that one fire, near the stern, was continuing to prove resistant to American firefighting, and the time lost in casting off to face Japanese aircraft appears to have been crucial in ensuring that this fire continued to burn; the *Morrison* simply did not have enough hoses to tackle it effectively. These various matters came together after 1515 when, at the third attempt, a line was passed from the *Birmingham* to the *Princeton*. At 1523, at the time when the *Birmingham* was tying up on the port side aft, the fire reached a stowage compartment aft of the hangar on the starboard side of the ship where torpedo flasks and spare bombs had been stored. The result was major damage to the *Princeton*, which lost part of her stern and the after part of the flight deck,[100] but the carnage wrought upon the *Birmingham* was worse. Her upper deck, packed with men fighting the fires, manning the anti-aircraft guns, and preparing the tow, was raked along the length of the ship, and half her company were killed or wounded. The scenes aboard the *Birmingham* invariably are described in some detail in all accounts of Leyte. Suffice it to note that the scene must have been appalling and the stoicism of wounded and dying is very moving; 229 officers and men were killed and 420 were wounded, 219 of these seriously. Incredibly, and with an appalling lack of tact, within a matter of minutes the *Princeton* requested that the *Birmingham* begin the tow,[101] but with the latter in no state to do so, at 1604 came recognition that "the fires had won."[102] With none of the escorts able to tow and the fires now working their way forward to the fuel tanks and main magazine, the decision was made to abandon the ship.[103] At 1645 Mitscher indicated to Sherman that with the carrier formations needing to head north the time had come for the *Princeton* to be sunk, and Sherman gave the order that she be dispatched by torpedoes. The *Irwin* was detailed to administer the *coup de grâce*, but with a torpedo director that had been pounded by the *Princeton* only the first of six torpedoes hit the carrier (at 1706) while the third and sixth broached and ran back to the destroyer, both missing her by less than ten yards.[104] The *Reno* thereupon came forward to fire two torpedoes at 1746, the first of which hit the *Princeton* below the forward aviation fuel tank: the resultant explosion of some 100,000 gallons of avgas literally blew the ship to pieces. She sank in less than a minute, her passing marked by a mushroom cloud.[105]

While Task Group 38.3 was thus committed, the battle developed along three separate lines. First, the various carrier groups took closer order during the morning of 24 October, and Task Group 38.4, the aircraft of which were considered not to have been particularly effective, was ordered to support Task Group 38.2, which, as previously noted, was the weakest of the three formations on line and the one closest to the San Bernardino Strait. The overall effect of this was to allow Nishimura's and Shima's formations free passage across the Sulu Sea after mid-morning. But Kinkaid and the support formations gathered off Leyte harbored no illusions about Japanese intentions and, having been afforded the better part of a day in which to make themselves ready, prepared to take station in the approaches to and in the Surigao Strait.

*   *   *

Second, in the course of the morning's operation the question of the where-abouts of the Japanese carrier force increasingly impinged upon American calculations. At this stage of proceedings Ozawa's formation had reached a position to the northeast of Luzon, and its intention was simply to attract American attention. Ironically, the operations by aircraft from Luzon and the damage inflicted on the *Princeton* distracted the one American carrier task group best placed to find Ozawa's formation.[106] The attacks by 2nd Air Fleet aircraft on the American carrier formations and Ozawa's attempt to draw off American formations from the area of the San Bernardino Strait were deliberate attempts to support Kurita's formation indirectly.[107] The Japanese lacked the numbers, quality, and operational technique to be able to provide continuous close air support for the battle formations, and therefore chose to strike at the American carrier forces and to lure them to the north in order to support Kurita's forces *en passant*.[108] The point, however, was that in the course of the morning Ozawa's formation, despite its best endeavors, was unable to play its role of sacrificial bait.

Dawn on 24 October found Ozawa's force committing aircraft to a search mission but without making contact with Sherman's task group. At 0910, however, Ozawa received a report from a land-based aircraft reporting the whereabouts of an American carrier formation, and in order to confirm this sighting Ozawa again committed aircraft to a reconnais-sance mission.[109] At 1115, however, Ozawa had the confirmation he sought and decided to launch what, given the paucity of aircraft numbers in the carriers, could be his only offensive mission of the battle.[110] Accordingly, beginning at 1145 the Japanese carriers began to launch their aircraft. It had been Ozawa's original intention that these would number six torpedo-bombers, twenty-eight dive-bombers, forty Zeke fighters, and two recon-naissance aircraft, the fighter and dive-bomber figures representing almost the sum of the Japanese carriers' establishment with these types of aircraft. But while most accounts of the battle state that these were the numbers flown off,[111] the fact was that a total of sixty-two aircraft were dispatched, and in two groups. The three light carriers between them provided twenty Zeke fighters and nine Zeke fighter-bombers—the *Chitose* seven fighters and two fighter-bombers, the *Chiyoda* five and four, and the *Zuiho* eight and three—and four Jills from either the *Chitose* or *Zuiho* or from both, while the *Zuikaku* contributed ten Zeke fighters, eleven fighter-bombers, six Jill torpedo-bombers, and two Judy dive-bombers, the latter also serving as scouts. Given the commitment of such numbers, what remained to the carriers must have been very slight indeed; for practical purposes Ozawa's force was bereft of both defensive and offensive capabilities.[112] The more immediate and important point, however, was that at or about 1245 the radar of the light carrier *Langley* detected the incoming Japanese aircraft at a range of about 105 miles and first four of the carrier's fighters and then another eight from the *Essex* were dispatched on a bearing of 035 degrees. The resultant clash is generally represented as having cost the Japanese about half their aircraft, but in fact six fighters, one Zeke fighter-bomber, and four Jills from the light carriers, and two fighters, five Zeke fighter-bombers, and one Jill from the *Zuikaku* were lost. Just three Japanese aircraft—a Zeke and a Jill from the *Chitose* and a Zeke fighter-bomber from the *Chiyoda*—returned to their carriers while thirty-nine aircraft flew to airfields on Luzon and, surprisingly, one fighter-bomber from the *Zuikaku* proceeded to Formosa.[113] But that was by the by. The real points of significance were that the Japanese aircraft had approached from seaward, not from Luzon, and in the course of the air battle American pilots reported that the Japanese aircraft had tailhooks.[114] Ozawa's formation, which had spent the previous day and the morning transmitting radio signals in the hope of attracting American attention, to no avail,[115] had at last achieved its objective. Its presence had been announced, and from this time the attention of Halsey and Task Force 38 was to be divided between the area to the northeast and Ozawa's carrier force, and the Sibuyan Sea and Kurita's battle force.

Third, and to return to the situation as it existed in the eighth and ninth hours of the day, the main American concentration was against Kurita's formation, which was subjected to successive major attacks in the course of the day. The majority of the accounts that have been written about this day invariably concentrate upon the attacks on and destruction of the battleship *Musashi* to the extent that the damage inflicted on other units of Kurita's force is seldom afforded proper accord. The heavy cruiser *Myoko* was torpedoed in the first American attack. With her two starboard shafts damaged and her speed reduced to fifteen knots, after transferring her admiral and his staff to the *Haguro* she turned back to Brunei and thence to Singapore. She was not afforded any destroyer as escort.[116] The battleship *Yamato* was damaged by one bomb that gouged a hole near the waterline on her port side and another that hit her on her forecastle deck and penetrated all decks before exploding, causing an estimated 3,000 tons of seawater to surge into the ship. She also suffered minor damage by a near-miss in the third attack. The battleship *Nagato* was hit amidships by single bomb hits in both the fourth and fifth attacks,[117] while the *Haruna* suffered minor damage as a result of no fewer than five near-misses,[118] and one destroyer is sometimes cited in accounts of these proceedings as having been damaged.[119] Perhaps more relevantly, and seldom properly considered, the claims of Task Group 38.2 were of the order of a *Yamato*-class battleship taking three torpedo hits and a sister ship one torpedo and two bombs, a *Nagato*-class battleship being hit by one torpedo and two bombs, a *Kongo*-class battleship being hit by two torpedoes and six bombs, a *Mogami*-class cruiser possibly sunk by a torpedo, and two heavy cruisers, one *Nachi*-class and the other *Tone*-class, both hit by single torpedoes. Task Group 38.4 reported a *Yamato*-class battleship probably sunk and a sister ship hit by perhaps as many as three torpedoes and four bombs, a *Kongo*-class battleship hit by a single bomb, one heavy cruiser damaged and one light cruiser sunk, one destroyer sunk and another probably sunk, with another four damaged. Task Group 38.3 claimed one battleship badly damaged and two others damaged, and four heavy and two light cruisers damaged.[120] The exaggeration of these claims, their duplication, and the fact that there was no way they could be properly collated and evaluated in a timely manner clearly was the basis of Halsey's belief that Kurita's force had been neutralized in the course of these attacks.[121]

The precise sequence of events and the number and type of aircraft involved in the individual attacks are not matters that command agreement and accord, though in truth the various discrepancies are of small account when set against the issues involved in the day's proceedings. These opened with the dawn with the Kurita's two task groups switching from cruise to battle formation.[122] With Kurita's 1st Task Group leading and some 12 km separating this formation from Suzuki's 2nd Task Group, this deployment involved two circles of warships around the flagships, the first with battleships and cruisers some 2 km and the second with destroyers another 1.5 km from the *Yamato* and *Kongo*.[123] The Japanese formations and their units were thus deployed when they were found by American search aircraft and subjected to attack. In the course of 24 October the American carriers launched four attacks. The first attack formation consisted of twenty-one Hellcats, twelve Helldivers, and twelve Avengers flown off the *Intrepid* and *Cabot* of Task Group 38.2 at or about 0910. These aircraft began their attack on the Japanese warships at 1026. The second attack formation consisted of nineteen Hellcats, twelve Helldivers, and eleven Avengers, again from the *Intrepid* and *Cabot*; these aircraft were flown off

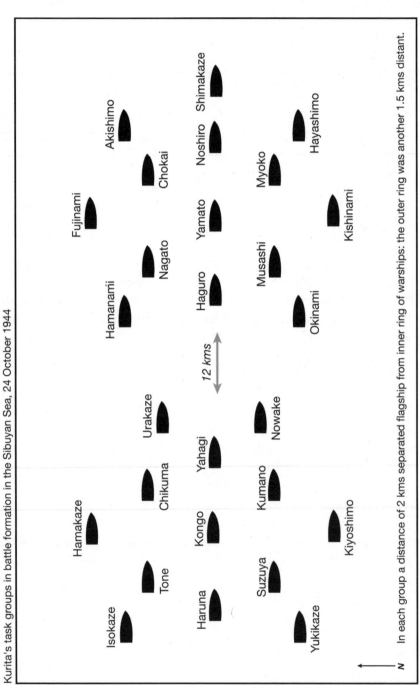

Kurita's task groups in battle formation in the Sibuyan Sea, 24 October 1944

In each group a distance of 2 kms separated flagship from inner ring of warships: the outer ring was another 1.5 kms distant.

Fig. 1. Admiral Chester W. Nimitz, USN, Commander in Chief, Pacific Fleet and Pacific Ocean Areas, puts on a battle helmet while visiting a U.S. Navy ship, circa 1944. *Collection of Fleet Admiral Chester W. Nimitz, USN. U.S. Naval Historical Center photograph.*

Fig. 2. Admiral William F. Halsey, USN, Commander, Third Fleet, on the bridge of his flagship, the battleship *New Jersey* (BB-62), while *en route* to carry out raids on the Philippines, December 1944. *Official U.S. Navy photograph, now in the collections of the National Archives.*

Fig. 3. Vice Admiral Thomas C. Kinkaid, USN, Commander, Seventh Fleet, watches landing operations in Lingayen Gulf, Luzon, from the bridge of his flagship, the *Wasatch* (AGC-9), circa 9 January 1945. Courtesy of Mrs. Thomas C. Kinkaid, 1976. When providing this view, she stated that it was Admiral Kinkaid's favorite photograph of himself. *U.S. Naval Historical Center photograph.*

Fig. 4. The fleet carrier *Essex* (CV-9) off Newport News in May 1943. Among the aircraft parked on her flight deck are twenty-four SBD scout bombers (parked aft), about eleven F6F fighters (parked in after part of the midships area), and about eighteen TBF/TBM torpedo planes (parked amidships). Having completed her trials, she sailed for the Pacific in May 1943 and was the first of the wartime fleet carriers to see service with the Pacific Fleet.   *Official U.S. Navy photograph, now in the collections of the National Archives.*

Fig 5. The battleship *Massachusetts* (BB-59) coming into Ulithi anchorage on 24 November 1944, during a break in operations off the Philippines. Photographed from the fleet carrier *Wasp* (CV-18). Fleet Admiral Chester W. Nimitz has autographed the original print.   *Collection of Fleet Admiral Chester W. Nimitz, USN. U.S. Naval Historical Center photograph.*

Fig. 6. The light carrier *Princeton* (CV-23) under way in the North Atlantic area during her shakedown cruise, 31 May 1943. Aircraft parked aft include nine SBD scout bombers and twelve F4F fighters. *Official U.S. Navy photograph, now in the collections of the National Archives.*

Fig. 7. The light cruiser *Santa Fe* (CL-60) operating out of the Philadelphia Navy Yard, Pennsylvania, on 7 March 1943, at about the time she went to the Pacific.   *Photograph from the Bureau of Ships Collection in the U.S. National Archives.*

Fig. 8. Vice Admiral Kurita Takeo, Imperial Japanese Navy. Portrait photograph, taken during World War II. Original photograph was in the files of Rear Admiral Samuel Eliot Morison, USNR. *U.S. Naval Historical Center photograph.*

Fig 9. The Japanese heavy cruiser *Chokai*. View of the ship's starboard side from just aft of the bow to the aircraft catapults, circa 1938. Probably photographed off the coast of China. The original photograph came from Rear Admiral Samuel Eliot Morison's World War II history project working files. *U.S. Naval Historical Center photograph.*

Fig. 10. The Japanese battleship *Yamato* running trials, 30 October 1941. This photograph was seized by occupation authorities in Japan following the end of World War II. *Official U.S. Navy photograph, now in the collections of the National Archives.*

Fig. 11. The Japanese fleet carrier *Zuikaku*, photographed 25 September 1941, the day she was completed for service. Courtesy of Mr. Hando Kazutoshi, 1970. *U.S. Naval Historical Center photograph.*

at or about 1045 and began their attack two hours later. The third attack formation, from the *Essex* and *Lexington* of Task Group 38.3, consisted of just sixteen Hellcats but twenty Helldivers and thirty-two Avengers. These aircraft left their carriers at or about 1050 and began their attack at about 1330. The fourth and final attack formation consisted of forty-two Hellcats, thirty-three Helldivers, and twenty-one Avengers. Of these, twenty-six Hellcats, twenty-one Helldivers, and eighteen Avengers were drawn from the *Franklin* and *Enterprise* of Task Group 38.4 while the balance came from the ubiquitous *Intrepid* and *Cabot*. These aircraft were flown off at or about 1313 and began their attacks an hour later at 1415.[124]

The sequence of subsequent events is somewhat confused, indeed as confused as two matters, the number of attacks to which the Japanese formations were subjected and the number of torpedoes and bombs that hit the *Musashi*. On the first matter, the four strikes flown off the American carriers sit uneasily alongside the five or six attacks that were conducted in most accounts of these proceedings. For example, the first attack began at 1025 or 1026, the second at 1138, the third at 1217, the fourth at 1253, the fifth at 1315, and the sixth and last attack at 1445. Only the first attacks are given in terms of duration, namely five and seven minutes respectively.[125] On the second matter, it was claimed by her executive officer that the *Musashi* was hit by as many as twenty-six torpedoes and thirty bombs,[126] and while it may well have seemed such numbers did indeed strike home and thereby confound the damage control efforts of Captain Kato Kenkichi, such numbers appear to have been exaggerated, but not overmuch. One of the most reliable sources suggests that the *Musashi* was overwhelmed by as many as twenty torpedo and seventeen bomb hits,[127] but it would seem that eleven of the torpedo and ten of the bomb hits were registered in the final attack,[128] by which time the battleship, having previously been hit by nine torpedoes and seven bombs, was in very real difficulty and on two counts. The use of counterflooding to correct the list could only be done by reducing buoyancy and trim, and with her bow down by some four meters the *Musashi* could not maintain speed and hence her position in formation. Though she was still able to make sixteen knots, she had lost speed, maneuverability, and her place in formation, and thus the protection afforded by the other Japanese warships, essential to any chance of survival. As it was, by the time of the attacks around 1253 only a quarter of the ship's 25-mm anti-aircraft guns remained operational, as American bombs and strafing exacted heavy casualties among the gun crews in these unprotected positions.[129] The use of the 18.1-in. guns of the main armament firing the *sanshiki-dan* 3,000-piece airburst rounds at incoming American aircraft at 1315 was inadvertent evidence that the battleship was already *in extremis*. The heavy wear and tear to the gun barrels caused by these rounds and the resultant adverse effects on their accuracy of fire meant that the initial request for their use was refused,[130] but final recourse to these weapons suggests that by this time she had already sustained such damage that her fate was all but sealed.

Inevitably, in various accounts there have been references to "the critical damage," an unhelpful concept since the *Musashi* was overtaken by cumulative damage, but clearly the damage sustained in the second and third attacks was singularly important. The *Musashi* was initially hit by a torpedo and then by another that penetrated through the hole that had been made.[131] The resultant explosion carried into the ship's innards, breaching the damage control system.[132] Thereafter the *Musashi*, which by the time of the final attack had already survived a scale of attack and damage which would have accounted for any other battleship then in existence, began to lose power as boiler and engine rooms were destroyed by individual torpedo hits while bombs destroyed her bridges, wounding her captain and killing seventy-eight of her crew, including various senior officers.[133] Even before the final attack there were suggestions that the *Musashi* should attempt to make her way to Coron Bay,[134] but after this attack, which flooded first the port outboard and then the inboard engine rooms and thus reduced the battleships to two shafts, the *Musashi* had been reduced to six knots and clearly was in a desperate state. Listing ten degrees to port, eight meters down by the bow, and flooded from forward main turret to bow, her list was reduced to six degrees but at the expense of further flooding. As her bow settled until it was eight meters below normal, the list increased while the loss of the starboard outer engine room meant her ability to pump was minimal. In any case, by this time there was more water in the ship than could be pumped out, and further counterflooding was halted. The battleship was ordered to try to make for San José,[135] and at this stage the heavy cruiser *Tone* and the destroyer *Kiyoshimo* were detached in order to try to escort her to safety, but after the final attack her captain was ordered by Kurita to beach her on a nearby reef in order that she might be able to function as a battery,[136] while the *Shimakaze* was sent to evacuate *Maya* personnel from the stricken battleship.[137] It may well have been that she did not have sufficient power to mount any submerged reef but in fact her steering and power died even before she reached any island, and without emergency lighting the *Musashi* was in darkness as

dusk approached. She asked for destroyers to come alongside to take off survivors, wounded and unwounded, but the two that were in company—by
this time the *Hamakaze* and *Kiyoshimo* because the *Shimakaze* and the
heavy cruiser *Tone* had returned to Kurita's formation—refused to do so,
obviously for fear of being caught as the battleship sank.[138] Amazingly, in
spite of the massive damage that had been inflicted on her, the *Musashi*
took nearly three hours after the last attack to sink. By 1915 she was listing
twelve degrees to port, and this increased to thirty degrees in a matter of
minutes. With all crew having been brought up from below, the order to
abandon ship was given at 1920. At 1935 the *Musashi* capsized to port, and
with men trying to run along her hull she rose until her stern was well clear
of the water. Thereafter

> crewmen started jumping off . . . the stern, which was sticking up like a tower
> from the ocean surface. Before they reached the ocean surface below, they were
> screaming in horror. Most of them hit the battleship's huge screws before they
> reached the water. Crewmen were running along the battleship, and several
> men who jumped off the sides were sucked into the huge holes made by the
> torpedoes.[139]

The ship disappeared below the surface of the sea with a deafening
roar, creating a swirling whirlpool that sucked untold numbers of seamen to
their deaths, and then she exploded, again killing an unknown number of
sailors who were flung skyward on a pillar of sea. What remained thereafter
were hundreds of men in the sea, many trapped in oil that was up to fifty
centimeters thick, and the destroyers *Hamakaze* and *Kiyoshimo* refusing
to close upon the scene of desolation for some three hours. It has been
suggested that when they did so they did not halt and that their propellers
accounted for more sailors in the water, but nonetheless a total of 1,376
officers and men from an original crew of 2,399 were rescued from the
sea's embrace, the process of rescue continuing until 0215 the following
morning.[140] Depending on perspective, this was a surprisingly high number
given the circumstances of the *Musashi*'s loss or a relatively small number
given the time she took to sink.

The sinking of the *Musashi* had three riders. The first, simply, was that "the
number of bomb hits and torpedoes required to sink the ship amazed U.S.
designers."[141] With the Americans using mixed depth settings between ten
and twenty feet and the eight Avengers from the *Enterprise* using torpedoes

set at twelve feet,[142] it may be that fewer torpedoes would have been needed to sink the *Musashi* had they been set lower, to hit below the armor belt. This, however, would seem to be at best a pedantic argument. A ship so large and well-protected was going to absorb a great deal of punishment before she succumbed, and there was another point that was more obvious to the U.S. carrier fraternity. There was a realization that the *Musashi*'s powers of resistance may have been exaggerated by the indiscriminate nature of the torpedo attacks to which she was subjected. The *Musashi* took thirteen hits to port and seven to starboard, but prior to the final attack the division was four to five. Subsequently the Americans laid emphasis on attacks against only one side of a ship in order to induce capsizing, and this doctrine was put into effect in April 1945 with the attacks that accounted for the *Musashi*'s sister ship, the *Yamato*, in the East China Sea in April 1945.[143]

The second is somewhat esoteric, indeed perverse, since clearly it was never intended thus, but in the last hours of her existence the *Musashi* in effect played the role of decoy and provided indirect cover against American air attack for the formation as a whole. In the first capacity she did this to greater effect than did Ozawa prior to this time and in the second capacity she was more effective than the 2nd Air Fleet. The point appears never to have been considered, and for good and obvious reason, but the fact is that the final overwhelming attack was directed against a ship if not doomed to sink then certainly not going to be involved in any forthcoming battle, and the American effort could well have been better directed against the *Yamato* or the *Nagato*, or even the *Kongo* or the *Haruna*. It is a point that has not commanded much attention, but during this day's attacks on Japanese warships in the Sibuyan Sea, the American carrier aircraft accounted for just one ship, albeit one of the greatest battleships ever built. Given that in real terms American carrier aircraft operated in conditions tantamount to total air supremacy and were unopposed in the air since it seems they never encountered more than four Japanese aircraft over Kurita's formation at any one time and a total of just ten for the whole of the day,[144] that the use of more than 250 aircraft—with no fewer than seventy-six Avenger torpedo-bombers in that number—resulted in the sinking of just one battleship and forced a heavy cruiser to turn back was, in many ways, scant return. The cost to the Americans—just eighteen American aircraft were shot down by Japanese warships while another two were lost operationally and ten more were lost in search, combat air patrol, and other missions—was just one fewer than the number of aircraft lost in the *Princeton*.[145] But the real point would seem to be that at least the final American attack on Kurita's formation was largely misdirected, and indeed was like a hunt. The gathering wolves attacked the doomed quarry rather than the unwounded beasts, and it was the latter that were the more important at this stage of proceedings.

The third is another point that is easily missed in accounts of this day's proceedings, though it was clearly understood on the Japanese side at the time. This was a simple but profoundly important point: the American efforts were getting bigger during the day.[146] The last attack was the largest of the day, and the point was that it engulfed the *Musashi* at or about 1445 when there was between three and four more hours of daylight remaining to the two sides. With his formation having shed the *Musashi*, at 1530, Kurita was persuaded by his operations officer, Commander Inao Otani, to turn back to the west, calculating that the Japanese formations had to put distance between themselves and American carriers that might be able to launch as many as three more strikes before dusk.[147] Even if this figure could be disputed, the basic point was well-made, though with one rider: in turning back, the Japanese formation encountered the near-helpless *Musashi*, and it does not take much imagination to realize the effect of seeing this ship reduced to such a state must have had upon her compatriots.[148] But even though the Japanese turnaway was reported by American search aircraft as early as 1600,[149] one other matter intruded upon the march of events. This was that in the course of the last attack on the *Musashi*, at 1640, search aircraft from Task Group 38.3 found Ozawa's carrier force in 18°10'North 124°30'East, some 130 miles east of Luzon, on a course 210 degrees and making an estimated fifteen knots. The composition of this formation, as finally reported, was four battleships, one with a flight deck aft, five to six cruisers, and six destroyers. Fortunately for the Americans, the Japanese carrier force was found almost immediately thereafter. When reported, this formation was stated to consist of two *Shokaku*-class carriers, one light carrier, three light cruisers, and three or more destroyers. These units were reported to be some fifteen miles north of a battleship force, and, in 18°25'North 125°28'East, almost one degree of longitude east of the other reported position.[150] What had happened was that the first sighting had been of the battleships and escorts from Ozawa's formation which had been detached with orders to proceed southward in a separate attempt to attract American attention and draw American carriers to the north. The division of Ozawa's force was to cause some confusion on the American part not least because if the sighting reports of Kurita's force were correct, this new formation could not have four battleships, but that was of relatively small account, and in any case the Japanese battle group rejoined Ozawa's carrier group about sunrise next morning.[151]

Finding Ozawa's formation represented the final piece of the strategic jigsaw for Halsey, Mitscher, and Task Force 38's carrier formations, and it came only after days of uncertainty and anxiety. In retrospect, with all the advantages of hindsight and full appreciation of the extent of Japanese weakness in terms of carrier air power at this time, it is easy to dismiss American concerns as grossly exaggerated, but even with the overwhelming victory in the air over the Philippine Sea in June and the evidence of Japanese weakness over the Philippines and Formosa in recent weeks, the American concerns were natural and correct. The fact that the Japanese had completed two new fleet carriers—the *Amagi* and *Katsuragi*—was known to U.S. naval intelligence,[152] but there was no way the extent of Japanese weakness could have been discerned. Accordingly, Halsey and his senior commanders saw Japanese carriers as the real threat to American naval and air superiority, and in this respect the sighting report that made reference to three fleet carriers and one light carrier did not merely suggest that Ozawa had a much more powerful force under command than was the case, but was part of a self-fulfilling cycle. From the time that Japanese carriers were positively identified American attention was held, exactly as Ozawa had intended.

But two other matters also impinged upon American deliberations at this stage of proceedings. The first, already noted, was that the first sighting of Ozawa's formation—actually the battleships and escorts which were separated from the carriers at the time—came at the very time when Halsey was informed that Kurita's force had turned away, "apparently in irreparable disarray (and) in either temporary or final retreat."[153] The second was the relative lateness of the hour when the Japanese formations were found. This unfortunate unfolding of events owed itself to two things. First, because Halsey suspected a Japanese carrier force might be to the north in the general direction of Formosa and Okinawa and because Mitscher suspected a Japanese carrier force might be to the west behind Luzon in the South China Sea, it was not until relatively late in the morning of 24 October that Sherman obtained permission to conduct a search to the north and northeast; by this time it was in the latter direction that Sherman expected to find the enemy.[154] Second, is the fact that the various Japanese raids to which Task Group 38.3 was subjected, when tied to the problem presented by the *Princeton*, meant that even though the formation was ordered by Mitscher at 1155 to conduct a search of the sector between 350 and 040 degrees with five groups each with one scout and two fighters, and was ready to do so by 1245, the need to use fighters assigned to this scouting mission for the defense of the task group ensured that it was not until 1405, and a few minutes after the end of what proved to be the last attack of the day on Task Group 38.3,[155] that unescorted Helldivers were dispatched.[156] The result was that Ozawa's formation was not found until it was too late in the day to conduct a strike; with sunset at 1815,[157] there was no possibility of any strike force being able to return to their carriers before dark. Herein was any irony seldom noted in histories of this battle. If Ozawa had been successful in attracting American attention at or about mid-day, then events might well have unfolded differently, and the Americans might have been able to deal with both Japanese formations, those of Ozawa and Kurita, that same afternoon. In such an eventuality, what was a decidedly unfortunate set of events for the Americans might have been averted.

Even before he was informed of Kurita's turnaway, Halsey at 1512 issued a warning order to the formations under his command, providing that four battleships, two heavy and three light cruisers, and two divisions of destroyers, all drawn from Task Groups 38.2 and 38.4, "will be formed as Task Force 34 under commander battle line. Task Force 34 engage decisively at long ranges. Commander Task Group 38.4 conduct carriers of Task Group 38.2 and Task Group 38.3 clear of surface fighting."[158] This signal, to which King and Nimitz were addressees, was obviously intended as the first, precautionary order to guard against the eventuality of a surface action against an enemy intent, and able, to negotiate the San Bernardino Strait. Kinkaid eavesdropped this signal, and took it to mean that Halsey would be forming a battle group in order to cover the Strait and thereby safeguard his formations gathered off Samar. This was the general interpretation placed upon the signal and presented no difficulties to all concerned, but after Kurita's force had been reported to have turned back to the west, Halsey, using short-range voice-radio, at 1710 informed the commanders of Task Groups 38.2 and 38.4 that "[i]f the enemy sorties [i.e. turns back to the east and attempts to transit the San Bernardino Strait] Task Force 34 will be formed when directed by me."[159] Kinkaid and Mitscher were not parties to this signal.[160] The discovery of Ozawa's force initiated the process that ensured that these intentions were overtaken by events.

When the search aircraft that had found the Japanese carrier force returned to the *Lexington*, Mitscher and his chief of staff, Commodore

Arleigh Burke, personally debriefed the pilots. Their conclusion was that to the northeast was a single Japanese formation, in two parts admittedly, with at least three carriers, four to six cruisers, six or more destroyers, and the battleships *Hyuga* and *Ise*.[161] It seems that at this stage Burke suggested that the battleships *Massachusetts* and *South Dakota*, with two light cruisers and destroyer squadrons, be detached from Sherman's Task Group 38.3 and sent north with a view to forcing a night action. Apparently, Mitscher accepted this proposal and at 1712 ordered Sherman to put such a plan into action with nightfall.[162] But before this could happen Halsey issued the order that in effect overruled such provision and thus set in train the sequence of events that brought the American forces gathered off Leyte to the brink of a very real but local defeat.

This episode would seem to raise three obvious questions. First, Halsey's orders were issued after 2000, by which time the ships assigned to this task could have parted company, but there is no evidence to suggest that they did. Second, it beggars belief that Mitscher would not have informed Halsey of this decision, yet there is no evidence to suggest that this was the case, and, moreover, there is one other related matter pertaining to Mitscher at this time. It was in the immediate aftermath of receiving the 1640 sighting report, at 1645, that Mitscher intimated to Sherman that the *Princeton* be scuttled "in view of contact to north."[163] Whether that was part of the Burke proposal or an anticipation of what Halsey would do is a moot point, but at 1723 Mitscher indicated to the task group commanders his intention to go north through the night.[164] Whether this was with just Task Group 38.3 or all the task groups is not clear, but it does not seem that the reference was about just the battleships. Third, even allowing for the clear superiority of the two American battleships relative to their aging opposite numbers, why Burke should suggest the use of just two battleships to deal with an enemy formation with both carriers and battleships—and which reports suggested had a minimum of seventeen and perhaps as many of twenty-four units—seems somewhat odd, even allowing for the fact that Task Group 38.3 had only two battleships to send.[165] Nonetheless, the suggestion stands in neat contrast to the main line of argument deployed in defense of Halsey's decision to send the three carrier groups north, in pursuit of Ozawa's formation, without leaving any force to cover the San Bernardino Strait.

This decision has been the subject of much discussion, and in an obvious sense it has a triple context. The first is provided by a double fact, that at this stage of the Pacific war the destruction of enemy carrier formations was a primary objective, perhaps the primary objective in a fleet action, and to this was the point, noted in the course of fleet staff discussions later that evening, that there seemed to be three Japanese forces moving in what seemed a coordinated and deliberate manner, and at speeds that suggested their concentration the next morning. Given this reading of the situation, not surprisingly Halsey chose to move against the main force, the carriers, in part because it was or seemed to be the main force and in part as the means of ensuring the disruption of Japanese intent. The second is provided by the three options that Halsey stated were open to him at the time. These were to divide the carrier groups and use the carriers, lightly screened, to go north while the battle line covered the Strait; to keep the whole of the three groups covering the Strait; and to keep the carrier groups together and to go north in full concentrated strength even though this would mean leaving the Strait unguarded.[166] The third is provided by the denunciations that had followed Spruance as a result of his decision, during the battle of the Philippine Sea in June, to decline contact and to stand off the threatened beachheads on Saipan and not to go after the Japanese carrier formations.[167] Most of the criticisms of Spruance were ill-directed and grossly overdrawn, but at this stage Halsey could not have been unaware of them.[168] Halsey chose the third and last option, and the justification he provided for this decision was concentration of force. To Halsey the critical matter was to avoid a division of force, clearly lest defeat overwhelm the weakened and divided parts, and to this end he was to use the argument that concentration of force constituted the basic, overriding principle of war, to be observed at all times.[169] To such an assertion there are two answers, one obvious and the other not. The obvious answer is that military genius in no small measure involves that element of judgment that sets aside the principles of war to better facilitate the task in hand. The not-so-obvious answer is that Halsey's own orders had contradicted the principle of concentration. The original 1512 order dealing with the formation of Task Force 34 had stated:

> Battle Plan: Battleship Division 7, *Miami, Vincennes, Biloxi,* Destroyer Squadron 52 less *Steven Potter* from Task Group 38.2 and *Washington, Alabama, Wichita, New Orleans,* Destroyer Division 100, *Patterson, Bagley* from Task Group 38.4 will be formed as Task Force 34 (under Vice Admiral Lee).[170]

Battleship Division 7 consisted of the *Iowa* and *New Jersey,* and the *Washington* and *Alabama* had been allocated to Task Group 38.4 from Task Group 38.3 on the previous day. This left the *Massachusetts* and *South*

Dakota—the two battleships with the carrier formation nearest Ozawa though the latter's presence was not known at the time—out of the frame. Clearly these two battleships had the time and the speed to be able to get to a position off the San Bernardino Strait and to join the other four had that been required, but this order was given at a time when the Americans knew that the Japanese force in the Sibuyan Sea had at least four battleships and a goodly number of cruisers. At best, it would seem that this instruction regarding the formation of a battle force envisaged battle on the basis of numerical equality with the enemy and without the full concentration of all the battleships that were available.[171] Equally clearly, it would seem that for Halsey the word "concentration" had various meanings, depending on convenience.

The whole issue of Halsey's decision has been beset by a number of matters of dubious relevance. For example, Kincaid's misunderstanding of Halsey's arrangement is wholly irrelevant. Kinkaid's was not the power of decision, and whether or not he misinterpreted Halsey's intention is wholly unimportant. Any misunderstanding on the part of Kinkaid had no bearing on the deployment of his forces in the sense that there was little that he could have done to provide himself with a guard against any force coming through the San Bernardino Strait. Likewise, naval historians who have blamed MacArthur for failing to ensure proper communications between Kinkaid and Halsey seem to have embraced a somewhat disingenuous argument.[172] One hesitates to write anything in defense of MacArthur, but for naval historians to blame an army general for a lack of proper communications between naval formations seems to be at the very limit of credibility. In any event, a theater commander can hardly be blamed for lack of communications between one of his forces and a counterpart in another theater; that responsibility and task, surely, fell to the Joint Chiefs of Staff, and specifically King, who bore executive responsibility for the Pacific. And, of course, it seems that King, after the war, went to some lengths to try to place responsibility for the errors of omission and commission upon Kinkaid.[173]

More immediately, however, are five matters that demand consideration. The first was Halsey's statement that when he made the decision to take his formations to the north he was convinced that "the northern force could not be left to operate unmolested . . . destruction of its carriers would mean much to our future operations." In this his views mirrored those of

Sherman: "As the sun went down the situation was entirely to my liking and I felt we had a chance to completely wipe out a major group of the enemy fleet, including the precious carriers, which he could ill afford to lose."[174] Both Halsey and Sherman glimpsed the opportunity, and the basic argument was one with which there can be no serious quarrel even if it was disproved by events; the *Kaigun* was so weak by this stage of the war that the destruction of its carriers was neither here nor there. But Halsey could not know that the Japanese carrier teeth had been drawn, and his obvious concern had to be the danger of being caught the next day by Japanese aircraft operating from both Luzon and Ozawa's carriers. But the second point, Halsey's argument that "the center force might sortie and inflict some damage," but that its fighting capacity had been "too badly impaired to win a decision,"[175] presents problems of comprehension. Leaving aside the point that this estimation of Japanese capabilities was based upon an uncritical acceptance of the claims of aircrew involved in the attacks on Kurita's formation, and that this was in no small measure the direct responsibility of Halsey's air officer,[176] it is difficult to resist the idea that Kurita's force was never going to transit the San Bernardino Strait unless its fighting capacity was more or less intact, reduced perhaps but nonetheless intact; indeed, there was no point in its attempting to pass through the Strait unless this was so. But this observation on the part of Halsey, and his subsequent statement that he did not believe that Kurita's force could reach Leyte Gulf in the hours of darkness and that in any case Kinkaid's forces could handle a force capable of no more than "merely hit and run,"[177] would seem to invite the observation that on his own admission Halsey was quite prepared to see Kinkaid's force take losses that would have been avoided if a battle line had been left off the Strait. Given that there was no way he or anyone else could have foreseen what losses might have been incurred, Halsey's statement invites the observation that it would seem to confirm the validity of the old saying that the difference between genius and stupidity is that genius has its limits.

The third point, however, is that even before Halsey gave the order for the three carrier formations to concentrate and move north, he was aware that Kurita's force had turned back to the east,[178] and subsequently the Americans became aware that the Japanese had switched on the navigation lights in the Strait.[179] Nothing could have been more obvious proof of Japanese intent, but both before and after his situation report, received by Kinkaid at 2024, that "[s]trike reports indicate enemy heavily damaged. Am proceeding north with three groups to attack enemy carrier force at dawn,"[180] Halsey's intention was being questioned within his own staff. Apparently a certain Lieutenant Matthews tried to tell Halsey twice during the night of 24–25 October of the danger of not leaving a covering force in position at the San Bernardino Strait by reference to reconnaissance reports that indicated that Kurita's force was coming east. At 2006 a Hellcat from the *Independence* reported a Japanese force coming east, a report that was passed by Halsey to Kinkaid, and at 2115 an aircraft reported Kurita's force between Burias and Masbate and therefore east of its previously reported position.[181] Moreover, it appears that various staff officers—obviously retiring early in order to be on hand throughout the next day—left the bridge in the belief that Task Force 34 was to be formed and left at the Strait and were astonished when they returned to the bridge in the early hours of the next morning and found the battleships in company.[182] If commanders such as Kinkaid were misled, or misled themselves, as a result of Halsey's signals, then they appear not to have been alone, for the misunderstanding even within Halsey's own staff in the *New Jersey* would seem to be beyond belief. As it was, and this is the fourth point, Kinkaid did ask Halsey if Task Force 34 had been formed and was off the San Bernardino Strait, but he elicited no response. Kinkaid's original belief, when informed that Halsey was going north with three groups, was that with four groups under command (i.e., the three carrier groups and the battle line), Halsey had detached the latter. Kinkaid ordered search missions by Catalinas based on the tender *Half Moon* off Cabugan Grande Island at the northern end of the Surigao Strait, but these amphibians found nothing. The one Catalina that passed directly over the San Bernardino Strait did so an hour ahead of the Japanese force, which it did not detect,[183] and the northernmost of the three escort carrier formations (Task Group 77.4) was ordered to undertake dawn search missions from Leyte Gulf to the San Bernardino Strait. It could not conduct night searches because the American escort carriers did not have night aircraft,[184] and by a singularly unfortunate set of circumstances the carrier that was given the order to conduct these searches, the *Ommaney Bay*, was not able to fly off its aircraft until thirty minutes after sunrise, by which time potential disaster was about to overwhelm the most northerly of the three American escort carrier groups off Samar.[185] But it was not until 0412, and then at the prompting of his operations officer, that Kinkaid asked Halsey if Task Force 34 was in position. By then it was too late for any appropriate countermeasures to be undertaken by Kinkaid's formations, and in any event there was no reply from Halsey's flagship until after 0648 when Halsey finally received Kinkaid's message.[186] By that time there was scarcely any need for an answer.

The fifth and last point, however, is the one that presents the most difficulty. It is a point that can be simply stated. When Halsey brought the carrier force to a position off the Philippines in order to provide direct support for the landings on Leyte, he had sent a signal to MacArthur—evidence that he could communicate directly when he wanted to—that stated:

> Since the South China Sea may suddenly become a critical area, information is requested as to what is the earliest estimate for a safe route to that sea via Surigao and Mindoro straits for (a) well-escorted oilers and (b) major combatant ships.[187]

This signal has attracted its share of attention not least because Nimitz immediately reminded Halsey that his task was to "cover and support forces of the Southwest Pacific" and specifically forbade any movement of Halsey's forces into central Philippine waters without direct orders from himself.[188] A certain misunderstanding seems to have entered the historical record on account of the general assumption that Halsey had intended to move through the San Bernardino Strait, whereas this was not the case.[189] The request for information specifically referred to the Surigao Strait—which was Kinkaid's area of responsibility whereas the San Bernardino Strait was not—and made no mention of the water that separates Luzon and Samar, though Nimitz's response applied equally and specifically to both. The point, however, would seem to be the utter inconsistency of Halsey. On 21 October it was vitally important for him to move through the Visayans, via the Surigao Strait and across the Bohol and Sulu Seas into the Mindoro Strait and hence to a position directly outside Manila Bay, in order to deal with any Japanese force that might be there. Yet on 24 October, and at a time when he knew that a Japanese force was in the Sibuyan Sea, Halsey did not consider it worthwhile to leave a covering force in position off the San Bernardino Strait. There would seem to be no way these two positions can be reconciled.[190]

At issue, of course, was the primary function of Halsey's carrier force, and the nature of the problem herein can be gauged by Halsey's own observation, in his battle report, that "to statically guard San Bernardino Strait until enemy surface and carrier air strikes could be co-ordinated would have been childish."[191] One wonders about the use of the last word, which would seem to reflect poorly on Halsey, but the situation was not an either-or, and it is this aspect of post-war analysis, when combined with what seems to have been a deliberate confusion of the issue, that makes this whole episode so perplexing. Amid the arguments about communications and misinterpretation, the critical issue was not command but role, and Halsey's role, unequivocally, was to "cover and support forces of Southwest Pacific in order to assist the seizure and occupation of objectives in the central Philippines." What Halsey always tried to claim was that his actions were covered by the provision in his orders that stated that his formation was "to destroy enemy naval and air forces in or threatening the Philippine area," and, critically, "in (the event the) opportunity for (the) destruction of (a) major portion of the enemy fleet offer(s) itself or can be created, such destruction becomes the primary task."[192] These provisions, written into Halsey's orders as a direct result of what had happened in the Philippine Sea in June, constituted the escape clause, as Halsey later wrote "it was not my job to protect the Seventh Fleet. My job was offensive, to strike with the Third Fleet."[193] This was not the case. The task of Halsey's carriers was not offensive. It was offensive only if the support and amphibious forces were secure. Blame might be attached to Kinkaid for not properly conducting detailed and extensive reconnaissance, and his battle line commander, Oldendorf, might be criticized for taking all his battleships into the Surigao Strait in an attempt to finish off damaged Japanese warships after the night action at the very time when his formation was needed to support the escort carriers. But given the lack of night search capability on the part of the escort carriers, such censure of Kincaid would seem to be misplaced, while Oldendorf can hardly be criticized for not knowing at this stage of proceedings that the San Bernardino Strait had been left unguarded and that Kurita's force was an hour or two from contact with Task Group 77.4, but in any case the primary role of Oldendorf's battleship formations was not to fight the likes of the *Yamato*. The destruction of any enemy forces that might seek to attack the amphibious and support formations at Leyte obviously presented the best possible guarantee of those formations, but two basic points nonetheless remain. First, the rider in Halsey's orders did not cancel the order to cover the other formations and did not make the destruction of any enemy formations the sole objective or an objective of such overriding importance that other tasks were of secondary or tertiary importance. Halsey, lest the point is missed, was not authorized to abandon the beachheads *en passant*.[194] Second, the simple fact was that on the afternoon and evening of 24 October, on a day when the fast carrier force's overwhelming concern had been the Japanese battle formation moving through the Sibuyan Sea, Halsey in effect dismissed further operations against this formation, and any form of direct support for the American forces off Samar, from further consideration.

Halsey's order for the carrier groups to go north with a view to dealing with their opposite number the next morning was given at 2024 by his chief of staff.[195] As early as 1630 Task Group 38.2 and Task Group 38.4 had effected a rendezvous in 13°36'North 126°01'East, tactical command thereafter being vested in Davison in the *Franklin*, but it was not until about 2330 that Task Group 38.3 joined company.[196] Sherman, by his own admission, had reluctantly obeyed Halsey's order because it involved his formation having to turn back to the southeast around 1900, and hence away from the Japanese carrier force, in order to join the other two groups.[197] From the time the three groups were together, tactical command was assumed by Mitscher, and shortly after midnight the American formations, which had been making twenty-five knots and were in 14°31'North 125°34'East at midnight, were slowed to sixteen knots to avoid the possibility of running past the Japanese force.[198] At 0030 the *Independence* launched one aircraft to conduct a night search, and this aircraft found one of the Japanese groups at 0205 and the second at 0235. Because of engine trouble it was unable to stay in contact, and because the other search aircraft in the *Independence* had radar problems no replacement could come on station.[199] The irony of such a situation is, of course, delicious. For all the numbers and strength of Halsey's fleet, in the final analysis obtaining contact with the enemy carrier force was reduced to a single aircraft and chance, and Halsey had no contact with the enemy force which he sought to destroy for some nine hours before this contact.

But there were in this period four matters relating to the carrier groups and Halsey's decision that need to be noted, and there was also a fifth matter, on the Japanese side and wholly unrelated to this precise sequence of events, that demands consideration. The first, previously noted but repeated here, is that Halsey provided a report to Kinkaid about what he was doing at 2024. It was precisely because Kinkaid presumed that Halsey had four formations under command, that his being informed of Halsey's intention to proceed north with three groups led naturally to the assumption that one group, the battle group, was being left to guard the San

Bernardino Strait. It has been argued that in reality there was no basis for Kinkaid's assumption that Halsey might have chosen to leave one carrier group behind. The primary reason cited in defense of such an eventuality was that a battle group would be left without air cover the next morning. This seems like special pleading. Kinkaid was not alone in making this assumption, and the fact that Nimitz and King also seemed to make the same assumption would suggest that whatever fault there may have been on this particular point does not pertain to Kinkaid.[200]

Second, in this period there were misgivings about these arrangements, and there were a number of attempts by Halsey's subordinates to have them reversed. In the *Franklin*, the commander of Task Group 38.4 and his chief of staff were less than impressed by what Halsey had ordered, but Davison assumed that Halsey had more information than he did and so made no protest.[201] Mitscher took the same line when wakened by his staff, and Burke apparently in the late evening of 24 October convinced himself that Ozawa's force was a decoy because the aircraft from the carrier force had not returned to the northeast. When signals were received in the *Lexington* indicating that Kurita's force had turned back to the east, Burke, along with the operations officer, reported to Mitscher, but like Davison he took the line that Halsey "has all the information we have. He may have more. . . . If he wants my advice, he'll ask for it."[202] As it was, Halsey had largely bypassed Mitscher for much of the day, having taken tactical command of the carrier groups himself, and clearly Mitscher's decision reflected that fact, at least in part. Lee, in the *Washington*, twice attempted to call Halsey by TBS to express his concern at the baring of the San Bernardino Strait. He was convinced that a couple of light carriers would be all that was required to cover a battle force deployed off the Strait, and in any case he seems to have seen through Japanese intention and realized that Ozawa's carrier formation was a decoy.[203] His attempt to express these views, repeated after the report from the scout from the *Independence* was received, was treated in a perfunctory, indeed dismissive, manner, after which Lee held his hand.[204] Quite independently, Bogan, the commander of Task Group 38.2 in the *Intrepid*, came to the same view when informed by the *Independence* that one of her scouts had found the navigation lights of the Strait on and Kurita's force coming east. Bogan attempted, again by TBS, to put across his view that Task Force 34 should be formed and his own group should be assigned the role of covering the battle line, but this was treated to the same curt indifference on the part of one of Halsey's staff officers as Lee's had been, and with the same result.[205] One would note, however, that perhaps this last line of argument would not have been likely to appeal to Halsey under any circumstances given that the New Jersey was in Task Group 38.2. But lest the overall point be missed, what these various episodes together meant was that Mitscher, the battle line commander, and two of the three carrier commanders clearly had reservations about what Halsey had put in hand, and the third carrier commander had reservations for another reason. The obvious question is just how Halsey and his staff could have devised and then held to a course of action so clearly unattractive to most senior commanders in the fleet.

Third, it needs be noted that the last chance to do something that would have ensured a different unfolding of events came as a result of a series of reports after 2304 by an aircraft from the Independence, and specifically the report that was received at 0011 on 25 October. This reported a Japanese battleship formation in column—a deployment that had been adopted at 1951 the previous evening when it was dark and clearly there was no danger of attack—between Burias and Ticao islands, i.e., less than forty miles from the San Bernardino Strait.[206] The report also stated that the force was headed to the northeast, which was incorrect, and did not give a time of sighting, an omission that did not amount to much because it was clearly within the previous hour. But what is interesting about this report was that when it was received in the New Jersey—when she was about 165 miles from the Strait and 220 miles from Leyte Gulf—the fleet staff officers made their calculations but no detail was changed. If this seems surprising because a battle force could probably have reached Samar ahead of Kurita's force, and presumably at this stage Halsey and his staff must have assumed that any losses incurred at the hands of this force would be inconsequential, then perhaps it is even more surprising that this final contact report was never forwarded to Kinkaid.[207]

The basic point is, however, that this third episode really was the last chance when things might have been shaped to a course different from what occurred. Put another way, after this, things were inevitable—or more accurately, certain things were inevitable. Once this moment had passed there was nothing that could have prevented Kurita's formation from negotiating the San Bernardino Strait and obtaining the contact it sought off Samar, but this fact of life prompts consideration of the fourth matter, Halsey's own comment on the U.S. carrier formations being reined in after midnight. According to Halsey, his reasoning was fear that Ozawa's carrier force "slipped past my right flank" and thence "would be able to shuttle-bomb me—fly from his carriers, attack me, continue on to his fields on Luzon for more bombs and fuel, and then attack me again on the way back." One would suggest that such an eventuality would have been impossible if the Japanese force had passed the American carrier formation, and in any event the experience off the Marianas in June 1944 should surely have pointed to this fear being exaggerated, but Halsey also stated, "If the enemy slipped past by my left flank, between me and Luzon, he would have had a free crack at the transports." Leaving aside the fact that the transports were not off Luzon, this observation defies belief. Halsey here is claiming that he could not expose the transports—and other forces gathered off Samar and Leyte—to attack by a carrier group at the very time when his own actions exposed the transports and their covering and support formations to attack by a battle force.[208]

The fifth and final matter was Japanese and, perversely, was not directly related to any of the Japanese naval formations making their way through or off the Philippines. It was a matter nonetheless linked to what had happened to Kurita in the Sibuyan Sea, and that at 1600, after having turned back to the west in an attempt to put distance between his formations and American carrier aircraft in the remaining hours of daylight, Kurita made a signal to Combined Fleet headquarters protesting the lack of air cover his formation had been afforded over the previous six hours.[209] He was not to be reassured on this matter, and the fact was that, various disingenuous claims notwithstanding, Kurita's force had been afforded whatever protection just ten fighters were able to provide. Such numbers, which was about the size of the standard combat air patrol for a single American carrier group at any one time, represented the total number that were available, and obviously at various times these would have been obliged to return to their airfields to refuel and rearm but for the fact that all seemed to have been destroyed by American fighters on their first appearance. It would seem that the maximum number of fighters ever put over Kurita's force was four, and to precisely no effect.[210]

Kurita's report that his force had turned back to the west and his complaint about lack of air cover elicited a response from the Combined Fleet commander which has assumed a certain notoriety: *TENYU WO KAKUSHIN SHI ZENGUN TOTSUGEKI SEYO*/BELIEVE IN GOD'S HELP: ALL FORCES CHARGE![211] It was, perhaps, the best possible evidence of the primacy in Japanese calculations of hope rather than reason, and it was afforded a reception by Kurita's staff that can only be described as derisory.[212] But the real point was that even before this signal, at 1714, Kurita had turned his formation back to the east,[213] and for one reason. The day's fighting had cost time, time that could not be afforded and which meant that the element of coordination between the central and southern battleship formations was coming adrift. The Japanese plan called for the Japanese formations to converge on Leyte Gulf at dawn on the following day, and in trying to fend off successive American attacks Kurita's force necessarily fell behind schedule. Accordingly, Kurita turned his formations back to the east, and in the day's last light, around 1900, passed the *Musashi* in the last minutes of her life.[214] Thereafter for Kurita and his formation there was no turning back, even if the company of American search aircraft for the remainder of the day was unwelcome. According to the signal of 2145 Kurita stated his expectation that his force would be in Leyte Gulf about 1100 the next day, some five hours later than had been envisaged under the terms of the original plan.[215] Herein was one point that was to be a foretaste of a more serious turn of events. The refueling of the formation in Brunei Bay rather than in Coron Bay meant that Kurita's formation could not attempt to make up lost time by a major increase of speed. It was not so much the battleships and cruisers that were the problem but the destroyers. Leyte Gulf represented extreme range for these warships, and thus there could be no real advance over most economical cruising speed for Kurita's force, which had to accept that its final approach would be conducted in daylight.[216]

Perhaps the most important word in Toyoda's signal was that though it was directed solely to Kurita, other commanders in the Philippines areas of responsibility and interest were on the distribution list. The clear expectation that what remained of the once-proud fleets were to be sacrificed in the attempt to inflict a real and lasting defeat on the Americans had obvious implications for what remained of the air formations based on Luzon, and in that evening, according to Toyoda, Onishi and Fukudome "decided that if the surface units are taking such desperate measures we too must take similar desperate measures, and started the first operation of the so-called Special Attack Force."[217] In truth the situation was a little bit more complicated than Toyoda suggests, but not much. The *kamikaze* option, as noted elsewhere, had been on the table since the defeat off the Marianas, and it had been seriously considered four days previously, on 20 October. Now, however, and one assumes partly because these senior commanders must have belatedly realized the ineffectiveness of conventional air attack on this and previous days, the two air fleet commanders decided to employ *kamikaze* attack the next morning.[218] A signal to that effect was

sent to Combined Fleet headquarters at 0008[219]—just three minutes before
American commanders received the report from one of their search aircraft that Kurita's force was approaching the San Bernardino Strait, and
two minutes before the first contact report placed Nishimura's force at
the entrance to the Surigao Strait.[220] Herein was a neat juxtaposition, not
that those involved had any awareness of their proximity and not that the
Japanese were in any position to appreciate the irony.

Thus was set, a kingdom—or rather an empire—for a stage, and History
to behold the swelling scene. Thus closed a day that had seen the sinking
of just two Japanese warships, a mighty 67,123-ton battleship and a lowly
1,1715-ton destroyer. It had seen also the *en passant* sinking of a 2,844-ton
army transport by carrier aircraft, and American submarines accounting for
two naval support units, one army transport, and five merchantmen west of
the Luzon Strait, and there had been the sinking of the *Princeton*. But as
the sands of time pointed to the passing of Tuesday, 24 October 1944, the
day that was to come was to be very different. It was "the day" of the battle
of Leyte Gulf, and it was the day when three of the four main actions that
constitute the battle were fought. But this coming day was something more.
It is generally known that 25 October witnessed the first deliberate and
systemic use of *kamikaze* attacks by Japanese land-based aircraft. Also it is
generally known that this day witnessed the last action between battleships,
thus closing a period of history that reached back more than four hundred
years. But not generally realized is that this day also witnessed the last
action between aircraft carriers, *Deo volente*. In truth, on these three separate matters this coming day, Wednesday, 25 October 1944 really represents
one of the most important single days in naval history, indeed in military
history generally, and not simply on account of these three matters. This
coming day was to witness, with the Japanese alone losing sixteen warships
and one submarine of 183,365 tons, one of the most expensive single days in
naval history in terms of losses by both warship numbers and by tonnage.[221]
But perhaps even more significant, and a point seldom noted, was the
spread of conflict, to which reference can be made simply in terms of the
sinking of the light cruiser *Tama* in 21°23'North 127°19'East and the light
cruiser *Mogami* in 09°40'North 124°50'East. Oddly, the *Tama* was both
the most northern and eastern and the heavy cruiser *Mogami* was both the
most southern and western of Japanese losses, and if the east-west spread of
Japanese losses was most modest, 02°29' of longitude, or about 160 miles,

11°43' of latitude, or about 760 miles, represents the north-south distance between the sinking of these ships. What were two of three parts of a single naval battle spread over some 120,000 square miles of ocean and islands have no obvious or immediate parallel. Perhaps the German submarine campaign against Allied and neutral shipping in the North Atlantic and the defeat of the Spanish armada in 1588 represent campaigns, and the Smyrna convoy debacle of June 1693 represents a battle, that could be held to stand comparison with the events that were to unfold with next day's dawn. But none of these have that combination of increased distance and reduced time that is the essence of Leyte Gulf, the conduct of operations over hundreds of miles during the hours of daylight in a single day, and over a number of successive days. It is difficult indeed to resist the idea that here, in the western Pacific, in an area of deployment and battle that reached from the Inland Sea to Singapore to northeast Mindanao and Dinagat, was something without precedent, that here indeed, as 24 October died, "the great day of wrath is come," and the Japanese would prove wholly unable to stand against it.[222]

CHAPTER SIX

THE GREAT DAY OF WRATH

25 October 1944

ACCOUNTS OF THE naval battle for the Philippines invariably follow the three sets of action of 25 October 1944 singly and in sequence, namely the action in the Surigao Strait involving the formations of Nishimura and Shima, the surface action off Samar that involved Kurita's battle formations, and the action off Cape Engaño that witnessed the destruction of Ozawa's carrier force. Such, in basic outline, was the manner in which events unfolded in terms of time, but in fact there were coincidences of timing, most obviously between the second and third actions, and there were follow-up actions against Japanese formations withdrawing through the straits. This account, rather than following the standard representation of this day's events, will set forth its account chronologically in order to better portray these actions.

The situation thirty minutes either side of midnight involved the "approach to contact" phase in three separate areas. In the north the approach was American because the Japanese carrier and battle formations, now certain of the following day's contact with American forces, had turned back to the north in an attempt to drag the American carrier forces farther to the north and away from the San Bernardino Strait. As the three American carrier groups came north, and speed was checked from twenty-five to sixteen knots, a search from the *Independence* ordered by Halsey's staff revealed that the Japanese battleship formation was but eighty miles to the north.[1] This report was received at or about 0200, and immediately thereafter, Burke, Mitscher's chief of staff, recommended that Task Force 34 be formed and should lead the advance to the north. At this stage it was presumed that the battle force might be able to make contact with the enemy at about 0430, but this schedule, which was somewhat optimistic, was set at naught when the order to form Task Force 34 was given at 0230.[2] Lee ordered that his units, which numbered six battleships, seven cruisers, and eighteen destroyers from three formations, slow and allow themselves to be passed by the other units, and once clear and gathered together, the units became a formation and proceeded northward at high speed to a position some ten miles ahead of the carrier groups. At the same time, the carriers were ordered to ready their deck loads of strike aircraft for immediate takeoff whenever ordered,[3] but events resolutely refused to unfold in the way the Americans had wished. The position of Japanese forces had been misreported and there was never less than 200 miles between American and Japanese formations at this stage of proceedings, and the first flights from the American carriers came around 0600, just before sunrise, with the dispatch of search aircraft.[4] With daylight, and without waiting for any contact report, Mitscher then ordered the flying of standard combat air patrols and sent off 180 aircraft in what was intended to be the day's first strike. Apparently the logic of this action was to have as little time between contact and attack as possible and, by holding the advantage of timing over the Japanese carriers, to conduct an attack before the Japanese had a chance to dispatch their own strike force. It seems that Mitscher calculated that in so doing the American carriers would not be exposed to any repeat of what had happened to the *Princeton*.[5]

In the center, Kurita's battle formations, their numbers reduced from thirty-nine that had sailed from Lingga Roads and from thirty-two that had left Brunei to just four battleships, six heavy and two light cruisers, and eleven destroyers,[6] entered the San Bernardino Strait, in single column, at 2320. In clear weather and with a bright moon the Japanese warships, which steamed at twenty knots,[7] began to emerge from the Strait at 0037. As they did so, the excitement of anticipation was mixed in equal measure with surprise and relief at not encountering an enemy battle line or submarines at the moment of maximum vulnerability before the ships could move into battle formation.[8] Thereafter the ships formed themselves into an extended cruising formation, some thirteen miles across the columns, preparatory to going into battle formation with the dawn.[9]

In the south, midnight found Nishimura's battle force southwest of Limasawa while Shima's formation was west of Camiguin, some forty miles astern.[10] By this time Nishimura's force had beaten off two attacks by groups of American PT boats and had passed another group without having been sighted,[11] but at this stage of proceedings it was divided into two groups, the *Mogami* and three destroyers having been sent forward to reconnoiter Panaon and the approaches to the Surigao Strait while the battleships, with the *Shigure*, hugged the southern coast of Bohol.[12] It was not until 0040 that the two groups effected a rendezvous and adopted an approach formation, the destroyers *Michishio* and *Asagumo* leading the formation abreast. The *Yamashiro*, flanked by the *Shigure* and *Yamagumo*, was some four kilometers astern, and she was followed, at one-kilometer intervals, first by the *Fuso* and then the *Mogami*.[13]

The situation in the south was the first to result in battle on the morning of 25 October, and events of previous days, obviously, form the essential background to this action. The problem herein, however, is not so much events but interpretation and argument, and one would suggest that over the years there have been four areas of interest that have not necessarily been the subjects of clarification and objectivity.

The first of these concerns the fact that Nishimura's formation was found on the morning of 24 October and was subjected to a single attack by carrier aircraft as it crossed the Sulu Sea and approached Negros. It has been suggested that many of the problems that were to inflict themselves upon Nishimura's force were self-induced, not least because Nishimura, by adopting the course and speed he did, compromised his own formation and unnecessarily revealed his presence and, by implication, intent. The basis of this argument is the claim that by 0905, when found some 215 miles from the Surigao Strait by search aircraft from Task Group 38.4, Nishimura's force was some six hours "further advanced than was either necessary or desirable," and that given the subsequent American pre-occupation with Kurita's battle formation in the Sibuyan Sea, it otherwise "might have reached all the way to Surigao before being detected."[14] This is an argument compounded by the second matter, namely a criticism of Japanese arrangements generally, but specifically of Nishimura's conduct of operations, with reference to lack of coordination between formations. The first of these two points has a certain superficial attractiveness, the main point being that a moderately paced final-phase approach to contact

Nishimura's task group in cruise and approach formation, 24–25 October 1944

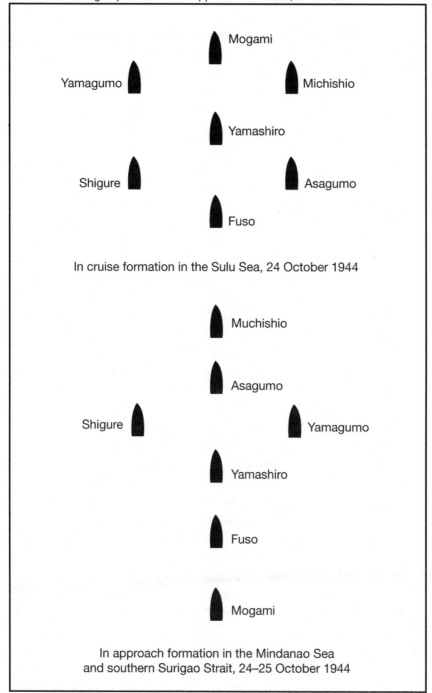

Mogami

Yamagumo   Michishio

Yamashiro

Shigure   Asagumo

Fuso

In cruise formation in the Sulu Sea, 24 October 1944

Muchishio

Asagumo

Shigure   Yamagumo

Yamashiro

Fuso

Mogami

In approach formation in the Mindanao Sea
and southern Surigao Strait, 24–25 October 1944

would have allowed Nishimura's force to have adopted a much slower advance across the Sulu Sea. Such an advance would have kept it beyond the range of American carrier aircraft that found it on the morning of 24 October only at the very limit of their range. The second, likewise, has a certain plausibility. Coordination between Nishimura and Shima was non-existent and between Nishimura and Kurita scarcely any better, consisting as it did of Kurita's periodic revision of his estimated time of arrival off Leyte and Nishimura's seeming utter indifference to any signal sent to him by Kurita.

The first of these points nonetheless leaves itself wide open to the "so what?" response. Even if Nishimura and Shima had led forces that crossed the Sulu Sea and came across the Mindanao Sea undetected, they would still have been obliged to negotiate the Surigao Strait, which had been subjected, at the point where it enters Leyte Gulf, to routine patrol by American battleships every night since 20 October.[15] The local command had deduced that any Japanese move against American amphibious shipping off Leyte would have to come through the Strait and had made provision accordingly. Not being detected in the Sulu and Mindanao Seas would not have altered this situation, and it is difficult to see what real advantage might have been visited upon the Japanese formations had the Americans been served notice of perhaps ninety minutes rather than eighteen hours. The second matter, however, is one on which it is difficult to be definitive, and for obvious reason. From the two Japanese battleships and three destroyers sunk in the Strait there were just twenty-eight survivors,[16] none from the formation staff and senior ranks of the flagship. Thus there is no source that can provide any authoritative evidence of the factors that shaped Nishimura's decisions, only subjective conjecture, and in truth a history of these events is confronted by the impossibility of discerning what were Nishimura's calculations and the reasoning that underpinned them.

Historical studies over the years have provided three possible explanations of Nishimura's conduct of operations. The first, simply, could be summarized by Racine's observation: *L'ivresse de malheur emporte la raison*—The frenzy of disaster/adversity (that) sweeps away all reason. This view would hold that Nishimura had already concluded that his force was being sent on what amounted to a suicide mission, and that the fatalism thus bestowed rendered the admiral immune to any development that did not accord exactly with a course of events on which he was already determined.[17] The second is a personal line of argument, which may be woven around the first. It is that Nishimura's only son had been killed in the

Philippines and his father, when given the task of leading a force through the Surigao Strait, saw in his own death a means of personal atonement and fulfillment.[18] Given the place of ritual suicide in the Japanese ethic, this line of explanation is perhaps not as fanciful as, *prima facie*, it might seem. The third explanation is different in that it notes the obvious point that there was very little point in seeking any form of synchronization with Kurita's force. The two formations were to mount a pincer attack, but the critical point was where they finished, not if one arm reached its destination ahead of the other. If one did so then that was of small account, and in any event no matter what time Kurita set out in successive revisions of his timetable, the fact was that, for Nishimura, the best possible time for negotiating the Surigao Strait had to be between midnight and dawn.[19] To have attempted to pass through the Strait in daylight, and thereby been subjected to successive attacks by carrier aircraft while having limited freedom to maneuver, could only have had one result. In fact, coming through the Strait under cover of dark proved just as bad, if anything even worse, than a daylight passage through the Strait, but Nishimura and staff could not be blamed for that. The fact was that, despite all the evidence of the previous fifteen months to the contrary, Nishimura and his staff clung to the idea of Japanese superiority over the Americans in night fighting, that indeed a night passage through the Surigao Strait promised either the best or only hope of the formation being able to enter Leyte Gulf. If this line of argument is accepted, and it is worth noting that according to the captain of the *Shigure*, Nishimura "was an old-style admiral and preferred a night engagement to a day engagement," then Nishimura's refusal to alter speed and his clear intention to be off the American beachheads "at dawn" on 25 October,[20] make sense, and other matters—chain of command, the fact that Nishimura and Shima came under separate commands, and various personal differences and antipathies that might have made cooperation between the two men impossible—can be discounted as having little or merely *en passant* relevance.

The third and fourth matters relating to historical treatment of the Surigao Strait episode are related and form two separate but linked aspects of American defensive arrangements. The Surigao Strait itself, by virtue of its physical dimensions, served to massively assist these arrangements. Some thirty miles in length and about twelve miles wide at its southern entrance and twenty-five miles wide in the north where it enters Leyte Gulf, the Strait was host to a five-knot current that worked against the Japanese, and it was bordered by rugged cliffs that were more than a match for *Kaigun* radar. Apparently during the action fought in the Surigao Strait, no Allied warship, not even those to the north across the channel, was detected by Japanese radar.[21] American units were able to shelter close to and against the background of the islands, and were all but invisible to Japanese eyes and radar, while the Japanese ships were obliged to negotiate the southern entrance and come north in column.[22] Exactly the same problem as the one that Kurita and his staff had anticipated in seeking to use the San Bernardino Strait—the prospect of emerging from the Strait in line formation and opposed by an enemy with overwhelming advantage of position—faced Nishimura and Shima in the Surigao Strait, but here, at the southern entrance to Leyte Gulf and unlike the situation at the eastern exit of the San Bernardino Strait, an American battle line was in position and ready to give battle.

The fourth matter relates to American strength and deployment. Put at its simplest, the Americans had two fire-support formations, a northern force with three battleships and three destroyers, a southern force with three battleships, three heavy and two light cruisers, and thirteen destroyers, and a third force which originally had been assigned the close cover role and consisted of one heavy and two light cruisers and six destroyers. In addition, one destroyer group, which had escorted landing ships and craft but presently was operating as the anti-submarine patrol across the northern end of the Strait, was on hand, and its commander, Captain Jesse G. Coward, was more than a little anxious to be involved in proceedings,[23] and there were also no fewer than thirty-nine PT boats on hand.[24] When ordered by Kinkaid to prepare "a welcoming committee" to meet a Japanese force that reportedly consisted of two battleships, three heavy and three light cruisers, and ten destroyers and which appeared to be seeking to reach Leyte Gulf through the Surigao Strait,[25] Oldendorf, the force commander in the light cruiser *Louisville*, set out his formations in an arrangement that was curiously similar to the trench system on the Western Front in the last year or two of the previous war. The outpost line was to be provided by two cruiser formations that were stationed on the flanks, with the western force,[26] next to Leyte, consisting of the Australian heavy cruiser *Shropshire* and the American light cruisers *Boise* and *Phoenix*.[27] The eastern force, patrolling in front of the battleships and covering the area between the main channel and Hibuson, had the secondary task of covering the eastern channel between Hibuson and Dinagat just in case the Japanese chose not to use the main one.[28] This force consisted of the heavy cruisers *Louisville*, *Portland* and the *Minneapolis* and the light cruisers *Denver* and *Columbia*, and was deployed some four miles to the south of the battle line, with the other cruiser force perhaps another mile farther forward.[29] The main line of resistance was to be provided by the concentrated battle force—the *West Virginia, Maryland, Mississippi, Tennessee, California* and the *Pennsylvania*—that, with its units a thousand yards apart, was to patrol across the main channel of the Strait, between Leyte and Hibuson Island.

Forward of these formations were to be destroyer flotillas gathered on the two sides of the Strait. With the battle line holding six destroyers as a screen, there were to be two formations that were to conduct a series of attacks upon the Japanese line as it came north. The more northern of these formations consisted of the destroyers that had been with the cruisers, and the more southern, and the first of the destroyer formations to contact the enemy, was Coward's itinerant group, which detached two of its number to patrol the channel between Hibuson and Desolation Point, Dinagat.[30] Ahead, reaching to and beyond the southern entrance of the Strait, were the PT boats, which were formed into thirteen three-boat sections. Three of these groups were deployed forward of Panaon Island and the entrance to the Strait, the most western of these being between Point Agio, eastern Bohol, and Camiguin Island. This was some fifty miles forward of the five sections gathered around Binit Point, southern Panaon, and around Bilaa Point, at the northern tip of Mindanao, across the entrance to the Surigao Strait. The remaining five sections were inside the Strait.[31] What Oldendorf was able to do, in the ample time he was allowed to make his deployment, was to prepare a defense in depth, with his heaviest artillery on the naval equivalent of a reverse slope, and thence to subject any advancing Japanese force to successive attacks. Through a combination of concentrated torpedo attacks in the narrow confines of the Strait and concentrated firepower where Strait and Gulf came together, Oldendorf aimed and clearly expected to overwhelm whatever Japanese force was met in a short and decisive action.[32] Much of the attention devoted to this action has concerned itself with the Americans' potentially overwhelming tactical advantage of having their main formations cross the enemy T, the classical naval configuration whereby a force was able to concentrate broadside fire against an advancing enemy that would be limited to returning fire only from forward turrets.[33] In effect, Oldendorf aimed to provide himself with a potentially telling advantage in successive actions over whatever Japanese forces were able to survive the torpedo-infested waters to the south, though in making such arrangements there were, inevitably, two riders. The PT boats, in effect an extended skirmish line, were under strict orders to stay south of latitude 10°North and to report contact, and once this was done they were free to proceed independently, i.e., to attack whether individually or together.[34] Clearly, while senior American commanders might hope the PT boats would be able to exact a toll on any Japanese formation that was encountered, they limited themselves to hope rather than expectation.

More seriously, though the Americans, in preparing for this action in the Surigao Strait, possessed potentially overwhelming advantages of numbers and position, the only battle that they could fight was a short one. The reason for this was that all the American units were low on fuel and ammunition. The need to provide close fire support for formations ashore meant that three-quarters of the shells carried by the battleships for their main armanent had been high-explosive rather than armor-piercing,[35] and it would seem, given that some units had just 12 percent of their high-explosive rounds left,[36] that fire support over the previous five days had been somewhat prodigal.[37] The relative shortage of armor-piercing shells available to the battleships meant that action had to be limited to less than twenty-five minutes, after which time a unit would exhaust its magazines. What is interesting is that 24 October had been set aside for the replenishment, both of oil and ammunition, of the various American formations, but while there was nothing that could have been done about remedying the shortage of armor-piercing rounds because such ammunition was not available in the support ships,[38] there seems to have been no refurbishment of the destroyers. Unless the support ships were well to the east and units could not make their way to and from the Strait and be back in time for a night action, why this should have been the case is not exactly clear. What is clear, however, is that the need for a short action dictated the fighting of any night action at an ideal range between 17,000 and 20,000 yards,[39] and it so happened that the northern of the destroyer formations tasked to conduct its attacks on the Japanese line did so at the time when the enemy was closing and roughly at that range from the American battle line.[40] Overall, the reception Oldendorf planned to afford Nishimura's battle force was summarized with the comment that always commands attention and inclusion in the record but seldom in full:

> My theory was that of the old-time gambler: Never give a sucker an even chance. If my opponent is foolish enough to come at me with an inferior force, I am certainly not going to give him an even break.[41]

Put another way,

> Oldendorf's disposition of forces would put the oncoming Japanese force into
> the jaws of several succeeding pincers as PTs and destroyers gnawed at his flanks
> along the way. This alone would have been a difficult gauntlet to run.[42]

Mixed metaphors notwithstanding, this was an accurate description of the
imbalance of advantages.

Nishimura's force, having driven off two sets of attackers, entered the
Surigao Strait at about 0130, as reported by the PT boats involved in the
first attack. Received by Oldendorf at 0026, this signal was the first report
of a contact with Nishimura's formation since the attack about 1000 the
previous morning. Because of technical difficulties, the contact report
from the second set of PT boats to mount an attack on Nishimura's ships
failed to reach Oldendorf until 0330, by which time the Allied battleships
and cruisers were well aware of the whereabouts of the Japanese formation.
After passing into the Strait, the Japanese ships, initially in line ahead with
the four destroyers leading, fought off seven successive attacks by the PT
boats without sustaining a single hit. In return, Japanese fire damaged ten
boats but ultimately accounted for only one, PT-493. She was heavily damaged and beached on southern Panaon, only to be claimed by high tide
the next morning. Her crew, having gone into a defensive laager overnight,
was rescued by PT-491.[43]

The Japanese were able to beat off these attacks by a combination of
firepower and turning toward their attackers, but from 0225, when Japanese units were sighted by the eleventh section of PT boats in the narrows
between Amagusan Point (southeast Leyte) and Pelotes Point on Dinagat,
the situation was on the point of undergoing fundamental change. The
PT boats were ordered clear by Coward,[44] and his five destroyers, divided
between the *McDermut* and *Monssen* on the west of the main channel
and the *Remey*, *McGowan* and the *Melvin* to the east, brought coordination and numbers to restricted waters, and to devastating effect. The five
destroyers were brought to General Quarters at 0206, then began to move
south, at twenty knots, at 0230.[45] At 0240 the Japanese were located by
radar at a range of 38,000 yards (twenty-two miles), and it is claimed that
at 0256 Coward's three-ship group was seen in the *Shigure*.[46] By this time
Coward had begun to turn his destroyers away, to the southeast, in order

to open the angle for firing torpedoes, his intention being that the *Remey* should fire her torpedoes at the *Yamashiro* and the *McGowan* and *Melvin* at the *Fuso* and *Mogami*. Between 0300 and 0302, a total of twenty-seven torpedoes were fired by the three American destroyers, after which Coward led his units clear via the channel between Dinagat and Hibuson. The Americans fired their torpedoes at a range of between 8,000 and 9,000 yards, in an eight-minute span, and it was around 0308 that the *McDermut* and *Monssen* turned toward the oncoming Japanese ships; between 0309 and 0310 both destroyers fired their full complement of ten torpedoes. The two American destroyers turned away immediately after carrying out their attack and ran north along the Leyte coast in the direction of Cabugan Grande island, narrowly avoiding a clash with PT boats.[47]

In the course of this second attack the *Monssen* was straddled but not hit, but what was so notable about these episodes was the ineffectiveness of Japanese fire—the *Remey*, *McGowan* and the *Melvin* drew fire but were not even subjected to near-misses—and the initial lack of any evasive action. The result was that one torpedo, apparently from the *Melvin*, hit the *Fuso*.[48] But in seeking to avoid the second attack, Nishimura turned his units away, toward the east, before turning back to the north, and in so doing he brought his ships directly into the path of the torpedoes fired by the *McDermut* and *Monssen*.[49] The result was that the salvo fired by the first of the two destroyers was among the most telling of the war. The *McDermut*'s torpedoes accounted for the *Yamagumo*, which blew up and sank almost immediately, reduced the *Michishio* to a sinking condition, and ripped the bow off the *Asagumo*.[50] With the *Fuso* having fallen out of formation as a result of the damage she had sustained,[51] the *Yamashiro* was hit by a single torpedo fired by the *Monssen*.[52] These hits were registered around 0320, some ten or eleven minutes after the *Fuso* had been hit, and it was about this same time that the PT boats registered their only hit of the night, not here in a supporting role and against Nishimura's ships, but at the expense of Shima's formation, which had entered the Strait at 0305.[53] At 0325 inside Binit Point, the PT-137, having aimed at a destroyer coming south to take position astern of the heavy cruisers *Nachi* and *Ashigara*, hit the light cruiser *Abukuma*. Ironically, the PT-137 had not sighted the latter and because of a smoke screen was not aware that her attack had been successful. Badly damaged and reduced to ten knots, the *Abukuma* could not maintain station and was abandoned by the other ships in Shima's formation, which increased their speed to twenty-eight knots immediately after the attack.[54] By this stage of proceedings, the various changes of course imposed on Nishimura's force in dealing with successive attacks and the higher speed of Shima's force as it had come across the Mindanao Sea meant that by the time the latter moved into the Surigao Strait it was only some twenty miles astern of Nishimura's formation. In a sense, elements of defeat were coming together.

This attack was followed immediately by one conducted by the six units of the 24th Destroyer Squadron. This formation was given its warning order to prepare to move at 0254 and at 0302 began to move south in two groups of three, the *Arunta, Killen* and the *Beale* from the area off Cabugan Grande and the *Hutchins, Daly* and the *Bache* farther to the south from the area off Bugho Point.[55] As they closed on the Japanese line, the explosion that destroyed the *Yamagumo*, at or about 0317, illuminated the whole of the Japanese formation, and between 0323 and 0326 the *Arunta, Killen* and the *Beale*, in that order, fired their torpedoes, the *Killen* being credited with a single hit on the *Yamashiro*, which was temporarily slowed to five knots.[56] The other three destroyers, having come past the Japanese formation, turned back northward, firing a total of fifteen torpedoes as they did. After turning through a complete circle, the American destroyers then closed on the Japanese line, engaging two Japanese destroyers—presumably the *Asagumo* and *Michishio*—with gunfire.[57] Coming north at 0349, the *Hutchins, Daly* and the *Bache* were ordered clear by their commander lest they foul the range of the battleships and cruisers,[58] but one minute later the *Hutchins* managed to fire a spread of five torpedoes at the *Asagumo*. Because she had started to turn even as the *Hutchins* had fired, these torpedoes missed her, but the *Michishio*, beyond her, was caught at 0358. She blew up and sank immediately.[59]

The order that the destroyers get clear of the battle area came at a time when the third destroyer formation available to Oldendorf was completing its attack, and the cruisers on both sides of the Strait and the battleships to the north were on the point of opening fire. The 56th Destroyer Squadron was ordered forward at 0335.[60] It consisted of three sections, each with three destroyers. The eastern section, with the *Robinson, Halford* and the *Bryant*, stayed close to Hibuson before launching its torpedoes between 0354 and 0359. The western section, consisting of the *Heywood L. Edwards, Leutze* and the *Bennion*, came down the main channel before making to the southwest and launching its torpedoes between 0357 and 0359.[61] The third and last section, which had the *Newcomb, Richard P. Leary* and the *Albert W. Grant* under command, advanced between the other two and to the east of the main channel and launched its torpedoes about 0404.[62]

In terms of timing, the first two of these attacks were probably the best executed of all the Allied torpedo efforts since they constituted a scissors attack, simultaneous and from two directions, which the previous destroyer attacks most definitely were not.[63] And, perhaps predictably, this was the one set of attacks that failed to register a single hit. Herein is a neat irony, a comment on execution of offensive operations that has a parallel in the American attacks that crippled three Japanese carriers at Midway in June 1944. The attacks that rendered the most damage in both actions were those noted for fragmentation of effort, inadequate coordination, and absence of concentration of force, i.e., both attacks represented the violation of the staff school's principles of war.[64]

To counter the last of these attacks, the *Yamashiro* backed from a northern to western course, briefly setting herself on a course parallel to but away from the American battle line to the north. By this stage, however, she was under fire from all three formations to the north. Off the Leyte coast the *Boise* and *Phoenix* opened fire at or about 0351, the *Shropshire* at 0356. The two American light cruisers checked fire at 0357 during their turn back to the west and resumed fire at 0400.[65] Also at 0351 the eastern cruiser force, which happened to be more or less due north of the Japanese and across the main channel, opened fire. The first to fire was the *Denver*, and three of the remaining four cruisers opened fire within a minute. At 0358 the *Portland* shifted fire to the *Mogami*, and the American cruisers, three of which were straddled but not hit, continued to fire until 0409—by which time the five units between them had fired an incredible total of 3,100 rounds of 8-in. and 6-in.—when Oldendorf gave the order for a cease-fire, whereupon the formation turned away to port, reversed course, and headed westward.[66] Of the battleships, three, the *West Virginia*, *Tennessee* and the *California*, which respectively were the first, fourth, and fifth in line, were equipped with the latest Mark VIII fire-control radar, and it was to be these three that made the greater part of the battle line's contribution to this battle. The *West Virginia* opened fire at 0353 and fired ninety-three 16-in. rounds in sixteen salvoes, and claimed that every salvo was a straddle. The *Tennessee* and *California* opened fire two minutes later, their respective contributions being sixty-nine and sixty-three 14-in. armor-piercing rounds, the *Tennessee* firing thirteen salvoes and the *California* nine. The other three battleships had Mark III radars and encountered problems finding the enemy. The *Maryland*, beginning at 0359, fired forty-eight 16-in. rounds in six salvoes. The *Pennsylvania* did not fire at all, while the *Mississippi* fired just one full, twelve-gun salvo at 0409, after the cease-fire order.[67] This proved to be the last of the battleships' contribution, and it proved to be the last time a battleship fired in battle with an enemy counterpart. Herein, of course, was irony. The destroyer attacks put something like 130 torpedoes into the water, and had there been success commensurate with the effort made there would have been no need for the American battleships to have given battle. In a real sense, the battleships could only play a part in this battle if the results of the PT boat and destroyer attacks were less than forthcoming. If, however, the results were all that could be wished, the battleships might have been involved in administering the *coup de grâce*, but, of course, some historians might argue that such, indeed, was the action in the Surigao Strait that night.

Even before Allied cruisers and battleships joined the fray, the Japanese formation was literally falling apart as damaged units tried to withdraw southward and the *Mogami* and *Shigure* tried to take station off the *Yamashiro's* starboard quarter, i.e., on the flagship's disengaged side and farthest from the American battle line. In truth, the Japanese formation was in some state of disorder, a state of affairs matched in various accounts of these proceedings. In the all-embracing darkness of a night action, one in which just one Japanese ship survived, a certain confusion is perhaps inevitable, but in the various accounts of this battle there have been two areas of interest notable for lack of clarity. The first is that some of these histories, mostly those written in the first decade after the end of the war, claim that it was not the *Fuso* but the *Yamashiro* that was hit and fell out of line, and that it was the *Fuso,* not Nishimura's flagship, that proceeded northward in a vain attempt to do battle with the enemy. This rendition of proceedings has been confirmed in one of the most recent histories of this battle.[68] The second relates to the *Michishio* and the obvious inconsistency that beset her loss. She was sunk some nine minutes of latitude, almost ten miles, north of where she was hit, i.e., in the general area where the *Yamagumo* was sunk. Yet supposedly she had been hit by a torpedo and wrecked; when torpedoed by the *Hutchins,* she was supposedly drifting southward.

It is difficult to see how these different accounts can be reconciled, and certainly the claims about the battleships are mutually exclusive. Suffice it to note two matters. With reference to the *Michishio,* the historian has little option but to set down the general—i.e., conventional and widely accepted—version of proceedings and add the Cromwellian "warts and all" approach: any final and definitive statement of what happened is not possible. On the fate of the *Yamashiro* and *Fuso,* however, the situation is different. The Japanese accounts, drawn from survivors, are definite. The *Fuso* was torpedoed at or about 0319, fell out of line, and at 0338 broke in two. It was the *Yamashiro* that continued northward,[69] with Nishimura apparently unaware of the plight of his flagship's sister.[70] Nishimura's signals of 0323 and, more importantly, of 0330 to Kurita and Shima, made after the *Yamashiro* had passed the *Michishio* and *Asagumo*, reported the presence of enemy destroyers and torpedo boats in the northern part of the Strait. The second signal reported that two of the destroyers had been disabled and that the flagship had been hit by one torpedo, but not so damaged as to affect performance.[71] Moreover, Nishimura also made another signal, his last, at 0352 in which he tried to report contact with the enemy battle line.[72] These would suggest, conclusively, that it was not the *Yamashiro* that had fallen out of formation, though in one matter the fate of the *Fuso* nonetheless does raise one obvious question. Even allowing for the fact that the *Fuso* was poorly compartmentalized,[73] which reflected that she had been laid down in March 1912, how she could have been split in two and both parts set on fire throughout their lengths by a single hit is somewhat surprising and apparently without parallel in the Second World War.[74] But the *Fuso* could not have been hit by any torpedo aimed at Japanese ships after 0320; her falling out of formation took her clear of the main areas of subsequent action, not that this affects the basic story one whit. From 0340 the *Fuso* was like a condemned prisoner awaiting execution, and her state was such that when his formation passed her two burning parts at 0410 Shima assumed these were the *Yamashiro* and *Fuso* and did not realize they were two parts of the same ship.[75]

The action involving the American battle line was but brief. By 0400 only the *Yamashiro* was coming forward and she was burning throughout her length,[76] and apparently by this time three of her turrets had been knocked out. The *Shigure*, "constantly trembling from the force of near-misses," had no gyrocompass and radio but nonetheless was set on a "charmed if somewhat aimless course." She was hit by just one shell, which failed to explode.[77] The *Mogami* turned to port at 0353 and then away to the south and increased speed at 0356. As she did so she was engaged by the *Hutchins*, *Daly* and the *Bache*, and in response, at 0401, she fired torpedoes at the American destroyers, all of which missed. As the American destroyers withdrew northward the *Yamashiro* took them under fire. The *Hutchins* and *Daly* were subjected to near-misses but between 0400 and 0405 both ceased fire as they moved clear of the immediate battle area.[78] By this time the *Portland* had shifted fire from the *Yamashiro* to the *Mogami*, and at 0402 the Japanese heavy cruiser was hit by a salvo that exploded in the bridge, killing virtually everyone on it and leaving the gunnery officer in command of the ship. She was also hit by shells that penetrated to the engine and fire rooms and all but brought her to a halt.[79] Immediately afterward the *Grant* was hit as she, along with her two companions, tried to get clear of the area between the American battle line and the *Yamashiro.* Hit for the first time at 0407 and some twenty times overall, she was brought to a halt by 0420 with 129 of her crew killed, wounded, and missing.[80]

By that time, however, the battle was more or less over, and for three reasons. First, the reversal of course on the part of the American battleships was not without incident, the *California* mistaking the order and changing course only 015 degrees, with the result that she was thrown out of line and the *Tennessee* had to reverse engines to avoid a collision. The latter was not able to fire for five minutes, and by the time order was restored with the *California* now astern of the *Tennessee,*[81] Oldendorf's cease-fire order was in effect. Second, as the fire from the battle line and cruisers died at 0409, the *Yamashiro,* making fifteen knots, turned to port to retire.[82] Apparently as she turned, at 0411, she was hit by two torpedoes—from those fired some seven minutes earlier by the *Newcomb, Leary* and the *Grant*—and within a matter of minutes she had capsized.[83] After sustaining shell and torpedo hits that were perhaps unprecedented in numbers and severity, she disappeared from the radar screens in several American ships at 0418, which was a minute before Oldendorf gave permission for units to resume fire.[84] At 0417, however, and as a direct response to a warning from the *Leary* that she had combed Japanese torpedoes as she came north,[85] the battleships of the original northern formation, namely the *West Virginia, Maryland* and the *Mississippi,* were ordered due north as a precaution lest the Japanese warships had fired a spread of torpedoes to cover their withdrawal.[86] This was a factor in the third reason why the battle died. With the Japanese running southward and the Allied battleships and cruisers holding their position or, in the case of the three battleships, opening range, contact was lost. By 0419, with the *Yamashiro* seeking the peace of the deep, there was no enemy to engage. The ten minutes in which fire had been halted had allowed the *Mogami* and *Shigure* to escape, or at least get clear of the immediate battle area, or, as one account has it, with no respect for historical or literary accuracy: "Leaving their doomed battleships behind, the decimated enemy ships fled."[87]

The loss of contact with the two retiring units from Nishimura's force at this time is perhaps surprising given that at 0350, before the cruisers and battleships joined the fray, American radars in the battleships had detected Shima's force.[88] Because of the various checks and turns that had plagued the battle formation's progress over the previous two hours, Shima's force had closed the distance between the two forces and was at that stage perhaps forty or fifty minutes behind Nishimura's force. By the time the *Yamashiro* sank and Oldendorf gave permission for fire to be resumed, Shima's formation and the *Mogami* and *Shigure* were separated by minimal time and distance, and, indeed, they were so close that the *Nachi* and *Mogami* literally ran into one another.

Shima's force came upon the scene in battle formation with the *Nachi* and *Ashigara* leading the four destroyers.[89] As it did so it came across the *Shigure* making her way from the scene of battle, and the meeting has become notorious over the years in light of the exchange between her and the *Nachi*. After Shima's flagship had identified herself, the *Shigure* did the same, adding that she had rudder difficulties. Her captain made no report because, as he explained after the war:

> The reason I did not communicate directly with Admiral Shima and inform him of the situation was that I had no connection with him and was not under his command. I assumed (he) knew of conditions of the battle . . . by sighting the burning ships *Fuso* and *Mogami*, and by seeing me on a retiring course.[90]

It was a comment that inadvertently provided a damaging insight into arrangements within the *Kaigun* and placed the alleged differences between Nishimura and Shima in some sort of perspective, and it bears noting that in his turn Shima did not see fit to make enquiries. But this matter notwithstanding, at this stage "Shima still thought he was hastening to the support of Nishimura . . . and all six ships were ready to fire torpedoes as soon as they found a target," a state of affairs which is difficult to reconcile given the restraints of geography and time. At 0420, which was the time when the forward part of the *Fuso* sank, Japanese radar detected what were assumed to be two enemy ships at a range of eight miles, and the two cruisers, after turning to the east, both fired eight torpedoes at 0424 at an estimated 9,000 yards from the enemy. These torpedoes proved to be the only contribution of Shima's force to the battle, and they were wholly ineffective. Two were later found having run ashore on Hibuson Island, and these, like several other torpedoes launched by Japanese warships over the previous two hours, might have been set to run too deeply to have any real chance of hitting destroyers or even cruisers. But as the *Nachi* and *Ashigara* launched their torpedoes, the burning *Mogami* was sighted from the *Nachi*. In Shima's flagship it was assumed that the *Mogami* was stationary, but in fact she was making something like eight knots but with minimal steering. With the attention of the *Nachi* for the moment concentrated upon its attack, and with Shima at 0425 sending an interestingly euphemistic signal that his formation "has concluded its attack and is retiring from the battle area to plan subsequent action,"[91] by the time attention switched back to the *Mogami* it was too late to avoid a collision. Full rudder was applied and engines stopped, but at 0430 the *Mogami* sliced into the stern of the *Nachi*.[92] For the *Mogami*, this was not the first time this had happened to her. She had plowed into the stern of her sister ship *Mikuma* more than two years previously off Midway and inflicted damage that had led to the *Mikuma*'s destruction. The *Ashigara* and the destroyers, following the *Nachi*, turned outside the flagship and the *Mogami*, the *Nachi* making smoke while the destroyers moved north in an attempt to contact the enemy.[93]

Within a matter of ten minutes, however, the *Nachi* and the *Mogami* untangled themselves and proceeded southward (0443), the *Nachi* being limited to about twenty knots. The damage his flagship had sustained ensured that Shima, prompted by one of his staff officers, could entertain no thought of seeking further action,[94] and with the destroyers recalled his force turned back to the south, leaving the *Asagumo* to her fate, the *Mogami* trailing and passing the *Shigure*, which had been brought to a halt because of loss of steering and which was left in the Strait for thirty minutes as she set about running repairs.[95] At this same time the Americans were also coming south. Oldendorf waited until 0431, a minute after the *Nachi* and *Mogami* collided, before ordering his formations south,[96] and presumably it was his decision to use the destroyers that had been with the battleships in the pursuit that meant that the torpedoes that had been fired by the *Nachi* and *Ashigara* and the foray of the Japanese destroyers to the north commanded no success; the Allied ships were too far to the north and beyond the range of torpedoes and warships alike. It was not until 0451 that the western cruiser formation started down the west side of the channel, but while the American units were able to regain radar contact with Shima's ships at a range of 25,500 yards, the latter quickly passed beyond range. The one ship that remained within range, the *Mogami*, was engaged. At 0519, just one minute before the stern of the *Fuso* disappeared beneath the surface of the Strait,[97] the units of the eastern cruiser formation, after a change of course across the channel which left them off Esconchada Point or roughly where the two Japanese cruisers had collided some fifty minutes before, took the *Mogami* under fire. For ten minutes the American heavy and light cruisers added to the *Mogami*'s agony, eliciting the comment from the captain of the *Columbia* that the ship, which was burning fiercely even before action was joined, was a worse sight than the battleship *Arizona* when she was sunk.[98] But with a last-gasp resilience, the *Mogami* was able to increase her speed to seventeen knots and get clear of an enemy formation that, with sunrise some thirty minutes hence, hesitated to come forward. With Oldendorf unable to identify warships hugging the coasts, it made no sense to try to risk an advance into the narrows, and possibly into "torpedo waters," when daylight was certain to reveal any Japanese unit in position.[99] At 0539, after just ten minutes of fire, Oldendorf ordered a cease-fire and in effect abandoned the pursuit.[100] At this stage the destroyers, which had needed thirty minutes to clear the battleships, gather in formation, and then come south, had still not been able to get into the battle and clearly would be unable to close on the enemy while it was still dark and when they would hold clear advantage. Moreover, when turning to the south, Oldendorf had sent a signal to Kinkaid urging that with the dawn, strikes by aircraft from the escort carriers be conducted against Japanese units to the south and west.[101] By this time, Oldendorf must have decided to place reliance on this particular way of taking the fight to the enemy. After sunrise, however, Oldendorf turned his formation back to the south and ordered the two light cruisers, with three destroyers, to proceed southward and deal with crippled enemy ships.[102] As a neat contrast, at about 0530 Shima's formation, at the southern entrance to the Strait, met the *Abukuma*, which amazingly had survived a number of contacts with PT boats and still persisted in an attempt to come north, though to what purpose, given her damage and lack of speed, is difficult to discern.[103] After meeting her, and with the *Shigure* by this stage in company, the Japanese units were forced to endure a series of disjointed and ineffective attacks by PT boats that remained in the vicinity, but despite the damaged condition of the *Nachi* and *Abukuma*, and later the *Mogami*, the Japanese ships negotiated the entrance into the Mindanao Sea without further mishap. In daylight the PT boats were wholly unable to register the results that had eluded them during the night.[104] Shima's force, hugging the northern Mindanao coast, hit but did not sink two of the PT boats, then dispatched the *Abukuma*, escorted by the *Ushio*, to Dapitan, northwest Mindanao.[105] The cruisers and destroyers sent forward by Oldendorf did encounter one straggler, the destroyer *Asagumo*. In a one-sided, three-minute encounter, the Japanese warship was dispatched at about 0718. In a manner that reflected credit on both sides, "her American adversaries watched in awe as the stern slipped in the sea with the after gun(s) still firing."[106] What remained thereafter was the attack—in fact the second of two—on the *Mogami* by carrier-based aircraft from Task Group 77.4 that finally halted her at 0910 and led to her being abandoned before being sunk by the *Akebono*,[107] and, the next day, the sinking of the *Abukuma* off southeast Negros. The latter represented the only sinking of a Japanese warship by land-based aircraft during the battle of Leyte Gulf,[108] but by this stage of proceedings the sinking of the *Asagumo*, *Mogami* and the *Abukuma* had been reduced to nickel-and-dime status. The focus of all attention even by the time the *Asagumo* was taken under fire had switched to the north, off Samar, with the news that Kurita's force, having passed through the San Bernardino Strait, was engaging an escort carrier formation. Oldendorf was obliged to set course to the north but with "fuel dangerously low, his torpedoes almost exhausted, and his ammunition near the vanishing point." This may be an overstatement, but not by much, and it leaves aside the little-appreciated fact that the battle force was limited to a maximum speed of sixteen knots, perhaps eighteen, because of the damage inflicted on three of her screws when the *West Virginia* ran aground on 21 October.[109]

At the time the *Mogami* and *Nachi* collided, the American carriers to the north were preparing their aircraft for search and strike operations with the dawn,[110] while to their north the two Japanese groups that together formed Ozawa's command were some ninety minutes from effecting their rendezvous. At 0600 they joined company and by 0700 had formed themselves into the two separate formations that were to meet the initial American attacks.[111] The more northerly of the two formations, Group 5, consisted of the *Zuikaku* and the *Zuiho*, with the battleship *Ise*, the light cruisers *Oyodo* and *Tama*, the destroyers *Akitsuki*, *Hatsutsuki* and the *Wakatsuki*, and the destroyer escort *Kuwa*, while the other formation, Group 6, consisted of the *Chitose* and *Chiyoda*, the battleship *Hyuga*, the light cruiser *Isuzu*, the destroyer *Shimotsuki*, and the destroyer escorts *Kiri*, *Sugi* and the *Maki*.[112] That, it would seem, would be about the only aspect of the Cape Engaño action that can be stated with any certainty. This action is seldom afforded much consideration in the various histories that have been written. The American attacks have never been afforded detailed accounts of the numbers of aircraft and parent carriers and a detailed analysis of their attacks relative to individual Japanese ships. Accounts of events in

Ozawa's carrier groups in battle formation off Cape Engaño, 25 October 1944

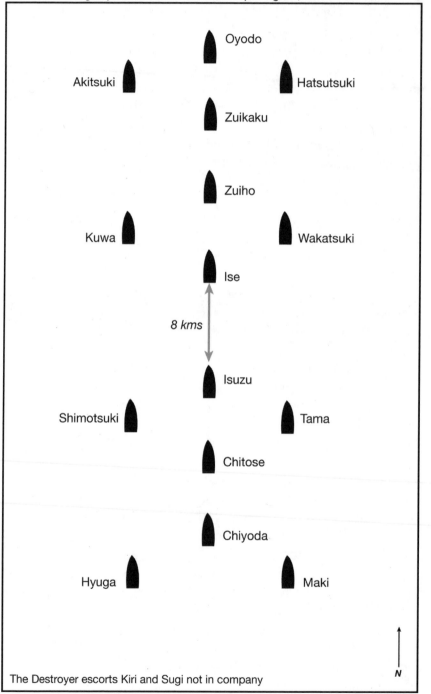

The Destroyer escorts Kiri and Sugi not in company

the north inevitably concentrate upon just one matter, the situation in the *New Jersey* that arose as a direct result of the signal from Nimitz that was received at 1000 and which in its turn was sent as a direct result of the situation that had developed by this time off Samar. The latter, namely the surface action between Kurita's formations and two U.S. escort carrier groups, plus Kinkaid's increasingly desperate and hopelessly unrealistic calls for help from Halsey's formations, prompted Nimitz to ask the whereabouts of Task Force 34, but this request was to become famous because of an unfortunate set of circumstances relating to its wording. This matter assumed a pre-eminence in American naval historiography in the immediate post-war period which it has never lost, and with two results. The first, simply, is that it has overshadowed the actions that were fought off Cape Engaño this day. These, generally afforded minimal treatment, have never assumed status other than "also ran" even though the day was, in terms of carriers sunk, the most expensive single day in history with four carriers, admittedly three of them light carriers, sunk. The second, however, is more difficult to define, but it is the manner in which these matters relating to Halsey and the Nimitz signal have distorted perspective. Thus the signal, and specifically its wording, "would have an inadvertent but terribly significant effect upon the Battle of Leyte Gulf . . . and was to alter the course of the two battles raging in the Philippines."[113] It is hard to discern the basis of such a view, which is not untypical of the general treatment of this episode. What followed from the Nimitz signal, the battle force's turn to the south, was irrelevant to the outcome of the action off Samar. The American formation failed to reach the San Bernardino Strait ahead of Kurita's formations and it had no influence upon the outcome of this particular battle other than that its warships accounted for one Japanese destroyer which otherwise would have escaped. Moreover, Task Force 34's turn probably did not have any real impact upon events to the north. The detachment of a battle force and its being sent south certainly had no effect in terms of subsequent actions that resulted in the sinking of the light carrier *Chiyoda* and destroyer *Hatsutsuki*, but whether an American battle force might have been able to overhaul Japanese groups and units farther to the north is doubtful. It may be that the American battle force would have caught the *Tama*, but, of course, she was caught anyway, and provided American submarines with their only (shared) sinking in this battle. Given the time it would have taken to sink such units as the *Chiyoda* and *Hatsutsuki* and the warning they would have conveyed to units to the north, it seems unlikely that the Americans would have sunk more warships than was the case.[114] On this day and to all causes, the Americans sank seven Japanese warships from Ozawa's command, and it is by no means clear, and certainly not obvious, that they would have been able to sink more but for the battle force being detached and sent south. Yet that eventuality alone—that had the battleships been retained in the north, American efforts would have accounted for more than the seven units that were sunk—might be justification for the view that the signal of Nimitz exercised so profound, indeed cataclysmic, influence upon events. It is difficult to consider the number of Japanese warships that might have been thus involved in terms of genuine importance, still less real strategic significance.

In the course of this day there were, depending on the source, five or six attacks mounted by American carrier aircraft, but at this stage in the recounting of events only the initial strike will be considered in order that the sequence of events, and Kinkaid's first signal that referred to contact with Kurita's battle forces, be considered properly and in parallel. Thus this story must begin with the approach of sunrise and the dispatch of search aircraft, which was followed by the American carriers flying off about 150 aircraft which were held, in formation, circling some fifty miles ahead of the carrier groups, waiting for sighting contact reports and guidance to their targets.[115]

The contacts came around 0712,[116] the *Zuikaku* and the *Hyuga*, from their different groups, sighting American search aircraft in their turn. The incoming attack, mounted from the sector between 130 and 210 degrees, was detected on Japanese radar at 0740 and began around 0813.[117] With the Japanese groups working up to twenty-four knots and seemingly surprised by the earliness of contact, the Japanese carriers were not able to dispatch all their aircraft before Hellcats arrived on the scene.[118] Directed by McCampbell, some fifty American aircraft attacked the southern group, with the *Chitose* and *Chiyoda*, and about eighty attacked the northern group, with the *Zuikaku* and *Zuiho*, these strikes lasting until 0859.[119] In the southern group both the light carriers were hit, but while the *Chiyoda's* damage was minor, the *Chitose*, initially attacked by aircraft from the *Essex* and then from the *Lexington*, was heavily damaged. Listing to port because one of the three bomb hits she sustained was below the waterline, she was left dead in the water.[120] To the north, the destroyer *Akitsuki* was hit by a bomb amidships, which caused a fire and which in turn set off an explosion that resulted in her sinking.[121] The *Tama*, hit by a torpedo and racked by a violent explosion, very quickly fell astern, never to rejoin.[122] The *Zuiho*, missed by Avengers from the *Essex* and *Lexington*, was hit amidships by a bomb from a Helldiver from the *Intrepid*, but the damage she incurred was not serious.[123] The *Zuikaku*, hit aft by a torpedo from an Avenger from either the *Intrepid* or *San Jacinto*, was left with a six-degree list and disabled steering; at one stage she was down to just one shaft. Restricted to just eighteen knots, the *Zuikaku's* lack of maneuverability was an obvious tactical handicap upon the group and in all probability would have resulted in her being abandoned, but the wrecking of her radio communications ensured that she could no longer function as a flagship.[124] It was not until 1100, however, that Ozawa and a seven-man staff were transferred to the *Oyodo*, and only after some difficulty. Apparently, Ozawa was initially disposed to remain with the *Zuikaku* on the basis that the role of decoy condemned all the ships in the command, and he thus saw no point in moving his flag. Ultimately, his staff persuaded him of his continuing responsibility to the formation rather than individual ships, and Ozawa allowed himself to be transferred by boat to the light cruiser.[125]

Aircraft from the first strike were still in the air when the American carriers began to launch aircraft for a second, and much more modestly proportioned, strike with about sixteen Avengers, six Helldivers, and fourteen fighters from Task Groups 38.3 and 38.4. The launch began around 0835, which was about the time the crisis of command began to unfold in the *New Jersey*. By the time the American carriers committed to the third strike of the day began to fly off the aircraft, around 1145,[126] the crisis was past in the sense that decisions had been made and put into effect and that for the most part what happened in the remainder of the day represented the playing out of a script, the final part of which had been written more or less between these times.

This crisis of command's first manifestation was the 0412 signal from Kinkaid to Halsey which informed him of a decisive success that had been registered in the Surigao Strait, though it would seem that such a claim was anticipatory, and asking the whereabouts of Task Force 34.[127] This signal was not received by Halsey until 0648, and it caused bewilderment because it was not understood how Kinkaid knew about this formation. Halsey nonetheless replied to this signal at 0705, informing Kinkaid that the battle line was with the carrier groups and not off the San Bernardino Strait.[128] Seven minutes earlier Kurita's formations had joined battle with one of the American escort carrier formations off northern Samar.

The first indication that things might be going awry was provided the Americans in the form of a radio interception of a Japanese radio conversation at 0637. This was noted in the *Fanshaw Bay*, but it was dismissed as a Japanese attempt to jam the fighter net.[129] At 0647, within a couple of minutes of the *Fanshaw Bay*'s radar picking up the Japanese ships on a bearing of 290 degrees at a range of eighteen and a half miles,[130] an aircraft on anti-submarine patrol from the *Kadashan Bay* reported she had drawn fire from a group of unidentifiable ships,[131] and this was followed all but immediately by an aircraft from the *St. Lo* that reported that this force included battleships and cruisers and was in a position some twenty miles north by northwest of the most northern of the escort carrier groups, Task Unit 77.4.3 (Rear Admiral Clifton A. F. Sprague).[132] Some ten minutes later, the distinctive pagoda masts of Japanese battleships began to break the northern horizon, and immediately the Japanese warships, while still hull-down, opened fire.[133] The first contact report was received by Kinkaid at 0704, and immediately the commander of the 7th Fleet undertook three measures. First, he signaled Halsey at 0707, informing him of what had happened and asking for immediate assistance on the part of the carrier force;[134] this was to be the first of three such signals sent by Kinkaid within fifteen minutes of his being informed of the contact with Japanese forces.[135] Second, he ordered Oldendorf to abandon the pursuit of Japanese forces in the south and to come north in order to stand in line across the entrance to Leyte Gulf; at the same time he ordered destroyers escorting transports back to Manus to return and fleet units in the Gulf to support the battle force.[136] Third, he ordered all the aircraft from the three escort carrier formations to concentrate against Kurita's formation.[137] With reference to the second arrangement, Kinkaid's action provoked dispute within his staff because in effect it abandoned Task Unit 77.4.3 and perhaps Task Unit 77.4.2 (Rear Admiral Felix B. Stump) and in any case would take some hours to be properly effective. It seems that Kinkaid's order for the battle force to come north was mixed with concern lest it suffer losses, the simple fact being that escort carriers could be replaced whereas battleships and heavy cruisers could not. Oldendorf's forces were ordered into a line barring the route into Leyte Gulf at 0953 and again, after the order was rescinded, at 1127, by which time it was unnecessary.[138] At best, it would seem that opposition to Kinkaid's original proposed course of action was

wholly misplaced because had the initial action been conducted with anything approaching a minimum level of competence on the Japanese part
there was absolutely nothing that could have been done by Oldendorf's, or
any other, formation to support Task Unit 77.4.3. With the Japanese formations possessing clear advantage of speed and firepower, the destruction
of the northern escort carrier formation should have been registered long
before Oldendorf's battleships were able to reach the northern entrance
to Leyte Gulf.

     With reference to the third measure, the directing of aircraft from the
escort carrier formations against Kurita's force, problems and opportunity
presented themselves equally. Escort carriers, because their primary roles
were close air support and anti-submarine operations, generally carried
very few armor-piercing bombs and between nine and twelve torpedoes.[139]
The capacity of the escort carrier formation to do battle with an enemy
fleet formation, even a battle line with no carrier capacity of its own, was
limited. Task Unit 77.4.3 was able to launch forty-four Avengers in the first
thirty minutes of action, but of the nine launched by the *Gambier Bay* only
two had torpedoes and one had so little fuel that it was obliged to ditch
within a matter of minutes of being launched. Most of the Avengers had
100-lb. bombs capable of registering nothing more than superficial topside
damage.[140] But against this was the fact that at the time when Kurita's forces
made contact with Task Unit 77.4.3, the most southerly of the three American escort carrier formations, Task Unit 77.4.1 (Rear Admiral Thomas L.
Sprague), with four escort carriers under command, had its Avengers being
armed with torpedoes and armor-piercing bombs in readiness for attacks
on Japanese units withdrawing from the Surigao Strait, while to the north
a number of Avengers from the escort carriers of Task Unit 77.4.2 were
already armed with torpedoes.[141] It was somewhat unfortunate that the first
of these two formations was more than sixty miles to the south of Task Unit
77.4.3, but if there was no escaping the general point that individual American escort carriers had few aircraft which could counterattack Kurita's
battleships and cruisers with any realistic hope of inflicting loss, the fact
remained that the sixteen escort carriers of these three formations between
them mustered the equivalent of two carrier task groups.[142] This latter fact
is but little appreciated and seldom afforded even passing acknowledgment
in most accounts of these events, but the reality was that even though the
escort carriers were caught dispersed and unprepared to fight a battle that
none had anticipated, between them they had the numbers that could
provide for sustained attack on Kurita's formations. As evidence of what

this meant, reference may be made to the operations of Task Unit 77.4.2 on this day. In the ninety minutes after the first dispatch of aircraft north, its carriers launched thirty-six fighters and forty-three Avengers, and in the course of the day aircraft from this formation's carriers launched forty-nine torpedoes, dropped 133 500-lb. SAP bombs, and fired 276 rockets at Japanese warships, and with some of her Avengers committed to support operations on Leyte, the *Marcus Island* played host to Avengers from Task Unit 77.4.1 and provided them with torpedoes.[143] There is no escaping the point that Task Unit 77.4.3 should never have survived its encounter with Kurita's battleships and cruisers; the Japanese warships possessed an advantage of sighting, speed, and firepower that should have resulted in the destruction of formations and units in short order. But the balance of advantage was perhaps a little more even-handed than is generally recognized, and in assessing Kurita's conduct of operations the sheer number of aircraft that attacked his force, and perhaps above all their persistence, must have been a major factor in his calculations during the events that were to unfold over the next three hours as he tried to deal with Task Unit 77.4.3.

Such were the *hors d'oeuvres* for a main course that was remarkable, indeed extraordinary, in a number of ways. The action fought off Samar on the morning of 25 October was extraordinary in terms of how it came to be fought in the first place, not simply with reference to sins of omission and commission (alleged) on the part of Halsey, but because, despite overwhelming American advantage in numbers, aircraft, radio, and radar, the Japanese battle forces managed not simply to come through the San Bernardino Strait but then steamed undetected for more than six hours before making contact, and indeed after the battle the greater part of the Japanese forces managed to escape, again without being seriously contacted during what remained of this day. It was extraordinary in terms of outcome, and the fact that there was no way the American task group in the north could have escaped utter, total, and immediate annihilation, yet it did so with the loss of just a single escort carrier, two destroyers, and one destroyer escort. Five escort carriers, one destroyer, and three destroyer escorts escaped if—in the case of one of the escort carriers—only for the moment. It was extraordinary in terms of the Japanese performance in this battle, specifically Kurita's conduct—or misconduct—of operations and the gunnery of the Japanese battleships and cruisers in this action. Even allowing that at least in the initial stages of the battle the Japanese warships shot well but were singularly unfortunate in registering many straddles but few hits, such matters as target identification, claims, fire distribution, and an undoubted ability to persistently miss the target at short ranges combine to place real question marks against the professional competence of formations which had spent weeks preparing for the very type of battle that presented itself off Samar. The captain of the *Hoel* commented, "It hardly seemed possible that during daylight a destroyer could close to ranges of 6,000 to 10,000 yards of a battleship or cruiser, launch torpedo attacks, and then remain afloat for more than an hour,"[144] and the fact that this did happen, and that the escort carrier *Kalinin Bay* survived an hour-long encounter with five Japanese destroyers not one of which recorded a single hit even though range was finally reduced to 10,500 yards,[145] makes the point because it most certainly would not have happened had the roles been reversed. It was extraordinary, too, in another sense, namely the treatment afforded this episode by history. The American performance, specifically that of the escorts in their attempt to shield the escort carriers from the advancing Japanese columns, was both outstanding and came to occupy a rightful place in service and national lore; in terms of overall accomplishment this achievement cannot be gainsaid. The escape of Task Unit 77.4.3 from the clutches of overwhelming disaster nonetheless has commanded uncritical acclaim, and seldom has there been proper attention paid to the fact that in the final analysis it was not so much that the Americans saved themselves as that the Japanese, and specifically Kurita, allowed what would have been—and say it very quietly—only a modest and temporary victory to slip through their fingers. Moreover, there are points of detail and one matter relating to context that demand comment. On the first of these two points one would note claims given official credence that border on the ridiculous. Thus in the U.S. Navy's own publication, in 1968, when the *Hoel* had closed

> to within 6,000 yards of the leading cruiser, [the] *Haguro*, the fearless destroyer [*sic*] launched a half-salvo of torpedoes which ran "hot, straight and normal." This time she was rewarded by the sight of large columns of water which rose from her target. Although Japanese records deny that these torpedoes hit the cruiser, there is no evidence to indicate any other explanation for the geyser effect observed.[146]

Thus a claim was raised to incontrovertible fact despite conclusive, irreversible evidence that the *Haguro* was not torpedoed in this action, and this goes alongside such claims that in advancing to do battle with approaching Japanese warships the destroyer *Johnston* fired 200 rounds in five minutes—this at ranges beyond 10,000 yards at which distance she fired her torpedoes—and in a subsequent action, at a time when two of her guns had been silenced and one was operating manually, she fired thirty rounds and made fifteen hits on an enemy battleship in just forty seconds.[147] The American performance is demeaned by the credence given to such exaggerated and clearly erroneous claims, especially credence given after more than twenty years when evidence to the contrary was available, but herein the matter of context presents itself for consideration. One of the more unfortunate aspects of this day's events was that partly because of the episode involving Nimitz's signal to Halsey and its wording, the portrayal of events always seems to go hand in hand with that of the second battle of Balaclava, the Charge of the Light Brigade, which took place on this same day in 1854. The parallel between the units of the screen advancing in order to place themselves between the escort carriers and the enemy and the ill-fated British cavalry action is obvious,[148] but it invites the obvious comment: perhaps the real parallel was between Kurita's formations, and perhaps even more tellingly Nishimura's force, and the British cavalry force of 1854. But with reference to matters literary, perhaps more telling is that whereas the U.S. Navy never completed its post-war study of one of the greatest battles in naval history, one Britisher did write a poem about the 1854 defeat in which heroic failure came close to victory, but even this pales alongside the fact that 25 October is the date of another battle, infinitely more famous than Balaclava and even Leyte. This was a battle that "from this day to the ending of the world" will be remembered, and about which one Englishman did write the play that encompasses the greatest battlefield speech in literature and the most beautiful line in all his work.[149]

The merits of literature aside, much of the difficulty that has attended the recounting of this battle has concerned the phase of battle that was now to unfold off Samar, and for obvious reason: what happened was largely inexplicable, and post-war interrogation and analyses failed to add to the understanding. The element of incomprehension begins with the first two orders issued by Kurita on contact with the enemy. These were for the formations to set course to the southeast and to conduct a general chase.[150] The latter in effect allowed the main units—the four battleships and six heavy cruisers—to engage targets of opportunity and not be limited to formation requirements, and the former seemingly had two main purposes. With the wind blowing from the northeast, for the Japanese to take up a position to windward was to prevent the American carriers from operating their aircraft, while to stand to the east of the carrier force would thereby both trap it against Samar and Leyte and prevent its escape into the vastness of the Philippine Sea. In terms of an approach to Leyte Gulf, adopting an initial course of 110 degrees and then coming round to the south and then the southwest, Kurita's choice of course, had something to commend it,[151] but against these considerations were two facts of life. While the initial American reaction was to turn the carriers to the east in order to fly off their aircraft, Task Unit 77.4.3 immediately turned back to the southwest with the result that in coming around the long left flank the Japanese battleships and cruisers, despite a clear advantage of speed, were not able to appreciably reduce range in the first hour of battle. Moreover, from early in the proceedings, the units of the American screen laid smoke. This effort took two forms, the use of purpose-generated white smoke and, by reducing the air-to-fuel feed, the laying of thick, heavy black smoke from their funnels. In the heavy humid air, the lack of any strong wind meant that the smoke stayed close to the surface of the sea and, with the Japanese battleships and cruisers to the northeast and later the east, the American carriers enjoyed a surprising degree of concealment from enemy view.[152] Had the Japanese formations set course to the southwest from the outset, the American destroyers and destroyer escorts from the screen could have provided some degree of cover with smoke only by standing on the disengaged side. In such circumstances, the Japanese units would have problems of sighting but would not have faced a screen mounting counterattacks in defense of the escort carriers. In reality, of course, these units would have been obliged to stand between the oncoming Japanese warships and the escort carriers, and the latter would not have been concealed by any smoke screens. The odd point about all this is that when the Japanese units made their first contact with the American formation they held the advantage of position and were on a course of 200 degrees, which was about the best possible course for them to effect a timely and comprehensive envelopment of the carrier force.

By his orders, Kurita in effect condemned his two battle formations to a long stern chase, though oddly in the first minutes of action, with the American carriers heading eastward, their courses were slightly converging, and it was not until 0750, or almost an hour after opening fire, that Kurita's force turned to the southwest.[153] It could be argued that Kurita could have done much better by either ordering his units into line or taking his battle formation—with the battleships *Yamato* and *Nagato* and heavy cruisers *Haguro* and *Chokai*—to the west and sending Suzuki's faster formation— with the *Kongo* and *Haruna* and the four remaining heavy cruisers—to the east in an attempt to envelop the enemy formation. The weakness of this latter argument is that Kurita could only have divided his force if he had wholly reliable and accurate, as well as immediate, knowledge of the identity of the ships his force had encountered, and such information, of course, was not available. In fact, the Japanese had the advantage of first sighting, at 0641 by the battleship *Nagato*,[154] but this was largely set aside by the one error that has rightly cast a long shadow over the question of *Kaigun* competence. This error was the misidentification of the American warships. While the enemy ships could not be seen from the bridge of the *Yamato*, reports from fire-control positions were of sightings of fleet carriers, cruisers, and even battleships. The operations and gunnery officers from Kurita's staff went to positions from which were sighted two carriers, while the *Kongo* reported the presence of four carriers and ten other warships.[155] In his post-war interrogation, Rear Admiral Koyanagi Tomiji, Kurita's chief of staff, summarized what was reported as "five or six carriers, a few battle-ships and a few cruisers."[156] How, in broad daylight, such errors could have been made defies ready explanation. Admittedly, to date there had not been any action involving Japanese fleet units and American escort carriers, and the differences in length and displacement between a light carrier and an escort carrier and between a light cruiser and destroyer were more modest than generally realized,[157] but how destroyers and destroyer escorts could have been confused with battleships and cruisers by gunnery officers,[158] and how Kurita failed to realize that range was closing as his formations gradually overhauled much slower ships, which they could not have done had they been in contact with fleet carriers, remain questions to which no obvious answers have been forthcoming in six decades.

Apparently at or about 0623, when the Japanese radar first detected American aircraft, Kurita gave the order for his units to assume anti-air-craft formation,[159] but accounts of proceedings and post-war charts from the Japanese Defense Agency clearly indicate that when contact with the American carrier formation was made, Kurita's force was still in the cruise formation which it had adopted when clear of the San Bernardino Strait.[160] It was in six columns with the three columns to port consisting of the destroyers, cruisers, and battleships of Suzuki's 2nd Task Group and the three columns to starboard consisting of the cruisers, battleships, and destroyers of Kurita's 1st Task Group, the two battle formations in the third and fifth columns being behind the others. The *Yamato* opened fire at 0659 and within a couple of minutes Japanese fire had been marched to the center of the carrier force, with the *Fanshaw Bay* and *White Plains*, the nearest and most obvious targets, drawing fire, the latter being straddled and shaken by a series of near-misses, one of which temporarily caused her to lose steering control.[161] In this phase the Japanese, in a manner not unlike the Italian navy, shot well but unluckily. Enemy ships were straddled, but it was not until after 0725, when Kurita made a signal to Combined Fleet headquarters announcing that his force had sunk an enemy cruiser,[162] that the first hit was recorded, on the destroyer *Johnston*. It was not untypical of the misfortune that dogged the Japanese seemingly at every turn in this action that, with the *White Plains* seemingly in trouble, their fire shifted to other targets, and in the respite the American carrier was able to effect running repairs and maintain herself on station.[163] Probably minimal attention paid to her at this stage would have resulted in her destruction, yet at this same time, at 0721, the American ships ran into a rain squall, one that has been described as a providential rain squall, which reduced visibility to about half a mile. In the fifteen minutes when the American units were shrouded by the rain, the accuracy of Japanese fire fell away markedly.[164] The *Johnston*, however, was on the edge of the cover provided by smoke, and was not simply the first of the American ships to be hit but the first to suffer appreciable damage and also the first both to lay smoke and launch torpedoes at the pursuing enemy. Finding herself in a position between the carriers and the Japanese formations, the *Johnston*, anticipating the order to lay smoke and, apparently as a result of the calculation that she could not risk being sunk with her torpedoes unused,[165] sought both to conceal the escort carriers and herself with smoke and to attack the leading Japanese units. Emerging from her smoke, the *Johnston* opened fire at 18,000 yards, a range at which she had not the least chance of inflicting the slightest damage, but with a converging speed of more than forty-five knots she came to a range of 10,000 yards from the heavy cruiser *Kumano* and turned, firing all ten of her torpedoes. Chasing salvo splashes, she headed at maximum speed back to the cover of the smoke screen, but around 0730 was hit first by shells from a battleship and then by shells from a light cruiser,[166] presumably the *Kongo* and the *Yahagi* respectively. Apparently saved by the fact that the Japanese use of armor-piercing rounds meant that the full explosive power of shells was not inflicted on the *Johnston*, she nonetheless lost one fire and engine room, her gyrocompass, and all power to her steering and three rear turrets.[167] In return, however, she did better than she realized. Her subsequent claim to have recorded two or three torpedo hits on the *Kumano* was disputed, the Japanese admitting to just a single hit at 0727,[168] but in fact this hit had the effect of removing two Japanese heavy cruisers from the battle, albeit one only temporarily. The *Kumano* was a flagship and the transfer of the flag to the *Suzuya* in effect took this second cruiser out of the battle for a short period, with the transfer of admiral and staff completed about 0800. The *Kumano*, however, was more seriously afflicted. She was hit just forward of the No. 10 frame and lost her bow, and while her engines and power were unaffected she was immediately reduced to just fourteen knots. After the transfer of admiral and staff was complete, she set course for the San Bernardino Strait and whatever safety and repair Coron had to offer.[169]

The *Johnston*'s attack was quickly followed by successive attacks by the other units from the screen. These attacks were notable for the series of near-misses recorded by various American ships as they raced into position. With visibility reduced to a hundred yards by rain and smoke, the various destroyers and destroyer escorts were fortunate not to accomplish what the Japanese had thus far signally failed to do. The *Heermann*, for example, in working her way from the disengaged side, narrowly avoided collisions with both the *Hoel* and *Samuel B. Roberts*.[170] These attacks, like those executed in the Surigao Strait by the *Newcomb*, *Richard P. Leary* and the *Albert W. Grant*, were notable for their fragmentation of effort, inadequate coordination, and absence of concentration of force, and were notably successful though not in the manner that one normally defines the term. These attacks failed to register a single torpedo hit upon any Japanese warship, but their success was measured by the check they imposed upon the Japanese battleships, the *Yamato* having to turn about in order to outrun three torpedoes and losing seven miles in the process.[171]

These various attacks were conducted over about thirty-five minutes, the *Hoel* following hard on the heels of the *Johnston* and launching a half-salvo of torpedoes soon after 0725, forcing the *Kongo* to turn away to port at 0733. Given that Japanese warships were beginning to appear on both sides, the *Hoel* deliberately chose to mount two efforts, initially against the battleships to the east and the second against the heavy cruisers to the west, and the *Heermann* chose to attack first cruisers and then battleships when she mounted her attack around 0754. The *Hoel*, which tried to engage the *Kongo* with gunfire at a range of 14,000 yards, made her first attack at a range of 9,000 yards and was massively damaged in the process. Her port engine was shattered by a direct hit and her three rear turrets were silenced, but even as she turned away she launched her remaining torpedoes at a range of 6,000 yards at the *Haguro*.[172] The *Heermann* used seven torpedoes in an attack on the *Chikuma* at a range of 9,000 yards, claiming that in turning away after this attack she raked the *Kongo's* superstructure with gunfire before closing to a range of 4,400 yards, at which point she fired her three remaining torpedoes, but to no effect.[173] Immediately thereafter she was followed into the attack by three of the four destroyer escorts. The class nameship, the *John C. Butler*, had been in a position most distant from the Japanese units and made no torpedo attack herself but supported her three sister ships with gunfire.[174] These three attacks were similar in that the American ships closed to what should have been so short a range that no escape was possible, but a combination of Japanese distraction, thick and effective smoke cover, and sheer good fortune ensured the survival of the American warships. One could suggest that here was an element of surprise that worked to American advantage, but this suggestion must be tempered by acknowledgment that while surprise is indeed one of the principles of war, these American attacks no doubt did not leave the Japanese surprised: amazed perhaps, but not surprised. The *Raymond* and *Dennis* attacked more or less together, and with the *Samuel B. Roberts*, which tagged along behind the *Hoel* and *Heermann* and was not inhibited by the initial refusal of the force commander to authorize a torpedo attack by the destroyer escorts, launched their three-torpedo attacks just before 0800.[175] The *Roberts* was credited with having closed to a range of 4,000 yards in attacking a Japanese cruiser and, during her withdrawal after 0805, firing on an enemy cruiser at ranges between 5,300 and 7,500 yards. Amazingly, she did not incur a single hit at this stage of proceedings.[176] Three torpedoes seen to pass astern of the *Haguro* were assigned to the *Raymond* in the official U.S. Navy account, having been launched at a range of 6,000 yards, while the *Dennis* launched her torpedoes at a range of 8,000 yards, probably at the *Chikuma* and *Tone*.[177]

The identity of ships on both sides is difficult to determine with any precision. For example, the *Chikuma* and *Tone* were identified as the second and third cruisers in column,[178] but with the *Kumano* and *Suzuya* not in the line at this stage the two Japanese cruiser formations both had two units, no more. But this matter aside, the significance of these attacks was twofold. The first point was that none of the American warships from the screen were sunk outright, and all were in position to continue to offer resistance. Put another way, the Japanese had yet to brush aside the screen in order to get to the carriers. The second point was that by this time a state akin to chaos was beginning to engulf the Japanese formations. Initially, Kurita had ordered the battleships and cruisers to engage the enemy; the destroyers were not afforded any offensive role at this stage.[179] But by about 0815 the Japanese warships were spread over a distance of some fifteen miles, and while it is difficult if not impossible to discern the meaning of such comments that "communications were understandably poor and it was most unfortunate that Kurita did not know that the heavy cruisers *Haguro* and *Tone* had opened a path for the destroyers to attack the enemy,"[180] the fact was that by this stage of proceedings another matter was imposing itself upon events, and to Japanese disadvantage. This was that by this time attacks upon Kurita's formation by aircraft were beginning to assume serious proportions.

One of the difficulties with any attempt to explain these events is to define the various factors that contributed to Japanese ineffectiveness in this first phase of the battle off Samar and then to explain aspects of interdependence and relative importance. One can discern perhaps six matters that came together, and three of these relate immediately to the American contribution to proceedings—the effectiveness of the smoke screens,[181] the counterattacks by the destroyers and destroyer escorts, and the attacks by aircraft.[182] To these points must be added a fourth, that at the level of individuals and crews the Americans proved more than a match for their Japanese counterparts. Inevitably in American accounts of these proceedings this element has been stressed, and it is very American: the greatest and best, accordingly afforded wholly disproportionate treatment. This war produced other examples of warships that without hesitation took on vastly superior enemy units, the most obvious examples being the *Glowworm* and the *Hipper* (April 1940) and the *Jervis Bay* and *Sheer* (November 1940) though perhaps the more relevant parallel, because of their inability to prevent the carrier *Glorious* from being sunk, was the *Acasta* and *Ardent* and the *Gneisenau, Scharnhorst, Hipper,* and four destroyers (June 1940). This short list could be lengthened by reference to the Mediterranean theater, but suffice it to note perhaps the most apt parallel with the American escorts' action off Samar is one that apparently seems to have evaded naval historians, namely the second German *gefechtskehrtwendung* at Jutland on 31 May 1916, which involved the commitment of destroyers to attacks on the British line in order to facilitate the escape of the battleships and battlecruisers. One merely makes the point that the bravery of American captains and crews is neither disputed nor demeaned, and the survival of this escort carrier formation was in no small way the result of the escorts having outfought their enemy in this initial phase. On the Japanese side, the misidentification of enemy ships and the vagaries of shooting to which reference has been made join to provide the fifth matter that contributed to these proceedings, and the last, again one that occupies two sides of the same coin, is the disorganization that afflicted the Japanese formations as the battle unfolded and the restraint of the Japanese destroyers in the course of this opening encounter. Given that there was a serious overesti-mation of enemy strength, the failure to unleash the destroyers was perhaps understandable, but in some ways that argument can be reversed upon itself. If the enemy was as strong as Kurita believed, that was good reason to commit the destroyers offensively in the hope and expectation that their torpedoes would reap their timely share of victims. One has no means of proving anything beyond all reasonable doubt, but one suspects that it was at this stage that the consequence of having refueled at Brunei Bay rather than off Coron manifested itself. On this third day of action, the Japanese destroyers did not have enough fuel to engage in high-speed chase, to make thirty knots in an attempt to envelop an enemy force and subject it to con-centrated torpedo attack. To make this argument is, in one sense, perverse. What might be seen as the critical element in proceedings is identified not in terms of what happened but what did not happen, and in any event this argument sits uncomfortably alongside the insipid performance of the Japanese destroyers when they did come in contact with their American opposite numbers. Perhaps the best that might have been expected were attacks that picked off individual American ships or slowed the flight of the American formation as a whole by forcing it to turn to avoid attack, but the basic point is that this is one aspect of the Japanese conduct of operations off Samar that has been afforded little historical consideration.

History, however, is concerned with what happened, not with what did not happen or with what might have happened, and the point of immediacy at this stage, soon after 0800, was that after an hour the Japanese forma-tions were at last beginning to close and to assume a potentially decisive positional advantage relative to Task Unit 77.4.3. The destroyers from the 1st Task Group, closest to the enemy, had at last begun to come within range—about 18,000 yards—of the American screen, and by 0830 the destroyers from the 2nd Task Group, on the other side of the Japanese formation, had similarly joined the action.[183] Moreover, at 0810, when the escort carrier *Gambier Bay* was first hit, the *Haruna*, at a range of more than twenty miles, sighted and opened fire on carriers of Task Unit 77.4.2, and both she and the *Kongo* gave chase to this new enemy.[184] This development, however, did not prevent the *Kongo* from claiming the destruction, at about 0825, of an *Enterprise*-class carrier from the original task group.[185] At about this same time the *Yamato* also claimed the destruction of a carrier, and between 0842 and 0852 the *Haguro* claimed to have destroyed a carrier which disintegrated under the impact of shells that allegedly hit her along her entire length. By this time the *Fanshaw Bay* had been hit twice but with no immediate consequence, and the *Kalinin Bay* had been hit by four shells, which knocked out her radio and radar but apparently without any adverse effect on her handling of aircraft.[186] The *Kitkun Bay, St. Lo* and the *White Plains* had not been hit,[187] but the *Gambier Bay* was both last in line and *in extremis*, her speed having been reduced to eleven knots because of flooding which reached into her boiler and engine rooms as a result of a series of hits.[188] She alone of the six carriers of Task Unit 77.4.3 had been severely damaged and was but minutes from destruction. By this time, however, events had conspired to bring Halsey to center stage.

This development was the inevitable result of the signals sent by Kinkaid in the first minutes after Kurita's force had contacted Task Unit 77.4.3. These signals had to be sent to Manus, from where they were retransmitted, with two results. More than an hour was lost between Kinkaid's dispatch and Halsey's receipt of any individual signal, and, all but inevitably with Manus having to handle hundreds of signals without necessarily being aware of priorities, there was no guarantee that signals would be received in the order they were sent. All were beset by seemingly unavoidable delays in retransmission.

In setting out the record two obvious problems exist, namely the distinction between the deliberations of the moment and *ex post facto* rationalization, and either the inability or the unwillingness of those caught in these proceedings to recognize the difference. For example, Halsey subsequently wrote that when he first received word that Kurita's force was engaging the escort carriers off Samar he was of the view that Kinkaid's force would be able to look after itself.[189] It is difficult to believe that this was a consideration of any real account. The simple fact was that there was nothing Halsey could do to help the escort carrier formations to the south.

About 400 miles separated the carriers and battleships in the north from the formations to the south, clearly beyond the range of the carrier aircraft of Task Force 38. By the time Halsey received these signals he and the formations with him were caught by the logic of the previous decision to take all groups north, and at this stage of proceedings there was nothing that could be done to unravel the consequences of that decision. It is hard to resist the conclusion that the view that Kinkaid's force would be able to look after itself was at best a makeweight or rationalization, not a throwaway line since clearly it was more than that, but not much more. Clearly it was not a reason to do nothing because apart from ordering Task Group 38.1 to move to the support of the formations in and off Leyte Gulf, there was nothing that could be done. Moreover, there is at least one matter that does beggar belief, namely the statement that Halsey was shocked by the information that Oldendorf's battleships were low on ammunition, the implication clearly being that they would not be able to fight any prolonged action in defense of the formations in and off Leyte Gulf.[190] Why this should have come even as a surprise to Halsey is unclear. The battleships with Kinkaid's fleet had been involved in close support operations for four days and then had spent the fifth readying themselves for the Surigao Strait action. Given that Halsey had been in command of southwest Pacific operations between October 1942 and June 1944,[191] and thence had been involved in the series of landings and operations that reached from the lower Solomons to northwest New Guinea, there seems no reason whatsoever why he should have been surprised, still less shocked, by this information. Both at the levels of the force commander personally and, perhaps even more tellingly, the fleet staff, this information, or at least the common prudence that should be a hallmark of staff deliberation and planning, should have been assumed at the very least, but the inadequacy of staff arrangements and neglect of standard operational procedures manifested themselves to greater effect within the next two hours.

At 0822, some twenty minutes after receiving Kinkaid's report that the Japanese formations that had attempted to transit the Surigao Strait were withdrawing and were being pursued by light forces, Halsey received his third signal of the morning from Kinkaid. This stated that Japanese battleships and cruisers were firing on Task Unit 77.4.3 from a position fifteen miles astern.[192] Halsey's stated view was that at this point he "wondered how Kinkaid had let [his escort carriers] get caught like this, and why [Task Group 77.4's] search planes had not given him warning," but that he was not perturbed. He claimed that it was at this time when he calculated that the escort carriers would be able to protect themselves until such time that Oldendorf's battleships arrived on the scene.[193] At 0830 Halsey received the next signal from Kinkaid, stating, URGENTLY NEED FAST BATTLESHIPS LEYTE GULF AT ONCE. It was at this point, according to his memoirs, that Halsey was surprised because "it was not my job to protect the Seventh Fleet." Halsey nonetheless ordered McCain to move directly to support Kinkaid's forces "at best possible speed," and he advised Kinkaid accordingly.[194] It was not until 1316, however, that aircraft from Task Group 38.1 arrived over Kurita's force.[195] At 0900 Halsey received his fifth signal of the morning from Kinkaid, which in fact was the first that had been sent after Kurita's force contacted Task Unit 77.4.3, which informed him, OUR ESCORT CARRIERS BEING ATTACKED BY FOUR BATTLESHIPS EIGHT CRUISERS PLUS OTHERS. REQUEST LEE COVER LEYTE AT TOP SPEED. REQUEST FAST CARRIERS MAKE IMMEDIATE STRIKE,[196] and at 0922, a full hour after that initial contact report had been received, Halsey received a signal, dispatched at 0725, which stated,

CTU 77.4.3 UNDER ATTACK BY CRUISERS AND BATTLESHIPS (AT) 0700 (IN) 11°40'NORTH 126°25'EAST. REQUEST IMMEDIATE AIR STRIKE. ALSO REQUEST SUPPORT BY HEAVY SHIPS. MY BATTLESHIPS LOW IN AMMUNITION.[197]

Halsey recorded that in response to this last message he sent a signal to Kinkaid inside of five minutes which stated that his formations were in contact with Ozawa's force and that Task Group 38.1, with five carriers and four heavy cruisers, had been ordered to provide immediate assistance. Halsey also stated his own position—in 17°18'North 126°11'East or some 400 miles north of Task Unit 77.4.3—in order "to show [Kinkaid] the impossibility of the fast battleships reaching him."[198] Regarding this last inclusion it is difficult not to feel some sympathy for Halsey because Kinkaid, from the time he was made aware that the battle force was not off the San Bernardino Strait and by clear implication had to have gone north with the carriers, must have realized that Task Force 38, whether in whole or in part, could not move to the support of the formations off Samar and Leyte. Why Kinkaid continued to send increasingly desperate messages to Halsey is not entirely clear, though the obvious answer is decidedly unflattering to Kinkaid and was provided in the signal that Halsey received at 1003. This simply stated, WHERE IS LEE SEND LEE.[199] That the signal had been sent in clear and not in code was a token of the desperation that underwrote it.

Kinkaid was grasping at straws, seeking help from all sources in an attempt to redeem a situation that was all but beyond recall.

The element of sympathy for Halsey noted herein nonetheless needs be tempered by one aspect of military planning that, while common today, can be transposed across time with some relevance. Military formations in action have areas of responsibility, which is their sector of operations, and they also have areas of interest, on their flanks where they meet their neighboring formations. Halsey's point about lack of warning from search aircraft carried an obvious implication: Kinkaid and Sprague were taken by surprise because of their neglect of their area of interest. The point cannot be dodged. The scale of search that was ordered was wholly inadequate and then beset by problems that confounded the effort. But, and here was the but, while adequate precaution was neither initiated nor put into effect this matter concerned an area of interest, not an area of responsibility. The weakness of this argument is that the definitions of such areas are primarily military rather than naval, but the basic similarity in terms of the unfolding of events permits a proper transposition of terms. The fact of the matter was that the San Bernardino Strait most certainly did not constitute Kinkaid's area of responsibility.

This, however, is but one of two matters that, unfolding in the course of the receipt of these signals, elicit a divided response, a certain sympathy for Halsey in terms of the situation in which he found himself at this point but also telling criticism and condemnation of both his previous decision to leave the San Bernardino Strait unguarded and his decisions both now and over the next couple of hours. In terms of sympathy, the situation can be stated simply. His formations perhaps stood some three or four hours from recording a victory of overwhelming proportions, and at this stage of proceedings Halsey did not need the distraction relating to matters about which his formations could do nothing. These groups had to conform to the old truism that one fights as one must rather than as one would. It is easy to overlook the extent of the opportunity that now presented itself and indeed the scale of the American achievement that was to be registered this day. The battle now being fought off Cape Engaño was to be the only occasion in history when four carriers were sunk in a single day, and if three of these were light carriers and did not really compare to the *Akagi* and *Kaga*, which were lost off Midway in June 1942, nonetheless they could be measured alongside the *Hiryu* and *Soryu*, also lost in that battle. Of course the other side of the coin is seldom fully appreciated. The Japanese were prepared to take unprecedented carrier losses, admittedly the loss of all but empty carriers, in an attempt to ensure that Kurita's formations were able to reach their intended prey. An acceptance of the loss of perhaps all four carriers really should be cause for thought. But if Halsey cannot be blamed for not appreciating the weakness of Japanese carrier forces—and if the various task group commanders could work this out then one wonders why Halsey and the fleet staff could not have done the same[200]—there is no doubting that by most standards the destruction of an enemy carrier force was clearly more important than the destruction of an enemy battle force. But if in this respect one must have a certain sympathy for Halsey on account of the nature and extent of a victory that was there for the taking, the point was that this victory could have been won without the San Bernardino Strait finesse, though perhaps this analogy is misplaced; one could never really imagine Halsey and finesse together.

The other point, the criticism and condemnation, has two strands and is provided in the comment that Ozawa's force "gravely threatened" not only the U.S. carrier and covering formations "but the whole Pacific strategy." Such an observation would seem to be grossly overstated because it is hard to see how, under any circumstances, a force that consisted of just four carriers could possibly have set at naught the whole of American strategic policy in the war against Japan. Indeed, this point can be developed in terms of what any *Kaigun* victory, whether in the north or south, might have achieved. It is hard to see what the Japanese could have done to have even slowed the American advance into the western Pacific, and that leaves aside the whole question of confounding American and hence Allied policy for the war against Japan. The comment would seem to have little appreciation of reality, a reality that surely should have been available to a person of Halsey's seniority and position at the time, but the comment was provided by Halsey in his 1947 autobiography, and to which reference has already been made:

> It was not my job to protect the Seventh Fleet. My job was offensive, to strike with the Third Fleet, and we were even then rushing to intercept a force which gravely threatened not only Kinkaid and myself, but the whole Pacific strategy.[201]

It is impossible to discern how Ozawa's force could be held to present any real threat to the 7th Fleet, and it is difficult to reconcile the denial of defensive responsibility with the implied but obvious claim that the latter was in the process of being achieved. But perhaps the real point lay elsewhere, specifically that in setting forth such a detailed argument Halsey condemned himself, if not from his own mouth then at least from the tip of his own pen. The whole of his arguments, ranging from his "childish" signal later that day to setting out this account of proceedings, inadvertently admitted if not dereliction on his part then certainly that there was a case to answer.

Such matters may be left for the moment, but suffice it to note that it was more or less around the time when Halsey had to deal with Kinkaid's 0725 signal that the *Chitose* sank. Only minutes before she sank, the light cruiser *Isuzu* had been ordered to take the carrier in tow, but clearly the imminence of her loss led to this order being cancelled in favor of a general retirement to the north, the destroyer *Shimotsuki* being ordered to rescue the crew of the *Chitose* while the *Isuzu* was directed to stand by the *Tama*.[202] The *Chitose* sank at 0937,[203] which was about twenty minutes before the second strike force flown from the American carriers moved into the day's second attack on Ozawa's force. This was the smallest attack of the day, involving sixteen Avengers, six Helldivers, and fourteen fighters, and it appears to have singled out the *Chiyoda*, which was hit by Helldivers from the *Lexington* and *Franklin* and left heavily afire and with a sharp list to port.[204] It has been suggested that she was hit by a bomb at 1018 that disabled her engines,[205] but over the next couple of hours, with the *Hyuga* and destroyer escort *Maki* standing by, her damage control parties made every effort to save the ship and appeared to be winning. At 1155, some five minutes after the *Tama* was ordered to proceed independently, the *Hyuga* was ordered to take the *Chiyoda* in tow. The *Isuzu*, when she rejoined, was given the same instruction; presumably this order was given to free the *Hyuga* for defensive duties. But the appearance of American aircraft at about 1320 heralded the start of the third attack of the day,[206] and it was the certainty of having to endure further assault rather than any more damage inflicted in this attack that spelled an end to Japanese efforts to save the *Chiyoda*. The *Isuzu* and *Maki* were instructed to remove the crew of the carrier and then to sink her, but they failed to do so for reasons that are not readily apparent. The carrier and her crew were simply left with some three hours of life remaining to them before American warships arrived on the scene.[207]

This second attack saw mounting Japanese disorganization. The Japanese ships seemed to have maneuvered independently, with little or no cohesion, while by its end Ozawa's formations and units were scattered over as much as sixty miles with perhaps only the ships in the company of the *Zuikaku* and *Zuiho* properly justifying the dignity of formation status as opposed to being a mere collection of ships.[208] By the time this attack drew to a close, the Japanese had lost a light carrier and destroyer and had two carriers and one light cruiser in a sorry state, but it was exactly this same period of time that saw the crisis of command engulf Halsey, though the irony of the situation that had developed went unappreciated. The crisis of command was concerned solely with Kinkaid's formations, but by this time the crisis of the battle—or at least the first and greater of the two crises of this battle and day—had passed. There was no way any of the senior American commanders could have known this, but because the disaster that threatened to overwhelm the formation off Samar had passed, Halsey's decision to send the battle force to the south represented effort wasted. By the time this decision was forthcoming, however, a second crisis, this time presented by the first deliberate Japanese use of *kamikaze* formations, had begun to unfold, but there was nothing the American formations could have done either to forestall or defeat this new form of attack.

In the period when Halsey received these various signals from Kinkaid, the Japanese formations under Kurita's command slowly began to overhaul Task Unit 77.4.3 to the extent that the initial fear of the American force commander, that "it did not appear that any of our ships could survive another five minutes of the heavy-calibre fire being received," seemed—perhaps belatedly—to be on the point of realization.[209] The reason for this situation was that Japanese warships slowly began to move abreast of the American units astern of the escort carriers and on both sides, the result being that first the *Hoel* was disabled and sunk and then Japanese ships closed to engage the *Fanshaw Bay* and *Gambier Bay*. The *Hoel* was hit at about 0830 by a shell from the heavy cruiser *Tone* that disabled her remaining engine, and as she slowed the order to abandon ship was given. Under a hail of fire, she capsized to port and sank at 0855,[210] perhaps the only real cause for wonderment being that she took twenty-five minutes to sink when subjected to the attention of a number of enemy ships at a range of some 7,000 yards. In her last minutes she earned the distinction of coming closer to the battleship *Yamato* than any other American warship. In certain accounts she, and other American units, separately closed to such short ranges that enemy battleships could not engage her with their main armament.[211] The *Heermann* and *Johnston*, moving across to the port quarter, tried to shield the *Gambier Bay* from Japanese attention, but the heavy cruisers *Chokai* and *Haguro* and the light cruiser *Noshiro* between them possessed advantage sufficient to set the destroyers' intention at naught and to subject the escort carrier to deliberate fire that quickly reduced her to a flaming wreck. At 0907 she capsized and sank, but surprisingly about 800 of her crew were rescued by patrol and landing craft from Leyte.[212] To the west, the *Butler* and *Roberts*, joined by the ubiquitous *Johnston*, were more successful in covering the *Fanshaw Bay*, but around 0850 the *Roberts* took the first of a series of hits until at 0900 she was literally disemboweled by two or three shells, from either the *Haruna* or *Kongo*, that ripped her open along the waterline, destroyed one engine room, and set off massive fires aft. All power was lost and one gun, being fired manually, malfunctioned and exploded, killing virtually the entire gun crew. The order to abandon ship was given at 0910 but she took time to sink; the ship was not finally abandoned until 0935 and did not sink until 1005.[213] The *Johnston*, despite all the damage she had incurred, was instrumental in ensuring that the torpedo attack launched by the *Yahagi* at about 0905 and by her destroyers some ten minutes later was unavailing despite the subsequent claim that "three enemy carriers and one cruiser were enveloped in black smoke and observed to sink one after another."[214] At the time, the destroyers claimed to have sunk one *Enterprise*-class carrier and severely damaged another, while the *Gambier Bay* had been defined by the *Kongo* as being of similar pedigree and the *Yamato*, despite the closeness of her encounter, identified the *Hoel* as a cruiser.[215] Immediately after these attacks, when the Japanese destroyers were free to concentrate on the *Johnston*, she was struck by a number of shells that knocked out her remaining engine room. All power was lost, but it was not until 0945 that the order to abandon ship was given, but like the *Hoel* and *Roberts* before her, she took her time in sinking. At 1010 she rolled over,[216] and her sinking gave rise to one of the more celebrated episodes of the battle. As one Japanese destroyer closed in order to administer the *coup de grâce*, which proved unnecessary, American survivors in the water saw an enemy officer on the bridge salute the sinking ship.[217] The other three units of the screen, which seldom get much of a mention in accounts of the battle—which invariably concentrate upon the actions involving the three units that were lost[218]—were also involved in these and other kindred operations. The *Dennis* was hit twice, at 0850 and 0900, and with two guns taking no further part in proceedings, she retreated behind the smoke provided by the *Butler*. The latter subsequently sought to protect the *Fanshaw Bay* from the *Tone*, but an ammunition shortage meant she had to cease firing at 0918 and in any case was ordered forward to lay smoke at this time. The *Raymond* was involved in action with Japanese units at different times, but alone among the units of the screen emerged from more than two hours' action without as much as a scratch, not even from a near-miss.[219]

The loss of these destroyers has commanded much attention in most American accounts of this battle, and for obvious reason. At the level of both ships and individuals this was a story of heroic endeavor enhanced by formation survival in the face of impossible odds. Such individuals as Evans of the *Johnston* entered the pantheon of American heroes, and for good and obvious reason. The improbable sequence of events that ensured the survival of Task Unit 77.4.3 was in no small measure the result of the gallantry and sacrifice of such men and the nameless members of the ships' crews who paid the full price in the process. It is important, therefore, to note that on the American side the survival of the escort carrier formation was the result of two complementary efforts, those made by the units from the screen and by the carrier aircraft from the three formations that made up Task Group 77.4. The point is that while various individual attacks were conducted almost from first contact and the main range-finding position in the *Kongo* was fortuitously smashed in one of the very first attacks,[220] in the first hour after battle was joined, the American effort in the air really amounted to the sum of individual attacks. But by the time Kurita's war-ships picked off the *Hoel* and seemingly were poised to speedily dispatch screen and escort carriers alike, the main effort by the latter's aircraft materialized.

The initial effort in the air was fragmented and of minor account. The Avengers aloft at the time of the initial contact between Kurita's formations and Task Unit 77.4.3 and those launched immediately thereafter were armed with depth charges or light general-purpose bombs, and while the shock of depth charges could damage range-finding equipment, the use of such weapons against surface units necessarily had to be something of a lottery, and there is no indication that in the first hour of battle the American aircraft were anything more than an irritant. Thereafter, however, two matters served to provide substance to the American air attacks. The use of the airfield at Tacloban, where there was a supply of 500-lb. bombs, and the support afforded Task Unit 77.4.3 by its sister formations meant that properly armed aircraft, and in some numbers, were able to move against Kurita's formations even as they tried to close around the screen and escort carriers of the northern formation. A token of this support for Task Unit 77.4.3 was that the *Manila Bay* played host to eleven itinerants this day, and at one stage had on board aircraft from five carriers—herself, the *Sangamon*, *Gambier Bay*, *Kitkun Bay* and the *White Plains*.[221] With Task Unit 77.4.3 on course to the southwest and thus unable to fly off aircraft in its own defense, and with Task Unit 77.4.1 to the south and in any case to be committed to air defense of all three escort carrier formations, Task Unit 77.4.2 in effect was the only possible source of support for its sister formation, though it needs to be noted that none of these formations had the weapons and numbers that would enable them to conduct sustained operations against Kurita's units; the individual escort carriers' supply of torpedoes could only be used once.

Nonetheless, even without torpedoes, the initial air attacks did better than was realized at the time. At about 0724 the heavy cruiser *Suzuya*, even before she became a squadron flagship, suffered a near-miss that damaged her fuel tanks and inner port shaft. She was immediately reduced to about twenty knots and was left with about 800 tons of oil, a little more than one-third capacity. An attempt to increase her speed to twenty-four knots resulted in such vibration that she was forced to reduce speed and fall out the chase.[222] It was not until about 0842, however, that what proved to be the main American effort was put together. Mounted by about thirty aircraft, it was directed against the heavy cruisers leading the Japanese formations and came through a rain squall, the enemy units thus having minimal time to put down fire or take evasive action. The *Chikuma* was caught in a scissors attack by just four Avengers, apparently from the *Kitkun Bay*,[223] and while combing one pair of tracks was hit aft and lost her rudder. She was left circling and not under control.[224] The *Chokai* was also hit, apparently by a bomb or bombs from aircraft from the *Kitkun Bay*, and her engines were disabled.[225] At this same time the *Haguro* was hit by a bomb on one of her forward turrets without any serious loss to her overall efficiency, and along with the *Tone*, the captain of which had been wounded in a strafing attack by one of the Wildcats at about 0828,[226] she had led the chase of the carrier formation to the position whereby, around 0900, Kurita's force should have been but minutes from the destruction of Task Unit 77.4.3. The point, so easily missed, was that in the two hours that had elapsed since first contact, no fewer than four heavy cruisers and three destroyers had been lost to the Japanese order of battle. First the *Kumano* and then the *Suzuya* and destroyer *Okinami* had fallen out of formation, and there-after, just as it was belatedly but literally on the point of victory, Kurita's formation lost two more heavy cruisers, plus the *Fujinami* and *Nowaki*, which were instructed to stand by the *Chokai* and *Chikuma* respectively.[227] The *Chokai*, however, sank at about 0930, some forty minutes after being hit;[228] the *Fujinami* rescued her crew but was to be sunk herself off Mindoro two days later by American carrier aircraft.[229]

Thus even before the *Gambier Bay*, *Johnston* and the *Roberts* were sunk, no fewer than four heavy cruisers and three destroyers had been forced from the battle, and with three of the heavy cruisers seriously damaged and in fact doomed, the battle thus far had the makings of an improbable American victory. But it was at this point, in the period when the *Yahagi* and her destroyers launched their abortive torpedo attacks, that the battle off Samar ended. It did so because at 0911 Kurita recalled all units, ordering them to take positions off the *Yamato* and *Nagato*, which he turned back to the north.[230] This proved to be the critical decision of the entire battle, not just of this day, and for one simple reason. By this decision, the Japanese broke off contact with Task Unit 77.4.3, and this contact, once broken, was never re-established. Whatever its logic and intention, this decision spelled the end of the last great surface action in history.

Even at a distance of sixty years, a lifetime, it is impossible to provide an explanation of this decision. There appears to have been no discussion between Kurita and his staff prior to this decision that would serve as a basis of explanation, and Kurita never provided any full or detailed statement of the factors that governed his thinking. Whatever comment he provided after the war was partial and incomplete, and seemingly served only to further mystify and bewilder post-war interrogators, historians, and other interested personnel. Inevitably the passing of time makes it wholly impossible to recreate, and thereby understand, the circumstances and thinking that gave rise to this decision, but suffice it to note that it was a decision that defies logic and rationality.

In seeking to set out the context and what may be a possible explanation of Kurita's decision, one would note one matter so it may be set aside before the decision itself is considered. After Kurita turned his force away, he was to take his formations in pursuit of a formation that was reported to the north. The exact terms of his signal were WE WILL SEEK OUT AND ENGAGE ENEMY TASK FORCE WHICH IS IN POSITION BEARING 005 DEGREES 113 MILES FROM SULUAN ISLAND LIGHTHOUSE. The clear implication, at least in some accounts of these proceedings, is that the two were related.[231] This was not the case. The order was given at 1236, three hours after the turn-away. It would appear, therefore, that the turnaway and a desire to go north to seek out an enemy formation were wholly unrelated, not least because after 0800 the *Yamato* had launched two seaplanes, one of which had searched to the north and had reported that she had not encountered any enemy formations.[232] Certainly it would seem that at the time Kurita took his force northward he had not received any sighting report that placed an enemy formation to the north, and in any event the lack of detail regarding the content of this order prompts three obvious questions which seemingly are never addressed, namely the source of this report, the time of receipt of the sighting report by Kurita in the *Yamato*, and the detail of the enemy force in this report. The only detail known of this report is the time of 0945, though whether this was the time of sighting or of the signal—whether sent or received—is not clear.[233] Without any answers to these questions, any attempt to make sense of this second order would suggest that, with some allowance for miscalculation of distance, the formation supposedly in this position north of Suluan Island, roughly in a position 12°North 126°East at some time that morning, must have been Task Unit 77.4.3. Such a suggestion borders on the bizarre, but it is one that pales beside the only other possible explanation: if it was not Task Unit 77.4.3 that was reported then it must have been Kurita's own formation. The problem with either or both of these suggestions is that Kurita was some sixty-four miles to the north of Suluan at 0645 and then came south,[234] and most certainly there was no formation nearer this reported position than Kurita's. The problem with these alternative suggestions is the obvious one: both are based on the premise that Kurita received a signal placing an enemy formation in this given position, and lest the point made in these lines be missed one would repeat it. At the time when Kurita turned his force away he had received no such report, and—to raise a point examined in detail later—certainly there is evidence to suggest that there was never any such signal, a state of affairs that would raise a whole number of unanswerable questions.

In seeking to address the factors that might have led Kurita to turn his force away at 0911 one has to address five related matters. The first four of these concern themselves directly with the conduct of battle, and simply stated would be, first, a belief that the Japanese force, having become widely dispersed over the previous two hours, had to be re-formed; second, a belief that a real victory had been won; third, a realization that a high-speed general chase could not be sustained; and fourth, a fear of what force, and specifically what aircraft numbers, might be brought against the Japanese formation over the next few hours and against which provision had to be made. The fifth and last point concerns the individual, specifically the personal and human elements of failure. The immediate difficulty with these matters is the historical problem of trying to guess what Kurita could see and what he knew at the time. One is reminded that at Jutland the British commander, Admiral Sir John Jellicoe, barely saw the enemy. Officers in control positions saw the enemy, but on the bridge the fleet commander seldom saw enemy ships and in one famous single incident thought that the enemy's disappearance was the result of worsening visibility when in fact it was the result of a turnaway. One suspects that Kurita saw little of the battle,[235] but even if he did there is no escaping the basic point that he was singularly badly served in terms of reports that were littered with misidentification of enemy ships and that grossly exaggerated, indeed grotesquely exaggerated, losses inflicted upon the enemy. There can be no doubt that Kurita was never in a position to contradict such reports, which came from virtually every one of his ships and indeed even from the gunnery control position in the *Yamato*. There can also be little doubt that by 0900 the deleterious effect of a general chase had begun to impress itself upon Kurita. By that time his force was spread over more than fifteen miles, and the *Yamato* and *Nagato* had no screening destroyers. If the Americans were able to put together a serious air attack the Japanese battleships would have been needlessly exposed.

One would suggest that these points cannot seriously be disputed and that they may well have been present in Kurita's calculations. Certainly concern about the formation's shape and its potential vulnerability would have been matters that properly intruded upon a force commander's calculations. Moreover, Kurita by 0900 must have realized that the course of action on which his force was embarked could not be sustained, and for two reasons that are easily missed. High-speed steaming at this stage had to be purchased in terms of range, and two hours' action, coming on top of the previous day's fight in the Sibuyan Sea, must have seriously emptied the magazines of Kurita's ships. In terms of both oil and ammunition, the Japanese chase was prodigal, and the fact that Kurita initially restricted his destroyers' operations would suggest that he was aware of this fact with respect to fuel. But by this time, around 0900 or about when Kurita made his decision to turn away, the Japanese ships must have been low indeed in anti-aircraft ammunition, while Ugaki noted that the *Haguro*, as she came south, was beset by an ammunition shortage.[236] One assumes she was not alone in this respect.

But these points pale alongside two inescapable facts. The first is that Kurita deliberately chose to break off an engagement when he was in contact with not one but two enemy formations. Certainly the second formation, Task Unit 77.4.2, had not been subjected to loss, and so his placing of distance between himself and these formations could not have granted any immunity to attack; in fact, breaking contact with enemy carriers could only result in increased attack by their aircraft. The second is that Kurita seems to have been convinced that his formation was in contact with an enemy fast carrier formation and that his ships were not overhauling it. This raises the obvious question of how, if this was the case, were Japanese destroyers now coming into range of the enemy. Undoubtedly there was an element of miscalculation and self-justification here, but even this argument contains within it an unanswerable question: If the formation that had been contacted off Samar really did have the units that were identified, then why did the American battleships and heavy cruisers not form themselves into line and fight, for want of a better word, "properly"? The various arguments paraded through time as the possible basis for Kurita's decision simply do not make sense and most certainly do not hang together, not least the decision to go north to seek out the enemy. How Kurita's force was supposed to contact a carrier formation for the second time on the same day, and why it should have broken contact with two such formations and two hours later set course for an enemy perhaps fifty or sixty miles to the north, defy rational explanation.

The personal element may provide an explanation, speculative and incomplete though it must be. There are three distinct strands here, and the first two can be woven together. It could be argued that Kurita, like Halsey, was simply overwhelmed by the sheer size and scale of this battle, and in truth nothing in his career could have prepared Kurita for such a battle. This was a battle in which formations were deployed over thousands of miles, where the area of battle extended over hundreds of miles, and where time was compressed in a way that defies ready understanding. One can only suggest this point because it could not be proved, but one would suggest that the very nature of this battle did affect its conduct, and perhaps on both sides.

The second, complementary, strand is the stress of battle and losses. It is easy to lose sight of the fact that here off Samar the Japanese force incurred its third set of losses in three days, and it bears repeating what had disappeared from the order of battle. In the Palawan Passage two days previously the heavy cruisers *Atago* and *Maya* had been sunk, the *Takao* had been seriously damaged and obliged to withdraw from the battle, while the destroyers *Asashimo* and *Naganami* had been detached. In the Sibuyan Sea on the previous day the battleship *Musashi* had been sunk, the heavy cruiser *Myoko* had been seriously damaged and forced to return to Brunei, and the destroyers *Hamakaze* and *Kiyoshima* had been detached. Now, off Samar, the count stood at four heavy cruisers and three destroyers. In little more than forty-eight hours, the Japanese order of battle was reduced from a total of thirty-two to just sixteen warships, from two formations which between them had five battleships, ten heavy and two light cruisers, and fifteen destroyers to two formations each with two battleships, one heavy cruiser and one light cruiser, Kurita's task group having five destroyers and Suzuki's task group just three.

Table 6.1. The Strength of Formations Assigned to the Center Force, 22–25 October 1944								
	Kurita's 1st Task Group				Suzuki's 2nd Task Group			
	BB	CA	CL	DD	BB	CA	CL	DD
Original strength	3	6	1	9	2	4	1	6
At 2359 on 23 October	3	3	1	7	2	4	1	6
At 2359 on 24 October	2	2	1	7	2	4	1	4
At 1201 on 25 October	2	1	1	5	2	1	1	3
Lost or detached	1	5	-	4	-	3	-	3

Key:
BB Battleships   CA Heavy Cruisers   CL Light Cruisers   DD Destroyers

In other words, sixteen warships, exactly half the units in these two task groups, had been lost from the order of battle.[237] If Kurita at this stage was rattled by such losses—and indeed if he was fully aware of the extent of the morning's reverses—then perhaps that would be wholly understandable. Equally, the mounting scale of air attack at this stage of proceedings could also have had an unnerving effect, and again not surprisingly so. There is evidence that after some two hours the persistence of American aircraft had an effect that passed beyond mere irritation. In post-war interrogation Kurita's operations officer, Commander Otani Tonosuke, stated that at this stage the attacks by American aircraft were

> almost incessant but the number of planes at any one instant [sic] was few. The bombers and torpedo-planes were very aggressive and skilful, and coordination was impressive: even in comparison with the experience of the American attack that we had experienced (the previous day in the Sibuyan Sea) this was the most skilful work of your aircraft,[238]

and there can be little doubt that he was not alone in these views.

To these points one could add "the human dimension." Apart from Mitscher, it seems that no one ever slept, and one wonders how far sheer fatigue might have been at work, and one would suggest another matter. Various accounts note that what might have been at work were the lingering effects of dengue fever and the immersion when the *Atago* was sunk. But one would suggest that perhaps a Newtonian exhaustion was at work, the equal and opposite reaction to the extreme stress of the previous day, of the passing through the San Bernardino Strait and then the excitement of con-tact. All accounts of the battle make reference to the extremes of gratitude and pleasure, the tears of joy at being able to fight a real enemy and not empty transports. "God has come to our assistance" clearly summarized feelings.[239] The Japanese, as they joined battle, were on an emotional high with the adrenalin racing, something that might have banished physical fatigue and mental exhaustion. Perhaps battle, coming on top of all these points that made for tiredness and error, had a massively draining effect, the reverse of unthinking exhilaration, and again a parallel with Jutland might be relevant. After his two decisions that had placed his force between the enemy and his home bases, Jellicoe was all but passive. He sat on the bridge and made no decision even though it should have been clear that the enemy was attempting to come astern of his battle force. It was as if Jellicoe's decisions represented a lifetime, or fifty-seven years, of effort and left the individual spent. With Kurita and 25 October 1944, one has no way of knowing if personal disorientation and exhaustion were at work in clouding judgment at this critical time, though one notes Kurita's subse-quent comments on these matters and his view that while he did not feel tired at the time, he "was exhausted both physically and mentally."[240] And on such matters, a view set forth in 1947

> Yet it is asking much to expect precise logic from one whose flagship has been
> sunk, who had endured one whole day of submarine attacks and alarms and
> another of devastating air strikes before being able to engage, and whose force
> had been reduced from 37 ships to eighteen, three of which had been detached
> to rescue survivors. No one who has been under faintly comparable strain can fail
> to realise how difficult accurate evaluation and assessment (had) become.

is hard to dispute. The figures may be dubious but not the conclusion.[241]

One is always wary of single-cause explanation. One's inclination is
to assume that at this stage of proceedings "all the little bits were coming
together" in shaping Kurita's decision. In an obvious sense, the line of argument that all these factors were in play says both everything and nothing at
the same time, but suffice it to note that definitive judgment in these matters is impossible. One would note, however, that the third strand, hitherto
not defined, is decidedly uncomplimentary to Kurita. It would suggest that
Kurita's exercise of command in the Palawan Passage was inept and that the
general chase order issued when Task Unit 77.4.3 was contacted was in the
same category. The decision to turn away was merely par for the course for
an admiral whose performance throughout the war was at best mediocre.
If this seems somewhat harsh, then the least that can be said was that this
decision to turn his formation away, to break contact with the enemy, conformed to a less-than-impressive record of command to date. One wonders
what Ozawa might have done had appointments been reversed.

This assessment of Kurita is unlikely to command much sympathy
given that for the better part of sixty years he has not been subjected to
proper, searching examination in Western histories. But the real difficulty
that presents itself in dealing with Kurita and this decision is that the analysis of the individual suggests any number of questions. One of the most
obvious concerns the statement by Kurita's chief of staff:

> Giving up the pursuit when we did amounted to losing a prize already in hand.
> If we had known the types and number of enemy ships, and their speed, Admiral
> Kurita would never have suspended the pursuit, and would have annihilated the
> enemy. Lacking this vital information, we concluded that the enemy had already
> made good his escape.[242]

How and on what possible basis it could have been concluded "that
the enemy had already made good his escape" when enemy units were still
within line of sight after two hours of action is hard to discern. Moreover,
the statement has to be read very carefully because it suggests that Kurita
and his staff would have pressed the action had they known that the enemy

formation was inferior, which clearly implies that if they had known that the enemy was equal or superior then the pursuit would have been abandoned. This, given the Japanese objective, raises any number of questions. But that matter aside, one is left with four unanswerable points. First, at the time Kurita gave his order for his force to turn to the north, there were still U.S. carriers afloat and operating their aircraft; putting distance between the Japanese ships and these carriers was not going to ensure the *Kaigun* units against continuing air attack. It is impossible to see any logic in breaking contact with the enemy on this particular score. Second, it is impossible to see what other target Kurita could have sought given that he believed he was in contact with an enemy fleet carrier formation, and it is hard to believe that at this stage Kurita genuinely believed that a real victory had been won. Even if the six carriers that had been encountered had been fleet carriers and sunk, this would not have been a real victory of the order that Japan needed at this stage. The moral effect may have been important but in terms of national power and service numbers even sinkings on this scale would not have had real strategic impact. Third, it is hard to understand why the Japanese force could not have been re-formed while still heading to the southwest and toward Leyte Gulf, but it is hard, if not impossible, to understand why the process of re-forming had to be completed while heading away from the designated target area.[243] Fourth, and last, it is difficult indeed to understand why Kurita should have persisted in taking his force away from the enemy after 0940 when he received a signal from Southwest Area Fleet informing him that the American formation which he had engaged had been sending signals in clear. This evidence of distress and desperation caused no recasting of intent, yet it is difficult to understand why Kurita should not have sought to take immediate advantage of such information.

But all these possible explanations pale beside one point and that, very simply, is that there is evidence to suggest that there was no 0945 signal. This is a matter which seems to have eluded two or three generations of Western historians and writers and has led to sharp divisions even within the narrowly based "naval history" community within Japan. There has developed within Japan a number of schools—the word "explanations" would seem to be misplaced in this context—with reference to Kurita's behavior and this 0945 signal, one of which is that there was no signal. This holds that this whole matter was pure invention on the part of Kurita and his staff that was intended, to mix metaphors, "to cover their tracks," i.e., the wrong decision to turn to the north rather than continuing the action with the American carrier formation and proceeding into Leyte Gulf to deal with transports and shipping that might be there. It must be assumed, since it is not clear from the evidence available to this writer, that this "covering of tracks" related to superior command, i.e., Kurita in dealings with Toyoda, but it may also be that the signal made by Kurita to the ships in his formation may have been made simply to give purpose, to still any wavering and doubts—and with the passing of time and no contact with the American enemy it would then be overtaken by events and consigned to the rubbish bin.

The counter to this argument is provided in the form of evidence from junior officers in the *Yamato* who saw "some staff officers arguing . . . over the credibility of the signal," i.e., a signal reporting the presence of an enemy force to the north. Again it is not clear whether this credibility refers to a signal *per se* or its contents, or both, and a second counter to this argument is the assertion that a signal did arrive but with no designator that revealed the identity of the originator. This second line of argument all but inevitably gave rise to "the conspiracy theory," that there was a signal and that it was sent by the Americans. It must be doubted that any American, whether an individual or a signals, intelligence, or command organization, could have put together such a signal in a matter of an hour or so, not so much in terms of devising such an idea but putting it through a chain of command which, at every stage, would have been forced to confront the reality that sending such a signal to Kurita would necessarily reveal American reading of Japanese signals. There is no evidence whatsoever to suggest that there was a false U.S. signal that lured Kurita to the north, but equally there is no evidence, from the available signals logs, that suggests that a signal was sent from Southwest Area Fleet headquarters to the *Yamato*. If such a signal was sent, and as a result of some report from a shore-based aircraft operating from the Philippines, then that signal could only have come from Mikawa's command. It is perhaps remotely possible that the *Yamato* might have picked up an aircraft sighting report, but this seems so unlikely—not least because it must be doubted that she had the codes and ciphers of another command that would have enabled her to read an aircraft's signals—that it may be dismissed from further consideration.

Quite obviously, there is a problem in seeking to make sense of these matters, and the fact that over the past few decades there has been no consensus within the ranks of Japanese historians, analysts, and commentators indicates that these poor lines are not likely to resolve matters. There would appear, however, to be three points of relevance. The first is that while the best account of these various arguments is set forth in a publication by a certain Fukuda Yukihiro, who was junior officer in the *Haguro* on 25 October and thus had no personal interest in these matters, the main source of the first line of argument, that there never was a signal received by the *Yamato*, was Kojima Kiyofumi, a signals officer in the *Yamato*. This fact cannot be considered conclusive. No single officer could be assured of having seen every signal received, and with three levels of command—Kurita, Ugaki, and the ship itself—obviously there is cause to hesitate in deciding upon the veracity of Kojima's evidence. But, like Fukuda, Kojima had no personal interest in this matter, and that cannot be said about Kurita and his staff. Herein lies the second point of relevance, and that is that it would seem, and one cannot go further than that, that Kurita was not beyond falsehood on this day. His signal informing Toyoda that he had not abandoned the intention to proceed into Leyte Gulf would seem—by the least exacting standard—somewhat misleading. The third point, one that would seem to emerge directly from this second one, is that if there was no signal then Kurita's staff certainly had no incentive after the war to come forward with the truth, and in an obvious sense this "explanation" of proceedings would make sense of Kurita's post-war accounts of proceedings. If, as was alleged a few pages ago,

> Kurita never provided any full or detailed statement of the factors that governed his thinking. Whatever comment he provided after the war was partial and incomplete, and seemingly served only to further mystify and bewilder post-war interrogators, historians, and other interested personnel,

then an explanation might be there: the deliberate attempt to cover tracks, to deflect attention from full and comprehensive examination of this episode. This would make sense, and the implications for Kurita's professional and person standards are serious and would obviously raise question marks about whether he ever had any real intention of fighting a battle of annihilation that would necessarily involve self-immolation. But these matters could not be asserted definitively. We have merely to accept that it is one possible explanation, for which we in the West should be grateful to Fukuda.[244]

Perhaps the real question that should emerge from any consideration of Kurita's decision relates to the role of the fleet staff, to which reference—negative reference—has been made. What is notable is the lack of any attention to any involvement in the decision-making process on the part of the staff. Kurita was quite specific on this matter in a post-war interview.[245] In this respect naval staffs differed from army staffs, and again, with reference to the British example, one is reminded that throughout his time as First Sea Lord, between 1904 and 1910, Admiral John Fisher resisted the proposal to have a proper staff within the Admiralty, and for one reason. He was never prepared to share the power of decision; a staff existed to implement decisions made by an all-seeing commander. Fisher's views were very much along Hitlerian lines, the great man in history and the refusal to tether genius through systemic organization. In these matters Jellicoe was the exception that proved the rule, the great commander who worked through a staff, but given the historical antipathy of navies toward such matters as education and staffs, one wonders if and to what extent the weaknesses that attended Kurita's decision could be attributed to a lack of staff involvement, any proper discussion of options and actions. And, of course, one wonders if the same point can be made about the crisis that was to engulf Halsey in the *New Jersey* within an hour of Kurita's decision.

If, as was indicated in the opening line of this book, the only two problems in the study of naval history are naval historians and naval officers, one would propose that in the American writing of history there is but one problem, the Carlyle legacy. The idea that history is the biography of great men, that "history is about chaps," has all the attractiveness of simplicity, but one would suggest that by the twentieth century the Carlyle school had really outlived its usefulness, especially in matters relating to war. The importance of the individual commander in terms of morale and individual decisions cannot be doubted, but war was systemic and possessed qualities of state organization and control which did not exist before the middle of the nineteenth century. Napoleon presents an obvious problem in this respect, and there are various eighteenth-century matters that might suggest a certain historiographical care, an avoiding of the shedding of the tyranny of one interpretation in favor of another. Be that as it may, the relevance of these comments exists in the historical accounts relating to the signals that were received by Halsey shortly after 1000.

The first signal was from Kinkaid and stated that his position was desperate and indicated that only Halsey's battleships and strikes from his carriers might be able to prevent the destruction of his own escort carriers and the Japanese formations from entering Leyte Gulf. This was merely one more in the series, and previous comments on the others can be applied once more. The second signal was from Nimitz, and it is the one that has always figured large in accounts of this battle, and as such, it has always been saddled with a certain notoriety.

The basic story behind this signal is well-known. Events were being followed both at Pacific Fleet headquarters and in Washington, and a number of individuals on Nimitz's staff expressed concern that Halsey had left the San Bernardino Strait unguarded.[246] On the morning of 25 October, the course of events, as set out by Kinkaid's signals, caused mounting concern on the part of Nimitz, and at 0944 a signal was sent to Halsey which read in full (with names added) as follows:

> TURKEY TROTS TO WATER. QQ. FROM COMMANDER-IN-CHIEF PACIFIC FLEET [Nimitz]. ACTION COMMANDER THIRD FLEET [Halsey]. INFORMATION COMMANDER-IN-CHIEF [King] AND COMMANDER TASK FORCE 77 [Kinkaid]. WHERE IS REPEAT WHERE IS TASK FORCE 34. RR. THE WORLD WONDERS.

There were three parts to this signal, and two were padding included in order to avoid starting signals in the same way and thus render them vulnerable to compromise. TURKEY TROTS TO WATER and THE WORLD WONDERS were the padding, and these should have been removed by the signals staff. The two double-letter designators marked the beginning and end of the signal.

Padding was supposedly nonsense and not to be confused with the content of a signal, but in this case the one chance in a million materialized. The padding was confused by the signals staff with the result that the signal that was passed to Halsey read: FROM CINCPAC ACTION COM THIRD FLEET INFO COMINCH AND CTF 77 WHERE IS RPT WHERE IS TASK FORCE 34 RR THE WORLD WONDERS. When Halsey received this signal he had what amounted to a screaming fit. Halsey himself wrote a section in his autobiography on this episode, and his version of events has been widely accepted and incorporated, usually in detail and at disproportionate length, in most accounts of the battle. Certainly what is purported to have happened has largely been stressed at the expense of serious and proper analysis of what did happen.

What happened was that at 1055, almost an hour after Nimitz's signal was received, Halsey directed Task Force 34 to turn back to the south at 1115, with Task Group 38.2 being ordered to cover this force.[247] But with Task Force 34 ordered to shed the heavy cruisers *New Orleans* and *Wichita*, the light cruisers *Mobile* and *Santa Fe*, and ten destroyers in order to better provide for the two carrier groups that were to remain in the north,[248] the battle force directed south numbered six battleships, three cruisers, and eight destroyers. Halsey informed both Nimitz and Kinkaid of what he had done, the latter being informed that Halsey was coming south with six battleships but that he did not expect to arrive until 0800 the following morning.[249] By his action Halsey ended the battleships' participation in the northern battle and thus ensured that any surface action, then seemingly but a few hours away, would have to be fought without them, but at the same time Halsey pointed to the fact that their ability to come to the help of Kinkaid's formation bordered on the non-existent.

What never seems to be afforded full and proper consideration of this episode are three matters. The first, simply, was that the course of action— to leave battleships covering the San Bernardino Strait—had been wholly unacceptable to Halsey the previous night. The battleships had to go north as the *sine qua non* of the battle the next day with the Japanese carrier force. Comment has already been made about this decision, but Halsey's defense of it may be quoted here in full. In his action report he wrote:

> It maintained the integrity of the . . . fleet; it adopted the best possibility of sur- prise and destruction of [the] enemy carrier force. It was particularly sound and necessary if the strength of the [enemy] northern force proved to be the maxi- mum reported. It was recognized that the [enemy] center force might sortie and inflict some damage, but its fighting power was considered too seriously impaired to win a decision. Finally, it was calculated that [the carrier] forces could return in time to reverse any advantage that the [enemy] center force might gain.[250]

The whole point is that the entire logic underpinning the original deci- sion was thrown overboard on receipt of one signal from Nimitz. Kinkaid had sent a number of appeals for help, wholly unrealistic appeals it must be stated, and in effect Halsey had disregarded them. But on receipt of one signal from Nimitz, and not because of any change of circumstances in the meantime, Halsey "saw the light" and reversed the logic of all the decisions made over the previous fifteen or so hours. Halsey subsequently stated that his awareness of Nimitz's concern "for the safety of the Seventh Fleet force was the final factor that influenced his decision" to send the battle force south,[251] a statement that is difficult to credit given that it is wholly impossible to discern what the other factors had been, and Halsey also subsequently stated that he regretted this reversal of policy, that it was wrong,[252] and there is little doubt that in one immediate sense it was wrong. There was little, if anything, that Task Force 34 could do to support

Kinkaid's formations; the calculations of the previous hour or so had been completely correct. At this stage of proceedings, the battle line should have been kept in the north.

The second point, however, if it does not contradict this conclusion, does cast a different light on proceedings. Halsey turned the battle force back to the south at 1115, more than an hour after he received the signal from Nimitz, thus costing Task Force 34 more than two hours to make it back to the position where it had been when Nimitz's signal had been received. But as the battle force came south it slowed to twelve knots so the battleships could top up the destroyers with fuel. This process took between 1345 and 1622,[253] after which time the formation was divided with Task Group 34.5 then being formed. This was to consist of the battleships *Iowa* and *New Jersey*, three light cruisers, and eight destroyers, and at 1701 this formation was ordered to proceed to the San Bernardino Strait. At this stage Task Group 38.2 was to the east of this new formation.[254] This force was to arrive off the Strait soon after midnight.

These arrangements invite the obvious critical comment. At this stage of proceedings Halsey could not have known that Kurita was to take his force back through the San Bernardino Strait, and these arrangements would have done little or nothing about the situation off Samar, though it should be noted that it was Halsey's intention that this new force would arrive off the Strait and then sweep southward around northern and eastern Samar. Perhaps more relevantly, this whole process took the better part of seven hours from the time Nimitz's signal was received in the *New Jersey*, and this consisted of two hours' lost time and five hours slow progress southward as the destroyers were refueled. It is hard to resist the thought that had Halsey ordered just the battleships and Task Group 38.2 forward from the outset, then all six battleships, the two fast battleships plus the *Alabama, Massachusetts, South Dakota* and the *Washington*, could have been off the San Bernardino Strait in early evening. Whether a separation of the two groups of battleships, with the six-knot speed differential, had any real point is debatable, but this whole process suggests that in losing many hours in refueling the destroyers Halsey adopted the one course of action that ensured that the battleships missed the main enemy formation as it moved westward through the San Bernardino Strait late in the evening of 25 October.[255]

The third point, however, is the most obvious one. These three sets of arrangements—the detachment of Task Force 34, its being divided between two subordinate formations, and the assignment of Task Group

38.2 as the covering force—represented what had been so wholly unacceptable the previous night. The whole point behind Halsey's taking the battle force north was concentration of force, yet here was not merely the repudiation of that principle but the adoption of its direct antithesis; at this time Task Force 38 consisted of six separate formations separated over hundreds of miles.[256] Halsey's actions simply cannot be reconciled the one with the others, and herein one returns to Halsey and his version of events regarding the receipt of Nimitz's 0944 signal. He wrote that while speculating on the effect of Kinkaid's signal in clear upon enemy calculations, Nimitz's signal

> drove all other thoughts out of my mind. I can close my eyes and see it today:
> From: CINCPAC.
> To: COM THIRD FLEET.
> THE WHOLE WORLD WANTS TO KNOW WHERE IS TASK FORCE 34.
>
> I was as stunned as if I had been struck in the face. The paper rattled in my hands, I snatched off my cap, threw it on the deck and shouted something that I am ashamed to remember. Mick Carney (the chief of staff) rushed over and grabbed my arm: "Stop it! What the hell's the matter with you? Pull yourself together!"
>
> I gave him the dispatch and turned my back. I was so mad I couldn't talk. It was utterly impossible for me to believe that Chester Nimitz would send me such an insult. He hadn't, of course, but I did not know the truth for several weeks. It requires an explanation of Navy procedure. To increase the difficulty of breaking our codes, most dispatches are padded with gibberish. The decoding officers almost always recognize it as such and delete it from the transcription, but CINCPAC's encoder was either drowsy or smart-alecky, and his padding—"The whole world wants to know"—sounded so infernally plausible that my decoders read it as a valid part of the message. Chester blew up when I told him about it; he tracked down the little squirt and chewed him to bits, but it was too late then: the damage had been done.[257]

It is this version of events that has imposed itself on accounts of the battle, but two points need be noted. First, the signal passed to Halsey, not the version given here, very clearly had THE WORLD WONDERS after the designator, and therefore should have been recognized by Halsey as not having been part of the message. Admittedly, the process of filter-up filter-out might well have meant that Halsey was not familiar with signals procedures and therefore did not realize the significance of the RR designator when he read the signal. That seems more than likely and indeed it makes sense of his being so distraught at the supposed insult.[258] But second, the most authoritative biography of Halsey wrote of this episode:

Halsey, speechless, handed the despatch to his chief of staff and turned away. A check with the New Jersey's [signals personnel] identified the final words of the despatch as padding.[259]

In other words, within a minute or two of having received this dispatch and having indulged himself in his tantrum, Halsey must have been aware of the truth, that Nimitz most definitely had not sent him a studied, very deliberate insult. Even allowing for the aftermath of misplaced indignation, and that for the immediate moment Halsey probably did need a few minutes to calm himself, the point must be that in his account of this episode Halsey seems to have been very discerning, and not just in the wording of a signal. It is hard to resist the conclusion that in setting out this version of events Halsey, if he did not lie and lie very deliberately, was very selective with the truth, and most definitely sought to cloud issues and to conceal the true sequence of events. Moreover, this is a conclusion that also would apply to the statement in his autobiography that the time between 1000 and 1115 "was spent in reshuffling the task force and refueling Bogan's nearly empty destroyers for our high-speed run"[260]—a claim which in any case should raise question marks as to how these destroyers, then involved in the chase of Ozawa's force, had been allowed to reach such a state in the first place. The destroyers from Task Group 38.2 may well have begun to take on fuel in this period, but there was no way they could have begun refueling at 1000 for a run to the south. This version of events in Halsey's autobiography seems to be mendacious[261] and wholly self-serving, and one suspects for obvious reason—to deflect attention from his own actions, which by this time threatened to have serious and unfortunate consequences.

Somewhat strangely, however, Kurita's turnaway off Samar and Halsey's decision to turn the battleships back to the south combined to spell the end of the battle, or at least what had threatened to become the main battle. There remained a whole number of actions that were to be fought during what remained of this fourth Wednesday of October 1944. In the north, the Americans completed a comprehensive victory over Ozawa's force. In the center, Kurita's force was subjected to two attacks by a total of 147 aircraft from Task Group 38.1, but other than the scuttling of heavy cruisers already badly damaged, the Japanese formations were able to get through what remained of the day without incurring further loss. The remainder of the day off Samar was to be dominated by the first *kamikaze* attacks, directed initially against Task Unit 77.4.1 but with the main effort made against Task Unit 77.4.3. The following day was to see further American offensive operations as Japanese warships were pursued as they steamed westward through the Philippines, and these operations were to result in the sinking of no fewer than three light cruisers and three destroyers while another two Japanese destroyers were sunk on the next day, 27 October. In truth, however, these two last days were little more than postscripts, the final stages of a battle in which three of the four main actions—in the Surigao Strait, off Samar, and off Cape Engaño—together resulted in the most destructive single day in modern naval history. This single day was to claim a total of seventeen Japanese units of 183,365 tons and five American units of 22,456 tons, and at its end the *Kaigun,* in real terms, had been reduced to little more than a local coastal defense force of minimal value and worth.

Halsey turned his battle force to the south at a time when Task Groups 38.3 and 38.4 were committed to continuing operations against Ozawa's formations. The second strike of the day was then in hand, and preparations for what was to be the third and largest strike of the day were under way, but one of the irritating aspects of the history of this battle is that this and subsequent attacks are given little attention. This may well have been because other events diminished their immediacy and importance, but it may also have been the product of another factor: in terms of the number of aircraft committed in these attacks, and the figure generally given for the third attack is about 200 aircraft, the results were decidedly modest. A certain care needs be observed because two Japanese carriers were dispatched, but in light of the numbers of aircraft that attacked, the paucity of Japanese defense which in this attack failed to account for a single aircraft, and the individual isolation of scattered Japanese warships, the results that were obtained were perhaps not all that had been hoped. In total the carriers launched 527 strike missions this day and 431 aircraft carried out attacks, claiming 153 hits,[262] but it is doubtful that the number of torpedo and bomb hits together entered double figures.

As it was, with three-quarters of its aircraft and aircrew having taken part in the first strike, this third strike was launched between 1145 and 1200 and arrived over its prey about 1310. Directed by Commander Hugh Winters from the *Lexington,* who on this day was to become one of the very few naval officers ever to witness the sinking of three aircraft carriers, aircraft from the *Lexington* attacked the *Zuikaku* while aircraft from the *Essex* concentrated on the *Zuiho*; aircraft from the *Langley* divided their attention between the two. The *Zuikaku* was caught by a minimum of three torpedo hits, though some sources suggest that in the course of all the attacks this day she was hit by as many as six torpedoes and seven bombs,[263] most of which seem to have been inflicted upon her during this third attack. Large fires were started by the bomb hits that were inflicted on the *Zuiho*, but while the *Zuikaku* rapidly lost way and was soon listing twenty degrees to port, the *Zuiho* was able to bring her fires under control quickly. As a result, Winters then ordered aircraft from the *Enterprise*, *Franklin* and the *San Jacinto* of Task Group 38.4 to direct their efforts against the light carrier. These aircraft apparently recorded hits that set off the fires again, but as the American attack aircraft turned for home, the *Zuiho* was still heading north under her own power.[264]

After the order to abandon ship was given at 1358, the *Zuikaku*, the last of the Japanese carriers that had conducted the attack on Pearl Harbor and the veteran of almost every major battle in the Pacific war, capsized and sank at 1414. She took with her 843 of her officers and men. More than an hour later, at 1526, the *Zuiho*, presumably subjected to progressive flooding which the inadequate subdivision of the *Shoho*-class light carriers could not contain, finally succumbed just as aircraft from the fourth strike of the day began to move to their attack positions. Both carriers went quietly, with no flame or explosion. The destroyer escort *Kuwa* rescued 847 officers and men from the *Zuiho* while the battleship *Ise* picked up another ninety-eight.[265] But by the time of this final attack on the two carriers American intention had undergone change. Mitscher decided at 1330 that the carrier formations would not go farther north, the nearest Japanese units then being some sixty miles distant. Apparently his caution was because there were no battleships in company, and at this stage of proceedings there was a wariness on the part of the commander of the cruiser and destroyer force that had been detached from Task Force 34 to venture forward, and for the same reason. By the time of the *Zuikaku*'s sinking, however, Winters had established that the Japanese units, including one battleship, that had been standing by their stricken companions were moving north. Winters, who spent more than six hours over the Japanese ships, then reported that two destroyers rescued survivors from first the *Zuikaku* and then the *Zuiho*.[266] Clearly, therefore, there was little danger of the American light units running into enemy battleships, and therefore Mitscher ordered the cruiser force north, and at 1429, just fifteen minutes after the *Zuikaku* had gone, a force with four cruisers and twelve destroyers stood toward the enemy at twenty-five knots. As this force moved north, aircraft from the carriers provided fighter cover and reconnaissance while its own six Kingfisher seaplanes searched for downed aircrew. The *Cotten* subsequently recovered two aviators and the *Callaghan* and *Bronson* one pilot each.[267]

The American formation was led to the *Chiyoda* by Winters, who fortuitously sighted it when he was over the Japanese carrier on his way back to the *Lexington*. He was able to assure the American warships that the *Chiyoda* was unsupported and to assume the role of spotter, with the *New Orleans* and *Wichita* opening fire at 20,000 yards at 1625, and the *Mobile* and *Santa Fe* closing to 15,000 yards before engaging.[268] Within fifteen minutes the *Chiyoda* had been reduced to a wreck with "great clouds of smoke with intermingling flashes of fire,"[269] and at 1642 the destroyers were ordered forward to administer the *coup de grâce*. At 1647, however, the *Chiyoda* rolled over to port and at 1650 sank before the destroyers could carry out their attack. Survivors were seen swarming over her side as she sank, and many were in the water, but the destroyers were refused permission to carry out any rescue operations, and the force was re-formed to continue northward.[270]

In the meantime two more strikes were staged by the carriers against Japanese units to the north. A total of ninety-eight aircraft were launched after 1600, the lateness of the hour presumably ensuring that the aircraft went forward as launched and attacked as they came upon the enemy with only minimal coordination. The air group from one carrier was to claim no fewer than thirteen hits on one battleship, and when the day's tallies were assembled it was found that one battleship had been hit no fewer than twenty-two times and the other fifteen times, and seven of these hits were by torpedoes. At best, three of the thirteen Avengers committed to this 1600 attack were armed with torpedoes, and with such numbers the chances of recording any significant result against the *Hyuga* and *Ise* were slim. During these attacks, the last of which began at 1510, the *Hyuga* appears to have been hit once and the *Ise* on her port catapult.[271] One cruiser was reportedly left "hopelessly damaged," and aircraft from the *Langley*, presumably trying to emulate Kurita's ships, claimed that one Japanese destroyer disappeared as a result of a strafing attack, though there was no claim that the victim had been seen to sink.[272] In fact, these strikes, the efficiency of which drew adverse comment from Captain Ohmae Toshikazu, chief of staff to Ozawa in the *Oyodo*,[273] registered no more than very slight damage from near-misses and may have delayed certain Japanese units as they ran northward, but two night fighters from the *Essex* led the cruiser force to a group of three Japanese warships, the destroyers *Hatsutsuki* and the *Wakatsuki* and the destroyer escort *Kuwa*.[274] These had been detected at a range of some thirty-five miles beyond where the *Chitose* had been sunk. Some thirty minutes after sunset the American cruiser force established contact by radar at a range of seventeen miles (31,000 yards) with these Japanese ships and opened fire at 1851. With one Japanese warship to the north of the other two, the heavy cruisers sought to catch the more distant enemy, but even though the *Wichita* worked up thirty knots, the Japanese ship was beyond range by 1906. Of the other two Japanese ships, one, likewise, was able to draw beyond range as its consort, hit for the first time at 1911, sought to slow the pursuing Americans by a series of turns to threaten her pursuers and to shield herself in smoke. By 1929 three American destroyers moved forward with the expectation of mounting a torpedo attack, but it was not until 2012, by which time the *Hatsutsuki* had been slowed by hits, that this attack was executed at a range of 6,800 yards, but apparently without success.[275] The Japanese destroyer continued to return fire for more than twenty minutes but as her speed fell to ten knots the American warships closed and, with the aid of star shell, subjected her to a merciless short-range pounding. The *Porterfield* was ordered to finish her by torpedo and began to close at 2057, but before she could attack the *Hatsutsuki* had gone, sunk by explosion at 2059.[276]

Though the *Hatsutsuki* straddled the *Santa Fe* several times without hitting the American light cruiser, her dogged fight and the fact that the two other ships were able to escape commanded a certain American respect, and her sinking in effect marked the end of the battle off Cape Engaño. There were, however, three matters that remained to be played out in this northern battle area during the hours that remained to this day. The last phase of the fight between the *Hatsutsuki* and the American cruiser force was accompanied by American night aircraft detecting two groups of Japanese warships to the north, the nearer being at a range of nearly fifty miles. With these two groups assessed as making about twenty knots, it was clear that there was little chance of catching up with either of these groups during the hours of darkness. Accordingly, at 2150, some twenty minutes after it had been re-formed into cruise formation, the cruiser force turned back to the south and a rendezvous with the carriers and replenishment.[277]

At the same time Ozawa had turned back to the south. He had received a distress call from the *Hatsutsuki* at 1915 and turned his flagship *Oyodo*, the battleships *Hyuga* and *Ise*, and the destroyer *Shimotsuki* back, but for what purpose it is hard to discern because he was, in a curious way, similarly placed with the *Hatsutsuki* as Halsey had been with Kinkaid's formations some hours previously. There was nothing that Ozawa's collection of ships could do to provide support or cover for the *Hatsutsuki*, but Ozawa maintained a search in this general area until just before midnight when, without any form of contact other than with the *Wakatsuki*, which joined company, Ozawa turned for the north. Just before he did so, and in the only episode during the battle that involved American submarines, the *Jallao* sank the *Tama*. Left to her own devices after being damaged that morning, the *Tama* had been making her way to Amami-o-Shima. At 2004 the *Jallao*, on her first operational patrol, established radar contact at a range of 27,000 yards. After calling in the other two submarines in her pack, the *Atule* and *Pintado*, the *Jallao* ran ahead of the Japanese cruiser while the *Pintado* moved around to the north. After securing visual contact in brilliant moonlight, when the target was provisionally identified as a battleship, the *Jallao* submerged at 2242, and as range closed the *Tama* was correctly identified as a light cruiser and torpedo settings were adjusted accordingly. Unfortunately for the *Jallao*, however, problems with her torpedo doors meant she was only able to fire three torpedoes from her bow tubes, and one apparently detonated prematurely. The *Tama* turned toward the explosion while the *Jallao* turned to bring her stern tubes to bear, and at about 700 yards the *Tama* turned away, thereby lining herself up for another salvo, again of three torpedoes.[278] This time all three torpedoes hit, one between bow and bridge, one amidships, and the third near her after mast. Burning throughout her length and enveloped in a thick black pall of smoke, the *Tama* sank immediately.[279] While other submarines were involved in patrols and one, the *Halibut*, was involved in a somewhat bizarre incident that defies explanation and for a time was credited with having sunk the *Akitsuki*,[280] the *Tama* was the only Japanese warship sunk by an American submarine during the battle.

*   *   *

In the north, therefore, events unfolded according to script. Ozawa's formation played out its decoy role and Mitscher's carriers, in association with the light formation, completed its destruction with the sinking of its four carriers. In the center, as Halsey turned and came south, the events of the morning, the action off Samar between Kurita's force and Task Unit

77.4.3, represented a hard act to follow, yet in a perverse sense what was to follow was scarcely less remarkable. What was astonishing about this morning's battle action was not simply that this was the only occasion in history when a formation with carriers was taken under enemy fire but that no fewer than five of the six carriers that were subjected to the fire escaped destruction, and in an obvious sense nothing can stand comparison with this fact. The best comment on this fact was provided by the American formation commander:

> At 0925 my mind was occupied with dodging torpedoes when near the bridge I heard one of the signalmen yell, "Goddamit, boys, they're getting away!" I could not believe my eyes, but it looked as if the whole Japanese fleet was indeed retiring. However, it took a whole series of reports from circling planes to convince me. And still I could not get the fact to soak into my battle-numbed brain. At best, I had expected to be swimming by this time.[281]

That the American carrier formation was still intact, and operating its aircraft, was truly extraordinary, and clearly at the time Kurita called off his units, the Americans in the ships under attack were crossing off the minutes that remained to them. But what was to follow was scarcely less incredible, and divided into two. There were the series of events and decisions affecting Kurita's command which together resulted in first the turning back to the southwest, toward Leyte Gulf, and then a second turnaway that was ultimately to lead to Kurita setting his force on a course that was to lead to its passing through the San Bernardino Strait about 2140,[282] and the attacks on Task Unit 77.4.3 by *kamikaze* aircraft. The element of incredulity that attaches itself to the latter, to the *kamikaze* attacks, is obvious, but one would suggest it is accompanied and complemented by a simple fact of life that was no less significant and in an obvious sense more immediately important and relevant: American sailors who fought to live outfought Japanese airmen who died in order to fight.

In fact the first *kamikaze* attack materialized even as Kurita's units joined battle with the carriers of Task Unit 77.4.3. The day's first operations by the latter's sister formation, Task Unit 77.4.1, which was some 130 miles to the south, was directed against Japanese warships withdrawing from the Surigao Strait, but when word came of developments to the north, the four carriers of this formation began to recover and rearm their aircraft in readiness for attacks on Kurita's force. At 0736 the *Santee* began launching five Avengers and eight Wildcats, and four minutes later she was hit on the port side of her flight deck by an A6M2 Zeke from a group of five such aircraft, with three A6M5 fighter escorts, from Davao. Distracted by their own operations, the American ships had failed to detect the incoming attack until the last moment, but the *Santee* was to be fortunate. The Japanese aircraft was armed with only a single light bomb and the force of impact had been dissipated by the time the Japanese aircraft reached the hangar deck. Fires were caused but they failed to ignite a nearby pile of eight 1,000-lb. bombs. Within eleven minutes these fires had been brought under control, but at 0756 the *Santee* was shaken by a heavy underwater explosion amidships which caused flooding and a six-degree list to starboard. At the time, and even after her first dockyard inspection, it was believed that she had been damaged by the denotation of one of her depth charges which had been lost overboard as a result of the *kamikaze* hit, and it was not realized until after the war that the *Santee* had been hit by a torpedo from the submarine I. 56 which was deflected and exploded some yards from the ship. As it was, emergency repairs were completed by 0935, and at a cost of just forty-three casualties the *Santee* maintained her place on station.[283]

At the same time as the *Santee* was hit, both the *Petrof Bay* and *Sangamon* were narrowly missed by *kamikazes*, both aircraft being shot down as they tried to crash into these two escort carriers.[284] The fourth and last of the carriers in this formation, the *Suwannee*, was not so fortunate. Apparently her gunners shot down two Japanese aircraft and hit a third, but the latter still managed to hit the carrier. The aircraft tore a hole in the flight deck and its bomb ripped open a larger hole in the hangar deck, but within two hours repairs had been made sufficient to allow the carrier to fight off two more attacks.[285] By this time, however, what proved to be the main *kamikaze* course of the day had unfolded to the north.

This was delivered again by five aircraft, these operating from Mabalacat airfield, part of the Clark Field complex on Luzon, and was directed against Task Unit 77.4.3. One *kamikaze* aircraft clipped the *Kitkun Bay* and crashed into the sea.[286] Two of the aircraft that sought to attack the *Fanshaw Bay* were shot down, as was one of two that tried to attack the *White Plains*. The second, though hit, redirected its attention to the *St. Lo*, and at 1051 penetrated the flight deck and exploded in a hangar deck, setting off seven explosions of torpedoes and bombs that ripped open the entire flight deck and threw deck, elevator, and aircraft hundreds of feet into the air.[287] The carrier was engulfed in flames throughout her length, and after a series of explosions which must have blown out her bottom and caused her list to

port to immediately become a thirty-degree list to starboard, she sank by
the stern within thirty minutes, "leaving a cloud of dense black smoke to
mark her watery grave." That 754 survivors were recovered from the water,
from a crew of 860 officers and men, is perhaps surprising given the extent
of her damage and the rapidity with which she was lost.[288]

As the *St. Lo* fell astern of the formation, however, another Japanese
attack materialized, and this time the escort carriers were without any
screen because the *Butler, Dennis* and the *Raymond* were standing by the
stricken unit. Apparently this attack was conducted by fifteen Judy dive-
bombers and was intended to be conventional, but while most of the Judys
carried out their attacks and escaped, five deliberately chose to attempt
to crash into the American carriers. One was shot down just short of the
Kitkun Bay, parts of the crashed aircraft peppering the forecastle, but the
Kalinin Bay was hit by two of the four aircraft that attacked her. One of the
kamikazes crashed into the port side of the flight deck, setting off fires that
were quenched within five minutes, while the other hit and destroyed her
aft port stack. The damage was quite extensive, but it was neither serious
nor a problem in terms of continuing operations. She counted only five
dead among her sixty casualties.[289]

These attacks took place between 1050 and 1110, but by 1120, when the
St. Lo sank, the American carriers that had been hit or been subjected to
near-misses had their repairs in hand and the two formations that had been
attacked were in the process of being re-formed preparatory to their next
flying operations. Task Unit 77.4.1 proceeded northward in what proved
to be a vain attempt to contact and attack Kurita's formation, but nonetheless late that night effected a rendezvous with its sister formation before
turning back to the south.[290] Perhaps strangely in light of the subsequent
reputation gained by the *kamikazes*, this operational debut was limited in
its effect. Just one escort carrier was sunk, and only one of four units of
the southern carrier formation was damaged, and not seriously, while of
the four surviving carriers in the northern formation, the *Fanshaw Bay*
emerged untouched while the other three were able to shrug off their damage. Nonetheless, the fact was that a couple of handfuls of *kamikaze* aircraft
in two attacks staged over three hours inflicted almost as much loss and
damage on American formations as Kurita's force had registered in three
days, and a by-product of these attacks on the carriers was distraction and
lack of cover which resulted in two LSTs being sunk that afternoon by
conventional bombing attack.[291]

Nonetheless, Task Unit 77.4.3 was in effect finished with this battle, and the next day set course, via Mios Woendi in the Schouten Islands on 29 October, for Manus, where it arrived on 1 November. From there the *Fanshaw Bay, Kalinin Bay* and the *White Plains* made their way via Pearl Harbor to the San Diego navy yard, the latter two never returning to combat duty.[292] Task Unit 77.4.1 was not so fortunate; it was subjected to further *kamikaze* attack the next day, but the *Suwannee* alone was hit. She was hit by an aircraft that crashed into an Avenger on the forward elevator, and the resultant explosions accounted for another nine aircraft, but despite fires that took many hours to bring under control and having almost a quarter of her crew killed or wounded, the carrier was able to survive. However, at this point the *Santee* and *Suwannee* were detached, with the former proceeding to Manus, reached on 31 October, while the latter proceeded to Kossol Roads, in the Palaus. Between 28 October and 1 November she underwent emergency repairs sufficient to ensure that she reached Manus.[293] The *Petrof Bay* and *Sangamon* remained on station for another two days before they, too, returned to Manus. The *Sangamon, Santee* and the *Suwannee* then returned to the West Coast for repair and overhaul.[294]

The Japanese recourse to "special attack" tactics invites three comments. The first, to which reference has been made, is to note that such was Japanese inferiority in the air at this stage of the war that the use of *kamikaze* tactics represented not the best but the only hope of inflicting loss on the American enemy, the *Princeton* notwithstanding. The results on 25 October may have been modest, but the fact was that fifty-seven bombers, escorted by ninety-seven fighters, were committed to attacks on that day without recording a single hit.[295] Second, the Americans did not properly grasp the full significance of this development and for obvious reason. The effort was small-scale, and, of course, Allied ships had been hit by damaged Japanese aircraft before, and therefore the full and proper realization that what had happened that morning was new and deliberate was not immediately forthcoming. Third, with these attacks the initial *kamikaze* effort was over. The morning had opened with Onishi's 1st Air Fleet having just four units with a total of just thirteen aircraft assigned the *kamikaze* role, three units at Mabalacat and one at Cebu.[296] The first attack, against the escort carriers of Task Unit 77.4.1, was not staged by a *kamikaze* unit *per se* but was an improvised attack by a unit that deliberately made use of special attack tactics; it was not a unit that had been deliberately selected for this role. The second attack, which accounted for the *St. Lo,* was staged by a *kamikaze* unit, the *Shikishima Unit,* and the attack the next morning was conducted by the *Yamato Unit* from Cebu. The obvious question that attaches itself to their use is just what could have been reasonably expected of these units. With such numbers it was totally impossible for the *kamikazes* to ensure the success of Kurita, yet this seems to have been the expectation as self-justifying logic applied itself. As it was, the returning fighters claimed that one light carrier had been hit twice and sunk, one light carrier had been damaged, and a light cruiser had been sunk; this claim was broadcast from Tokyo.[297] Obviously, overstatement was not confined to Kurita's warships, but in real terms the point was that with the two attacks on the morning of 25 October this particular Japanese effort was spent, for the moment.

Thus the focus of attention in the final part of this chapter returns to Kurita and his battle formation off Samar after the turnaway at 0911. After this turnaway, Kurita steered a figure-eight course while gathering the various warships together, and it took his force two hours to re-form itself. Such a length of time, not far short of the length of time the Japanese warships had been in action, seems extraordinary but no doubt was at least in part the result of the Japanese destroyers presiding over the last rites of sinking American ships. There were also losses among the heavy cruisers, and the assignment of destroyers to rescue crews, that likewise served to slow the regrouping of Kurita's formation. When first hit and forced out of line just before 0900, the *Chikuma* and *Chokai* were simply left with no destroyers assigned to stand by them. At this stage of the battle the immediacy of the action against the American carrier force precluded such assignment, but once the pursuit was abandoned the *Fujinami* was detailed to stand by the *Chokai,* which sank within a matter of minutes, and the *Nowaki* was ordered to stand by the *Chikuma.* As the gathering of warships together neared completion, the *Suzuya* was attacked by aircraft, and while even the few accounts that set out these events cannot be reconciled, she incurred such damage that she was obliged to transfer her admiral—for the second time that morning—to the *Tone* at 1157, and thereafter began to settle. Accounts of what happened to her differ, but she was hit either by three torpedoes at about 1100 or by bombs around 1114 which set off an uncontrollable fire in the torpedo compartment which in turn set off the torpedoes.[298] When she was passed by aircraft from Task Unit 77.4.2 seeking out Kurita's force, she was listing so badly to starboard, with her main deck awash, that it was clear she was doomed, and she was not attacked.[299] At 1300, after Kurita had made his second and last turnaway of the day, the *Okinami* was ordered to sink her. She sank at 1322, the third and last of the Japanese heavy cruisers to be sunk this day, and thereafter the *Okinami*, with her survivors, rejoined.

In the meantime, at 1120 to be precise, Kurita, with his battle force now re-formed, set course to the southeast and Leyte Gulf.[300] It seems that Kurita's intention was to break into the Gulf and deal with whatever warships and transports were found there. *En route* at 1205 he so advised Combined Fleet headquarters,[301] but at 1148 an episode occurred that passed beyond the merely bizarre and which inadvertently must cast doubts upon this intention. The presence of a *Pennsylvania*-class battleship and four destroyers was reported almost due south of the *Yamato* and at a range of twenty-four miles,[302] but there was no attempt to verify this report and there was no attempt to close or to open fire. Given the relative slowness of the *Pennsylvania*-class battleships and the advantage of range of the *Yamato*'s main armament, the failure to engage seems as odd as the fact that this sighting was still being recorded as undisputed fact in one Japanese history even in 1956.[303] The truth is that the sighting was mere imagination. One would have thought that an action against such an isolated and unsupported American battleship would have been precisely the type of action the Japanese sought at this stage of proceedings, but at 1236 Kurita turned his formation back to the north,[304] abandoning any intention of entering Leyte Gulf and indicating that the formation would seek battle with the enemy formation reportedly off northeast Samar.

Herein lies the final act of the two personal issues that arose from this day, because it was this decision that marked the end of the battle. There were to be a series of attacks on Kurita's formation by carrier aircraft, from both the escort carriers of Task Group 77.4 and the carriers of McCain's Task Group 38.1, but these achieved nothing of any consequence though there is no doubt that they served to confirm for Kurita the wisdom of his decision to turn back and set course for the San Bernardino Strait. Just one short gunnery action remained to be fought in this central sector after this time, and the focus of historical attention inevitably has concentrated upon Kurita's 1236 decision.

※   ※   ※

Kurita's force was less than two hours from the beachheads on Leyte Gulf and had the advantage of position in standing to the east of any American formations, including Task Unit 77.4.3 and Oldendorf's battle force, that might be encountered, but the decision not to proceed, to turn back, seemingly was occasioned by one consideration. This was Kurita's belief that his force could not accomplish more than it had thus far and the additional calculation that with the Americans using the Tacloban airfield his force would be subjected to mounting and irresistible attack. The basis of this calculation, inevitably, had to be the belief that a real victory had been won, and the fact was, to borrow a memorable comment on which it is hard to improve: "outfought by pygmies, he yet thought he had conquered giants."[305] Yet, interestingly, Kurita's action report notes that while his formation had been in contact with an enemy force that mustered six or seven carriers accompanied by many cruisers and destroyers, three or four carriers, including one of the *Enterprise* class, two heavy cruisers, and some destroyers were deemed to have been "definitely sunk."[306] One is left to wonder the pedigree of the two or three carriers that were not of the *Enterprise* class, and it is perhaps worth noting, *en passant*, that at this stage of the war the *Enterprise* class consisted of just one carrier, the nameship. It is easy to miss the point that Kurita in this report admitted that in an action lasting two hours two or three enemy carriers had escaped, but if what Kurita claimed really was the extent of success, then it is difficult to see the basis for the belief that a real victory, one that would materially improve Japan's political or strategic position, had been won. It is even more difficult to see the basis of Kurita's claim that the issue he faced was "a question of what good I could do in the Gulf,"[307] since only there might he find carrier formations the destruction of which would justify the annihilation of his force. But this whole issue is befuddled by the claim that in the situation in which he found himself:

> The wiser course was deemed to be to cross the enemy's anticipation by striking at his task force which had been reported (to the north). We believed that to turn about . . . in search of this (force) would prove to be to our advantage in subsequent operations. Having so determined, we turned northward.[308]

By the least exacting standard, this claim does not make sense.

Any careful consideration of Kurita's decisions would seem to indicate that the major reasons for the turnaway at 0911 were the state of disorganization then enveloping his formation and the belief that the enemy carriers were not being closed. That the *Tone* had closed to only 10,000 yards was not relevant when set alongside Kurita's belief that the range had not been closed. As a consequence, the pursuit was abandoned, and after 1120, as Kurita's formation headed southwest toward Leyte Gulf, it could see American aircraft taking off and landing on carriers that were beyond the horizon; these carriers, however, were not pursued. Kurita then abandoned the intention to move into the Gulf, where the enemy's—and the Japanese—freedom of maneuver would be limited, in order to move against an enemy formation reported to have been about ninety miles to the north almost three hours previously. This enemy formation would be on the open sea with unencumbered freedom of maneuver while the Japanese formation's advance to contact was certain to be tracked by carrier aircraft from "beyond the horizon." Admittedly Kurita clearly pinned considerable hope upon shore-based aircraft inflicting significant damage on the force he sought to engage, and he made a signal requesting such strikes at 1150, a full forty-six minutes before he turned his force northward.[309] But if this sequence is interesting and indeed perhaps significant, the overall intent must be considered hopelessly flawed; a very considerable amount of hope is no basis for an operational plan.

In seeking to explain Kurita's decision there are two basic problems. The first, simply, is Kurita's own account of proceedings; it has been noted that he himself, when asked why he turned his formation away,

> had difficulty answering the question in two days of interrogation by American naval officers. He gave his reasons, to be sure—perhaps too many reasons. But he left enigma as thick as a smoke screen in the wake of some of them.[310]

The second, no less simply, is that these American officers were looking for an answer, and probably just one answer and even more probably one answer that made sense. It is quite possible, perhaps even likely, that there was no real answer, and certainly not one single and simple answer, and it was an answer at variance with formal logic.

Kurita himself stated that he was determined to lead his formation into Leyte Gulf until "the second bombing attack," which one of the earliest accounts suggests began around 1140 and was conducted by aircraft from all three American escort carrier formations but primarily from Task Unit 77.4.2.[311] The problem with such reckoning, however, is that this attack began at 1240 and therefore could not have been a reason for that turnaway. In any event, though as many as thirty-seven Avengers, with a similar number of Wildcats, were committed to this attack, it is difficult to discern why it was important given that no Japanese warship sustained any real damage, notwithstanding the unsubstantiated allusions of the U.S. Navy's official history.[312]

It seems more than likely that Kurita's memory was at fault and that he confused the timing and sequence of events. It also seems more than likely that what he meant was not that this was the attack that led him to turn away, but that it was at this point, as a result of the cumulative effect of successive attacks, none of which possessed singular significance, that he was led to abandon his recast intention. These attacks would have been those conducted by the escort carriers after the 0911 turnaway, but even this interpretation of events does not address one matter. While Kurita was marking time gathering his units he received signals that informed him of Kinkaid's signals in clear begging Halsey for support.[313] By an inverted process of logic, Kurita appears to have taken this to mean that his force could expect to come under sustained attack by Halsey's carrier aircraft. Kincaid's desperation seems to have had no effect in terms of seeking to complete an unfinished task, and if indeed Kurita's force was to come under sustained attack—and knowledge of Kinkaid's request does pose the question of what Kurita thought his force had engaged that morning—then closing on the enemy was perhaps a suitable means of defense.

What compounds problems of explanation and interpretation is that Kurita seemed unperturbed by the prospect of abandoning his primary mission, but at different times indicated that in turning back to the north it was his intention to seek out the reported enemy formation or to effect a rendezvous with Ozawa's formation. The least that could be said about these is that the first and third do beggar belief. The abandonment of the primary mission was at best questionable, but the abandonment of the primary mission in order to go to the assistance of a formation that had been deliberately sacrificed as the means of ensuring that Kurita could discharge the primary mission presents real problems of comprehension. In addition, the abandonment of the primary mission because the American "landing had been confirmed and I (Kurita) therefore considered it not so important as it would have been before," i.e., the forewarned transports would have cleared the area, should invite the obvious rejoinder: the American landing had been confirmed before Kurita's force sailed from Brunei Bay. The implications of Kurita's using this argument are considerable indeed.

*   *   *

During post-war interrogation Kurita also stated that he desired "to be at the San Bernardino Strait at sunset to get through and as far to the west as possible during the night."[314] This is perhaps the only statement by Kurita on the whole vexed question of turnaway and intention with which there can be no serious quarrel, but the obvious question that emerges is when this calculation first intruded upon Kurita's deliberations. It would appear that Kurita settled on this course as a direct result of the attack by aircraft from McCain's Task Group 38.1, to which previous reference has been made, even though this attack, involving nineteen Avengers, thirty-three Helldivers, and forty-six Hellcats, resulted in just a single hit on the *Tone* by a bomb, which failed to detonate.[315] The Japanese may have been able to emerge all but unscathed from this attack because the Avengers, operating at extreme range, had to be armed with bombs rather than torpedoes. Two of the Avengers that were on flight decks and armed with torpedoes were not allowed to take part in this strike despite the representations of their crews.[316]

One would suggest that notwithstanding its lack of results, this attack reflected well upon Task Group 38.1. Before it was staged, McCain, ignoring all signals security procedures, sought information about airfields on Leyte and the availability of flight decks with Task Group 77.4 for his aircraft, and it was a measure of the extreme range that the *Hancock* dispatched twelve Helldivers and only three were able to get back to their ship while two ditched short of Task Group 38.1. Four landed with the escort carriers of Task Unit 77.4.2 and two landed at Tacloban, one being written off in the process. The twelfth and last of these dive-bombers was shot down. Overall, three aircraft from this attack were shot down and nine proceeded to Leyte and its airstrips.[317]

The point about this attack is that it was the first in a series of attacks on Kurita's force that were staged throughout the remaining hours of daylight by aircraft from both Task Groups 38.1 and 77.4. This first strike was improvised and not concentrated, the problems of range and fuel forcing the aircraft to attack immediately upon contact, but after another two hours' high-speed closing, the carriers of Task Group 38.1 launched a second strike that was not quite so pressed in such matters. The carriers began to launch their aircraft at 1245, before the first strike had reached and attacked the enemy, and these aircraft numbered thirteen Avengers, twenty dive-bombers, and twenty-seven fighters. Unfortunately the aircraft from this second strike became lost and when finally directed to the Japanese force by the carriers of Task Group 77.4 the groups had become separated from one another and their attacks were not coordinated. Together the two strikes conducted by Task Group 38.1 claimed four hits on the *Yamato*, another four on either the *Haruna* or *Kongo*, a single hit on the *Nagato*, perhaps five hits on one or more unidentified battleships, and a number of hits on several of the cruisers and destroyers,[318] but in terms of damage and loss inflicted on the enemy this second attack represented no improvement over its predecessor. The subsequent attacks by aircraft from the escort carriers likewise registered no real results. There were three sets of attacks between 1600 and 1723, but while some of the twenty-six Avengers (in the company of twenty-four Wildcats) from Task Unit 77.4.2 in the last strike were armed with torpedoes,[319] the fact that most of the attacking bombers were armed with only general-purpose bombs and rockets meant there was never any real chance of the aircraft conducting anything more than harassing attacks. The only result was a series of near-misses which split some bilges and caused many of the Japanese ships to trail oil as they headed for the San Bernardino Strait.[320] By this stage of proceedings only the destroyer *Yukikaze* had not been damaged in some way, but she was always thus. With the hard-earned reputation of being a lucky ship, she emerged from a series of actions throughout the war unscathed and was to remain so until 30 July 1945 when she was mined, but not sunk, in the Sea of Japan off Miyazu.[321]

The events to the north off Cape Engaño had still to run their course, but with Kurita leading his formations back to the San Bernardino Strait, the naval battle for the Philippines was over but for one action. The following days were to see a series of operations as American aircraft took the tide of battle to Kurita's force as it moved through the Visayans, and there was the hunting of various fugitives, most obviously in the south. The one action that remained was to involve one last Japanese destroyer and was to be fought just after midnight off the San Bernardino Strait, but before considering this action and drawing this chapter to its close, one other point may be made.

Any consideration of the American carrier operations against Kurita's force during the afternoon of 25 October should reveal one point, namely that its whereabouts was known throughout the hours of daylight. It was found again at 2140 as it entered the Strait in single column, this time by an aircraft from the light carrier *Independence*.[322] But with the last attack by escort carrier aircraft being made against Kurita's force in the last full hour of daylight when it was off northeast Samar, the impartial observer is left to wonder why perhaps one strike mission was not mounted by Task Group 38.2 during this afternoon. Any careful consideration of their respective positions and courses would suggest that after 1500 the carriers of Task Group 38.2 were nearer to Kurita's force than were the carriers of Task Group 38.1, which, after committing nearly 150 aircraft to two strikes, was in no position to launch a third, not in the hours of daylight that remained and with the welcoming decks of Task Group 77.4's escort carriers and airstrips on Leyte no longer in position to afford a home away from home. But even allowing for refueling and the need to have the carriers of Task Group 38.2 in a position to cover the battle force that had been directed to the south, the fact that Task Group 38.2 never undertook any search and strike operations on this afternoon is perhaps surprising, and one is left to wonder, with all the advantages of hindsight, if Halsey would not have been better served to have left Task Group 38.2 in the north, to deal with what remained of Ozawa's formation, and to have gone south with Task Groups 38.3 and 38.4, one of which could certainly have undertaken one strike operation, perhaps even two, during these final hours of battle. As it was, Halsey can hardly be faulted for leaving two carrier groups in the north to deal with Ozawa's formation while going south with one, though the fact that he divided his battle force does raise two very interesting points. Halsey's embrace of the principle of concentration of force does not sit easily alongside the division of the battleships and an arrangement that left four battleships wholly without any cruisers and destroyers as screen, and just what the advanced force of just two battleships, three light cruisers, and eight destroyers was expected to do against an enemy that numbered four battleships presents a problem of understanding. These two battleships, members of the *Iowa* class, represented the best battleships built by any nation, the *Yamato* and *Musashi* not excluded, and their firepower, by virtue of their radar and ranging equipment, was massively superior to any other battleships, the *North Carolina* and *South Dakota* classes excepted. One can well believe that the *Iowa* and *New Jersey* would not have encountered too many problems with the *Haruna* and *Kongo*, but against four Japanese battleships, the obvious question presents itself. It is perhaps not idle to speculate what might have happened had Halsey sent all six of his battleships forward without losing time refueling their cruisers and destroyers. Such a force, making perhaps twenty-five knots, certainly would have arrived off the San Bernardino Strait ahead of Kurita's formation, and in those circumstances it is difficult to resist a conclusion that, *prima facie,* seems arrogantly overweening:

> Apart from the accidents common to naval warfare, there is every reason to believe that (such a force) would have crossed Kurita's T and completed the destruction of Centre Force.[323]

The corollary is easily missed: if Halsey had sent the battleships forward then Kurita's turnaway at 1236 would have availed his force nothing. Ah! The mighty "ifs" accumulate. . . .

Midnight found Task Group 34.5 steaming south at twenty-eight knots and some forty miles from the San Bernardino Strait, and by this time the realization that despite having steamed about 300 miles north and then the same distance south they had missed both sets of enemy forces must have been impressing itself on Halsey and indeed all the officers and men of the ships in this formation. At about this time, however, one of the search aircraft from the *Independence* had a radar contact with what she reported as a destroyer—in fact the *Nowaki*—and indicated that this ship might be off the entrance to the Strait at or about 0100. The destroyer *Lewis Hancock* was ordered forward to serve as radar picket, and at 0028, some three minutes after the formation turned to the southeast, she reported a contact, almost due south and at a range of 29,000 yards, with a ship heading to the west at a speed of twenty knots.[324] The formation's three light cruisers, along with two destroyers,[325] were detached with orders to deal with the enemy unit, with the *Iowa* and *New Jersey* and the remaining destroyers turning north to clear the area. The cruisers, apparently undetected by an unsuspecting enemy, closed to a range of 17,000 yards before opening fire at 0054, the destroyers restraining themselves until the range had fallen to 11,000 yards. About 0059 the American cruisers checked their fire; the Japanese ship had slowed to about thirteen knots and by this time was illuminated by a dull red glow. The cruisers resumed fire and by 0103 the enemy unit was in flames from bow to stern and was dead in the water. With the cruisers pulling clear, the *Miller* and *Owen* went forward, and at a range of about 4,400 yards, the latter fired a half-salvo of five torpedoes, all of which seem to have missed. The two destroyers then closed and opened rapid fire at little more than point-blank range until at 0132 the Japanese ship suffered a massive explosion that sent debris hundreds of feet into the air and lit up the entire battle area. As the flames died, the two American destroyers resumed fire, to what purpose is unclear, until at 0135 there was a second explosion after which the enemy disappeared from American radar screens.[326] The American destroyers rejoined their formation.

One of the peculiarities of military accounting is that armies lose men and navies lose ships. The Japanese unit was the destroyer *Nowaki*, and in one way her fate was similar to that of the *Hatsutsuki*, which had been sunk some four hours earlier. The latter, along with the *Wakatsuki*, had rescued a total of 866 officers and men from the *Zuikaku*[327] and may well have had seven hundred, perhaps eight hundred, men aboard. The *Nowaki* had been detached from Kurita's command to stand by the *Chikuma* and never rejoined. With a crew of about 300 officers and men, she may well have had perhaps eleven hundred sailors packed into her when caught by the American units. In separate actions, both the *Hatsutsuki* and *Nowaki* were lashed by protracted fire, torn apart by a hail of high-explosive hatred. God knows of the scenes on board those two destroyers. We, fortunately, do not.

CHAPTER SEVEN

THE NAVAL BATTLE
FOR THE PHILIPPINES

The Postscript,
26 October–30 November 1944

HISTORICALLY, BATTLE, WHETHER on land or at sea, has possessed three terms of reference: it has been fought in line of sight, at very short range, and within the hours of daylight of a single day. When making such a definition, the exceptions that prove the rule immediately and forcefully present themselves. Battles do not unfold with due observation of a twenty-four-hour schedule, and history is littered with battles that have lasted more than a day. There are naval battles that have lasted more than a day, but they have been rare, as indeed has been the naval battle of annihilation. Any casual acquaintance with naval history would note that in the Age of Sail, naval battles between fleets were few, and overwhelming success seldom attended such actions. Trafalgar, for example, is generally considered to be the greatest of British naval victories and its place in history is secure, but at the 1805 battle the French and Spanish fleets together mustered thirty-three line-of-battle ships, of which eighteen were taken, with eleven reaching the safety of Cádiz. The extent of the British victory in this action can be gauged by reference to other great British naval victories. At the Glorious First of June in 1794, which was a running fight that extended over four days, the French lost seven of thirty ships of the line; at the battle of the Saints in 1782, the French lost seven of twenty-nine ships of the line; and at Quiberon Bay in 1759, seven of twenty-one. Battles such as Tsushima, in May 1905, were the exception in that this battle was a battle of annihilation, but, without in any way denigrating the Japanese achievement off the Donkey's Ears, one would suggest that Tsushima was not a fleet action. It was a battle between a fleet and a collection of ships, and the overwhelming nature of the Japanese victory reflected this disparity.

The historical perspective is important because it serves to illustrate the significance of 25 October, specifically in terms of losses. At day's end, stretched conveniently to include the sinking of the *Nowaki*, the *Kaigun* had lost one fleet and three light carriers, two battleships, four heavy cruisers, one light cruiser, and six destroyers to add to the losses of the previous two days, and this bare statement of losses does not include three cruisers grievously damaged and the destroyers that had been detached to attend to these and the survivors from sunken ships. The extent and significance of these losses may be measured against the total of four carriers, seven battleships, fourteen heavy and seven light cruisers, thirty-one destroyers, and four destroyer escorts with the four formations with which the Japanese gave battle. But when this battle ended is quite another matter.

The battle of Leyte Gulf is generally afforded the dates of 23–26 October 1944,[1] while the single date of 25 October is generally recognized to be the anniversary of the battle. The claims of this day cannot be diminished in any way. The starting line of 23 October is obvious in terms of the action in the Palawan Passage, but one would suggest the previous day is perhaps more relevant in terms of the deployment that led to this episode and the battle overall. One would suggest that the point of ending should be marked by continuity of losses among the formations that fought the battle. For this latter reason one would suggest that the proper date for the end of this battle is 28 October, when the U.S. destroyer escort *Eversole* and the Japanese submarine I. 45 were sunk, the former by the latter.[2] Losses had been taken by Japanese units over each of the previous three days, but 29 October—when the *John A. Johnson* became the first American merchantman sunk by a Japanese submarine during 1944[3]—was the first day in seven when no units from the various formations that had fought the main actions that go under the name of Leyte Gulf were lost. It was also the first day American carrier formations were not involved in action, having withdrawn from the battle area.

Thus this account of the naval battle for the Philippines has been afforded the dates of 22–28 October 1944 and will follow the course of events over the three days after 25 October at least in terms of sinkings. The follow-up phase of the battle is not to be lightly dismissed, yet in many accounts of proceedings is afforded cursory treatment, as indeed are many of the events of the second half of 25 October, the Cape Engaño action included. But the point about this action was its relevance in terms of what it provided the Americans. If one looks at such battles as Trafalgar or Jutland, and even more contentiously Midway, the victor emerged from these battles with nothing that was not previously within its grasp. British command of the sea was neither diminished nor augmented by the victories of 1805 and 1916. The British came into possession of nothing they did not have before these battles were fought; it merely took eight years in one case and thirty months in the other for the finality of victory to be properly realized. Midway is more difficult in terms of historical interpretation, not least because of public requirement for "the decisive battle" or "the turning point." Wars of many years' duration do not have decisive battles, and one single battle never possesses singular importance in terms of Fortune and her changing sides. Midway is best seen as one battle, the most important single battle, in a series of actions fought between May and November 1942 that, along with other matters such as time and distance, resulted in the initiative changing hands. After Midway the initiative was like a gun lying in the street; it was there for either side to pick up and use. But it was to take a whole series of actions, between warships, between warships and submarines, between aircraft, and between aircraft and warships to complete the process, and the Japanese defeat was not simply one of losses. It embraced a deepening disorder in terms of the breakdown of formations and the commitment of shipping on a scale that could not be sustained. The Japanese could not sustain their effort in the lower Solomons after mid-November 1942, but their defeat, while obviously marked by their losses in the first and second naval battles of Guadalcanal, was the result of the coming together of different aspects of defeat.

Leyte was different in one respect. Note has already been taken of the strangest aspects of this battle, namely that it was the greatest naval battle of the war and that it was fought after the issue of victory and defeat at sea, and in the war generally, had been decided. But even when the issue of victory and defeat has been resolved, battles remain to be fought and victories have to be won, because success is not commanded. Leyte was part of this process, but in its winning the Americans came into possession of one aspect of victory seldom afforded real consideration because it defies ready definition: position. The American naval victory, coming with the securing of positions on Leyte itself that meant that victory on the island was merely a matter of time and the only question was at what price, placed the Americans in a situation whereby they could take the tide of war into and through the Visayans to Luzon, and in so doing place themselves astride Japanese lines of communication between the southern resources area and the home islands. The calculation that had been so important in shaping the Japanese decision to seek battle—that the loss of the island group would represent a defeat virtually indistinguishable from an invasion and conquest of the home islands—was correct.

For the Americans, there was no single moment of advantage, no point in time when the various aspects of victory came together, though in one sense the sortie of the carrier force into the South China Sea in January 1945 after the landings in Lingayen Gulf does see the various pieces of the victorious jigsaw falling into place. In that month, all forms of Allied action and natural and unknown causes accounted for eighteen Japanese naval and sixteen military freighters and transports of 68,038 and 65,227 tons respectively, and seventy-two merchantmen of 229,313 tons. Of these totals, twenty of the service vessels of 98,622 tons and forty-four merchant-men of 158,105 tons were sunk in the southern resources areas, primarily by carrier aircraft. The latter accounted for seven naval and six army ships of 33,266 tons and 36,830 tons, plus thirty-seven merchantmen—twenty-two on a single day—of 131,949 tons. The significance of such loss for a nation that ended 1944 with just 2,842,000 tons of shipping but needed some ten million tons to meet its pre-war import needs requires little elaboration, and this makes no allowance for the fact that on 31 December 1944 about 800,000 tons of Japanese shipping was not in service.

The process whereby, in the aftermath of battle, the Americans moved into and through the Philippines rightly forms part of the follow-up phase of the battle of Leyte Gulf. In the battle itself the Japanese fleet was worsted and reduced to a state that denied it the means of offering continuing resistance worthy of the name. Before and after the battle, the American carrier force stripped the Philippines of air cover and as a result the Americans were able to move directly against escorts, minesweepers and patrol vessels, and service and merchant shipping on a scale and at a tempo unprecedented in the Pacific war. In terms of sinkings in a single day, the attack on Truk was never equaled, and 17 February 1944 remained the most destructive single day of the war in terms of service and merchant shipping, but the point was that the performance of January 1945 was never repeated and for obvious reason. After January 1945 the Japanese had so few ships that what were available were primarily concentrated on local routes, specifically from Manchoutikuo, and the Allied move against Okinawa in late March 1945 closed the shipping links between Japan and the resources area for which she had gone to war.

Certainly the follow-up phase of this battle extends through the middle of November 1944, the time of the American carrier raids over Manila Bay, and should properly include the sinking of the battleship *Kongo* and destroyer *Urakaze* by the submarine *Sealion* off northwest Formosa in the early hours of 21 November.[4] The link between this sinking and the battle lies in the paucity of the protection afforded the *Kongo*, *Nagato* and the *Yamato* when they sailed from Brunei on 16 November for home waters. Such was the extent of Japanese losses, overall and not just in the October battle, that these three battleships had just the light cruiser *Yahagi* and four destroyers in company. But chronological neatness suggests that the follow-up phase should cover the whole of November, not least in order to return to the point made in the first chapter, the fact that with aircraft and submarines now released from fleet operations and ranging over and around the Philippines almost at will, the Americans in November 1944 inflicted almost as much loss on the Japanese as they had in the previous month. In October 1944 the *Kaigun* lost sixty-three warships of 347,222 tons and a total of 118 service and merchant ships of a staggering 478,489 tons. In November 1944 the *Kaigun* actually lost one more warship than in October, but the tonnage loss, 224,429 tons, reflected not just the loss of the *Kongo*, the 17,500-ton escort carrier *Shinyo*, and two heavy cruisers, but, on 29 November, the greatest single loss of the entire war, the sinking of the fleet carrier *Shinano* by the submarine *Archer-fish*. Losses among service and merchant shipping in November 1944 totaled ninety-eight ships of 414,591 tons. The following month, when Japanese losses totaled thirty-five warships of 61,520 tons and forty-five service and merchant ships of 177,685 tons, represented a slackening of pace after the massive successes of the previous two months and a gathering of American strength before the renewal of a major offensive effort with the new year.

The follow-up phase of the battle of Leyte Gulf thus divides into two parts, the first, 26–29 October, being the immediate aftermath of the main actions, in which time the Americans completed the immediate victory through the sinking of the light cruisers *Abukuma* and *Noshiro* and the destroyer *Hayashimo* on the 26th, and of the destroyers *Fujinami* and *Shiranui* on the 27th. As noted elsewhere, on the first of these two days, 26 October, as the Japanese sought to bring reinforcements to the island, American carrier aircraft accounted for the light cruiser *Kinu*, the destroyer *Uranami*, and LSM T. 102 off Ormoc in western Leyte. In addition, the official U.S. accounts indicate that the Japanese lost three submarines at this time. After having lost the I. 54 to the destroyer escort *Richard M. Rowell* from the screen of Task Unit 77.4.1 in a position some seventy miles east of Surigao in northeast Mindanao, on the morning of 24 October, the Japanese were to lose the I. 46 and then the I. 26 and I. 45. The first was noted as missing on the 27th and the other two on the following day. The cause of the I. 46's loss has never been established. It has been assumed that the I. 45 was sunk in a position some 120 miles northeast of Surigao on the morning of the 28th by the destroyer escort *Whitehurst* after the Japanese submarine had sunk the *Eversole,* and that the I. 26 was sunk in roughly the same position that afternoon by the *Gridley* and *Helm,* destroyers in the screen of Task Group 38.4.[5] The second part of follow-up operations, 30 October–30 November, was punctuated by the main carrier operations of 11, 13–14, 19, and 25 November that were primarily directed against warships and shipping in the Visayans and off northwest Luzon. These attacks exacted a major toll of Japanese warships—two light cruisers, eight destroyers, two destroyer-transports, one minesweeper, and five landing ships—but the point was that this was part of an offensive effort directed against Japanese warships, service, and merchant shipping throughout the Philippines that involved submarines from bases in both the central Pacific and Australia, land- and carrier-based aircraft, and, at the very end of November 1944, American warships which had presented themselves on the "wrong"—that is, western—side of Leyte. The American carrier aircraft provided perhaps the most important single dimension of this assault on Japanese warships and shipping, but the real point was that this assault represented the coming together of different efforts against an enemy stripped of virtually every means of defense, while the movement of American warships around to Ormoc Bay provided notice of the American intention, and ability, to move into the central and western Philippines.

On the morning of 26 October, the main American naval effort took two forms. First, with Task Groups 38.3 and 38.4 ordered to replenish themselves from the oilers in 16° 10' North 129° 30' East after turning back from the north,[6] Task Groups 38.1 and 38.2 effected a rendezvous at 0500 before beginning to launch their first strike of the day one hour later. The two formations were under McCain's command, and he was determined to mount successive strikes from the earliest possible time and to send the initial strike force in the direction of Mindoro.[7] These calculations were based upon the realization that Kurita's force would be within striking range briefly at best and that it was essential to find and make the first strikes as soon after first light as possible. But it was not until 0810 that Kurita's force was found in the Tablas Strait approaching Semirara Island. A second strike was immediately flown off, but it was not until 1245 that a third strike could be mounted.

Second, the escort carriers of Task Group 77.4, despite the trials and tribulations of the previous day, mounted a dawn reconnaissance, and while the initial American hope and expectation was that contact might be re-established with the Japanese forces that had withdrawn from the Surigao Strait, soon after sunrise two American scout aircraft came across the light cruiser *Kinu*, the destroyer *Uranami*, and four transports.[8] These had collected some 2,000 troops of the 30th Infantry Division from Cagayan, in northern Mindanao, and had safely delivered them to Ormoc just before dawn that morning. Then, sailing from Ormoc at about 0500, they had sought to put distance between themselves and American aircraft as they set course via the Visayan Sea for Coron Bay and an oiler. For reasons which are not immediately clear but which seemingly concerned themselves with the mounting of combat air patrol, close support for the forces on Leyte, and the search to the south, the morning passed with no American strike, and it was not until around noon that American aircraft began a series of attacks by bombers armed only with light general-purpose bombs and rockets. The initial target was the *Uranami*, and she was undone by a series of near-misses and sank at about 1224. The *Kinu* was caught around 1300 by a hit that wrecked her steering, but it was not until 1730 that she sank.[9] One of the landing ships, the T. 102, was also sunk, but the other transports escaped with one, the T. 10, having rescued survivors from the two warships.[10] The cost of this success was borne by escort carrier *Suwannee*, which was hit by a *kamikaze* about noon. The Japanese were to claim that three *kamikaze* aircraft from the Yamato Unit on Cebu penetrated the combat air patrol, two of them hitting a carrier that was "definitely sunk" and the third hitting a carrier that was not.[11] In reality, the *Suwannee* was hit by a Zeke that crashed into an Avenger that had just landed, the resultant explosion engulfing nine other aircraft. Though fires raged for several hours before being brought under control, the *Suwannee* was fortunate that depth charges burned but did not detonate,[12] but with 245 killed, wounded, and missing, she was taken off station at the end of the day. Task Unit 77.4.1 withdrew to Kossol Roads on 28 October, then sailed for Manus on 1 November. After five days of repairs, the *Suwannee* then sailed for the Puget Sound navy yard via Pearl Harbor.[13]

The attacks by aircraft from Task Groups 38.1 and 38.2 thus straddled the efforts of the escort carriers, but for all the numbers that were sent against Kurita's force—a total of 174 aircraft from Task Group 38.1 and 83 from Task Group 38.2, only slightly less than the total number of aircraft committed two days earlier to the battle in the Sibuyan Sea—the results were disappointingly meager. After initial contact by scout aircraft between 0750 and 0800, the attack groups were directed to Kurita's formation as it left the Sibuyan Sea on a southerly course off northwest Panay. The *Nagato* obtained radar contact with these aircraft at around 0825, and the first attack of the day took place between 0834 and 0900.[14] The *Yamato* was twice hit by bombs in the bow and was fairly extensively damaged—Koyanagi, Kurita's chief of staff, was badly wounded by splinters—but the light cruiser *Noshiro* took a torpedo in one of her starboard boiler rooms and lost way. Her admiral transferred immediately to the destroyer *Hamanami*, but the *Noshiro* was caught in the second attack and hit by one bomb on one of her forward turrets. Progressive flooding and perhaps near-misses in this second attack caused her to sank at 1113 off Batbatan Island; the destroyer *Akishimo* rescued 328 of her crew of 730 officers and men.[15] At this same time the straggler *Hayashimo*, having taken on fuel from the *Okinami* in order to reach Coron Bay where a tanker was waiting, was attacked by American carrier aircraft and hit by a single bomb that must have wrecked her engine rooms or steering. She was beached on Semirara Island, south of Mindoro, and was used by American aircraft for bombing practice for the next six weeks.[16] B-24 Liberators from Morotai also attacked some of Kurita's ships west of Panay and claimed a series of hits on the *Nagato*, *Kongo*, and an unidentified light cruiser. Neither of these two battleships was hit, and whether these heavy bombers contributed to the sinking of the *Nishiro* is not clear but seems unlikely.[17]

Also on this day, the battleship *California* and light cruiser *Louisville* were hit but not seriously damaged by *kamikaze* aircraft off Leyte,[18] while the *Abukuma*, which had been subjected to a series of attacks by land-based bombers on the previous day, was sunk. She and the *Ushio* sailed for Coron from Dapitan at 0605 but were sighted by an army bomber and after 0918 were subjected to three attacks by a total of forty-four B-24 Liberators from the 5th Air Force based on Noemfoor and B-25 Mitchells from the 13th Air Force based on Biak. The first resulted in a single hit that set off a number of fires, but the second, delivered at low level in a manner not unlike what had happened more than eighteen months previously in the Bismarck Sea, resulted in two more hits which resulted in the *Abukuma*'s loss of steering and speed. The third attack resulted in no hits, but with fires spreading, power was lost. At 1100 the *Ushio* was ordered alongside and at 1128 the order to abandon ship was passed. The *Abukuma* sank at 1242,[19] and with her sinking there remained just three of the ships that had been members of the task force that had conducted the raid on the U.S. Pacific Fleet at Pearl Harbor in December 1941.[20]

These actions were random. The Japanese ships that were attacked were targets of opportunity on a day when there was no pattern to operations other than the pursuit of Japanese formations as they came through the Visayans. But a certain order was to be brought to proceedings the next day, and primarily as a result of three developments. First, most Japanese formations moved beyond the range of American carrier aircraft in the course of 26 October, with the result that the next day the toll exacted by these aircraft was modest. Second, on 26 October, with Task Unit 77.4.3 somewhat the worse for wear but before the troubles of Task Unit 77.4.1 manifested themselves, Kincaid asked Halsey to provide combat air patrol for the escort carriers. Third, even as Japanese formations moved clear of the battle area, the commitment to reinforce and supply forces on Leyte had to be maintained. The result was that even as Task Group 38.1 was ordered for a second time to withdraw to Ulithi and Task Group 38.3 was also ordered to retire, with the other two carrier groups obliged to remain on station, the focus of American attention after 27 October was correspondingly reduced. On this day, 27 October, with Task Group 38.2 refueling, aircraft from task Group 38.3 registered their last successful attack before withdrawal. The *Fujinami*, packed with survivors from the *Chokai*, was sunk off Mindoro[21] while the *Shiranui*, after reaching Coron, was ordered to return to rescue survivors from the *Kinu* but was caught and sunk in the Sibuyan Sea, just to the east of Tabias, by aircraft from the *Essex*.[22]

The sinking of the *Fujinami* and *Shiranui* were the last losses sustained by Japanese formations in this battle. Kurita's force, the last of the Japanese formations to be attacked, passed beyond the range of American carrier aircraft around noon on 27 October. But even putting distance between

himself and the American carrier formations did not ease Kurita's problems, and two were immediate and pressing. The first and lesser problem was that the destroyers were desperately short of oil by this stage of
proceedings, and Kurita had to make a decision on where he was to lead his
force. Brunei Bay, the point to which Japanese oilers and munitions ships
were to go, was the obvious choice, but it was within range of American
land-based bombers, and the suggestion came from within his staff that
the battle force should make its way to Camranh Bay. But the second and
more serious problem for Kurita was that the prospect of attempting to
return to Brunei Bay via the Palawan Passage was cause enough to hesitate,[23] and he instead chose to lead his formation across the Dangerous
Ground, the *Haruna* and *Nagato* respectively refueling the *Yukikaze* and
Isokaze in the process. The other destroyers, the *Akishimo, Hamanami,
Kishinami, Shimakaze* and the *Urakaze*, proceeded to Coron Bay.[24] There
they took on fuel from the *Nichiei Maru* and *Yuho Maru*, which apparently
were the only oilers from the original groups available to the Japanese at
this stage.[25] With the *Banei Maru, Hakko Maru* and the *Omurosan Maru*
in Brunei Bay and the *Ryoei Maru* at Makou in the Pescadores, on this
day the *Nippo Maru* and *Itsukushima Maru* were both torpedoed in the
Balabac Strait: the *Nippo Maru* was sunk but the heavily damaged *Itsukushima Maru* managed to reach Marudu Bay, northern Borneo, where she
sank four days later. With the destroyers that went to Coron not rejoining
them, Kurita's battleships, cruisers, and two destroyers passed through
the shallows without mishap and arrived at Brunei Bay shortly after 2000
on 28 October and immediately began to refuel,[26] but it was not until 6
November that ammunition, and specifically 40 mm anti-aircraft ammunition, arrived for the warships courtesy of the aircraft carrier *Junyo* and
light cruiser *Kiso*. It was not until the evening of the following day that the
unloading of the *Junyo* was completed.[27] Two days earlier, on 4 November,
the inspection of units and their damage had revealed that a basic division
between destroyers going to Singapore and Soerabaja and battleships and
cruisers returning to dockyards in the home islands could be applied, but
of course tactical considerations precluded so neat an arrangement.[28] But
what is perhaps the most surprising aspect of events at Brunei was that it
was not until the evening of 7 November that the *Ashigara* arrived at Brunei
Bay "from her hideout in the Palawan Islands," and the Japanese force,
including the *Junyo*, put to sea the following day. It did so partly because
an air raid was feared and partly as a means of distracting American attention when the needs of the Leyte convoys were pressing, but no raid took

place and the Japanese force clearly failed in its decoy role. Perhaps most significantly, the lack of oilers meant that the formation had to shed units, with the *Ashigara, Oyodo* and the *Kiyoshimo* returning to Brunei[29] while the main units in the formation were forced to try to refuel at Miri on 11 November; *Rikugun* restrictions on the amount of oil made available to the *Kaigun* meant that the *Hakko Maru* was able to supply the warships with only 4,000 tons of oil, and 700 tons of it went to the *Yamato.*[30] Such a development can be said to have marked the end of the line, but the withdrawal of units from Brunei was punctuated by the loss of the *Kongo* and *Urakaze,* but that in its turn was bracketed by the American bomber raids on Japanese warships in Brunei Bay on 16 and 22 November. These attacks recorded minimal damage, with no ships hit and only minor damaged inflicted by near-misses,[31] at least on 16 November. It was during the evening of that day that the *Kongo* and her company sailed from Brunei, and the remaining ships sailed the next day for Lingga Roads.[32] It is worth noting, if only *en passant*, that sailing units to Lingga Roads all but brought them into range of other Allied aircraft, because on 5 November, when the *Nachi* was sunk and Manila raided, fifty-three B-29 Superfortresses based at the Kharagpur airfield outside Calcutta, in a deliberate attempt to deny the Japanese warships docking and repair facilities, mounted an attack on the King George VI graving dock at Singapore, inflicting sufficient damage to ensure that it was out of action for three months.[33] With the death at this time of Wang Ching-wei, head of the collaborationist regime in Nanking, and on 22 November the formation at Ceylon of the British Pacific Fleet,[34] defeat indeed must have seemed to the Japanese to have been a seamless web, casting itself around them at every turn.

Regarding the units the Japanese dispatched to Leyte, the success the Americans registered against the *Kinu* and *Uranami* and one or two of their charges proved isolated; only the landing ship T. 101 was sunk, on 28 October, in the week that followed the destruction of the 16th Cruiser Division. The relative immunity this Japanese effort enjoyed was in no small measure the result of the fact that few aircraft could be based on airfields on Leyte before 31 October, and the carrier formations on station clearly had problems meeting all the demands placed upon them. The American problem with the airstrips on Leyte was twofold: between 17 October and 25 November no less than thirty-five inches of rain fell at Dulag, and the beaches were hopelessly congested with engineers unable to find required

equipment.[35] As it was, though the first fighters were flown to the Tacloban
airstrip on 27 October, it was not until the last day of the month, when
eighty P-38 Lightnings and a dozen P-61 Black Widow night fighters were
flown in,[36] that the contribution of land-based aircraft to the battle could
be anything other than minimal. Thereafter, as aircraft numbers rose—
with 119 on the island on 10 November[37]—sinkings off Leyte recorded
by aircraft based on the island mounted, but nonetheless they remained
decidedly modest: the 7,191-ton transport *Noto Maru* on 2 November,
the 8,407-ton transport *Kashii Maru* and 5,350-ton landing ship *Takatsu
Maru* on the tenth, the landing ships T. 111 and T. 160 on the 24th, and
the 2,880-ton transport *Shinsho Maru* five days later represented the sum
of the sinkings by land-based aircraft in the immediate Leyte area during
November 1944. In part, however, these relatively small returns reflected
the fact that in the second week of November whatever success came the
way of American aircraft based on Leyte was overtaken by the return of the
carriers to the fray. The carriers were able to take the tide of battle beyond
Ormoc, Leyte, and immediately adjacent waters, and, crucially, in the second week of November 1944 they brought the Japanese to the realization
that the battle for the island of Leyte had been lost.

The crucial episode in this process came in the wake of the Japanese
success in getting most of the 1st Infantry Division into Leyte without
loss during the last week of October and first week of November while
barges brought minor units from other islands in the Visayans. A number
of barges and minor landing craft were destroyed, but only with the dawn
and after the Japanese had been able to come ashore.[38] Success in getting
troops and supplies into Leyte—ultimately 45,000 men and 10,000 tons of
supplies from nine convoys were put ashore[39]—encouraged the Japanese
naval command in the Philippines to attempt to send two major convoys
from Manila to Ormoc, the first with supplies and the second with about
10,000 troops from the 26th Infantry Division. The two convoys were to
be separated by a twenty-four-hour gap, and the first one was to be the
less well-protected. It was to cede its three destroyers to the second convoy
during its final approach to Leyte, and the latter then would have seven
destroyers, one minesweeper, and a chaser as escorts, a scale of protection
virtually unknown to military convoys since the heady days of early 1942.
The result was disastrous. The first convoy lost two of its transports on
the 10th as they tried to withdraw from Leyte after getting most of their
supplies ashore but, with the carriers of three of Task Force 38's four task
groups some 200 miles off the San Bernardino Strait, the second convoy

was found soon after dawn on 11 November. Within forty-five minutes of the first sighting report, the first of 347 aircraft were launched in an attack that deliberately singled out the transports for destruction, the result being that all five transports were sunk along with no fewer than four of the destroyers—the *Hamanami*, *Naganami*, *Shimakaze* and the *Wakat-suki*—and the minesweeper W. 30. Two days later American carrier aircraft followed up their success by sinking two of the three destroyers that had escaped their attention, plus another light cruiser and two destroyers, inside Manila Bay.[40]

These losses came two days after the Japanese army high command in Southeast Asia first considered whether to abandon the fight for Leyte, and in truth the Japanese had no real option; on 10 November the Japanese formations on Leyte had fewer than ten artillery pieces in service.[41] But, perhaps predictably, the proposal to write off Leyte by General Yamashita Tomoyuki, the commander in the Philippines, was overruled by Field Marshal Terauchi Hisaichi, commander in Southeast Asia, with the result that the Leyte effort was sustained to ever less effect and arguably at an increasing cost to Japanese defensive capacity throughout the Philippines in general.[42] In contrast, the Americans were ultimately to have about 200,000 soldiers on Leyte, though the majority of these were air base and service personnel and combat troops preparing themselves for next-phase landing operations on Mindoro and Luzon. The disparity of strengths and resources between Japan and the United States, between the Japanese and the American military, was perhaps never more obvious than in this one short campaign for this island, but the point of immediate relevance at this stage of proceedings was obvious: the Americans no longer had to face a Japanese fleet, and by mid-November with their carrier force established with three task groups, they were in a position to move across the whole of the board. In between times, however, American carrier strength fell. The maintenance of just two task groups on station at the end of October has been noted, but this fell to a single group—with just one fleet carrier and two light carriers, one of which was configured for night operations—by the beginning of November. Task Group 38.3 was allowed just two days at Ulithi before it and Task Group 38.1—with McCain having assumed command in place of Mitscher on 30 October—were ordered back to the Philippines.[43] On 5 November, however, with Task Force 38 restored to three carrier groups on station and aircraft from Task Group 38.2 committed over the Sibuyan Sea and Mindoro and from Task Group 38.1 over southern and central Luzon, Task Group 38.3 put its aircraft over Manila

Bay.[44] The heavy cruiser *Nachi* was sunk in the course of the day—by aircraft from the *Lexington*—as was the escort P. 107,[45] but any sinkings on this day were completely overshadowed by the Americans' domination of the skies over Manila. The moral and political significance of this fact was all-important, and in an immediate sense more than offset two other matters. The first of these was that in the aftermath of the actions off Leyte on 10–11 November the Americans had to accept that the immediate naval priority had to be the Philippines. Until this time the naval high command had been thinking of using the carrier force in raids on the home islands and letting the campaign in the Philippines—with aircraft established in bases ashore—look after itself. But adverse weather and the relatively slow preparation of airstrips meant that Task Force 38 could not be freed for operations to the north. The latter had to await February 1945, but in real terms there was little loss in such delay.[46] The second matter was that, inevitably, the American carriers after 25 October were in the position of having to fight a battle the terms of which were not theirs to dictate. They had to fight the battle as it was rather than as they would, and it was one that took the form of attacks staged by *kamikaze* aircraft.

After the sinking of the *Fujinami* and *Shiranui* on 27 October, Task Group 38.3 withdrew in order to refuel, with Task Groups 38.2 and 38.4 assuming operations over southern Luzon and the Visayans. The latter formation, with the *Enterprise, Franklin, Belleau Wood* and the *San Jacinto*, assumed the main offensive role and conducted a number of strikes against shipping off Cebu. Its units were attacked by both Japanese aircraft and submarines, and some of its aircraft were obliged to land at Dulag airstrip and were lost as a result, but in real terms these various air operations were low-key. On 29 October, with Task Group 38.2 assuming the primary role, American carrier aircraft attacked Japanese airfields in the Manila area and claimed to have destroyed seventy-one in the air and another thirteen on the ground for the loss of eleven of their own number. A *kamikaze* aircraft, however, hit a port gun position in the *Intrepid*, killing or wounding sixteen but causing no overall loss of operational efficiency.[47] On 30 October, with Task Group 38.2 off Samar and Task Group 38.4 off Leyte, the *Franklin* and *Belleau Wood* were hit by *kamikazes*. The *Franklin* was attacked by five *kamikazes*, one of which crashed into her side but fell into the sea before exploding. A second penetrated the flight deck and exploded in the gallery deck, wrecking the rear elevator and destroying thirty-three aircraft. A third *kamikaze*, hit during its approach, switched its attention to the *Belleau Wood*, but even though it was shot down, parts of the aircraft crashed onto the flight deck and set off ammunition that was being used to service aircraft, a dozen of which were destroyed. Major fires were started and were contained only with difficulty. With ninety-two killed and missing and another fifty-four seriously wounded, the *Belleau Wood's* casualty list was longer than that of the *Franklin*, but the immediate point was that with just the *Enterprise* and *San Jacinto* operational, Task Group 38.4 was obliged to withdraw from the battle. It set course for Ulithi, the *Franklin* thereafter proceeding to Puget Sound and the *Belleau Wood* to Hunter's Point and to their respective yards.[48] It was the withdrawal of Task Group 38.4 because of extensive damage to two of its four carriers that obliged Task Group 38.3 to return to the fray without the benefits of rest.

On the following day, 1 November, *kamikaze* aircraft struck at destroyers in the Surigao Strait. At 0950 the *Claxton* was extensively damaged when a *kamikaze* crashed into the sea alongside.[49] Two minutes later the *Ammen* was hit, but fortunately for her the two-engined Fran bounced over the side and exploded,[50] and the *Killen* was hit by a single bomb; both remained on station while the damage incurred by the *Claxton* was repaired at Tacloban and Manus. The latter was obliged to withdraw from the battle area, however, not as a result of the damage she had sustained but on account of the 187 survivors she had rescued from the *Abner Read*. The *Read* was hit first by a bomb that penetrated down her after funnel and exploded in a fire room and then by the stricken Judy that had aimed this bomb at her. Fires engulfed the destroyer's stern and one of her magazines. The resultant explosion left her sinking and she was abandoned at 1358; she sank seventeen minutes later.[51]

The *Abner Read* was the first of thirteen destroyers to be sunk as a result of deliberate *kamikaze* attack, another nine being extensively damaged and scrapped unrepaired at war's end.[52] In addition, two destroyer escorts, three minesweepers, and five high-speed transports were sunk outright by *kamikaze* attack with another destroyer escort and five minesweepers left in a state similar to the nine destroyers. But the success of 25 October, the sinking of an escort carrier, was not to be repeated until 1945 when the *Ommaney Bay* was sunk off Mindoro on 4 January 1945 and the *Bismarck Sea* was sunk off Iwo Jima on 21 February 1945. A *kamikaze* aircraft clipped the *Lexington* on 5 November, but no fleet or light carrier was ever sunk as a result of *kamikaze* attack, and with the three carrier groups, the Americans were able to work over the airfields of Luzon between 3 and

6 November and largely eliminate the *kamikaze* attack at source, albeit only temporarily. Apparently on 4 November *kamikazes* accounted for a fleet carrier which was seen to settle and also set a light carrier on fire,[53] but perversely the Americans never noticed these developments, though they had noted that the light cruiser *Reno,* in the screen of Task Group 38.3, had been torpedoed and all but sunk by the submarine I. 41 just before midnight on 3–4 November; the *Reno* was the first American warship in a carrier or battle formation to be torpedoed by a Japanese submarine for more than two years.[54] In the course of these operations over Luzon, American pilots claimed to have destroyed 439 aircraft, most of them on the ground, while losing thirty-six of their own aircraft. Another nine air-craft were lost in the attacks on the Japanese supply and troopship convoys, and twenty-five more were lost in the operations of 13 and 14 November over Luzon, after which Task Group 38.3 returned to Ulithi.[55] With three formations on station, the attacks on Luzon were resumed on 19 Novem-ber and, with Task Group 38.4 staging a diversionary attack on Yap on the 22nd, were continued on 25 November by Task Groups 38.2 and 38.3. On that day American carrier aircraft finally accounted for the *Kumano.* She had been bombed on 26 October and reduced to just one engine and five knots but nonetheless had reached Coron Bay and then made her way to Manila, where she was afforded temporary repairs sufficient to allow her to return to home waters. In the company of the likewise badly damaged *Aoba,* the *Kumano* sailed with seven freighters in convoy Mata 31, but she ran across a patrol line consisting of the submarines *Bream, Guitarro* and the *Raton,* with the *Ray* also on hand. All four submarines attacked her on the morning of 6 November, and the various accounts suggest that the *Kumano* must have been hit by at least two torpedoes from each of the four American submarines. One Japanese source indicates that the *Kumano* was hit by two torpedoes and lost power and steering. One submarine, the *Ray,* attempted to close on the *Kumano* but she grounded while submerged and had to abandon her effort. The *Kumano* was towed by a tanker either to Santa Cruz, where immediate repairs were effected, or directly to Dasol Bay, where she was beached. In either case, it was in Dasol Bay that she was caught on 25 November by eight Hellcats, thirteen Helldivers, and nine Avengers from the *Ticonderoga.* Few details of what happened are available, but one account suggests that she was hit by four bombs and five torpedoes and another that she was hit by no fewer than six torpedoes and sank within four minutes of the first hit. Whatever the situation, she was finally destroyed that day. Whether she was "accounted for" on 6 November

and the events of 25 November were merely the *coup de grâce*, and whether the agency of sinking was submarines, carrier aircraft, or shared, is difficult to determine.[56]

This success, however, was upstaged by *kamikaze* aircraft, which by deliberately tagging along behind returning American aircraft and thus being afforded protection from the combat air patrol because of congested radar screens, hit the *Essex*, *Hancock*, *Intrepid* and the *Cabot*. The damage sustained by the *Hancock* and *Essex* was minor, the latter's fires being extinguished within twenty minutes,[57] and the *Cabot* was hit by a *kamikaze* that crashed into anti-aircraft gun positions and suffered a near-miss which showered her port side with splinters and burning debris. The *Intrepid*, however, was hit just before 1300 by two *kamikazes* that penetrated to her hangar deck and set off fires that took two hours to bring under control. With her flight and hangar decks wrecked, blazing aviation fuel pouring down her sides from ruptured lines, and 154 of her crew killed, wounded, or missing, the *Intrepid* nonetheless stayed on station for what remained of the day:[58] she was singularly fortunate to have had no fewer than seventy-five of her aircraft in the air when she was hit. These were recovered by the *Hancock*, *Essex* and the *Ticonderoga* before being flown into the airstrip at Tacloban.[59] But with the *Independence* subjected to self-inflicted damage when one of her aircraft crashed on landing, Task Group 38.2 had no option but to withdraw; the formation reached Ulithi on 28 November. The *Cabot* was subjected to local repairs and returned to the battle on 11 December,[60] but the *Intrepid* was obliged to make her way to San Francisco for major repairs and did not return to action until mid-March 1945. After Task Group 38.2's departure, just one carrier group remained on station, but by this time the focus of American attention had shifted toward Mindoro and Lingayen Gulf.

The operations of 25 November provide a point where the story of the aftermath of the naval battle for the Philippines can be brought to a close, and for two reasons. This day coincided, within a twenty-four-hour period, with the first direct support of ground forces on Leyte by aircraft on the island and with the first raid by B-29 Superfortresses on the Japanese home islands from bases in the Marianas.[61] It was not until March 1945, by which time the Americans had abandoned the precision-attack doctrine in favor of massed low-level area bombardments, that this offensive assumed serious proportions, and it was in this month that the last tanker reached the home islands from the south. Regarding this latter fact, one point needs to be noted. The Pacific war opened with a Japanese attack across the whole width of the western Pacific, but after February 1943 there was a steady, remorseless ebbing of Japanese power. The movement of the "frontline" was simply in one direction, toward the home islands, the exception being on the border between Burma and India, and but briefly, and in southern China in 1944. It is not an oversimplification to state that by August 1945 the Japanese fleet had ceased to exist and what naval units remained to Japan were gathered in home waters, where they were powerless to stop or even inflict any real loss on the enemy. October–November 1944 was part of this process in terms of the collapse of Japanese convoy arrangements and the enfeeblement of Japanese escort formations. The General Escort Command, hopelessly underestablished in terms of the number and quality of escorts and aircraft, had not been created until November 1943, and almost immediately was forced to abandon routes through the Marshalls and Carolines and to Rabaul. By May 1944 most of the convoy routes directed through the Palaus had been abandoned, and by September all convoy routes east of the Philippines, and to western New Guinea, had been abandoned as the tide of American conquest swept westward. With the American landings in the Philippines, notice was served that Japanese convoy routes to the south would soon be no more, and while certain routes south from Indo-China and along the Malay Barrier remained until the end of the war, by the end of 1944, the General Escort Command had abandoned virtually all the convoy routes between the Japanese home islands and the southern resources areas. Moreover, with the virtual demise of the Japanese fleet, Allied submarines were free to concentrate almost all their attention against Japanese shipping, with results that were significant in one respect. In September 1944, submarines sank a total of forty-one service transports and auxiliaries and merchantmen of 157,793 tons. In October 1944, even as the demands of battle ensured a division of attention and effort, submarines nonetheless accounted for sixty-three service and civilian ships of 324,765 tons. This proved to be the peak of the submarine effort in terms of returns in any calendar month, but November 1944 nonetheless saw a respectable toll of Japanese shipping exacted by submarines. A total of fifty-three ships of 238,872 tons were sunk by submarines in that month, but of these no fewer than twenty-five service and merchant ships of 104,683 tons were sunk in the waters that washed the Kuriles, the home islands, and in the East China Sea. Such losses were unprecedented—just. Japanese losses in these waters had amounted to nineteen ships of 97,734 tons in October 1942 and to twenty-four ships of 104,277 tons in September 1943, but in both months about three-fifths of the losses had been in the East China Sea. About nine-tenths of the toll exacted in November 1944 by submarines was in home waters, demonstrating the enfeeblement of Japan by this stage of proceedings. Of course Japanese losses in home waters, after a fall, rose again in March 1945 and then between May and August 1945 reached disastrous levels under the impact of the mining campaign, with carrier operations in this final stage of the war supplementing Operation STARVATION. Herein lay the significance of the events of November 1944 in terms of the finality and totality of Japan's ultimate defeat. That defeat was primarily inflicted by the United States, though the importance of China in terms of the continuity of conflict and open-ended commitment of Japanese resources is not to be underestimated any more than the importance of Soviet intervention in the last days of the war should be derided. The contribution of other allies—Australia, Britain, Canada, France, the Netherlands, and New Zealand—was small, whether individually or collectively, but it was nonetheless a contribution, and at various times very welcome to the United States. Japan's defeat at sea encompassed both her fleet and her shipping, and in terms of the latter it involved submarines, land-based aircraft, warships, mines, and carrier aircraft, with all these individual efforts coming together to produce an overall result disastrous for Japan both in terms of the unfolding of events and at these events' end. For Japan, the naval battle for the Philippines in October 1944 represented comprehensive defeat, an unmitigated disaster. There were three main actions, and all were massive Japanese defeats. The defeat off Cape Engaño was sought but nonetheless represented carrier losses that were more or less on a par with those sustained at Midway and at the Philippine Sea, and from which there could be no recovery. In the south, in the actions in the Surigao Strait and thereafter, two Japanese formations were, in numbers alone, halved in a series of actions over a two-day period, and for minimal return; at no stage did either Japanese formation come anywhere near the realization of aim. In the center, the Japanese formation lost ten of its units, including one of the greatest battleships in the world and no fewer than five heavy cruisers, yet it managed to sink just one of six escort carriers it engaged and, simply, was outthought and outfought by the Americans. The commander of Task Unit 77.4.3 famously remarked that American survival and success in this battle on 25 October was in no small measure the result of the partiality of Almighty God,[62] but in truth what was undoubtedly one of the bravest and most glorious episodes in American naval history should never have been because the Japanese should have prevailed in this action without breaking a sweat. But they did not, and it was on the basis of this improbable victory—and, lest they be forgotten, the victories that had been won in the Sibuyan Sea, off Cape Engaño, and in the Surigao Strait—that the Americans were then able to carry the tide of battle to Mindoro and Luzon and later the other islands of the Philippines, and to Iwo Jima, Okinawa, and the home islands. Herein lay the significance of the naval battle of the Philippines and its immediate aftermath. In each of these two parts, the Americans were able to win comprehensive victories, the results obtained after 28 October made possible by the previous victory but at the same time supplementing that victory and adding to its dimension and significance. In truth, here was a victory that must rank with the greatest ever won in the course of history, and which, on the reverse side of the coin, ultimately provided the *Kaigun* with its chance to bloom as flowers of death.

CHAPTER EIGHT

TO PAUSE AND CONSIDER

*Blame, Responsibility,
and the Verdict of History*

THIS ACCOUNT OF the naval battle for the Philippines has sought to avoid the problems normally associated with accounts of the battle of Leyte Gulf. It has sought to provide full and detailed coverage of the four main actions, 24–25 October, that together constitute the battle, and it has sought to properly set out both the preliminaries and the follow-up actions. In so doing it has set out the course of events at the expense of the inconsequential details that litter most accounts of these actions, which, *prima facie*, seem to want to record every single hit on an American ship or deal with individuals and their actions in disproportionate detail to their importance, significance, and effect.

This latter point is crucial in setting out the terms of reference of this work, since these are not concerned with individuals *per se*, and for one reason: the emphasis placed on individuals in so many accounts of this battle has served to obscure what should be the proper basis of analysis and understanding. In any examination of the naval battle for the Philippines, what is important is not Halsey and Kurita and their various decisions, but the basic question of how nations wage war and how armed forces fight. The Carlyle approach is not merely of little value, but it is positively misleading since the basis of understanding lies in the correct appreciation of the basis of the American way of war, which, from the time of Grant, lay in the combination of mass, firepower, and shock action. Demographic, economic, industrial, and financial superiority over all enemies has meant that the American way of war, for a hundred years, stressed superiority of numbers, concentration of massed firepower, and seeking battle as the means of ensuring the defeat of an enemy. This formula lacked subtlety and possessed little in the way of finesse, but the yardstick by which it must be measured is effectiveness and success, and it stood the United States in good stead until she fundamentally failed to understand the nature of the war she sought and of the enemy she faced in Southeast Asia in the 1960s. But if the American way of war was basic, one can argue that for subtlety, elegance, and sophistication, there are few examples in warfare in the twentieth century to rival the opening Japanese moves, across nine time zones and 7,000 miles, that brought war to Southeast Asia and the Pacific in December 1941. The Japanese put together a plan involving successive attacks by forces operating behind a front secured by land-based air power and then penetrated to the Malay Barrier with an effort remarkable in terms of economy and lack of overall superiority of numbers, but which commanded massive local superiority over enemies defensively dispersed and unable to cooperate to any real effect. And, of course, the war that Japan thus initiated was a war that she lost.

Japan lost the war in the Pacific because her high command made one fundamental error: it failed to understand the nature of the war it initiated in December 1941. This basic error can be said to pre-date December 1941. It could be said to apply to July–September 1937 when Japan chose to pick up an open-ended commitment in China in the belief she could win a victory on the continental mainland, and it was from this fundamental error, in underestimating the problems of fighting a war in China and the nature of the enemy, that all other problems followed. Certainly by 1941 Japan was saddled with a commitment in China that was self-defeating and which could not be ended, and it is this that provides the basis of any understanding of the subsequent absurdities that gripped the process of Japanese policy making. Unable to win a war in China, Japan sought to secure British and Dutch possessions in Southeast Asia, and therefore attacked the only country in the world that could ensure her defeat. Japan failed to understand that the alternative to victory in the limited war she initiated was not defeat in a limited war but defeat in a total war. She failed to realize that the terms of reference of this war were not hers to determine. With no experience of defeat, Japan could not envisage defeat, and she failed to understand the nature and temper of the American enemy.

The basis of the American victory both in this battle and in the Pacific war in general lay in the acquisition of strength in depth that was remarkable. Seldom in history have polities been defeated by sea power, and even more seldom have been defeats of polities across an ocean; probably only the Spanish destruction of the Aztec empire stands comparison with the United States' prosecuting a war across the whole of the Pacific and taking the tide of battle to the home islands. In terms of the application of force—as distinct from the basis of national power—the basis of American success lay primarily in sea and air power. The naval and air forces that were to take the tide of war across the central and southwest Pacific were more or less in place by November 1943, less than two years after the Japanese attack on the U.S. Pacific Fleet at its Pearl Harbor base, and what is so notable about the subsequent campaigns and this naval battle of October 1944 is not so much the failures and the things that went wrong but that so many things went right. If one looks at the massive expansion of the U.S. Navy between 1941 and 1944, from a navy that possessed seven fleet carriers and one escort carrier at the time of Pearl Harbor to one with twelve fleet, nine light, and sixty-five escort carriers on 1 October 1944—and it had another eight fleet and ten escort carriers that were to be commissioned before the end of the Japanese war—then what is truly remarkable is the lack of any dilution of professionalism. The point can be easily missed, but between December 1941 and September 1945 the war at sea underwent a series of massive changes, the cumulative effect of which was profound. Radar, TBS voice radio, the qualitative and quantitative changes in gunnery, massed carrier formations capable of taking on and defeating shore-based air power, and the development of amphibious assault capability constituted profound change, and herein is the relevance of the naval battle for the Philippines. The U.S. Navy was in the forefront of most of these changes; it stayed abreast of them and was equal to the challenge they represented. What is so notable about this battle is, with one caveat, the effectiveness of the American carrier formations in the prosecution of operations that would have been unthinkable in 1941. The caveat, which cannot be proven, is the belief that this battle of October 1944 lasted one day too many for the American carrier formations. Any consideration of American air operations on 25 October should raise the point that the number of hits on and the destruction of enemy units were probably not wholly in accordance with what might have been expected in light of the numbers of aircraft that undertook offensive operations, the lack of opposition in the air, and the relative ineffectiveness of Japanese anti-aircraft fire. The results that were registered over the next two days can be subjected to the same comment—which, presumably, would have to be

amended to three days too many. Exhaustion, after some three weeks of
action that involved ships and crews at general quarters and in action for
days at a time, worked by 25 October to lessen returns, but it needs to be
noted that even if this was the case, American carrier aircraft nonetheless
accounted on this day for three carriers and a destroyer and shared in the
destruction of another carrier and light cruiser off Cape Engaño, while
the escort carriers accounted for three heavy cruisers off Samar. These
comments leave themselves open to the obvious rejoinder—that if such
losses were indeed inflicted on the enemy by tired, exhausted air groups,
then what might have been the scale of losses had the enemy been attacked
by fresh formations not worn down by days of constant action?—but that,
perversely, is exactly the point.

The naval battle for the Philippines represented as comprehensive and
total a victory as any that had been won at sea over the previous 373 years,
and the extent and totality of this victory is but seldom properly appreciated. Battles of annihilation are basically a military preserve; whether in the
Age of Sail or of Steam, naval battles very seldom are thus. But the naval
battle for the Philippines should be considered in such terms, and on four
separate but related counts. The Japanese fleet was destroyed; what was
left was little more than an auxiliary force, without any real capability and
so reduced that it barely existed. The Japanese naval and army air forces
were overwhelmed in a series of actions—the Americans claiming to have
destroyed 1,559 enemy aircraft in the air, over the naval formations, and in
attacks on airfields—that amounted to the beginning of the end, and both
were reduced to defensive roles with their only hope vested in "a weapon of
despair."[1] The Japanese escort forces and shipping, stripped of support and
cover, were simply overwhelmed in the months that were to follow, while
the American victory, as noted elsewhere, in reaching into the western
Pacific and hence in securing islands astride Japanese maritime lines of
communication to the south, possessed an element of totality. There is no
way these aspects of victory can be quantified or defined, but the extent
of the American victory can perhaps be best understood in terms of what
happened to the Japanese units that survived this battle.

As noted elsewhere, in November 1944 all agencies of destruction,
but primarily carrier aircraft, accounted for the destroyers *Wakatsuki* and
Shimotsuki from Ozawa's northern force; the destroyers *Hamanami, Naganami, Shimakaze, Akishimo* and the *Okinami*, the battleship *Kongo*, the
destroyer *Urakaze*, and the heavy cruiser *Kumano* from Kurita's force; and
the heavy cruiser *Nachi* and destroyers *Akebono* and *Hatsuharu* from the

southern and other detached formations. This is a total of one battleship, two heavy cruisers, and ten destroyers, plus two submarines, in just one month as the Americans moved to consolidate and improve upon their victory, and these were losses just from the formations that had been involved in the battle; other units from other formations—escorts, patrol vessels, minesweepers, and amphibious vessels—must be added to the list. What remained from the formations that had offered battle in defense of the Philippines was a total of five battleships, six heavy and three light cruisers, ten destroyers, four escorts, and eight submarines, and of this total of thirty-six warships and submarines no fewer than twenty-seven were to be destroyed. Just nine remained to be surrendered at war's end and of these, two heavy cruisers had been rendered *hors de combat*: in real terms the total was seven. But two points emerge from this statement of fact. The sheer scale of the victory that was won, specifically on 25 October, has overshadowed the victory that was won in the follow-up phase. The victory won over and in the waters that washed the Philippines in November was every bit as extensive and real as that won in the week of the battle. It was not a victory on the scale of the victory won in the battle and in terms of the type of Japanese warship that was sunk there was obvious difference, but the point is that the success that was registered in this follow-up phase did not present itself as an alternative to the success that had previously been recorded; this success complemented the previous victory, and together they provided the basis for subsequent offensive action that amounted to the annihilation of the Imperial Navy. It took until the end of July 1945 and the great raids over the Inland Sea for this victory of annihilation to be finally recorded, but from the time of this battle the Japanese warships that escaped destruction were no more than fugitives on the run; perhaps condemned men awaiting execution might be the better analogy.

The reverse side of the coin also presents itself for proper consideration, and this was a defeat wholly lacking in any redeeming qualities. For Japan the defeat was a disaster, unmitigated and absolute, yet it is not straining the bounds of credibility to make the obvious point that the battle was lost, or should have been lost, before it was joined, and the truly incredible point about this battle was that one Japanese force did come within reach, and should have grasped, a local victory. But amid the various American analyses of this battle, there seldom seems to be much account taken of one obvious point: there was no victory the Japanese could have won which would have materially affected the course, still less the outcome, of the war in the Pacific. The loss of every warship in Task Unit 77.4.3 would have represented, for the Americans, no more than a strategic hiccup, and it is hard, if not impossible, to see what real delays might have been inflicted upon the American strategic timetable even if all three of Kinkaid's escort carrier groups had been annihilated. The U.S. Navy had other escort carriers that no doubt would have found themselves on the frontline as opposed to training, ferrying, and local escort duties, and perhaps the United States would have been obliged to seek the return of a number of escort carriers that had been made available to Britain, but the U.S. Navy at this stage of proceedings possessed a strength in depth that would have enabled it to shrug off such losses. Put in a slightly different way, the number of units that were launched or commissioned between 22 and 28 October more than made good the losses that were incurred on these days.[2] There may well have been some political fallout, and no doubt heads would have rolled, but in terms of the nation waging war, and the services fighting, there was no victory that the Japanese could have won in the fourth week of October 1944 that would have wrought any real and lasting change in the nature and conduct of this war. In an obvious sense, the Japanese should have sought some form of negotiated surrender after the defeat in the Philippine Sea in June 1944, because that defeat, more than any other single defeat, pointed unmistakably to what was to come. But, of course, states seldom act in so logical a manner, and in any case it is doubtful that any attempt by Japan to seek a way to end the war she had initiated could have been successful. The minimum Allied demand would have been unconditional surrender, and it seems unlikely indeed that such a demand would have been acceptable to the Japanese high command at that time. Indeed there is overwhelming evidence to suggest that this would have been the case. If, as was the case, the Japanese high command could not bring itself to sue for peace, to surrender, even after the devastation of almost sixty of Japan's major cities, the attacks on Hiroshima and Nagasaki, and the Soviet entry into the war, then there was no real prospect of its accepting defeat in 1944.

The problem with such interpretation, however, is obvious. The demands of public expectation and national historiography inevitably focus attention upon individuals, in this case Kurita and Halsey. Regarding the Japanese admiral, one is pressed to develop arguments already set down. Two arguments have not been used to date, and these are that Kurita's turnaway was in part the result of the realization that Nishimura's force was no more and concern about fuel remaining to his ships. These were not included in the previous examination of Kurita's actions for one simple reason: they seem so inconsequential. Given the lack of organization within the Imperial Navy, and specifically the lack of any attempt on the part of Kurita and Nishimura to coordinate their operations, that Kurita might have been persuaded to turn back a second time, away from Leyte Gulf, because disaster had overwhelmed the southern force would seem dubious. Regarding fuel, Koyanagi indicated that it was a consideration and Kurita indicated it was not, but it is hard to believe that concern about oil could have been a major factor in Kurita's calculations. It is hard to believe that it was not a consideration because admirals, staffs, and ships' captains invariably, and at all times, express their concerns on the subject. Ships never have enough oil, not even when they have just completed their replenishment. But given all the other considerations that beset Kurita, it is difficult to believe that fuel was more than a secondary consideration at best. The problem of interpretation of Kurita and his actions nonetheless remains, and there is no satisfactory answer, and one is left to consider alternative explanations such as ineptitude and incompetence or loss of nerve at the moment of opportunity. The one point that seemingly must be beyond dispute is that once Kurita turned back north the second time, at 1236, there was no real alternative to his seeking to get his formation past Cape Espiritu Santo and through the San Bernardino Strait that evening, and the reason for this was fuel concerns because it was only at Coron that Kurita could avail himself of the fuel needed for his ships. This is not to assert, however, that concern about fuel prompted the 1236 turnaway in the first place. His immediate concern must have been the certainty of potentially overwhelming attack by carrier aircraft on the following day, but one wonders whether what was at work was a basic instinct for survival, very un-Japanese though it may have been at this time. It is worth noting, for example, that while Kurita was condemned for want of fighting spirit by Ugaki, who admittedly was never backward in castigating all and sundry, Ohmae, Ozawa's chief of staff, expressed the view that Kurita "should have been braver and gone on to Leyte."[3] It would seem that at the time at least some Japanese entertained dark thoughts about Kurita's motives and reasoning. As one historian has noted, the temptation to brand Kurita a coward is very real,[4] and hence there is additional reason for caution in noting that Kurita's sudden withdrawal from the battle off Samar was not "when victory was within his grasp." Kurita's withdrawal came when a victory was within his grasp, and at very best it would have been a minor victory of no strategic consequence.

Halsey presents problems of a different kind, in part because he could never bring himself to admit error and never admitted that Ozawa's force had been bait. The only mistake he ever claimed to have made in this battle was to have turned the battle force to the south when it stood on the brink of victory over Ozawa's broken formation,[5] but one would suggest that as serious an error was his post-war writings and version of events that alienated most of his peers and turned Kinkaid from a lifelong friend into an embittered foe.[6] What is so notable about these matters is not so much Halsey's stridency in setting out his case but the support he enjoyed from sources that one would have thought would have been less than enthusiastic about his conduct. At various times King was supportive of Halsey, at least until Halsey's antics proved too much, and Nimitz seemingly never reproached Halsey on any count. Over the years such individuals as John Thatch, McCain's air officer,[7] and the historian Stanley L. Falk[8] supported the decision to take the battle force north with the carriers and to leave the San Bernardino Strait unwatched and unguarded.

There would seem to be two basic issues that need to be addressed when considering Halsey's conduct and decisions, and to these, two more general points need be added in order to provide perspective. The first issue, simply, was role. The primary role of Task Unit 77.4.3 was the provision of close air support for the two divisions ashore in northern Leyte. The secondary role was providing combat air and anti-submarine patrols for itself and the transport and amphibious forces in its area of responsibility. It was to cooperate with Task Units 77.4.2 and 77.4.1 in carrying out these functions, but in terms of "role and missions" these were its duties, and they did not include fighting an enemy battle fleet.[9]

The second issue has commanded virtually no historical attention, but it is the signal of 2145 on 24 October from an aircraft from the *Independence* that reported that Kurita's force was in 12°45'North 123°22'East and hence farther to the east than at any previous time, clearly intent on making its way through the San Bernardino Strait. This signal was received by Halsey at 2320, and its significance is obvious. It was the basis of the decision to proceed north on the proviso, cited by Halsey in his report and noted elsewhere:

it was calculated that [the carrier] forces could return in time to reverse any advantage that the [enemy] center force might gain.

The observation is grotesque because there was no way Halsey could know what losses an unimpeded Japanese battle force might have been able to inflict on American formations if it fought its way into Leyte Gulf, and Halsey's statement would certainly seem to dismiss as of little or no account those Americans who might be killed before the carriers could intervene to reverse the balance of advantage against the Japanese. But this fact pales alongside the second issue, that of communcations: it seems that the 2145 signal was not passed to Kinkaid.[10]

If the signal was passed to Kinkaid then Halsey is not excused for taking his force to the north even though he knew Kurita's force was making for the San Bernardino Strait, but responsibility for what then happened has to be shared because Kinkaid, clearly, had been forewarned—at least in part. But there is no evidence that the signal was passed to Kinkaid, and certainly the deliberations of Kinkaid and his staff in the early hours of 25 October would suggest strongly that this was the case. Indeed, it is difficult to make sense of these deliberations if the contents of the 2145 signal had been known. Certainly the 0412 signal asking Halsey the whereabouts of Task Force 34 would make no sense if the 2145 signal had been received. It appears that Halsey deliberately continued with his forces to the north despite knowing that Kurita's battle formation would be passing through the San Bernardino Strait and deliberately neglected to warn Kinkaid of these developments. Halsey might well have a reasonable argument that Kinkaid's formations should have conducted a proper reconnaissance on the morning of 25 October, and that point cannot be denied, but that was small change when set alongside the fact that Kinkaid was not alone in assuming Halsey had left a battle force on station. The fact is that Halsey never kept any force off the Strait even though he knew that the enemy would pass through it during the night and never informed Kinkaid either of his actions or those of the enemy. The whole issue of command, communications between the 3rd and 7th Fleets, and errors of omission and commission on the part of Kinkaid are wholly irrelevant when set alongside what seems to have been willful and deliberate refusal on the part of Halsey both to discharge the primary function with which he had been entrusted—the defensive commitment to cover the amphibious, transport, and support formations—and to warn Kinkaid of Kurita's movements. Kincaid's communications failure is irrelevant when set alongside Halsey's

refusal to communicate on so important a matter as the movement of
Kurita's formation, while any attempt to deflect criticism of Halsey by
claiming the correctness of his decision to go north sits uneasily alongside
one inescapable fact that is best summarized by the caption to a photograph in Cutler's *The Battle of Leyte Gulf.* The photograph is of Kinkaid,
and the caption reads:

> Vice Admiral Thomas C. Kinkaid, commander of the Seventh Fleet. Given
> primary responsibility for the landing operations, his forces would ultimately
> face the bulk of the Japanese Fleet alone, while Halsey's Third Fleet pursued
> the northern decoy force.

Whatever Halsey might have claimed, this was not what should have
happened, and primary and overwhelming responsibility for such a state of
affairs was his. It bears recall, in any consideration of the account of events
on the part of those involved in these proceedings, that "the Devil can cite
Scriptures for his purpose."[11]

But if indeed the curse of this battle is the issue of personality, which
has served to deflect attention from real issues, the general matters to
which reference has been made, but which were undefined, remain to be
addressed. The first two of these concern the individual—the individual
being Halsey—and the system. On the first score, one wonders how much,
if at all, the faults that attach themselves to Halsey's conduct of the battle
derive from a lack of system. Reference has been made to the concept of
the great man and to the staff systems, and the fact is that the staff system
came late to navies. Armies had to adopt the general staff system in the last
three decades of the nineteenth century because of the massive increase
in the size of armies and the example that was set by the Prussian army.
The staff system, even within ministries and departments of state, was only
slowly adopted by navies, and one suspects that for most of Halsey's career
prior to 1941 he had very little dealing with a staff system at sea. Any casual
reading of accounts of Halsey's deliberations and decisions at Leyte Gulf,
whether by historians, commentators, or indeed Halsey himself, invite the
conclusion that for Halsey the staff was there to implement his decisions,
that the staff was merely chorus, there to make up the numbers, and he had
the answers. Any casual reading of accounts of Spruance's deliberations
and decisions invite the conclusion that for Spruance the staff consisted
of *dramatis personae*, individuals with genuine roles, and that Spruance

himself was always struggling with the questions. This is not to assert that Spruance did not make decisions, because clearly he did, but the point that seems to present itself is that Spruance, and commanders such as Kinkaid, Lee, and Mitscher, worked through the staff system in a way that Halsey could not or did not. It is impossible to prove this point, but one wonders if Halsey's error in going north with the battle force, leaving the San Bernardino Strait unwatched and unguarded, could have occurred had any of the other senior American commanders in Task Force 38 in this battle—Mitscher, McCain, Bogan, Sherman, Davison, or Lee—been in Halsey's place. If one looks at accounts of the deliberations of these men, the element of continuity between them and the present time is evident in a way that eludes Halsey. It is as if Halsey belonged to a time that had passed, a throwback to a simpler time which, by October 1944, was no more.

On the second score, and still dealing with the individual and the system, one wonders why Halsey was never held to account for his conduct in this battle. To any impartial and objective observer, without service interest and with a distance from events bequeathed by the passing of the years, what is strange about subsequent events is that neither King nor Nimitz seriously questioned, still less held reservations, about Halsey's exercise of command. King, when he met Halsey for the first time in January 1945, stopped Halsey when the latter raised the subject of the battle with the comment, "You don't have to tell me any more. You've got a green light on everything you did."[12] This observation by King is curious since it is more or less word for word the same as his comment to Spruance when the subject of the latter's conduct of operations in the battle of the Philippine Sea was raised, and even more curiously, the observation seems to be the same as the assurance given by King's deputy, Rear Admiral Charles H. Cooke, to Kinkaid at this time. It is difficult to believe that Cooke could have spoken thus to Kinkaid without King's explicit approval and consent, but while the comments to Spruance with respect to the June 1944 battle and to Halsey with respect to the October 1944 counterpart are not wholly incompatible and irreconcilable, the giving of the same assurance to both Halsey and Kinkaid at this time does present problems of understanding. Nimitz, it seems, never reproached Halsey in any way for what had happened, or not happened, off the San Bernardino Strait, but any examination of the two books which which Nimitz was associated, namely *The Great Sea War: The Story of Naval Action in World War II* and *Sea Power: A Naval History*, cannot but note a tone that is not exactly sympathetic to Halsey.

It is worth noting, perhaps, that these books were published in 1960 and Halsey died in 1959, and perhaps in these books Nimitz placed a certain distance between himself and a person who had long been a friend. But the problem in making sense of this lies in a comment attributed to Nimitz to the effect that

> when he sent Spruance out with the fleet he was always sure he would bring it home; when he sent Halsey out, he did not know precisely what was going to happen.[13]

If this really was the case, and one suspects that in one sense this might well have been a throwaway line, albeit one with a certain undercurrent of truth, then one is left to wonder why Nimitz could have entrusted Halsey with any force, still less a fleet. One would think such a comment could only suggest that Halsey was unfit to command.

King's behavior lends itself to one obvious interpretation, and that was simply that a war remained to be fought and won and he was not prepared to allow what was, in the final analysis, a matter of small account to intrude upon more important proceedings. Certainly to have pressed the issue at that time might well have proved embarrassing for King personally and for the U.S. Navy as an institution, and while King does appear to have been irritated and puzzled by the episode, it was not until Halsey's post-war antics really began to goad him that he expressed himself forcefully, but privately. King's behavior also lends itself to another obvious interpretation, and that is that by this stage of proceedings Halsey was so well-established in terms of public stature that he could not be removed or moved into some secondary post. In terms of press and public acclaim, Halsey's position was secure, in some ways not unlike that of MacArthur, and one can reasonably question the basis of that security since both men came to command a public standing in a period when their own actions most certainly never merited such treatment. Halsey came to the fore at a time of defeat, when America needed a hero. He was to enjoy such stature because he was "quotable." He exuded aggression, and most certainly there was a nasty-mindedness and racism that was not out of place in the America of that time. In the six months after the Japanese attack on the U.S. Pacific Fleet at Pearl Harbor, a period of mounting defeats, Halsey may well have embodied an American determination to prevail and become a symbol of ultimate victory, but what he did in those six months to merit such status is difficult to discern. The carrier attacks on Japanese installations in the Marshall

Islands in January 1942, on Wake in February, and on Marcus in March, and the Doolittle raid hardly constitute an achievement commensurate with the acclaim he was afforded, and the treatment he was then granted regarding the southwest Pacific campaign seems at variance with fact. It is possible to see that all the elements that were to make for the American victory in the lower Solomons in November 1942 were more or less in place on 18 October when Halsey assumed command at Noumea, New Caledonia. Certainly Halsey's impact on morale must have been important, breathing new confidence throughout the warships in theater, but what else constituted Halsey's contribution to victory is difficult to determine, and most certainly the treatment afforded Halsey contrasts sharply with the dismissive, indeed contemptuous, treatment afforded Vice Admiral Frank J. Fletcher at this same time. Slightly wounded in the battle of the Eastern Solomons in August 1942, Fletcher after

> the outbreak of the Pacific war . . . commanded in three major battles. Since April three carriers under his command had been torpedoed, and two of them, the *Lexington* and *Yorktown*, had gone down. With such a record, it was generally agreed that he must be extraordinarily unlucky or extraordinarily inept.[14]

In fact, Fletcher commanded American forces in the first three carrier battles that were ever fought and was never on the losing side, yet the comments here are remarkable in the assumption of American invulnerability. There is simply no acknowledgment that the military profession is alone in that an individual may make a whole number of decisions, each and every one correct, and still be killed, because the enemy has the same rights. This is a point that is particularly relevant at the present time because no state can carry out attacks on other states and enjoy automatic immunity from counterattack, yet here, and at the present time, is an assumption of assured success and victory with no real cost. It was not in Fletcher's power, indeed it was not in the power of any individual, to ensure the U.S. Navy against loss as it did battle with the enemy, yet Fletcher was moved into the backwater of the north Pacific, to Dutch Harbor and the Aleutians, and Halsey could go forward to lose more ships to typhoons than to enemy action and never be held to account. As it is, the portrayal of Fletcher in the terms outlined above sits uneasily alongside the recurring theme in so many American histories, namely the heaviness and severity of American losses. American losses were of small account. On 25 October, Task Groups 38.3 and 38.4 between them lost just ten aircraft to Japanese anti-aircraft fire,[15] a total that needs be set again the four carriers, one light cruiser, and one destroyer that were sunk by American aircraft, in whole or in part. Moreover, such a total needs be set against the fact that at the peak of aircraft production in March 1944 American factories completed an aircraft every five minutes, and given that such output included two- and four-engine bombers, the loss of ten single-engine naval aircraft represents less than fifty minutes' output. Moreover, the total of 2,803 Americans casualties—473 killed, 1,110 missing, and 1,220 wounded—in this battle[16] represents the toll of Soviet dead exacted every 212 minutes on the Eastern Front between 22 June 1941 and 12 May 1945.

In an obvious sense these comments conform to the issue of personality even as their basic argument seeks to set aside the issue in favor of nations and navies, power and force, systems and personalities, but any consideration of the naval battle for the Philippines should note a number of matters relating to the battle, and to the American and Japanese conduct of the battle, that are not related in any way to the issue of personality. In terms of the battle, as distinct from the conduct of one side or another, two points are of immediate significance. The first, and to which en passant reference has been made in the sixth chapter, is that one fights as one must rather than as one would, and the relevance here is the battle that unfolded in and off the Philippines in this fourth week of October 1944 did not conform to what either side had expected or sought. In the case of the Japanese this is all too obvious, and the great irony is that for the whole of the inter-war period the Kaigun had prepared itself for the gunnery action and here in the naval battle it fought two such actions and was beaten in both. In the case of the Americans this is not so obvious, but arguably this battle encompassed four fleet actions and only the action against Kurita's force in the Sibuyan Sea on 24 October and the action against Ozawa's formation the next morning were battles for which the U.S. Navy had prepared itself and wished to fight. The action off Samar was most certainly neither anticipated nor sought, and the action in the Surigao Strait was not one that anyone on the American side could have anticipated before they sailed. The basic point is that for all the American superiority of numbers and potentially overwhelming advantage in the air, the nature of the battle that unfolded was elusive. The second point, again one to which en passant reference has been made, goes hand-in-hand with the first, that it was not until the afternoon of 24 October that the Americans had all the enemy formations in their sights. The Americans possessed massive advantage in terms of reconnaissance capability and, lest it be forgotten, signals intelligence, and it was quite extraordinary that it was not until—figuratively—the last minute that the Americans were able to identify enemy forces to the north, in the center, and to the south and were able to divine Japanese intention. One suspects that the basic point is that always in battle there is the element of the unknown, the other side of the hill, and that no country or armed services can ever fully read and understand an enemy's meaning and purpose. It is not in the power of states, services, and individuals to command perception and success.

The most obvious point regarding the American conduct of battle, and one therefore so seldom addressed, relates directly to the reading of the battlefield, and what was really a lamentable failure of reconnaissance. There are three dimensions to this single aspect of operations, the first being the setting aside of the reconnaissance report regarding Kurita, Brunei Bay, and 20 October. The sequence of events—the expectation that the Japanese would be found, the Japanese being found where and when expected, and the report being discarded seemingly because it did not correspond exactly with what had been anticipated—represents an extraordinary development, yet it ran in parallel with the second matter: the withdrawal of submarines *Besugo, Ronquil* and the *Gabilan* from the reconnaissance role off the Bungo Strait before any Japanese force had the opportunity to sail, and the parallel fact that the *Darter* and *Dace* were under orders to watch the Balabac Strait but instead chose to attack Kurita's force even at the cost of abandoning their primary mission. Together these provide a strange—but understandable—coincidence, yet what seems so perverse is that no American submarine or submarines were deployed off the San Bernardino Strait. Of course the American expectation of their carrier forces being able to dominate these waters must have meant that submarine efforts had to be concentrated to the west, and there must have been a desire not to have a friendly submarine in this area for obvious reason. But the lack of any submarine off the Strait nonetheless does seem somewhat curious. It is doubly curious in that for the Philippine Sea battle in June the Americans had eleven submarines gathered around the exits from Tawi Tawi, seventeen off the Bonins and home islands, and fifteen in the Philippines and western Carolines. The disparity of numbers between June and October—when there were seventeen deployed in the reconnais-

sance role—is striking, but scarcely less so is that on 15 June, in the preliminaries to the battle of the Philippine Sea, the Japanese carriers were found
by the *Flying Fish* as they emerged from the San Bernardino Strait.

The remaining two matters on the American side relate to Halsey's
decisions, the first being that if it was so important for Halsey that he enter
the San Bernardino Strait in order to hunt down and destroy Japanese warships in the Visayan Sea, then it is difficult if not impossible to understand
how the Strait became so unimportant as not to require a guard force even
though he knew that Japanese forces were on the other side of it. Not even
the lure of a carrier force can really explain things when set out in this way.
The second is to question Halsey's logic that resulted in the ordering of two
groups, which represented three-fifths of the combat capacity of Task Force
38, to withdraw to Ulithi at a time when the first indications of the Japanese being on the move were received. Even allowing for one of the groups
returning to the fray, the one that missed the battle represented something
like two-fifths of Task Force 38's combat capacity—and this was voluntarily
relinquished by Halsey without any certainty that there would be no battle.
This latter point has been overshadowed by subsequent events, and it needs
be noted that formations had to be rotated, had to be withdrawn from the
battle at some time. It needs be noted, moreover, that the American carriers
had been at sea for more than two weeks, and had been in action over the
previous ten days, when Halsey made his decision on 21 October to detach
two formations, but the subsequent performance of Task Group 38.1 when
it tried to strike at Kurita's force in the early afternoon of 25 October hardly
suggests that it had been essential to dispatch it in the first place, whether for
reasons of rest and recuperation for ships' crews or depletion of air groups.

On the Japanese side, everything pales into insignificance when set
alongside Kurita's breaking off the pursuit of the carrier formation off
Samar; it was a moment, to borrow the saying, "when the world turned."
Yet one wonders, when one reads such statements as

> Had the [Japanese] plan succeeded the effect on the Allied troops on Leyte in all
> likelihood would have been calamitous, for these troops would have been isolated
> and their situation would have been precarious indeed. If it had been victorious
> in the naval battle, the Japanese fleet could have leisurely and effectively carried
> out the destruction of shipping, aircraft and supplies that were so vital to Allied
> operations on Leyte. An enemy naval victory would have had an adverse effect of
> incalculable proportions not only upon the Leyte operation, but upon the overall
> plan for the liberation of the Philippines as well.[17]

of the validity of the *Far Side* cartoon showing a cow on a psychiatrist's couch and saying to the psychiatrist, "Some times I think it's me, but most of the time I know it's the rest of the herd." There was no victory the Japanese could have won that would have wrought such effects, and at best the damage that even a victorious Japanese force might have inflicted on warships and shipping in the Gulf and off the beachheads could never have been anything but minor and of temporary effect. "Calamitous" and "incalculable proportions" might have a certain resonance but do not accord with reality. As it was, with the Japanese knowing that the main U.S. carrier strength was off Luzon, one wonders why there appears to have been no consideration of the option of sending the whole battle fleet into action via the Surigao Strait. Likewise, given the paucity of destroyer numbers with Kurita's formation, one wonders why Shima's formation was not directly attached to Kurita's force. The separation of the formations of Nishimura and Shima is often the subject of adverse comment and rightly so, but it beggars the imagination as to why, if both formations were committed to the Surigao Strait, Shima's formation was not ordered to lead. Overall, and making a choice between these various options, it seems that Shima's formation could have been best employed as part of Kurita's formation rather than being sent as an independent force to the Surigao Strait. Moreover, and as noted elsewhere, given the all-embracing seriousness of the battle force's mission and the paucity of destroyers, Kurita's detachment of destroyers to stand by the *Takao* and *Myoko* after they had been torpedoed seems bizarre, but when set against his two turnaways these matters are of little real account.

These lines have not dealt kindly with either Halsey or Kurita, and perhaps the only comment that might do both some measure of justice at this late stage is to suggest that had their roles been reversed, and an American of Kurita's persuasion and a Japanese of Halsey's temperament been in command then perhaps we might have seen a Japanese battle force close on Task Unit 77.4.3 rapidly and decisively and then move directly against Task Unit 77.4.2 and American forces in Leyte Gulf—if it could have evaded or outfought the American force left to watch over the exit of the San Bernardino Strait. Perhaps such an analogy is more relevant or easily understandable than allusions to the Japanese need for a Hotspur rather than a Hamlet,[18] but at the end one point needs to be made. The Americans won the battle of Leyte Gulf not because of Halsey and not in spite of him, and all considerations of the role of the individual in this battle come back to one basic point: result. The American victory in this battle was overwhelming.

The naval battle for the Philippines saw American carrier aircraft, land-based aircraft, warships, and submarines—or American shells, torpedoes, and bombs—account for a total of thirty Japanese warships and submarines, another two submarines being lost to causes that remain unknown. Admittedly two Australian warships were in the fray, but their presence does not in any way detract from the fact that this was an American victory, and was perhaps the most comprehensive single naval victory in the two world wars of the twentieth century. In numbers of ships sunk the American victory overshadowed those won off Midway atoll in June 1942 and west of Saipan two years later, and it was a victory that literally all but stripped the Imperial Navy of its remaining strength in every type of fleet unit. In overall terms, and with the U.S. Navy losing the light carrier *Princeton*, the escort carriers *Gambier Bay* and *St. Lo*, the destroyers *Hoel* and *Johnston*, and the destroyer escorts *Eversole* and *Samuel B. Roberts*, at the battle's end the Imperial Navy was left with the battleships *Hyuga*, *Ise*, *Nagato*, *Haruna*, *Kongo* and the *Yamato*; the fleet carriers *Junyo*, *Shinano*, *Amagi*, *Katsuragi* and the *Unryu*; the light carrier *Ryuho*; the escort carriers *Kaiyo* and *Shinyo*; the training carrier *Hosho*; the heavy cruisers *Aoba*, *Ashigara*, *Haguro*, *Myoko*, *Nachi*, *Takao*, *Kumano* and the *Tone*; the light cruisers *Kitakami*, *Kiso*, *Isuzu*, *Kashima*, *Kashii*, *Yahagi*, *Sakawa*, *Oyodo* and the *Yasojima*; and some twenty destroyers plus escorts, minesweepers, and patrol vessels. That all the carriers, battleships, and cruisers that remained to the Imperial Navy could be cited in a little more than five lines, and that of these the heavy cruisers *Aoba*, *Myoko* and the *Takao* were *hors de combat* and no fewer than seven—the battleship *Kongo*, the fleet carrier *Shinano*, the escort carrier *Shinyo*, and two heavy and two light cruisers—were sunk in November 1944 was evidence of the nature and extent of the American victory and Japanese defeat in both the war in general and this battle in particular. Battles at sea do not produce the immediately tangible result that attend victories won by armies; ground is not held, towns, cities, and positions are not taken. The battle at sea, like the battle in the air, is continuous in a way that the land battle is not; the same battle has to be fought over the same area in a way that the land battle does not. The nature of the American victory in October 1944 is difficult to define in the sense that just as what is termed "The Battle of the Atlantic" was not won until May 1945, so the naval battle for the Philippines was one part of a process that came to realization in July 1945. That was the bottom line of the victory that was won by the Americans in October 1944, its full extent taking some months to be realized, and herein is the point of Japanese losses at, and what was left to the *Kaigun* after, the naval battle for the Philippines. The reduction of the Imperial Navy to such a weakened state was a process that reached over three years, and in the battle of Leyte Gulf what was left to the Imperial Navy was literally put to the sword. In this battle the Japanese formations lost a total of three battleships, one fleet and three light carriers, six heavy and four light cruisers, and eleven destroyers, representing a total of 305,452 tons of warships, or 13.22 percent of the total *Kaigun* tonnage losses in the war.[19] It was certainly a defeat from which there could be no recovery because Japan simply lacked the numbers of ships that could form the nucleus of a reconstituted navy, and the Americans, with the ability to take the war to the home islands by carrier- and land-based aircraft, were never going to allow her time to look anew to her defenses. For the Imperial Navy the seas that washed the Philippines indeed proved to be "a fitting place to die," but this battle was much more. The battle of Leyte Gulf, the naval battle for the Philippines, was the last battle between fleets in history. It was the greatest battle in modern naval history in numbers of ships, the area of battle, the area of deployment, and length. It was a battle of three parts, and, too easy to miss, in each part there were surface actions and there were actions between aircraft and warships, and in each of these three separate actions warships sank and were sunk by warships and by aircraft; these actions were not separately and singularly fought. It was the last battle in which capital ships fought one another, and thus was the final act in a period of history that reached back to the sixteenth century. And it was the last battle in which carriers did battle with one another. Hopefully, so it will remain.

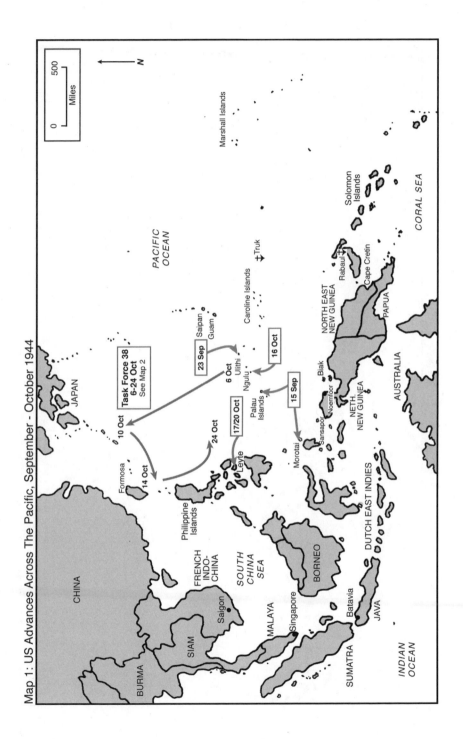

Map 1: US Advances Across The Pacific, September – October 1944

Map 2: The Western and Southwest Pacific: The American Approach to Contact

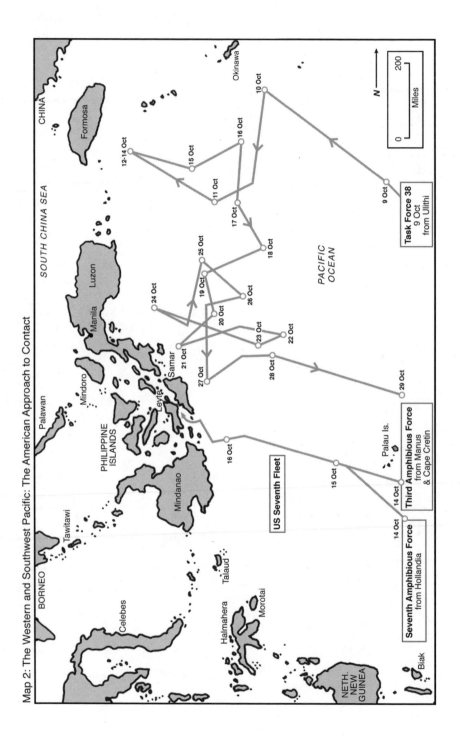

Map 3: The Western and Southwest Pacific: The Japanese Response

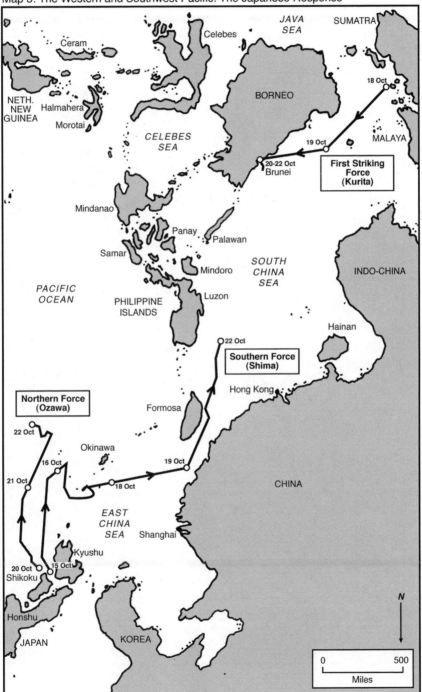

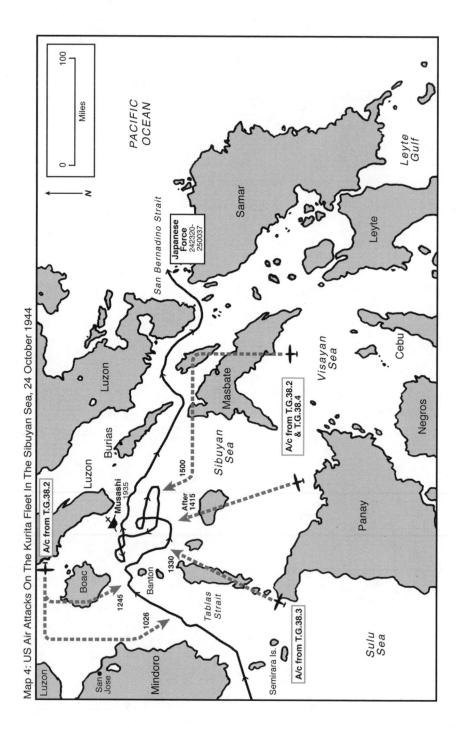

Map 4: US Air Attacks On The Kurita Fleet In The Sibuyan Sea, 24 October 1944

PACIFIC
OCEAN

Leyte
Gulf

Samar

Leyte

San Bernadino Strait

Japanese Force
242320-
250037

N

0   100

Miles

Luzon

Luzon

Burias

Masbate

Cebu

Visayan
Sea

A/c from T.G.38.2
& T.G.38.4

Musashi
1935

1500

Sibuyan
Sea

After
1415

A/c from T.G.38.2

Boac

1245

Negros

Panay

1026

Banton

1330

Tablas
Strait

San
Jose

Mindoro

Semirara Is.

A/c from T.G.38.3

Sulu
Sea

Map 5: The Surigao Strait Action

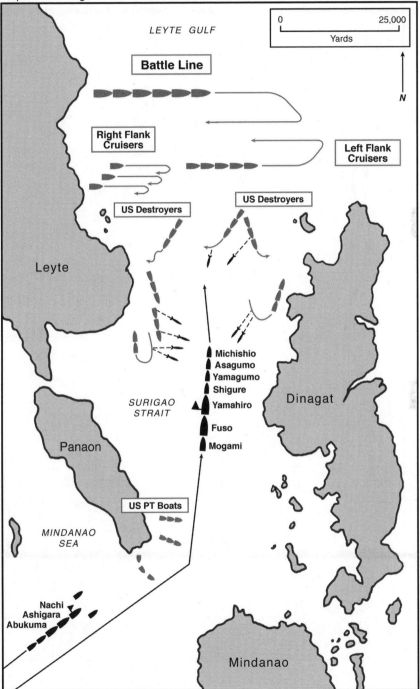

LEYTE GULF

Battle Line

Right Flank
Cruisers

Left Flank
Cruisers

US Destroyers

US Destroyers

Leyte

0   25,000
Yards

N

Michishio
Asagumo
Yamagumo
Shigure
Yamahiro
Fuso
Mogami

Dinagat

SURIGAO
STRAIT

Panaon

US PT Boats

MINDANAO
SEA

Nachi
Ashigara
Abukuma

Mindanao

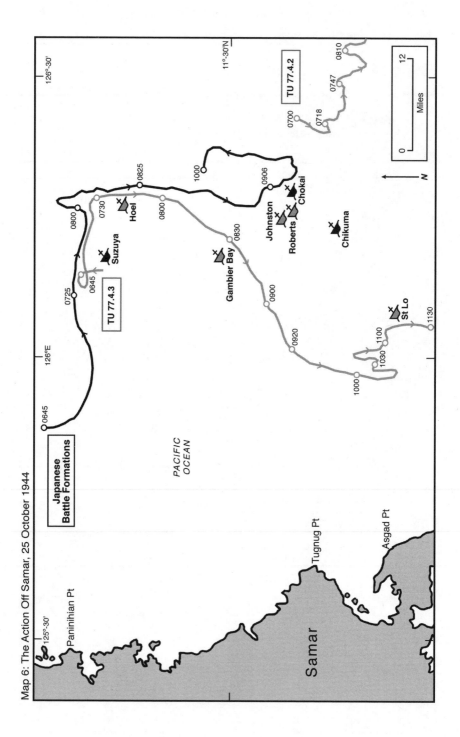

Map 6: The Action Off Samar, 25 October 1944

Map 7: The Action Off Cape Engaño, 25 October 1944

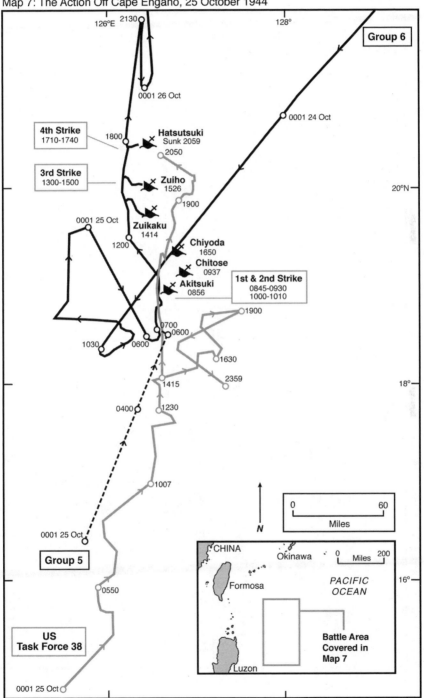

126°E

2130

128°

Group 6

0001 26 Oct

0001 24 Oct

20°N

4th Strike
1710-1740

1800

Hatsutsuki
Sunk 2059

× 2050

3rd Strike
1300-1500

× **Zuiho**
1526

1900

× **Zuikaku**
1414

0001 25 Oct

1200

Chiyoda
1650

Chitose
0937

× **Akitsuki**
0856

1st & 2nd Strike
0845-0930
1000-1010

1900

0700

0600

1630

1030

0600

2359

1415

18°

0400

1230

1007

N

0   60
Miles

0001 25 Oct

Group 5

CHINA   Okinawa

0   200
Miles

**US
Task Force 38**

0550

Formosa

*PACIFIC
OCEAN*

16°

**Battle Area
Covered in
Map 7**

0001 25 Oct

Luzon

Map 8: The American Carrier Operations After The Battle (1)

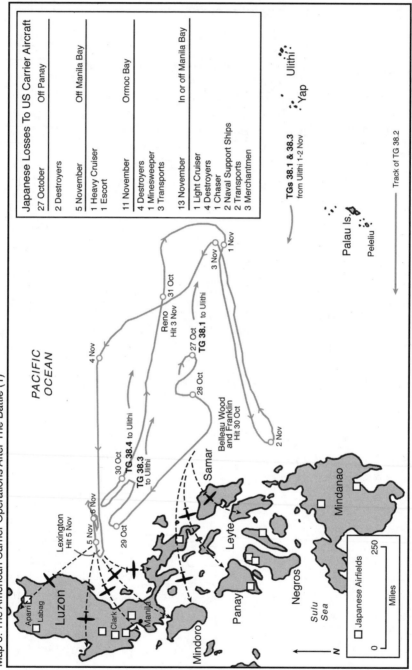

Japanese Losses To US Carrier Aircraft

27 October	Off Panay	
	2 Destroyers	
5 November	Off Manila Bay	
	1 Heavy Cruiser	
	1 Escort	
11 November	Ormoc Bay	
	4 Destroyers	
	1 Minesweeper	
	3 Transports	
13 November	In or off Manila Bay	
	1 Light Cruiser	
	4 Destroyers	
	1 Chaser	
	2 Naval Support Ships	
	2 Transports	
	3 Merchantmen	

Map 9: The American Carrier Operations After The Battle (2) 12 - 27 November 1944

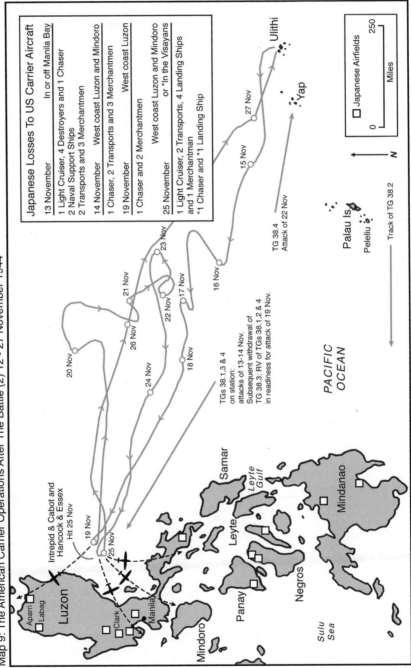

Japanese Losses To US Carrier Aircraft

13 November   In or off Manila Bay

1 Light Cruiser, 4 Destroyers and 1 Chaser
2 Naval Support Ships
2 Transports and 3 Merchantmen

14 November   West coast Luzon and Mindoro

1 Chaser, 2 Transports and 3 Merchantmen

19 November   West coast Luzon

1 Chaser and 2 Merchantmen

25 November   West coast Luzon and Mindoro
                   or *In the Visayans

1 Light Cruiser, 2 Transports, 4 Landing Ships
and 1 Merchantman
*1 Chaser and *1 Landing Ship

☐ Japanese Airfields

0   250

Miles

N

Ulithi

27 Nov

15 Nov

Yap

TG 38.4
Attack of 22 Nov

Palau Is.

Peleliu

Track of TG 38.2

PACIFIC
OCEAN

23 Nov

21 Nov

20 Nov

26 Nov

22 Nov

24 Nov

17 Nov

18 Nov

16 Nov

TGs 38.1,3 & 4
on station:
attacks of 13-14 Nov.
Subsequent withdrawal of
TG 38.3: RV of TGs 38.1,2 & 4
in readiness for attack of 19 Nov.

Intrepid & Cabot and
Hancock & Essex
Hit 25 Nov

19 Nov

25 Nov

Aparri
Labag

LUZON

Clark

Manila

Mindoro

Samar

Leyte
Gulf

Leyte

Panay

Negros

Mindanao

Sulu
Sea

THE ORDER OF BATTLE OF JAPANESE FORMATIONS INVOLVED IN THE NAVAL BATTLE FOR THE PHILIPPINES, 22–28 OCTOBER 1944

TASK FORCE MAIN BODY (VICE ADMIRAL OZAWA JISABURO IN THE FLEET CARRIER *ZUIKAKU*)

3rd Carrier Division (Vice Admiral Ozawa Jisaburo in the fleet carrier *Zuikaku*): The fleet carrier *Zuikaku* (Rear Admiral Kaizuka Takeo), and light carriers *Chitose* (Captain Kishi Yoshiyuki), *Chiyoda* (Captain Zyo/Jyo Eiichiro) and the *Zuiho* (Captain Sigiura Kuro).

4th Carrier Division (Rear Admiral Matsuda Chiaki in the hybrid battleship *Hyuga*): The battleship-carriers *Hyuga* (Rear Admiral Nomura Tomekichi) and *Ise* (Rear Admiral Nakase Noboru).

31st Escort Squadron (Rear Admiral Edo Heitaro/Hyotaro in the light cruiser *Isuzu*): The light cruiser *Isuzu* (Captain Matsuda Gengo) with the destroyer escorts *Kiri* (Commander Kawabata Makoto), *Kuwa* (Commander Yamashita Masamichi/Masanori), *Maki* (Commander Ishizuka Sakae) and the *Sugi* (Commander Kikuchi Toshitaka) from the 43rd Destroyer Division (Captain Kanma Ryoukichi in the *Maki*) in company.

61st Destroyer Division (Captain Amano Shigetaka in the destroyer *Hatsutsuki*): The destroyers *Akitsuki* (Commander Ogata Tomoe), *Hatsutsuki* (Commander Hashimoto Kanematu) and the *Wakatsuki* (Commander Suzuki Yasuatsu) with the destroyer *Shimotsuki* (Commander Hatano Kenichi) from the 41st Destroyer Division (Captain Wakita Kiichiro) in company.

Attached units: The light cruisers *Oyodo* (Captain Mudaguchi Kakurou) and *Tama* (Captain Yamamoto Iwata).

The oiler formation operating in support of this force consisted of the destroyer *Akikaze* (Commander Yamazaki Jintaro), the corvettes C.D. 22 (Lieutenant-Commander Haneba/Haba Ryo), C.D. 29 (Lieutenant-Commander Morishima Makinosuke), C.D. 31 (Lieutenant-Commander Kubo Takeshi), C.D. 33 (Lieutenant-Commander Morimoto Masaharu), C.D. 43 (Lieutenant-Commander Saito Yuichi) and the C.D. 132 (Commander Takemura Sou), and the oilers *Jinei Maru* and *Takane Maru*.

1ST STRIKING FORCE:
VICE ADMIRAL KURITA TAKEO IN THE HEAVY CRUISER *ATAGO*.

1st Task Group: Vice Admiral Kurita Takeo in the heavy cruiser *Atago*.

1st Battleship Division (Vice Admiral Ugaki Matome in the battleship *Yamato*): The battleships *Musashi* (Rear Admiral Inoguchi Toshihara), *Nagato* (Rear Admiral Kobe Yuji) and the *Yamato* (Rear Admiral Morishita Nobue).

4th Cruiser Division (Vice Admiral Kurita Takeo in the heavy cruiser *Atago*): The heavy cruisers *Atago* (Captain Araki Tsutau), *Chokai* (Captain Ariga Kosaku/Tanaka Jyo), *Maya* (Captain Oe Ranji) and the *Takao* (Captain Onoda Sutejiro).

5th Cruiser Division (Vice Admiral Hashimoto Shintaro in the heavy cruiser *Myoko*): The heavy cruisers *Haguro* (Captain Sugiura Kaju) and *Myoko* (Captain Ishiwara Itsu).

2nd Destroyer Squadron (Rear Admiral Hayakawa Mikio in the light cruiser *Noshiro*): The light cruiser *Noshiro* (Captain Kajiwara Sueyoshi) and destroyer *Shimakaze* (Commander Doi Hiroshi).

2nd Destroyer Division (Captain Shiraishi Nagayoshi in the destroyer *Hayashimo*): The destroyers *Akishimo* (Commander Nakao Kotaro) and *Hayashimo* (Commander Hirayama Toshio).

31st Destroyer Division (Captain Fukuoka T. in the destroyer *Kishinami*): The destroyers *Asashio* (Commander Sugihara Kyoshiro), *Kishinami* (Commander Mifune Toshiro), *Naganami* (Commander Toda/Tobita Kiyoshi) and the *Okinami* (Commander Akino Tan).

32nd Destroyer Division (Commander Aoki Hisaji in the destroyer *Fujinami*): The destroyers *Fujinami* (Commander Matsuzaki Tatsuji) and *Hamanami* (Commander Motokura Masayoshi).

2nd Task Group: Vice Admiral Suzuki Yoshio in the battleship *Kongo*.

3rd Battleship Division (Vice Admiral Suzuki Yoshio in the battleship *Kongo*): The battleships *Haruna* (Rear Admiral Shigenaga Kazutaka) and *Kongo* (Rear Admiral Shimazaki Toshio).

7th Cruiser Division (Vice Admiral Shiraishi Kazutaka in the heavy cruiser *Kumano*): The heavy cruisers *Chikuma* (Captain Norimitsu Saiji), *Kumano* (Captain Hitomi Soichiro), *Suzuya* (Captain Teraoka Masao) and the *Tone* (Captain Mayuzumi Haruo).

10th Destroyer Squadron (Rear Admiral Kimura Susumu in the light cruiser *Yahagi*): The light cruiser *Yahagi* (Captain Yoshimura Masatake) and destroyers *Kiyoshima* (Commander Kajimoto Kai) and *Nowaki* (Commander Moriya Setsuji).

17th Destroyer Division (Captain Tanii Tamotsu in the destroyer *Urakaze*): The destroyers *Hamakaze* (Commander Maekawa Manei), *Isokaze* (Commander Maeda Sadasho), *Urakaze* (Commander Yokota Yasuteru) and the *Yukikaze* (Commander Terauchi Masamichi).

3rd Task Group: Vice Admiral Nishimura Shoji in the battleship *Yamashiro*.

2nd Battleship Division (Vice Admiral Nishimura Shoji in the battleship *Yamashiro*): The battleships *Fuso* (Rear Admiral Ban Masami) and *Yamashiro* (Rear Admiral Shinoda Katsukiyo).

5th Cruiser Division: The heavy cruiser *Mogami* (Captain Tooma Ryo) and the destroyer *Shigure* (Commander Nishino Shigeru) from the 2nd Destroyer Division.

4th Destroyer Division (Captain Takahashi Kameshiro in the destroyer *Michishio*): The destroyers *Asagumo* (Commander Shibayama Kazuo/Ichio), *Michishio* (Lieutenant-Commander Tanaka Tomoo) and the *Yamagumo* (Commander Ono Shiro).

SOUTHWEST AREA FORCE (VICE ADMIRAL MIKAWA GUINICHI)

2nd Striking Force: Vice Admiral Shima Kiyohide in the heavy cruiser *Nachi*.
21st Cruiser Division (Vice Admiral Shima Kiyohide in the heavy cruiser *Nachi*): The
    heavy cruisers *Ashigara* (Captain Miura Hayao) and *Nachi* (Captain Kanoka Empei).
1st Destroyer Squadron (Rear Admiral Kimura Masatomi in the light cruiser *Abukuma*):
    The light cruiser *Abukuma* (Captain Hanada Takuo).
7th Destroyer Division (Commander Iwagami Jiichi in the destroyer *Akebono*): The destroy-
    ers *Akebono* (Commander Yoda Shiro) and *Ushio* (Commander Araki Masatomi).
18th Destroyer Division (Captain Inoue Yoshio in the destroyer *Shiranui*): The destroyers
    Kasumi and *Shiranui* (Commander Aratei Saburo).

DETACHED FORMATIONS

16th Cruiser Division (Vice Admiral Sakonju Naomasa in the *Aoba*): The heavy cruiser
    Aoba (Captain Yamazumi Chusaburo), the light cruiser *Kinu* (Captain Kawasaki
    Harumi) and the destroyer *Uranami* (Commander Sako Kaei).
This formation was assigned the task of escorting transports bound for Mindanao and did
    not take part in the battle; the transports were the T. 6, T. 101, T. 102 and the T. 131.
21st Destroyer Division (Captain Ishii Hisashi in the *Wakaba*): The destroyers *Hatsuharu*
    (Commander Okuma Yashunoshuke), *Hatsushimo* (Commander Sakaku Masazo/
    Sakakou Tsunezo) and the *Wakaba* (Commander Ninokata Kanefumi).

ADVANCE SUBMARINE FORCE

A total of fourteen submarines were available under the command of Vice Admiral Miwa
    Shigeyoshi in the *Tsukushi Maru* at Kure and operated off the Philippines against U.S.
    main formations. The submarines were organized thus:

A DIVISION
The I. 26 (Lieutenant-Commander Nishiuchi Masakazu/Shoichi), I. 45 (Lieutenant-
    Commander Kawashima Mamoru), I. 53 (Lieutenant-Commander Toyomasu Kiyohachi/
    Seihachi), I. 54 and the I. 56 (Lieutenant-Commander Moringa Masahiko).

B DIVISION
The I. 38 (Lieutenant-Commander Shimose Yoshiro), I. 41 (Lieutenant-Commander
    Kondo Fumitake), I. 44, I. 46 (Lieutenant-Commander Kawaguchi Koukaburo), Ro. 41
    (Lieutenant-Commander Shizuka Mitsuo), Ro. 43 (Lieutenant-Commander Tsukikata
    Masaki) and the Ro. 46 (Lieutenant-Commander Suzuki Shokichi/Masayoshi).

C DIVISION
The Ro. 109 (Lieutenant-Commander Masuzawa Seiji/Kiyoshi) and Ro. 112 (Lieutenant-
    Commander Ueshugi Kazuaki).

Two submarines were used to convey midget submarines for the attack on U.S. ships in
    the Ulithi anchorage. These were the I. 36 (Lieutenant-Commander Teramoto) and I.
    47 (Lieutenant-Commander Orita Zenji).

NAVAL AIR FORMATIONS

5th Base Air Force: c. 35 aircraft on 18 October (Vice Admiral Onishi Takijiro).
6th Base Air Force: c. 200 aircraft on 23 October (Vice Admiral Fukudome Shigeru).

E. & O. E.

Notes:

It was not possible to identify the commanding officers of the destroyer *Kasumi* and submarines I. 44 and I. 54 and of the oilers and transports cited herein.

The transliteration of many of the names was exceedingly difficult; some are dated and cannot be definitively cited. Such names are given with alternative renditions.

With due and unreserved acknowledgment to Kobayashi Go, currently at the University of Glasgow; Shindo Hiroyuki of the Military History Department, National Institute for Defence Studies; and Professor Tohmatsu Haruo, Tamagawa University, for all the help they afforded in the completion of this order of battle.

THE ORDER OF BATTLE OF THE 3RD FLEET, 9 OCTOBER 1944

3RD FLEET (ADMIRAL WILLIAM FREDERICK HALSEY, JR.,
IN THE BATTLESHIP *NEW JERSEY*)

TASK FORCE 38
(VICE ADMIRAL MARC ANDREW MITSCHER IN THE FLEET CARRIER *LEXINGTON*)

Task Group 38.1 (Vice Admiral John Sidney McCain in the fleet carrier Wasp)
Task Unit 38.1.1: The fleet carriers *Hornet* (Captain Austin Kelvin Doyle) and *Wasp* (Captain Oscar Arthur Weller) and the light carriers *Cowpens* (Captain Howard William Taylor, Jr.) and *Monterey* (Captain Stuart Howe Ingersoll).
Task Unit 38.1.2: Cruiser Division 6 (Rear Admiral Charles Turner Joy): The heavy cruiser *Wichita* (Captain Douglas Ancrum Spencer) and Cruiser Division 10 (Rear Admiral Lloyd Jerome Wiltse in the heavy cruiser *Boston*): The heavy cruisers *Boston* (Captain Ernest Edward Herrmann) and *Canberra* (Captain Alexander Rieman Early, Jr.) and the light cruiser *Houston* (Captain William Wohlsen Behrens).
Task Unit 38.1.3 (Captain Carl Frederick Espe in the destroyer *Izard*):
Destroyer Squadron 46 (Captain Espe in the *Izard*): The destroyers *Bell* (Commander John Sterett Crittenden Gabbert), *Burns* (Commander Jacob Thompson Bullen, Jr.), *Charrette* (Commander Gerald Patrick Joyce), *Conner* (Commander William Eugene Kaitner) and the *Izard* (Commander Milton Theodore Dayton), Destroyer Division 92 (Captain William Merton Sweetser in the *Boyd*): The destroyers *Boyd* (Commander Ulysses S. Grant Sharp, Jr.) and *Cowell* (Commander Charles William Parker), and Destroyer Division 100 (Captain Wallace Joseph Miller in the *Cogswell*): The destroyers *Caperton* (Commander George Kennedy Carmichael), *Cogswell* (Commander Robert Elmore Lockwood), *Ingersoll* (Commander Alexander Craig Veasey) and the *Knapp* (Lieutenant-Commander William Butler Brown).
Destroyer Squadron 12 (Captain William Page Burford in the *McCalla*): The destroyers *Brown* (Commander Thomas Henry Copeman, Jr.), *Grayson* (Commander William

Veazie Pratt, II), *McCalla* (Lieutenant-Commander Eli Vinock) and the *Woodworth* (Commander Charles Robert Stephan).

Task Group 38.2 *(Rear Admiral Gerald Francis Bogan in the fleet carrier* Intrepid)
Task Unit 38.2.1: The fleet carriers *Bunker Hill* (Captain Marshall Raymond Greer), *Hancock* (Captain Fred Clinton Dickey) and the *Intrepid* (Captain Joseph Francis Bolger) and the light carriers *Cabot* (Captain Stanley John Michael) and *Independence* (Captain Edward Coyle Ewen).
Task Unit 38.2.2: Battle Division 7 (Rear Admiral Oscar Charles Badger in the battleship *Iowa*): The battleships *Iowa* (Captain Allan Rockwell McCann) and *New Jersey* (Captain Carl Frederick Holden, Jr.) and Cruiser Division 14 (Rear Admiral Francis Eliot Maynard Whiting in the *Vincennes*): The light cruisers *Miami* (Captain John Graybill Crawford), *Oakland* (Captain Kendall Sturtevant Reed), *San Diego* (Captain William Evans Anthony Mullan) and the *Vincennes* (Captain Arthur D. Brown).
Task Unit 38.2.3 (Captain John Philip Womble, Jr., in the destroyer *Owen*):
Destroyer Squadron 52: Destroyer Division 103 (Captain Womble in the *Owen*): The destroyers *Miller* (Lieutenant-Commander Dwight Lyman Johnson), *Owen* (Commander Carlton Benton Jones), *Stephen Potter* (Commander Leonidas Walthall Pancoast), *The Sullivans* (Commander Ralph Jacob Baum) and the *Tingey* (Commander John Odgers Miner), and Destroyer Division 104 (Captain William Talty Kenny in the *Hickox*): The destroyers *Hickox* (Commander Joseph Hawes Wesson), *Hunt* (Commander Halford A. Knoertzer), *Lewis Hancock* (Commander William Marvin Searles) and the *Marshall* (Commander Joseph Dwight McKinney).
Destroyer Squadron 53 (Captain Harry Bean Jarrett in the *Cushing*): Destroyer Division 105 (Captain Harry Bean Jarrett in the *Cushing*): The destroyers *Benham* (Commander Frederic Seward Keeler), *Colahan* (Commander Donald Taylor Wilber), *Cushing* (Commander Louis Frank Volk), *Halsey Powell* (Commander Sidney Douglas Buxton Merrill) and the *Uhlmann* (Commander Selden Gain Hooper), and Destroyer Division 106 (Captain Benjamin Francis Tompkins in the *Stockham*): The destroyers *Stockham* (Commander Ephraim Paul Holmes), *Twining* (Commander Ellis Kerr Wakefield), *Wedderburn* (Commander Charles Hansford Kendall) and the *Yarnall* (Commander James Henry Hogg).

Task Group 38.3 *(Rear Admiral Frederick Carl Sherman in the fleet carrier* Essex)
Task Unit 38.3.1: The fleet carriers *Essex* (Captain Carlos Wilhelm Wieber) and *Lexington* (Captain Ernest Wheeler Litch) and the light carriers *Langley* (Captain John Fred Wegforth) and *Princeton* (Captain William Houck Buracker).
Task Unit 38.3.2: Pacific Fleet Battleships (Vice Admiral Willis Augustus Lee, Jr.): The battleship *Washington* (Captain Thomas Ross Cooley, Jr.), Battle Division 8 (Rear Admiral Glenn Benson Davis): The battleship *Massachusetts* (Captain William Walter Warlick), Battle Division 9 (Rear Admiral Edward William Hanson in the *South Dakota*): The battleships *Alabama* (Captain Vincent Raphael Murphy) and *South Dakota* (Captain Charles Bowers Momsen), and Cruiser Division 13 (Rear Admiral Laurence Toombs DuBose in the *Santa Fe*): The light cruisers *Birmingham* (Captain Thomas Browning Inglis), *Mobile* (Captain Christopher Chaffe Miller), *Reno* (Captain Ralph Clonts Alexander) and the *Santa Fe* (Captain Jerauld Wright).
Task Unit 38.3.3 (Captain Carlton Rice Todd in the destroyer *Porterfield*):
Destroyer Squadron 50 (Captain Edwin Richard Wilkinson in the *Clarence C. Bronson*): The destroyers *Clarence C. Bronson* (Commander Gifford Scull), *Cotten* (Commander Philip Wallace Winston), *Dortch* (Commander Richard Edwin Myers), *Gatling*

(Commander Alvin Franklin Richardson) and the *Healy* (Commander John Connor Atkeson).

Destroyer Squadron 55 (Captain Carlton Rice Todd in the *Porterfield*): Destroyer Division 109 (Captain Todd in the *Porterfield*): The destroyers *Callaghan* (Commander Charles Marriner Bertholf), *Cassin Young* (Commander Earl Tobias Schreiber), *Irwin* (Commander Daniel Byrd Miller), *Porterfield* (Lieutenant-Commander Don Wesley Wulzen) and the *Preston* (Commander Goldsborough Serpell Patrick), and Destroyer Division 110 (Commander Merle van Metre in the *Laws*): The destroyers *Laws* (Commander Lester Orin Wood), *Longshaw* (Commander Robert Hursey Speck), *Morrison* (Commander Walter Harold Price) and the *Prichett* (Commander Cecil Thilman Caulfield).

Task Group 38.4 (Rear Admiral Ralph Eugene Davison in the fleet carrier Franklin*)*

Task Unit 38.4.1: The fleet carriers *Enterprise* (Captain Cato Douglas Glover, Jr.) and *Franklin* (Captain James Marshall Shoemaker) and the light carriers *Belleau Wood* (Captain John Perry) and *San Jacinto* (Captain Michael Holt Kernodle).

Task Unit 38.4.2: The heavy cruiser *New Orleans* (Captain Jack Ellett Hurff) and the light cruiser *Biloxi* (Captain Paul Ralph Heineman).

Task Unit 38.4.3 (Captain Victor Dismukes Long in the destroyer *Maury*):

Destroyer Squadron 6 (Captain Long in the *Maury*): The destroyers *Gridley* (Commander Philip Decatur Quirk), *Helm* (Commander Selby Krauss Santmyers), *Maury* (Commander Joseph William Koenig) and the *McCall* (Lieutenant-Commander John Blake Carroll), Destroyer Division 12 (Captain Karl Frederick Poehlmann in the *Mugford*): The destroyers *Bagley* (Commander William Henry Shea, Jr.), *Mugford* (Commander Martin Adams Shellabarger), *Patterson* (Lieutenant-Commander Walter Andrew Hering) and the *Ralph Talbot* (Lieutenant-Commander William Stewart Brown), and Destroyer Division 24 (Captain Alvord John Greenacre in the *Wilkes*): The destroyers *Nicholson* (Commander Warfield Clay Bennett, Jr.), *Swanson* (Commander William Ratliff) and the *Wilkes* (Lieutenant-Commander Fred Earl McEntire, Jr.).

Task Group 30.8 (Captain Jasper Terry Acuff initially in the destroyer John D. Henley*)*

The escort carriers *Altamaha* (Captain Alfred Clarence Olney, Jr.), *Barnes* (Captain Daniel Nicol Logan), *Cape Esperance* (Captain Robert Wurts Bockius), *Kwajalein* (Captain Robert Crawford Warrack), *Nassau* (Captain Norman Wyatt Ellis), *Nehenta Bay* (Captain Horace Bushnell Butterfield), *Rudyard Bay* (Captain Curtis Stanton Smiley), *Sargent Bay* (Captain William Theodore Rassieur), *Shipley Bay* (Captain Edgar Tilghman Neale), *Sitkoh Bay* (Captain Robert Green Lockhart) and the *Steamer Bay* (Captain Steadman Teller) with replacement aircraft.

The oilers *Atascosa* (Commander Horace Leland de Rivera), *Aucilla* (Commander Charles L. Cover, Jr.), *Cache* (Lieutenant-Commander Coleman R. Cosgrove), *Caliente* (Lieutenant-Commander Allen E. Stiff), *Chicopee* (Commander Charles O. Peak), *Chikaskia* (Lieutenant-Commander George Zimmerman), *Cimarron* (Lieutenant-Commander Henry G. Schnaars, Jr.), *Escambia* (Lieutenant-Commander Richard Goorgian), *Guadalupe* (Commander Herbert Augustus Anderson), *Kankakee* (Lieutenant-Commander Walter G. Frundt), *Kaskaskia* (Lieutenant-Commander William F. Patten), *Kennebago* (Lieutenant-Commander Charles W. Brockway), *Lackawanna* (Commander Alfred James Homann), *Manatee* (Lieutenant-Commander Joseph B. Smyth), *Marias* (Commander Jens G. Olsen), *Mascoma* (Captain Cyril C. Eden), *Merrimack* (Captain Vaughn Bailey), *Millicoma* (Commander George E. Ely), *Mississinewa* (Commander Philip G. Beck), *Monongahela* (Commander Frederick Joseph Ilsemann), *Nantahala*

(Captain Palmer Mackenzie Gunnell), *Neches* (Commander Hedley G. Hansen), *Neosho* (Lieutenant-Commander Francis P. Parkinson), *Niobrara* (Commander Ralph C. Spaulding), *Pamanset* (Commander Dona J. Houle), *Patuxent* (Lieutenant-Commander Frank P. Ferrell), *Pecos* (Lieutenant-Commander George Washington Renegar), *Platte* (Commander Francis Stephenson Gibson), *Sabine* (Lieutenant-Commander Hans C. von Weien), *Saugatuck* (Lieutenant-Commander James F. Ardagh), *Sebec* (Lieutenant-Commander Howard M. Elder), *Taluga* (Commander Hans M. Mikkelsen), *Tappahannock* (Commander Chester Arthur Swafford) and the *Tomahawk* (Captain Benjamin Watkins Cloud).

The destroyers *Aylwin* (Lieutenant-Commander William Kittredge Rogers), *Capps* (Commander Bruce Edward Scofield Trippensee), *Dale* (Lieutenant-Commander Stanley Michael Zimny), *David W. Taylor* (Commander William Harry Johnsen), *Dewey* (Lieutenant-Commander Charles Raymond Calhoun), *Dyson* (Commander Lawrence Ernest Ruff), *Evans* (Commander Floyd Charles Camp), *Farragut* (Lieutenant-Commander Charles Conway Hartigan, Jr.), *Hailey* (Commander Parke Howle Brady), *Hall* (Commander Laurence Charles Baldauf), *Hobby* (Commander George Washington Pressey), *Hull* (Lieutenant-Commander James Alexander Marks), *John D. Henley* (Commander Clyde Wendell Smith), *Monaghan* (Commander Waldemar Frederick August Wendt), *Paul Hamilton* (Commander Leo George May), *Thatcher* (Commander William Arthur Cockell), *Thorn* (Lieutenant-Commander Frederick Henry Schneider, Jr.) and the *Welles* (Lieutenant-Commander John Sim Slaughter).

Notes:

Listed with these units are certain formation commanders but it is not clear which ships belonged to these formations. The commanders named were Captain Benjamin Van Meter Russell, commanding officer of Destroyer Division 102, in the *Capps*, Captain Preston Virginius Mercer, Destroyer Squadron 1, apparently in the *Dewey*, and Captain Joe Brice Cochran, Destroyer Division 38, in the *Hobby*.

Assigned to the screen at different times were the destroyer escorts *Acree* (Lieutenant-Commander Clement O. Davidson), *Bangust* (Lieutenant-Commander Charles F. MacNish), *Crowley* (Lieutenant-Commander Thomas J. Skewes, Jr.), *Donaldson* (Lieutenant-Commander Henry G. Hartmann), *Elden* (Lieutenant-Commander Frederick Charles Hartman, Jr.), *Halloran* (Lieutenant-Commander James G. Scripps), *Hilbert* (Lieutenant-Commander John B. Burnham), *Kyne* (Lieutenant-Commander Carroll F. Sweet, Jr.), *Lake* (Lieutenant-Commander Arthur D. Weekes, Jr.), *Lamons* (Lieutenant-Commander Charles Kenneth Hutchison), *Levy* (Lieutenant-Commander William G. Clarenbach), *Lyman* (Lieutenant-Commander James Woodrow Wilson, III), *McConnell* (Lieutenant-Commander Loris C. Oglesby), *Mitchell* (Lieutenant-Commander Jim K. Carpenter), *Osterhaus* (Lieutenant-Commander Victor D. Burton), *Parks* (Lieutenant-Commander Milford McQuilkin), *Rall* (Lieutenant-Commander Crittenden Battelle Taylor), *Reynolds* (Lieutenant-Commander Edward P. Adams), *Riddle* (Lieutenant-Commander Francis P. Steel), *Samuel S. Miles* (Lieutenant-Commander Henry Gilmore Brousseau), *Swearer* (Lieutenant John M. Trent), *Waterman* (Lieutenant-Commander John H. Stahle), *Weaver* (Lieutenant-Commander William Allen Taylor) and the *Wesson* (Lieutenant Henry Sears).

In addition, in company were the ammunition ships *Australian Victory* (Master C. N. Olsen), *Lassen* (Commander John E. Wade), *Mauna Loa* (Commander George Dewey Martin), *Mount Hood** (Commander Michael Toal), *Sangay* (Lieutenant-Commander Homer C. Taylor) and the *Shasta* (Commander William Lynch Ware) and the fleet tugs *Hitchiti* (Lieutenant-Commander Harry Alonzo Guthrie), *Jicarilla* (Lieutenant-Commander Winfred B. Coats), *Mataco* (Lieutenant Cecil O. Hall), *Menominee* (Lieutenant John A. Young), *Molala* (Lieutenant Rudolph Lee Ward), *Munsee* (Lieutenant-Commander John Francis Pingley), *Pawnee* (Lieutenant-Commander Howard C. Cramer), *Sioux* (Lieutenant Leonard Mac Jahnsen), *Tekesta* (Lieutenant Paul D. Petrich) and the *Zuni* (Lieutenant Ray Edward Chance).

Morison, p. 429, states that the destroyer escorts *O'Neill* and *Stern* were in company, but the *O'Neill* did not enter the Pacific until 31 October and the *Stern* did not arrive at Pearl Harbor until 23 November 1944; neither was in Philippine waters in the period of the battle and immediate aftermath and thus have been excluded from this order of battle.

* The *Mount Hood* was destroyed by an accidental explosion on 10 November 1944 while in Seeadler harbor, Manus.

APPENDIX THREE THE STRENGTH OF THE MAIN AMERICAN FORMATIONS
WITH THE 3RD AND 7TH FLEETS, OCTOBER 1944

(fleet units, escorts, minesweepers and minelayers, submarines, and oilers only)

	CV	CVL	CVE	a/c	BB	CA	CL	DD	DE	PF	CM	AM/DMS	SS	AO
T.F. 38														
T.G. 38.1	2	2	–	244	–	3	1	15	–	–	–	–	–	–
T.G. 38.2	3	2	–	339	2	–	4	17	–	–	–	–	–	–
T.G. 38.3	2	2	–	253	2	–	4	14	–	–	–	–	–	–
T.G. 38.4	2	2	–	241	2	–	2	11	–	–	–	–	–	–
T.F. 77														
T.G. 77.1	–	–	–	–	–	–	1	4	–	–	–	–	–	–
T.G. 77.3	–	–	–	–	–	2	2	7	–	–	–	–	–	–
T.G. 77.4	–	–	18	507	–	–	–	9	14	–	–	–	–	–
T.G. 77.5	–	–	–	–	–	–	–	–	3	–	2	22	–	–
T.G. 77.7	–	–	–	–	–	–	–	–	–	–	–	–	–	8
T.F. 78														
T.G. 78.1	–	–	–	–	3	–	–	3	–	–	–	–	–	–
T.G. 78.2	–	–	–	–	–	–	–	4	–	–	–	–	–	–
T.G. 78.3	–	–	–	–	–	–	–	3	–	–	1	–	–	–
T.G. 78.4	–	–	–	–	–	–	2	5	–	2	–	–	–	–
T.G. 78.6	–	–	–	–	–	–	–	2	–	2	–	–	–	–
T.G. 78.7	–	–	–	–	–	–	–	4	–	2	–	–	–	–
T.G. 78.8	–	–	–	–	–	–	–	5	–	4	–	–	–	–

APPENDIX THREE (CONTINUED)

	CV	CVL	CVE	a/c	BB	CA	CL	DD	DE	PF	CM	AM/DMS	SS	AO
T.F. 79														
T.G. 79.3					3	3	1	13						
T.G. 79.4								8						
T.G. 79.11								10						
T.F. 17								7					22	
T.G. 71.1													7	
T.G. 30.2			11	c.300		3		6	26					34
T.G. 30.8								18						
Total numbers	9	8	29	c. 1884	12	11	17	169	43	10	3	22	29	42

CV   Fleet carriers   BB   Battleships   DE   Destroyer escorts   SS   Submarines

CVL   Light carriers   CA   Heavy cruisers   PF   Frigates   AO   Oilers

CVE   Escort carriers   CL   Light cruisers   CM   Minelayers

a/c   aircraft   DD   Destroyers   AM/DMS   Minesweepers

APPENDIX FOUR   JAPANESE WARSHIP, SERVICE, AND MERCHANT SHIPPING LOSSES BETWEEN 1 AUGUST AND 30 NOVEMBER 1944

	In the Philippines				In all other theaters				Overall losses in all theaters			
	Ships	%	Tonnage	%	Ships	%	Tonnage	%	Ships	%	Tonnage	%
1–31 August 1944												
Warships	11	(35.48)	31,107	(62.38)	20	(64.52)	18,763	(37.62)	31		49,870	
Naval support shipping	9	(52.94)	83,342	(78.83)	8	(47.06)	22,385	(21.17)	17	(21.79)	105,727	(31.69)
Military transports	3	(16.67)	14,540	(26.11)	15	(83.33)	41,138	(73.89)	18	(23.08)	55,678	(16.69)
Merchantmen	16	(37.21)	80,586	(46.78)	27	(62.79)	91,665	(53.22)	43	(55.13)	172,251	(51.63)
Total shipping losses	28	(35.90)	178,468	(53.49)	50	(64.10)	155,188	(46.51)	78		333,656	
1 September–21 October 1944												
Warships	48	(65.75)	29,522	(46.31)	25	(34.25)	34,233	(53.69)	73		63,755	
Naval support shipping	28	(62.22)	133,415	(71.54)	17	(37.78)	53,076	(28.46)	45	(23.20)	186,491	(26.40)
Military transports	44	(77.19)	190,478	(82.63)	13	(22.81)	40,033	(17.37)	57	(29.38)	230,511	(32.64)
Merchantmen	59	(64.13)	179,109	(61.92)	33	(35.87)	110,170	(38.08)	92	(47.42)	289,279	(40.96)
Total shipping losses	131	(67.53)	503,002	(71.22)	63	(32.47)	203,279	(28.78)	194		706,281	
22–28 October 1944												
Warships	33	(94.29)	325,021	(98.82)	2	(5.71)	3,883	(1.18)	35		328,904	
Naval support shipping	5	(55.56)	33,883	(58.54)	3	(37.50)	24,001	(41.46)	8	(22.86)	57,884	(38.15)
Military transports	4	(57.14)	12,586	(55.05)	3	(42.86)	10,276	(44.95)	7	(20.00)	22,862	(15.07)
Merchantmen	8	(40.00)	45,877	(56.49)	12	(60.00)	25,091	(43.51)	20	(57.14)	70,968	(46.78)
Total shipping losses	17	(48.57)	92,346	(60.87)	18	(51.43)	59,368	(39.13)	35		151,714	

APPENDIX FOUR (CONTINUED)

29 October–30 November 1944

Warships	49 (73.13)	119,655 (52.71)	18 (26.87)	107,346 (47.29)	67	227,001
Naval support shipping	12 (37.50)	52,262 (37.08)	20 (62.50)	88,685 (62.92)	32 (31.37)	140,947 (32.34)
Military transports	17 (65.38)	85,951 (69.70)	9 (34.62)	37,366 (30.30)	26 (25.49)	123,317 (28.30)
Merchantmen	18 (40.91)	68,913 (40.17)	26 (59.09)	102,644 (59.83)	44 (43.14)	171,557 (39.36)
Total shipping losses	47 (46.08)	207,126 (47.53)	55 (53.92)	228,695 (52.47)	102	435,821

Overall losses in the period 1 September–30 November 1944

Warships	130 (73.45)	474,198 (76.24)	47 (26.55)	147,790 (23.76)	177	621,988
Naval support shipping	45 (52.33)	219,560 (56.09)	41 (47.67)	171,829 (43.90)	86 (25.75)	391,389 (30.05)
Military transports	65 (72.22)	289,015 (76.72)	25 (27.78)	87,675 (27.78)	90 (26.95)	376,690 (28.93)
Merchantmen	85 (53.80)	293,899 (55.02)	73 (46.20)	240,233 (44.98)	158 (47.31)	534,132 (41.02)
Total shipping losses	195 (58.38)	802,474 (61.62)	139 (41.62)	499,826 (38.38)	334	1,302,211

Under the heading "Warships" are included warships, auxiliary warships, and amphibious units.

The losses in other theaters and total losses in all theaters within the overall totals have been adjusted to include two warships of 2,328 tons, one naval support ship of 6,067 tons, and two merchantmen of 2,417 tons sunk either on dates or in areas that are not known.

Percentage figures relate to totals in specific phases other than the final figures; these refer to losses in the entire period.

APPENDIX FIVE   TABULAR REPRESENTATION OF JAPANESE WARSHIP, NAVAL, MILITARY, AND CIVILIAN SHIPPING LOSSES, 7–8 DECEMBER 1941–31 OCTOBER 1943

		Northern Pacific Theater		Japanese Home Waters		East China Sea		Central Pacific Theater		Southwest Pacific Theater	
To Central Pacific Submarines	Warships	5	5,607	13	29,647	2	3,654	15	41,467	3	5,965
	Naval support shipping	1	2,824	11	51,716	9	75,448	28	177,894	6	24,804
	Military transports	-	-	6	20,983	12	61,648	9	41,861	3	12,963
	Merchantmen	4	14,214	73	270,831	23	120,261	6	22,324	-	-
To Other Submarines	Warships	-	-	-	-	-	-	5	12,829	7	22,968
	Naval support shipping	-	-	-	-	-	-	8	44,469	7	4,970
	Military transports	-	-	-	-	-	-	13	62,781	12	44,627
	Merchantmen	-	-	-	-	-	-	-	-	-	-
To Carrier-based Aircraft	Warships	-	-	1	116	-	-	9	127,348	8.75	42,007
	Naval support shipping	-	-	-	-	-	-	1	6,567	-	-
	Military transports	-	-	-	-	-	-	-	-	2	12,931
	Merchantmen	-	-	-	-	-	-	-	-	-	-
To Shore-based Aircraft	Warships	1.50	2,574	-	-	-	-	1	1,772	26.25	66,033
	Naval support shipping	2.50	18,276	-	-	-	-	1	1,200	23	103,477
	Military transports	1	5,863	-	-	-	-	1	285	39	130,936
	Merchantmen	4	19,848	-	-	-	-	-	-	14	38,772
To Warships	Warships	3.50	7,107	-	-	-	-	1	3,311	35.50	114,720
	Naval support shipping	0.50	4,286	-	-	-	-	-	-	-	-
	Military transports	1	3,121	-	-	-	-	1	3,019	-	-
	Merchantmen	-	-	-	-	-	-	-	-	-	-

APPENDIX FIVE (CONTINUED)

Cause		No.	Tons	No.	Tons	No.	Tons	No.	Tons	No.	Tons
To Mines	Warships	-	-	-	-	-	-	-	-	5	9,361
	Naval support shipping	-	-	-	-	-	-	-	-	1	6,417
	Military transports	-	-	2	10,712	-	-	-	-	1	2,913
	Merchantmen	-	-	2	9,179	1	6,893	-	-	-	-
To Natural Causes, Accidents	Warships	2	2,575	2	40,760	1	217	2	1,976	2.50	3,545
	Naval support shipping	1	5,950	3	8,423	2	25,487	3	5,918	-	-
	Military transports	-	-	1	2,240	1	3,178	-	-	-	-
	Merchantmen	-	-	22	66,327	4	19,702	-	-	1	543
To Unknown Causes	Warships	1	2,434	1	148	-	-	1	2,198	2	2,382
	Naval support shipping	-	-	2	2,215	-	-	1	2,926	1	394
	Military transports	-	-	2	5,059	2	9,765	2	2,400	1	543
	Merchantmen	1	3,366	13	40,436	-	-	1	3,158	1	3,393
To Other Causes	Warships	-	-	-	-	-	-	3	3,393	-	-
	Naval support shipping	-	-	-	-	-	-	-	-	-	-
	Military transports	-	-	-	-	-	-	-	-	2	13,576
	Merchantmen	-	-	-	-	-	-	-	-	-	-
Total Losses	Warships	13	21,307	17	70,671	3	3,871	37	194,294	90	266,981
	Naval support shipping	5	31,376	16	64,354	11	100,935	42	238,974	38	169,062
	Military transports	2	8,984	11	38,994	15	74,591	26	110,346	60	218,489
	Merchantmen	9	37,428	110	386,773	28	146,856	7	25,482	16	42,708

Average monthly losses during a period of 22.75 months: 8.75 warships of 27,556 tons, 6.55 naval auxiliaries of 34,729 tons, 7.78 military transports of 31,873 tons, and 9.41 merchantmen of 34,849 tons; overall shipping losses, excluding warships, of 540 ships of 2,308,012 tons, an average of 23.74 ships of 101,451 tons per month.

APPENDIX FIVE (CONTINUED)

		Southern Resources Area	Indian Ocean Theater	Riverine China	Other and Unknown Theaters	Total Losses
To Central Pacific Submarines	Warships	1 / 2,904	–	–	–	39 / 89,244
	Naval support shipping	–	–	–	–	55 / 332,726
	Military transports	3 / 15,658	–	–	–	33 / 153,103
	Merchantmen	4 / 23,968	–	–	–	110 / 451,598
To Other Submarines	Warships	10 / 19,202	1 / 2,130	–	–	23 / 57,102
	Naval support shipping	17 / 114,887	1 / 3,967	–	–	33 / 198,293
	Military transports	31 / 140,274	5 / 38,008	–	–	61 / 285,690
	Merchantmen	17 / 69,199	–	–	–	17 / 69,199
To Carrier-based Aircraft	Warships	1 / 10,600	–	–	–	19.75 / 180,071
	Naval support shipping	–	–	–	–	1 / 6,567
	Military transports	–	–	–	–	2 / 12,931
	Merchantmen	–	–	–	–	–
To Shore-based Aircraft	Warships	6 / 2,773	1 / 355	–	–	35.75 / 73,517
	Naval support shipping	5 / 17,571	1 / 4,468	1 / 776	–	33.50 / 144,768
	Military transports	4 / 7,587	7 / 26,778	1 / 130	–	53 / 171,579
	Merchantmen	4 / 8,202	2 / 4,872	2 / 4,692	–	26 / 58,015
To Warships	Warships	3 / 10,730	2 / 11,580	–	–	45 / 147,448
	Naval support shipping	3 / 17,759	–	–	–	3.5 / 22,045
	Military transports	1 / 9,192	1 / 335	–	–	4 / 15,667
	Merchantmen	1 / 5,175	–	–	–	1 / 5,175

APPENDIX FIVE (CONTINUED)

		No.	Tonnage	No.	Tonnage	No.	Tonnage	No.	Tonnage	No.	Tonnage
To Mines	Warships	8	6,916	1	341	-	-	-	-	14	16,618
	Naval support shipping	4	9,786	-	-	-	-	-	-	5	16,203
	Military transports	2	2,440	2	10,702	-	-	-	-	7	42,970
	Merchantmen	4	13,009	-	-	-	-	-	-	7	29,081
To Natural Causes, Accidents	Warships	-	-	-	-	-	-	-	-	9,50	50,073
	Naval support shipping	1	472	-	-	-	-	-	-	10	46,250
	Military transports	1	1,871	-	-	-	-	-	-	3	7,289
	Merchantmen	2	6,078	-	-	1	5,822	-	-	30	98,452
To Unknown Causes	Warships	2	494	-	-	-	-	1	389	8	8,045
	Naval support shipping	1	14,050	2	1,062	-	-	1	589	8	23,236
	Military transports	1	5,307	2	10,468	-	-	-	-	10	33,542
	Merchantmen	3	8,982	1	165	-	-	3	3,393	23	62,893
To Other Causes	Warships	2	1,382	-	-	-	-	-	-	5	4,775
	Naval support shipping	-	-	-	-	-	-	-	-	-	-
	Military transports	2	4,976	-	-	-	-	-	-	4	14,552
	Merchantmen	-	-	-	-	-	-	-	-	-	-
Total Losses	Warships	33	55,001	5	14,379	-	-	1	389	199	626,893
	Naval support shipping	31	174,525	4	9,527	1	776	1	589	149	790,088
	Military transports	45	187,295	17	86,291	1	130	-	-	177	725,120
	Merchantmen	35	134,613	3	5,037	3	10,514	3	3,393	214	792,804

		Northern Pacific Theater	Japanese Home Waters	East China Sea	Central Pacific Theater	Southwest Pacific Theater
To Central Pacific Submarines	Warships	1 / 860	5 / 26,107	3 / 1,835	16 / 84,129	- / -
	Naval support shipping	4 / 12,266	15 / 70,313	1.50 / 15,055	50 / 236,700	- / -
	Military transports	7 / 28,575	7 / 30,446	4 / 23,454	30 / 145,971	- / -
	Merchantmen	3 / 6,574	19 / 57,273	15.50 / 71,963	11 / 39,611	- / -
To Other Submarines	Warships	- / -	2 / 5,345	- / -	6 / 13,543	- / -
	Naval support shipping	- / -	1 / 6,925	- / -	12 / 51,485	1 / 11,621
	Military transports	- / -	- / -	- / -	10 / 50,274	2 / 5,239
	Merchantmen	- / -	- / -	- / -	- / -	- / -
To Carrier-based Aircraft	Warships	- / -	-	-	37 / 59,344	2 / 2,725
	Naval support shipping	- / -	-	-	60.50 / 370,296	2 / 7,980
	Military transports	- / -	-	-	11 / 37,568	- / -
	Merchantmen	- / -	-	-	3 / 4,375	- / -
To Shore-based Aircraft	Warships	- / -	-	- / -	10 / 2,123	21 / 11,372
	Naval support shipping	- / -	-	1 / 3,202	9 / 22,884	15 / 65,297
	Military transports	- / -	-	1 / 6,385	2 / 5,952	28 / 59,279
	Merchantmen	- / -	-	2 / 3,448	3 / 2,222	2 / 2,754
To Warships	Warships	1 / 1,630	-	-	26 / 36,378	11 / 16,157
	Naval support shipping	- / -	-	-	1.50 / 5,565	1 / 812
	Military transports	- / -	-	-	1 / 839	- / -
	Merchantmen	1 / 4,960	-	-	- / -	1 / 475

APPENDIX SIX (CONTINUED)

Cause	Type	No.	Tons	No.	Tons	No.	Tons	No.	Tons	No.	Tons
To Mines	Warships	1	222	–	–	–	–	–	–	–	–
	Naval support shipping	–	–	–	–	–	–	2	11,774	2	–
	Military transports	–	–	–	–	–	–	–	–	–	–
	Merchantmen	–	–	1	875	–	5,307	–	–	–	4,055
To Natural Causes, Accidents	Warships	1	720	1	2,198	–	–	3	2,032	–	–
	Naval support shipping	1	657	2	7,058	–	–	–	–	–	–
	Military transports	–	–	1	670	–	–	–	–	–	–
	Merchantmen	–	–	16	26,547	–	5,342	–	–	–	–
To Unknown Causes	Warships	–	–	3	1,039	1	318	3	2,076	3	3,951
	Naval support shipping	–	–	–	–	–	–	1	439	–	–
	Military transports	–	–	–	–	0.50	2,644	2	2,022	5	3,222
	Merchantmen	–	–	4	10,081	0.50	2,644	2	5,874	1	521
To Other Causes	Warships	–	–	–	–	–	–	–	–	–	–
	Naval support shipping	–	–	–	–	–	–	–	–	–	–
	Military transports	–	–	–	–	–	–	–	–	–	–
	Merchantmen	–	–	–	–	–	–	–	–	–	–
Total Losses	Warships	4	3,432	11	34,689	4	2,153	101	199,625	37	34,205
	Naval support shipping	5	12,923	18	84,296	2.50	18,257	136	699,143	21	89,765
	Military transports	7	28,575	8	31,116	5.50	32,483	56	242,626	35	67,740
	Merchantmen	4	11,534	40	94,776	20	88,704	19	52,082	4	3,750

Average monthly losses during a period of eight months: 24.50 warships of 41,881 tons, 28.19 naval auxiliaries of 139,424 tons, 21.75 military transports of 83,417 tons, and 19.31 merchantmen of 64,898 tons; overall shipping losses, excluding warships, of 554 ships of 2,301,909 tons, an average of 69.25 ships of 287,739 tons per month.

APPENDIX SIX (CONTINUED)

		Southern Resources Area		Indian Ocean Theater		Riverine China		Other and Unknown Theaters		Total Losses	
To Central Pacific Submarines	Warships	5	4,937	-	-	-	-	-	-	30	117,868
	Naval support shipping	8	51,883	-	-	-	-	-	-	78.50	386,217
	Military transports	12	58,965	-	-	-	-	-	-	60	287,411
	Merchantmen	21	108,268	-	-	-	-	-	-	69.50	283,689
To Other Submarines	Warships	15	27,706	6	13,193	-	-	-	-	29	59,787
	Naval support shipping	20	121,873	4	5,604	-	-	-	-	38	197,508
	Military transports	32.50	163,099	4	9,703	-	-	-	-	48.50	228,315
	Merchantmen	18.50	81,476	1	2,658	-	-	-	-	19.50	84,134
To Carrier-based Aircraft	Warships	3	1,235	-	-	-	-	1	2,095	43	65,399
	Naval support shipping	1	993	1	2,722	-	-	-	-	64.50	381,991
	Military transports	-	-	1	778	-	-	-	-	12	38,346
	Merchantmen	-	-	-	-	-	-	-	-	3	4,375
To Shore-based Aircraft	Warships	4	4,134	-	-	-	-	1	1,805	35	17,629
	Naval support shipping	4	13,363	-	-	-	-	1	499	30	106,551
	Military transports	9	23,683	-	-	-	-	-	-	41	95,798
	Merchantmen	10	37,591	1	3,180	5	7,775	-	-	23	56,970
To Warships	Warships	-	-	2	2,723	-	-	1	1,144	41	58,032
	Naval support shipping	-	-	-	-	-	-	-	-	2.5	6,377
	Military transports	-	-	-	-	-	-	-	-	1	839
	Merchantmen	-	-	-	-	-	-	-	-	2	5,435
To Mines	Warships	1	2,090	-	-	-	-	-	-	2	2,312
	Naval support shipping	-	-	1	1,400	-	-	-	-	5	17,229
	Military transports	1	2,197	-	-	-	-	-	-	1	2,197
	Merchantmen	2	6,768	1	554	-	-	-	-	5	13,504

APPENDIX SIX (CONTINUED)

		No.	Tons	No.	Tons	No.	Tons	No.	Tons	No.	Tons
To Natural Causes, Accidents	Warships	1	1,685	-	-	-	-	-	-	6	6,635
	Naval support shipping	1	5,135	-	-	-	-	-	-	4	12,850
	Military transports	-	-	-	-	-	-	-	-	1	670
	Merchantmen	2	3,328	-	-	-	-	1	6,932	20	42,149
To Unknown Causes	Warships	1	5,141	-	-	-	-	-	-	10	7,384
	Naval support shipping	-	-	-	-	-	-	1	1,086	3	6,666
	Military transports	2	5,869	-	-	-	-	-	-	9.5	13,757
	Merchantmen	4	8,924	-	-	-	-	1	887	12.5	28,931
To Other Causes	Warships	-	-	-	-	-	-	-	-	-	-
	Naval support shipping	-	-	-	-	-	-	-	-	-	-
	Military transports	-	-	-	-	-	-	-	-	-	-
	Merchantmen	-	-	-	-	-	-	-	-	-	-
Total Losses	Warships	29	41,787	8	15,916	-	-	2	3,239	196	335,046
	Naval support shipping	35	198,388	6	9,726	-	-	2	2,891	225.5	1,115,389
	Military transports	56.50	253,813	5	10,481	-	-	1	499	174	667,333
	Merchantmen	57.50	246,355	3	6,392	5	7,775	2	7,819	154.5	519,187

APPENDIX SEVEN TABULAR REPRESENTATION OF JAPANESE WARSHIP, NAVAL, AND MILITARY SHIPPING LOSSES, 1 JULY 1944–31 MARCH 1945

		Northern Pacific Theater		Japanese Home Waters		East China Sea		Central Pacific Theater		Southwest Pacific Theater	
		No.	Tons	No.	Tons	No.	Tons	No.	Tons	No.	Tons
To Central Pacific Submarines	Warships	2	2,198	29	118,253	13	64,465	8	3,064	-	-
	Naval support shipping	4	10,208	9	17,946	8	34,232	7	12,047	-	-
	Military transports	3	16,890	10	54,697	13	45,033	3	8,858	-	-
	Merchantmen	4	7,947	43	147,240	19	97,008	1	1,916	-	-
To Other Submarines	Warships	-	-	-	-	-	-	1	2,111	-	-
	Naval support shipping	-	-	-	-	-	-	-	-	-	-
	Military transports	-	-	-	-	1	2,345	-	-	-	-
	Merchantmen	-	-	1	5,244	-	-	-	-	-	-
To Carrier-based Aircraft	Warships	-	-	4	1,158	22	10,999	20.5	16,903	-	-
	Naval support shipping	-	-	1	2,217	9	24,082	8	22,266	-	-
	Military transports	-	-	1	10,605	13	42,682	2	9,736	-	-
	Merchantmen	-	-	6	7,084	30	60,367	1	530	-	-
To Shore-based Aircraft	Warships	1	130	-	-	2	1,220	4	699	3	351
	Naval support shipping	-	-	-	-	2	3,175	-	-	1	542
	Military transports	-	-	-	-	-	-	-	-	2	764
	Merchantmen	2	348	3	2,598	2	1,364	4	2,732	-	-
To Warships	Warships	-	-	5	3,216	-	-	21.5	31,115	-	-
	Naval support shipping	-	-	-	-	-	-	-	-	-	-
	Military transports	-	-	-	-	-	-	-	-	-	-
	Merchantmen	-	-	-	-	-	-	-	-	-	-

APPENDIX SIX (CONTINUED)

Cause	Type	No.	Tonnage	No.	Tonnage	No.	Tonnage	No.	Tonnage	No.	Tonnage
To Natural Causes, Accidents	Warships	1	1,685	-	-	-	-	-	-	6	6,635
	Naval support shipping	1	5,135	-	-	-	-	-	-	4	12,850
	Military transports	-	-	-	-	-	-	-	-	1	670
	Merchantmen	2	3,328	-	-	-	-	1	6,932	20	42,149
To Unknown Causes	Warships	-	-	-	-	-	-	1	1,086	10	7,384
	Naval support shipping	1	5,141	-	-	-	-	1	-	3	6,666
	Military transports	2	5,869	-	-	-	-	-	-	9.5	13,757
	Merchantmen	4	8,924	-	-	-	-	1	887	12.5	28,931
To Other Causes	Warships	-	-	-	-	-	-	-	-	-	-
	Naval support shipping	-	-	-	-	-	-	-	-	-	-
	Military transports	-	-	-	-	-	-	-	-	-	-
	Merchantmen	-	-	-	-	-	-	-	-	-	-
Total Losses	Warships	29	41,787	8	15,916	-	-	2	3,239	196	335,046
	Naval support shipping	35	198,388	6	9,726	-	-	2	2,891	225.5	1,115,389
	Military transports	56.50	253,813	5	10,481	-	-	1	499	174	667,333
	Merchantmen	57.50	246,355	3	6,392	5	7,775	2	7,819	154.5	519,187

APPENDIX SEVEN TABULAR REPRESENTATION OF JAPANESE WARSHIP, NAVAL, AND MILITARY SHIPPING LOSSES, 1 JULY 1944–31 MARCH 1945

		Northern Pacific Theater		Japanese Home Waters		East China Sea		Central Pacific Theater		Southwest Pacific Theater	
To Central Pacific Submarines	Warships	2	2,198	29	118,253	13	64,465	8	3,064	-	-
	Naval support shipping	4	10,208	9	17,946	8	34,232	7	12,047	-	-
	Military transports	3	16,890	10	54,697	13	45,033	3	8,858	-	-
	Merchantmen	4	7,947	43	147,240	19	97,008	1	1,916	-	-
To Other Submarines	Warships	-	-	-	-	-	-	-	-	-	-
	Naval support shipping	-	-	-	-	-	-	1	2,111	-	-
	Military transports	-	-	-	-	-	-	-	-	-	-
	Merchantmen	-	-	1	5,244	1	2,345	-	-	-	-
To Carrier-based Aircraft	Warships	-	-	4	1,158	22	10,999	20.5	16,903	-	-
	Naval support shipping	-	-	1	2,217	9	24,082	8	22,266	-	-
	Military transports	-	-	1	10,605	13	42,682	2	9,736	-	-
	Merchantmen	-	-	6	7,084	30	60,367	1	530	-	-
To Shore-based Aircraft	Warships	1	130	-	-	2	1,220	4	699	3	351
	Naval support shipping	-	-	-	-	2	3,175	-	-	1	542
	Military transports	-	-	-	-	-	-	-	-	2	764
	Merchantmen	2	348	3	2,598	2	1,364	4	2,732	-	-
To Warships	Warships	-	-	5	3,216	-	-	21.5	31,115	-	-
	Naval support shipping	-	-	-	-	-	-	-	-	-	-
	Military transports	-	-	-	-	-	-	-	-	-	-
	Merchantmen	-	-	-	-	-	-	-	-	-	-

APPENDIX SEVEN (CONTINUED)

		No.	Tons	No.	Tons	No.	Tons	No.	Tons	No.	Tons
To Mines	Warships	-	-	2	450	-	-	1	648	-	-
	Naval support shipping	-	-	2	1,868	-	-	1	549	-	-
	Military transports	-	-	1	111	1	3,120	-	-	-	-
	Merchantmen	-	-	2	7,744	1	5,396	-	-	-	-
To Natural Causes, Accidents	Warships	1	769	1	130	1	950	2	2,635	-	-
	Naval support shipping	-	-	1	2,728	1	6,530	-	-	-	-
	Military transports	-	-	-	-	1	495	-	-	-	-
	Merchantmen	-	-	10	14,719	-	-	-	-	-	-
To Unknown Causes	Warships	-	-	4	831	1	122	6	3,483	2	245
	Naval support shipping	-	-	4	10,620	1	223	-	-	-	-
	Military transports	-	-	1	887	2	6,032	1	572	-	-
	Merchantmen	1	1,937	12	22,895	2	3,575	4	6,504	2	2,092
To Other Causes	Warships	-	-	-	-	-	-	-	-	-	-
	Naval support shipping	-	-	-	-	-	-	-	-	-	-
	Military transports	-	-	-	-	-	-	-	-	-	-
	Merchantmen	-	-	-	-	-	-	-	-	-	-
Total Losses	Warships	3	2,328	45	124,038	39	77,756	63	199,625	5	596
	Naval support shipping	5	10,977	17	35,379	21	68,242	16	699,143	1	542
	Military transports	3	16,890	13	66,300	29	91,936	7	242,626	2	764
	Merchantmen	7	10,232	77	207,524	55	170,055	10	52,082	2	2,092

Average monthly losses during period of nine months:
46.56 warships of 98,561 tons, 18.67 naval auxiliaries of 77,590 tons, 20 military transports of 80,121 tons, and 45.67 merchantmen of 148,609 tons; overall shipping losses, excluding warships, of 759 ships of 2,756,884 tons, an average of 84.33 ships of 306,320 tons per month.

APPENDIX SEVEN (CONTINUED)

		Southern Resources Area		Indian Ocean Theater		Riverine China		Other and Unknown Theaters		Total Losses	
To Central Pacific Submarines	Warships	19.50	42,900	-	-	-	-	-	-	71.50	230,880
	Naval support shipping	22.50	127,699	-	-	-	-	-	-	50.50	202,132
	Military transports	13	86,865	-	-	-	-	-	-	42	212,343
	Merchantmen	33	190,125	-	-	-	-	-	-	100	444,236
To Other Submarines	Warships	49	131,325	7	3,301	-	-	-	-	56	134,626
	Naval support shipping	34	202,446	-	-	-	-	-	-	35	204,557
	Military transports	25	129,895	3	7,340	-	-	-	-	28	136,235
	Merchantmen	55	262,841	3	5,014	-	-	-	-	60	275,444
To Carrier-based Aircraft	Warships	100	289,587	-	-	-	-	-	-	146.50	318,647
	Naval support shipping	24.50	112,294	1	830	-	-	-	-	43.50	161,689
	Military transports	35	156,281	-	-	-	-	-	-	50	219,304
	Merchantmen	74.50	258,947	-	-	-	-	1	245	112.50	327,173
To Shore-based Aircraft	Warships	38	27,798	-	-	3	1,054	-	-	51	31,252
	Naval support shipping	15	67,114	1	1,500	-	-	-	-	19	72,331
	Military transports	33	93,357	1	394	2	1,210	-	-	38	95,725
	Merchantmen	26.50	51,878	-	-	8	12,750	-	-	45.50	71,670
To Warships	Warships	19.5	114,140	2	840	-	-	-	-	48	149,311
	Naval support shipping	-	-	1	398	-	-	-	-	1	398
	Military transports	-	-	-	-	-	-	-	-	-	-
	Merchantmen	-	-	-	-	-	-	-	-	-	-

APPENDIX SEVEN (CONTINUED)

To Mines	Warships	2	1,085	5	968	1	625	-	-	11	3,776
	Naval support shipping	3	22,659	-	-	1	1,674	-	-	6	26,201
	Military transports	2	12,274	-	-	1	2,000	-	-	6	18,054
	Merchantmen	14	50,819	4	6,386	9	19,761	-	-	30	90,106
To Natural Causes, Accidents	Warships	4	3,498	-	-	-	-	-	-	8	7,213
	Naval support shipping	-	-	-	-	1	600	-	-	4	10,627
	Military transports	1	2,893	-	-	-	-	-	-	2	3,388
	Merchantmen	7	22,360	-	-	-	-	1	1,735	18	38,277
To Unknown Causes	Warships	10	5,109	1	872	-	-	-	-	24	10,662
	Naval support shipping	2	2,481	-	-	-	-	1	6,067	8	19,391
	Military transports	9	24,020	-	-	-	-	2	3,533	15	5,044
	Merchantmen	20	38,911	1	2,333	-	-	3	11,791	45	90,038
To Other Causes	Warships	3	681	-	-	-	-	-	-	3	681
	Naval support shipping	-	-	1	984	-	-	-	-	1	984
	Military transports	-	-	-	-	-	-	-	-	-	-
	Merchantmen	-	-	-	-	-	-	-	-	-	-
Total Losses	Warships	245	616,123	15	5,981	4	1,679	-	-	419	887,048
	Naval support shipping	101	534,693	4	3,712	2	2,274	1	6,067	168	698,310
	Military transports	118	516,361	4	7,734	3	3,210	2	3,533	181	726,443
	Merchantmen	230	875,881	8	13,733	17	32,511	5	13,771	411	1,337,481

APPENDIX EIGHT   JAPANESE WARSHIP,
SERVICE, AND MERCHANT SHIPPING
LOSSES, 7 DECEMBER 1941–31 MARCH 1945

	Overall Losses		Monthly Average	
7–8 December 1941–31 October 1943				
WARSHIPS	199	626,893	8.75	27,556
NAVAL TRANSPORTS AND SUPPORT SHIPS	149	790,088	6.55	34,729
MILITARY TRANSPORTS	177	725,120	7.78	31,873
MERCHANTMEN	214	792,804	9.41	34,849
OVERALL SHIPPING LOSSES	540	2,308,012		
AVERAGE MONTHLY SHIPPING LOSSES			23.74	101,451
1 November 1943–30 June 1944				
WARSHIPS	196	335,046	24.50	41,881
NAVAL TRANSPORTS AND SUPPORT SHIPS	225.5	1,115,389	28.19	139,424
MILITARY TRANSPORTS	174	667,333	21.75	83,417
MERCHANTMEN	154.5	519,187	19.31	64,898
OVERALL SHIPPING LOSSES	554	2,301,909		
AVERAGE MONTHLY SHIPPING LOSSES			69.25	287,739
1 July 1944–31 March 1945				
WARSHIPS	419	887,048	46.56	98,561
NAVAL TRANSPORTS AND SUPPORT SHIPS	170	698,310	18.67	77,590
MILITARY TRANSPORTS	181	726,443	20.11	80,716
MERCHANTMEN	411	1,337,481	45.67	148,609
OVERALL SHIPPING LOSSES	762	2,762,234		
AVERAGE MONTHLY SHIPPING LOSSES			84.44	306,915
Overall Losses **7–8 December 1941–31 March 1945**				
WARSHIPS	814	1,848,987	20.48	46,515
NAVAL TRANSPORTS AND SUPPORT SHIPS	544.5	2,603,787	13.70	65,504
MILITARY TRANSPORTS	532	2,118,896	13.38	53,306
MERCHANTMEN	779.5	2,649,472	19.61	66,653
OVERALL SHIPPING LOSSES	1,856	7,372,155		
AVERAGE MONTHLY SHIPPING LOSSES			46.69	185,463

Formations and Units	Fighters and various specialist derivatives						Dive-bombers			Level-altitude bombers				Total
	F6F-3	F6F-3N	F6F-3P	F6F-5	F6F-5N	F6F-5P	F6F-3	F6F-5	SB2C-3	TBF-1C	TBF-1D	TBM-1C	TBM-1D	
T.G. 38.1														
CV Hornet	11	2	1	21	2	3	-	-	25	1	-	17	-	83
CV Wasp	30	3	2	7	1	-	3	7	25	5	1	11	1	96
CVL Cowpens	-	-	-	25	-	1	-	-	-	-	-	9	-	35
CVL Monterey	-	-	-	21	-	-	-	-	-	-	-	9	-	30
Formation total	41	5	3	74	3	4	3	7	50	6	1	46	1	244
T.G. 38.2														
CV Bunker Hill	27	4	-	14	4	-	-	-	24	-	-	17	1	91
CV Hancock	-	-	-	37	4	-	-	-	42	-	-	18	-	101
CV Intrepid	-	5	-	36	-	3	-	-	28	-	-	18	-	90
CVL Cabot	3	-	-	18	-	-	-	-	-	1	-	8	-	30
CVL Independence	3	-	-	2	14	-	-	-	-	-	-	-	8	27
Formation total	33	9	-	107	22	3	-	-	94	1	-	61	9	339

APPENDIX NINE (CONTINUED)

Formations and Units	Fighters and various specialist derivatives						Dive-bombers			Level-altitude bombers				Total
	F6F-3	F6F-3N	F6F-3P	F6F-5	F6F-5N	F6F-5P	F6F-3	F6F-5	SB2C-3	TBF-1C	TBF-1D	TBM-1C	TBM-1D	
T.G. 38.3														
CV *Essex*	22	3	2	23	1	-	-	-	25	15	-	5	-	96
CV *Lexington*	14	2	1	22	1	1	-	-	30	-	-	18	-	89
CVL *Langley*	19	-	-	6	-	-	-	-	-	-	-	9	-	34
CVL *Princeton*	18	-	-	7	-	-	-	-	-	-	-	9	-	34
Formation total	73	5	3	58	2	1	-	-	55	15	-	41	-	253
T.G. 38.4														
CV *Enterprise*	-	4	-	36	-	-	-	-	34	-	-	19	-	93
CV *Franklin*	1	3	-	30	1	4	-	-	31	-	-	18	-	88
CVL *Belleau Wood*	-	-	-	24	-	1	-	-	-	-	-	9	-	34
CVL *San Jacinto*	14	-	-	5	-	-	-	-	-	-	-	7	-	26
Formation total	15	7	-	95	1	5	-	-	65	-	-	53	-	241
Task Force 38 TOTAL	162	26	6	334	28	13	3	7	264	22	1	201	10	1,077
Total by types	569						274			234				1,077

Source: S. E. Morison, *History of United States Naval Operations in World War II*, vol. XII: *Leyte, June 1944–January 1945*, pp. 424–429.

APPENDIX TEN JAPANESE LOSSES DURING AND AFTER THE NAVAL BATTLE FOR THE PHILIPPINES, 22–28 OCTOBER 1944

Original order of battle	Formations and Units	Sunk between 22 and 24 October 1944	Sunk 25 October 1944	Sunk between 26 and 28 October 1944	Sunk between 29 October and 30 November 1944	Sunk between 1 December 1944 and 15 August 1945	Survived and surrendered August–September 1945
	Northern Force						
2	Battleships	-	-	-	-	2	-
1	Fleet carriers	-	1	-	-	-	-
3	Light carriers	-	3	-	-	-	-
-	Heavy cruisers	-	-	-	-	-	-
3	Light cruisers	-	1	-	-	2	-
4	Destroyers	-	2	-	2	-	-
4	Escorts	-	-	-	-	1	3
17	Total	-	7	-	2	5	3
	Central Force						
5	Battleships	1	-	-	1	2	1
10	Heavy cruisers	2	3	-	1	2	2
2	Light cruisers	-	-	1	-	1	-
15	Destroyers	-	-	3	6	5	1
32	Total	3	3	4	8	10	4
	Southern Forces						
2	Battleships	-	2	-	-	-	-
3	Heavy cruisers	-	1	-	1	1	-
1	Light cruisers	-	-	1	-	-	-
8	Destroyers	-	3	1	1	2	1
14	Total	-	6	2	2	3	1
	Detached Forces						
1	Heavy cruisers	-	-	-	-	1	-
1	Light cruisers	-	-	1	-	-	-
4	Destroyers	1	-	1	1	1	-
6	Total	1	-	2	1	2	-

APPENDIX TEN (CONTINUED)

Original order of battle	Formations and Units	Sunk between 22 and 24 October 1944	Sunk 25 October 1944	Sunk between 26 and 28 October 1944	Sunk between 29 October and 30 November 1944	Sunk between 1 December 1944 and 15 August 1945	Survived and surrendered August–September 1945
	TOTALS						
9	Battleships	1	2	-	1	4	1
1	Fleet carriers	-	1	-	-	-	-
3	Light carriers	-	3	-	-	-	-
14	Heavy cruisers	2	4	-	2	4	2
7	Light cruisers	-	1	3	-	3	-
31	Destroyers	1	5	5	10	8	2
4	Escorts	-	-	-	-	1	3
	OVERALL						
69	**TOTAL**	**4**	**16**	**8**	**13**	**20**	**8**
	Remaining	65	49	41	28	8	-
14	Submarines	1	-	3	2	7	1
13	Escorts	-	-	-	1	7	5
10	Oilers	-	1	1	4	4	-

APPENDIX ELEVEN — THE FATE OF JAPANESE WARSHIPS, SUBMARINES, AND OILERS INVOLVED IN THE SHO OPERATION

Date	Unit	Location and General Area of Loss		Agency of Destruction
		Units with or Detached from the Four Main Formations		
23 October 1944	CA *Atago*	In 09°28'North 117°17'East	In the Palawan Passage	The submarine *Darter*[1]
	CA *Maya*	In 09°29'North 117°20'East	In the Palawan Passage	The submarine *Dace*[1]
24 October 1944	BB *Musashi*	In 12°50'North 122°35'East	In the Sibuyan Sea	Carrier aircraft[2]
	DD *Wakaba*	In 11°50'North 121°25'East	Off Panay	Carrier aircraft
	CV *Zuikaku*	In 19°20'North 125°15'East	Northeast of Cape Engaño	Carrier aircraft
	CVE *Chitose*	In 19°20'North 126°20'East	Northeast of Cape Engaño	Carrier aircraft
	CVE *Chiyoda*	In 18°37'North 126°45'East	Northeast of Cape Engaño	Carrier aircraft & warships
	CVE *Zuiho*	In 19°20'North 125°15'East	Northeast of Cape Engaño	Carrier aircraft
	BB *Fuso*	In 10°25'North 125°23'East	In the Surigao Strait	Surface action
	BB *Yamashiro*	In 10°22'North 125°21'East	In the Surigao Strait	Surface action
	CA *Chikuma*	In 11°22'North 126°16'East	Off Samar	Carrier aircraft
	CA *Chokai*	In 11°26'North 126°15'East	Off Samar	Carrier aircraft
25 October 1944	CA *Mogami*	In 09°40'North 124°50'East	South of Bohol	Surface action
	CA *Suzuya*	In 11°50'North 126°25'East	Off Samar	Carrier aircraft
	CL *Tama*	In 21°23'North 127°19'East	Northeast of Cape Engaño	Carrier aircraft & the submarine *Jallao*
	DD *Akitsuki*	In 20°29'North 126°30'East	Northeast of Cape Engaño	Carrier aircraft
	DD *Asagumo*	In 10°04'North 125°21'East	In the Surigao Strait	Surface action
	DD *Hatsutsuki*	In 20°24'North 126°30'East	Northeast of Cape Engaño	Surface action[3]
	DD *Michishio*	In 10°25'North 125°23'East	In the Surigao Strait	Surface action
	DD *Yamagumo*	In 10°16'North 125°23'East	In the Surigao Strait	Surface action

Date	Unit	Location and General Area of Loss		Agency of Destruction
26 October 1944	CL *Abukuma*	In 09°20'North 122°30'East	Off Negros	Warships & land-based aircraft
	CL *Noshiro*	In 11°35'North 121°45'East	Off northwest Panay	Carrier aircraft
	CL *Kinu*	In 11°46'North 123°11'East	Between Panay and Masbate	Carrier aircraft
	DD *Hayashimo*	In 12°05'North 121°21'East	On Semirara island	Carrier aircraft
	DD *Nowaki*	In 13°00'North 124°54'East	Off San Bernardino Strait	Surface action
	DD *Uranami*	In 11°50'North 123°00'East	Between Panay and Masbate	Carrier aircraft
27 October 1944	DD *Fujinami*	In 12°00'North 122°30'East	Off southern Mindoro	Carrier aircraft[4]
	DD *Shiranui*	In 12°00'North 122°30'East	Off northern Panay	Carrier aircraft[4]
5 November 1944	CA *Nachi*	In 13°50'North 120°20'East	Entrance to Manila Bay	Carrier aircraft
11 November 1944	DD *Hamanami*	In 10°50'North 124°35'East	Off Ormoc Bay, Leyte	Carrier aircraft
	DD *Naganami*	In 10°50'North 124°35'East	Off Ormoc Bay, Leyte	Carrier aircraft
	DD *Shimakaze*	In 10°50'North 124°35'East	Off Ormoc Bay, Leyte	Carrier aircraft
	DD *Wakatsuki*	In 10°50'North 124°35'East	Off Ormoc Bay, Leyte	Carrier aircraft
13 November 1944	DD *Akebono*	In 14°35'North 120°50'East	In Manila Bay	Carrier aircraft
	DD *Akishimo*	In 14°35'North 120°50'East	In Manila Bay	Carrier aircraft
	DD *Hatsuharu*	In 14°35'North 120°50'East	In Manila Bay	Carrier aircraft
	DD *Okinami*	In 14°35'North 120°50'East	In Manila Bay	Carrier aircraft
21 November 1944	BB *Kongo*	In 26°09'North 121°23'East	Off northwest Formosa	The submarine *Sealion*[5]
	DD *Urakaze*	In 26°09'North 121°23'East	Off northwest Formosa	The submarine *Sealion*[5]
25 November 1944	CA *Kumano*	In 15°47'North 119°52'East	Dasol Bay, northwest Luzon	Carrier aircraft[6]
	DD *Shimotsuki*	In 02°21'North 107°20'East	In the South China Sea	The submarine *Cavalla*
3 December 1944	DE *Kuwa*	In 10°50'North 124°35'East	In Ormoc Bay, Leyte	Surface action
4 December 1944	DD *Kishinami*	In 13°12'North 116°37'East	Northwest of Palawan	The submarine *Flasher*
26 December 1944	DD *Kiyoshimo*	In 12°20'North 121°00'East	Off southwest Mindoro	Warships & land-based aircraft
24 January 1945	DD *Shigure*	In 06°00'North 103°48'East	Off eastern Malaya	The submarine *Blackfin*

Date	Unit	Location and General Area of Loss	Agency of Destruction
7 April 1945	BB *Yamato*	In 30°22'North 128°04'East	Southwest of Kyushu	Carrier aircraft
	CL *Isuzu*	In 07°38'South 118°09'East	In the eastern Java Sea	Submarines *Charr* and *Gabilan*
	CL *Yahagi*	In 30°47'North 128°08'East	Southwest of Kyushu	Carrier aircraft
	DD *Asashimo*	In 31°00'North 128°00'East	Southwest of Kyushu	Carrier aircraft
	DD *Hamakaze*	In 30°47'North 128°08'East	Southwest of Kyushu	Carrier aircraft
	DD *Isokaze*	In 30°46'North 128°29'East	Southwest of Kyushu	Carrier aircraft
	DD *Kasumi*	In 31°00'North 128°00'East	Southwest of Kyushu	Carrier aircraft
16 May 1945	CA *Haguro*	In 05°00'North 99°30'East	Southwest of Penang	Surface action with British
8 June 1945	CA *Ashigara*	In 01°59'North 104°57'East	South of Singapore	The British submarine *Trenchant*
24 July 1945	BB *Hyuga*	In 34°10'North 132°33'East	In Kure harbour, Honshu	Carrier aircraft[7]
	CA *Tone*	In 34°14'North 132°27'East	Off Kure in Inland Sea	Carrier aircraft
28 July 1945	BB *Haruna*	In 34°15'North 132°29'East	Off Kure in Inland Sea	Carrier aircraft[8]
	BB *Ise*	In 34°12'North 132°31'East	In Kure harbour, Honshu	Carrier aircraft[8]
	CA *Aoba*	In 34°12'North 132°31'East	In Kure harbour, Honshu	Carrier aircraft
	CL *Oyodo*	In 34°13'North 132°25'East	In Kure harbour, Honshu	Carrier aircraft
30 July 1945	DD *Hatsushimo*	In 35°33'North 135°12'East	In Miyazu Bay, Honshu	Mine

Units That Were Surrendered after 2 September 1945[9]

BB *Nagato*	Badly damaged by carrier aircraft at Yokosuka on 18 July 1945. Transferred to the United States on 20 September 1945 and expended as target in Bikini tests of 1 and 24 July 1946. Foundered on 29 July 1946 in 11°40'North 165°15'East.
CA *Myoko*	Severely damaged in the Sibuyan Sea by carrier aircraft on 24 October 1944 and in South China Sea by attack by the submarine *Bergall* on 13 December 1944. *Hors de combat* at Singapore navy base. Scuttled in 03°05'06"North 100°04'06"East, in the Strait of Malacca east of Kuala Lumpur, on 8 July 1946.[10]
CA *Takao*	Severely damaged in the Palawan Passage by submarine *Darter* on 23 October 1944. *Hors de combat* at Singapore navy base and again severely damaged by attacks by British midget submarines XE-1 and XE-3 (respectively from the submarines *Spark* and *Stygian*) on 31 July 1945. Scuttled on 29 October 1946 in the Strait of Malacca.[11]

DD *Ushio*	Badly damaged in Manila Bay by carrier aircraft on 14 November 1944. Towed to and *hors de combat* at Yokosuka. Decommissioned 15 September 1945. Scrapped at "Shimasaki Docks"; process complete 4 August 1948.[12]
DD *Yukikaze*	Mined off Miyazu (north coast of central Honshu) on 30 July 1945. Refitted and then employed on repatriation service between 10 February and 18 December 1946. Arrived at Shanghai 3 July 1947 and transferred to Nationalist China three days later. In service (until 1965?) as the *Tang Yan/Tan Yang*. Ran aground in storm in May 1970. Stricken and scrapped at Kao-hsiung, southwest Taiwan, dates unknown.
DE *Kiri*	Badly damaged off Ormoc, Leyte, by carrier aircraft on 12 December 1944 but apparently fully repaired; classified as "undamaged" at war's end. Decommissioned 5 October 1945 and used thereafter on repatriation duties. Transferred to Soviet Union at Nakhodka on 29 July 1947; subsequent fate unknown.
DE *Maki*	Badly damaged off northwest Kyushu by submarine *Plaice* on 9 December 1944 but apparently fully repaired; classified as "undamaged" at war's end. Decommissioned 5 October 1945 and used thereafter on repatriation duties. Transferred to Britain on 14 August 1947 at Singapore and scrapped thereafter, dates unknown.
DE *Sugi*	Damaged off northwest Formosa by carrier aircraft on 21 January 1945. Decommissioned 5 October 1945 and used thereafter on repatriation duties. Transferred to Nationalist China on 31 July 1947 and in service as the *Hui Yang* until 1962. Lost as a result of running aground, whereabouts and place unknown; not salvaged.

Date	Unit	Location and General Area of Loss	Agency of Destruction
Warships and Units from the Oiler Formations			
(* denotes units with Ozawa's carrier formation.)			
25 October 1944	AO *Jinei Maru**	In 30°15'North 129°45'East	Southwest of Kyushu	The submarine *Sterlet*[13]
27 October 1944	AO *Nippo Maru*	In 07°17'North 116°45'East	In the Balabac Strait	The submarine *Bergall*
30 October 1944	AO *Takane Maru**	In 30°14'North 132°50'East	Off southeast Kyushu	The submarines *Trigger, Salmon & Sterlet*[14]
1 November 1944	AO *Itsukushima Maru*	In 06°45'North 116°55'East	In Marudu Bay, northern Borneo	The submarine *Bergall* & land-based aircraft[15]
3 November 1944	DD *Akikaze**	In 16°48'North 117°17'East	Off northwest Luzon	The submarine *Pintado*
8 November 1944	AO *Banei Mar*	In 13°53'North 119°26'East	Southwest of Manila Bay	The submarine *Hardhead*
26 November 1944	AO *Yuho Maru*	In 04°54'North 114°07'East	Off Miri, Sarawak	The submarine *Pargo*

Date	Unit	Location and General Area of Loss	Agency of Destruction
4 December 1944	AO *Hakko Maru*	In 13°12'North 116°37'East	The submarine *Flasher*
22 December 1944	AO *Omurosan Maru*	In 15°07'North 109°05'East	Southeast of the Paracels	The submarine *Flasher*
6 January 1945	AO *Nichiei Maru*	In 06°57'North 102°57'East	East of Singora[16]	The submarine *Besugo*
12 January 1945	Esc *Chiburi* Esc C. D. 19 Esc C. D. 43*	In 10°20'North 107°50'East In 10°20'North 107°50'East In 11°13'North 108°48'East	Off Cape St. Jacques Off Cape St. Jacques South of Cape Padaran	Carrier aircraft Carrier aircraft Carrier aircraft
14 January 1945	CMC *Yurijima*	In 05°51'North 103°16'East	East of Kota Bharu	The submarine *Cobia*
5 March 1945	AO *Ryoei Maru*	In 16°47'North 108°41'East	Off Da Nang, Indo-China	The submarine *Bashaw*
28 March 1945	Esc C. D. 33*	In 31°45'North 131°45'East	Off southeast Kyushu	Carrier aircraft
14 April 1945	Esc C. D. 31*	In 33°25'North 126°15'East	Off Namkwan, Quelpart Island, in Korean Strait	The submarine *Tirante*
3 May 1945	Esc C. D. 25	In 33°56'North 122°49'East	Between Tsingtao and Quelpart in Yellow Sea	The submarine *Springer*

Units That Were Surrendered after 2 September 1945

Esc *Kurahashi*	Officially decommissioned 30 November 1945; committed to repatriation duties from following day. Also given as having been employed as minesweeper 1945–1947. Transferred to Britain on 14 September 1947, and thereafter scrapped at Nagoya.
Esc C. D. 22*	Decommissioned at Maizuru 24 August 1945. Employed on repatriation duties 30 September 1945–4 February 1946 and then as minesweeper until 1 August 1946; then laid up at Sasebo. Transferred to the United States on 5 September 1947, and thereafter scrapped at Sasebo.
Esc C. D. 27	Undergoing repair after 6 August 1945 and decommissioned 20 November 1945 at Sasebo. Used on repatriation service (primarily between Okinawa and Shanghai and the home islands) between 13 April and 21 October 1946. Transferred to Britain on 14 August 1947, and thereafter scrapped at Singapore.
Esc C. D. 29*	Mined off Sasebo on 28 May 1945; engines badly damaged. Laid up at Sasebo and stricken 20 November 1945. Scrapped at Sasebo between November 1947 and March 1948.

| Esc C. D. 132* | Decommissioned 5 October 1945. Employed on repatriation duties (primarily between Shanghai, Pusan and Manila, and the home islands) between 31 October 1945 and 6 April 1946 and thereafter laid up at Sasebo. Sailed to Nagasaki 20 February 1948 and scrapped; completed in July 1948. | | |

Submarines That Were Committed to Operations in and off the Philippines

	SS I. 46	Missing east of Leyte Gulf after 27 October 1944.[17]		
	SS I. 26	Possibly sunk in 10°56'North 127°13'East, east of Leyte Gulf, by destroyers Gridley and Helm on 28 October 1944.[17]		
	SS I. 54	Possibly sunk in 10°58'North 127°13'East, east of Leyte Gulf, by destroyers Gridley and Helm on 28 October 1944.[17]		
	SS I. 45	Probably sunk in 10°10'North 127°28'East, off Surigao, by destroyer escort Whitehurst on 29 October 1944.[17]		

Date	Unit	Location and General Area of Loss		Agency of Destruction
12 November 1944	SS I. 38	In 08°04'North 138°03'East	South of Yap	The destroyer Nicholas
18 November 1944	SS I. 41	In 12°44'North 130°42'East	East of Samar	The destroyer escort Lawrence C. Taylor & aircraft from escort carrier Anzio
11 February 1945	SS Ro. 112	In 18°53'North 121°50'East	In the Luzon Strait	The submarine Batfish
26 February 1945	SS Ro. 43	In 25°07'North 140°19'East	Northwest of Iwo Jima	Aircraft from escort carrier Anzio
23 March 1945	SS Ro. 41	In 22°57'North 132°19'East	Southeast of Okinawa	The destroyer Haggard
	SS I. 44	Given as possibly sunk in 23°12'North 132°23'East, off Okinawa, by destroyer escort Fieberling on 10 April 1945[18]		
	SS I. 56	Given as sunk in 26°22'North 126°30'East, west of Okinawa, by destroyers Collett, Heermann, McCord, Mertz and the Uhlmann on 5 April 1945. More likely sunk in 26°42'North 130°38'East, east of Okinawa, by these same destroyers plus aircraft from the escort carrier Bataan on 18 April 1945.[18]		
	SS Ro. 46	Possibly sunk in 21°58'North 129°35'East, southeast of Okinawa, by destroyer escort Horace H. Bass on 25 April 1945.[19]		
	SS Ro. 109	Probably sunk in 24°15'North 131°16'East, southeast of Okinawa, by aircraft from the escort carrier Tulagi on 29 April 1945.[19]		

Unit That Was Surrendered after 2 September 1945

| | SS I. 53 | At Kure at war's end. Scuttled off the Goto Islands, off northwest Kyushu, on 1 April 1946. | | |

Notes:

1. These positions are the ones given in Ikeda Masae, *Taiheiyou Sensou Chibbiotu Kansen. Itai Chousa Taikan/Encyclopaedia of ships sunk in the Pacific War;* other sources give different positions.

2. This position is the one given in the Japanese official history, and other sources give different positions; for example, Jentschura gives the *Musashi* as having been sunk in 12°50′North 122°35′East.

3. This is the position of loss as given in Japanese sources; the contemporary American source gave the position as 20°14′North 126°11′East. See ADM 199.1494, p. 173.

4. These positions are American; Japanese records do not give positions for the loss of these two ships but note that that the *Fujinami* was sunk "off Mindoro, northwest of Panay Island" and the *Shiranui* "north of Panay Island."

5. The position given is the one presented in all standard reference books but cannot be correct; one of the Japanese ships might have been sunk in this position, but more than two hours separated the sinking of the two ships, in which time the *Kongo* was steaming at something like sixteen knots.

6. This position is Japanese; the American position is some four minutes to the west.

7. Raised and scrapped in 1952.

8. Raised and scrapped at Harima in 1946.

9. There seems to be considerable confusion in standard reference books regarding the surrender of Japanese warships. In part this seems to have stemmed from the fact that so many Japanese accounts of the war end with the Imperial broadcast of 15 August and simply do not deal with events after that date—i.e., the Soviet campaigns in the Kuriles and on Sakhalin and the surrender ceremony in the *Missouri* on 2 September. Such lassitude was fairly common and would seem to be the basis of the assertion that various ships—such as the *Yukikaze* and the *Kiri, Maki* and the *Sugi* in Jentschura, pp. 149 and 152—were surrendered in August 1945.

   It is possible that Japanese ships were surrendered at Yokohama on 29–30 August 1945 but apart from the fact that the national surrender necessarily involved the surrender of individual warships it seems that very few Japanese warships were physically surrendered. The warships that were involved in minesweeping and repatriation duties worked under Allied control and direction but remained Japanese and were operated by Japanese crews until July 1947, when the process of transfer to individual Allied powers began. The *Nagato* must have been one exception to this basic rule, as might have been the *Myoko* and *Takao*. The two Japanese heavy cruisers were *hors de combat* at Singapore at war's end, and the base and city were returned to British possession at the surrender of 12 September; they nonetheless retained caretaker Japanese crews until the time when they were scuttled.

   The warships that were to be transferred were gathered at Sasebo in the first half of 1947 and then sailed for their designated port of transfer; these were Shanghai for China, Hong Kong or Singapore for Britain, Tsingtao for the United States, and Nakhodka for the Soviet Union. Japanese warships bound for these ports sailed on 1 July or 26 July or 25 August or 30 September–1 October, and were then transferred some days later. Other warships were transferred to the Allies but remained in Japan and were scrapped.

   This explanation of what happened does not address the thorny question of legal ownership as distinct from physical possession; technically all Japanese warships that were passed to the Allied powers should have been the subject of proceedings in a prize court by the recipient country, but one suspects that such process, given that many of these ships were immediately scrapped, was not properly observed.

10. It seems that the *Myoko* left Singapore on 5 July.

11. Most accounts give the date of the scuttling of the *Takao* as 27 October 1946, but that is the date when she left Singapore under tow. She sank at 1818 on 29 October.

12. The whereabouts of the "Shinasaki Docks" is unknown, but given her damaged condition and probable difficulties of movement it may be that she was scrapped locally at Yokosuka in a yard that has since disappeared.

13. The American record, as given in *DANFS*, VI, p. 622, indicates that this ship, identified as the *Jinei Maru*, was sunk by the *Sterlet* on 25 October 1944; Roscoe, pp. 416 and 557, gives the position 30°15'North 129°45'East, southwest of Kyushu. Neither source cites the *Jinei Maru* as having been an oiler to Ozawa's force, and the *Japanese naval and merchant ship losses during WW2 to all causes: Joint Army-Navy assessment committee* names this civilian ship, not a fleet oiler, as the *Ikutagawa Maru*.

    Morison's official history, p. 430, cites the *Jinei Maru* as a member of the oiler force with Ozawa's force and marks her as having been sunk during the battle, but there is no other reference to her and there is no reference either to the *Sterlet* having sunk an oiler on 25 October or to her contribution to the sinking of the *Tanake Maru* five days later.

14. The record of this sinking is contradictory and incomplete.

    The American record, in the form of *DANFS*, VII, p. 279, indicates that the submarine *Trigger* torpedoed and seriously damaged an oiler, named as the *Tanake Maru*, on 30 October 1944. Morison, p. 407, Roscoe, p. 422, and *DANFS*, VI, p. 269, all state that on this same night the *Salmon* was engaged in an action with four escorts after she had torpedoed an oiler which was not named by Morison and Roscoe. This oiler, stated to have been previously damaged by the *Trigger*, was identified as the *Jinei Maru* in the *Salmon*'s entry. *DANFS*, VI, p. 623, states that on 31 October 1944 the *Sterlet* administered the *coup de grâce* reference an unnamed oiler previously damaged by the *Trigger*.

    Japanese naval and merchant ship losses during WW2 to all causes: Joint Army-Navy assessment committee indicates that the oiler was a civilian merchantman, type undefined, named the *Korei Maru*. It appears that this name was a mistransliteration, and that the ship was the *Tanake Maru*.

15. The record of this sinking is contradictory and confusing.

    The *Itsukushima Maru* is given as having been sunk in 07°17'North 116°45'East, cause undefined, on 27 October 1944 in *Kaiyou Roudou Kyoukai/Marine Labour Society, Nihon Syousen Senji Sounan Si*, and Ikeda Masae, *Taiheiyou Sensou Tinbotu Kansen Tyousa*. She is given in Watts and Gordon, p. 508, as having been sunk on 27 October 1944, cause not given, and in Jentschura, p. 252, as having been sunk on 27 October 1944 in the Balabac Strait by the submarine *Bergall*.

    Roscoe, pp. 412 and 529, makes reference to the *Nippo Maru*, the *Bergall* having sunk the *Nippo Maru*, but there is no reference to her having attacked, still less having torpedoed and sunk, a second oiler on this date.

    Other Japanese sources indicate that the *Itsukushima Maru* was torpedoed and left drifting in the same attack that accounted for the *Nippo Maru* and that she was then sunk by aircraft, presumably shore-based aircraft, on any one of three dates: 29 October, 31 October, and 1 November. The USAAF combat chronology gives no indication of when an American land-based aircraft may have completed the destruction of a Japanese oiler on any of these dates. One official Japanese history indicates that she entered Marudu Bay, northern Borneo early on 28 October.

The *Japanese naval and merchant ship losses during WW2 to all causes: Joint Army-Navy assessment committee* gives the *Itsukushima Maru* as having been sunk by aircraft on 29 October, a detail that is repeated in *Vessels lost or damaged by war causes while under Japanese control*; the copy in the Admiralty Library has a penciled addition which states that while she was sunk in a position slightly to the west of the Balabac Strait, she was "being broken up at Hong Kong in September 1954."

One Japanese source indicates the loss of the *Itsukushima Maru* as 11 January 1945, but it seems that this was the date when she was stricken.

The most careful research, undertaken within the NDHS by Shindo Hiroyuki and forwarded to the author by e-mail on 13 August 2004, states that she was torpedoed by the submarine *Bergall* on 27 October in the position cited but that she managed to reach Marudu Bay, northern Borneo, "where she was bombed by PB4Ys of the American VPB-115 on 29 October, and sank on 1 November 1944."

16. Japanese and American positions of sinkings often differ by a minute or two but in this case this American and the Japanese position, given as 04°30'North 103°30'East off Kuantan, represents a major difference (of something approaching 250 miles) that cannot be reconciled.

17. In *DANFS*, III, p. 159 the *Gridley* and *Helm* are credited with the sinking of I. 46. The Japanese records indicate that the I. 46 was lost after 27 October, cause known, while Jentschura (pp. 175–177) states that the I. 54 was sunk by the destroyer escort *Richard M. Rowell* in 09°45'North 126°45'East, east of Leyte Gulf, on 24 October, that the I. 54 was credited with the sinking of I. 54 on 28 October, but on p. 294 the *Helm* and *Gridley* are credited with the lost to causes unknown, and that the I. 26 was probably sunk by the *Gridley* and *Helm* and the I. 45 by the *Whitehurst* on 28 October. But the *Rowell*'s entry in *DANFS*, VI, p. 98, makes reference to an action against an enemy submarine on 26 October but does not claim that she sank the enemy boat. The only safe comment is that the cause of loss of these four boats would seem to be uncertain but that between them the *Gridley* and *Helm* accounted for one Japanese submarine and the *Whitehurst* another, probably the I. 45 and on 29 October. See *DANFS*, VIII, p. 272.

18. Japanese sources give the I. 56 as sunk by these American units on 5 April 1945, but the American record—for example the *DANFS*, III, p. 286 entry for the *Heermann*—makes no reference to any action on this day and gives the 18 April date. The problem herein is that Japanese sources also give the I. 44 as sunk by the *Heermann, McCord, Mertz* and the *Uhlmann* on 18 April 1945. In addition, it is perhaps worth noting that the *DANFS*, II, p. 404 entry for the *Fieberling* makes no reference whatsoever to any incident, still less any claim to having sunk an enemy submarine, on 10 April 1945.

19. Japanese records, primarily drawn from *Nihon Kaigun Sensuikansi Kankou Kai* and *Nihon Kaigun Sensuikansi Sinkousya*, reverse these two Japanese units; dates, whereabouts, and causes are the same, but the submarines have been exchanged.

THE ORDER OF BATTLE OF THE 7TH FLEET, 17 OCTOBER 1944

7TH FLEET (VICE ADMIRAL THOMAS CASSIN KINKAID IN
THE AMPHIBIOUS FORCE FLAGSHIP *WASATCH* WITH DEPUTY
COMMANDER VICE ADMIRAL THEODORE STARK WILKINSON IN
THE AMPHIBIOUS FORCE FLAGSHIP *MOUNT OLYMPUS*)

TASK FORCE 77 (VICE ADMIRAL THOMAS CASSIN KINKAID IN THE AMPHIBIOUS
FORCE FLAGSHIP *WASATCH*)

Task Group 77.1 (Vice Admiral Kinkaid in the Wasatch*)*
The amphibious force flagship *Wasatch* (Captain Alfred Marcellus Granum), the light
   cruiser *Nashville* (Captain Charles Edward Coney), and the destroyers *Abner Read*
   (Commander Arthur Montgomery Purdy), *Ammen* (Commander James Harvey Brown),
   Bush (Commander Rollin Everton Westholm) and the *Mullany* (Commander Albert
   Otto Momm).

Task Group 77.3 (Rear Admiral Russell Stanley Berkey in the light cruiser Phoenix*)*
The Australian heavy cruisers *Australia* (Captain Emile Frank Verlaine Dechaineux) and
   Shropshire (Captain Charles Alfred Godfrey Nichols) and the U.S. light cruisers *Boise*
   (Captain John Summerfield Roberts) and *Phoenix* (Captain Jack Harlan Duncan).
Destroyer Squadron 24 (Captain Kenmore Mathew McManes in the *Hutchins*): The U.S.
   destroyers *Bache* (Commander Robert Cameron Morton), *Beale* (Commander Doyle
   Murray Coffee), *Daly* (Commander Richard Gerben Visser), *Hutchins* (Commander
   Caleb Barrett Laning) and the *Killen* (Commander Howard Grant Corey), and the
   Australian destroyers *Arunta* (Commander Alfred Edgar Buchanan) and *Warramunga*
   (Lieutenant-Commander John Melvill Alliston).
Note: The *Warramunga's* commanding officer was originally Commander Neil Alex-
ander Mackinnon, who fell ill as a result of contracting some form of tropical fever at
the end of September 1944. Lieutenant-Commander Alliston was transferred from the

Shropshire to assume temporary command, and he and Mackinnon exchanged command five times before Alliston finally assumed full command on 17 October. He remained with the *Warramunga* until April 1945.

Task Group 77.4 (Rear Admiral Thomas Lamison Sprague in the escort carrier Sangamon*)*
Task Unit 77.4.1 (Rear Admiral T. L. Sprague in the *Sangamon*):
Task Unit 77.4.11/Carrier Division 22 (Rear Admiral T. L. Sprague in the *Sangamon*): The escort carriers *Chenango* (Captain George van Deurs), *Sangamon* (Captain Maurice Eugene Browder), *Santee* (Captain Robert Edwin Blick, Jr.) and the *Suwannee* (Captain William David Johnson, Jr.).
Task Unit 77.4.12/Carrier Division 28 (Rear Admiral George Raymond Henderson in the *Saginaw Bay*): The escort carriers *Petrof Bay* (Captain Joseph Lester Kane) and *Saginaw Bay* (Captain Frank Carlin Sutton).
Task Unit 77.4.13 (Captain Ira Hudson Nunn in the *McCord*): The destroyers *Hazelwood* (Commander Volckert Petrus Douw), *McCord* (Commander Fred Daniel Michael) and the *Trathen* (Commander John Raymond Millett), and the destroyer escorts *Coolbaugh* (Lieutenant-Commander Stuart T. Hotchkiss), *Edmonds* (Lieutenant-Commander John S. Burrows, Jr.), *Eversole* (Lieutenant-Commander George Elliott Marix), *Richard M. Rowell* (Commander Harry Allan Barnard, Jr.) and the *Richard S. Bull* (Lieutenant-Commander Alfred Wiltze Gardes, Jr.).
Task Unit 77.4.2 (Rear Admiral Felix Budwell Stump in the escort carrier *Natoma Bay*):
Task Unit 77.4.21/Carrier Division 24 (Rear Admiral Stump in the *Natoma Bay*): The escort carriers *Manila Bay* (Captain Fitzhugh Lee II) and *Natoma Bay* (Captain Albert Kellogg Morehouse).
Task Unit 77.4.22/Carrier Division 27 (Rear Admiral William Dodge Sample in the escort carrier *Marcus Island*): The escort carriers *Kadashan Bay* (Captain Robert Nisbet Hunter), *Marcus Island* (Captain Charles Frederic Greber), *Ommaney Bay* (Captain Howard Leyland Young) and the *Savo Island* (Captain Clarence Eugene Ekstrom).
Task Unit 77.4.23 (Captain Luther Kendrick Reynolds in the *Haggard*): The destroyers *Franks* (Commander David Richard Stephan), *Haggard* (Commander David Alonzo Harris) and the *Hailey*, and the destroyer escorts *Abercrombie* (Lieutenant-Commander Bernard H. Katschinski), *LeRay Wilson* (Lieutenant-Commander Matthew V. Carson, Jr.), *Oberrender* (Lieutenant-Commander Samuel Floyd Spencer), *Richard W. Suesens* (Lieutenant-Commander Robert Wallace Graham) and the *Walter C. Wann* (Lieutenant-Commander John W. Stedman, Jr.).
Task Unit 77.4.3 (Rear Admiral Clifton Albert Frederick Sprague in the escort carrier *Fanshaw Bay*):
Task Unit 77.4.31/Carrier Division 25 (Rear Admiral C. A. F. Sprague in the *Fanshaw Bay*): The escort carriers *Fanshaw Bay* (Captain Douglass Pollock Johnson), *Kalinin Bay* (Captain Thomas Binney Williamson), *St. Lo* (Captain Francis Joseph McKenna) and the *White Plains* (Captain Dennis Joseph Sullivan).
Task Unit 77.4.32/Carrier Division 26 (Rear Admiral Ralph Andrew Ofstie in the escort carrier *Kitkun Bay*): The escort carriers *Gambier Bay* (Captain Walter Victor Rudolph Vieweg) and *Kitkun Bay* (Captain John Perry Whitney).
Screen (Commander William Dow Thomas in the *Hoel*): The destroyers *Heermann* (Commander Amos Townsend Hathaway), *Hoel* (Commander Leon Samuel Kintberger) and the *Johnston* (Commander Ernest Edwin Evans), and the destroyer escorts *Dennis* (Lieutenant-Commander Samuel Hansen), *John C. Butler* (Lieutenant-Commander John Edward Pace), *Raymond* (Lieutenant-Commander Aaron Frederick Beyer, Jr.) and the *Samuel B. Roberts* (Lieutenant-Commander Robert Watson Copeland, Jr.).

Task Group 77.5 (Commander Walter Rowe Loud in the high-speed minesweeper Hovey)
Alternatively designated the Minesweeping and Hydrographic Group, this formation
consisted of the minelayers *Breese* (Lieutenant-Commander David Barney Cohen)
and *Preble* (Lieutenant-Commander Edward Francis Baldridge), the high-speed mine-
sweepers *Chandler* (Lieutenant Frank M. Murphy), *Hamilton* (Lieutenant-Commander
John Clague), *Hovey* (Lieutenant Albert A. Clark, Jr.), *Howard* (Lieutenant-Commander
Onofrio Frederick Salvia), *Long* (Lieutenant Stanley Caplan), *Southard* (Lieutenant
John E. Brennan) and the *Palmer* (Lieutenant William E. McGuirk, Jr.), the mine-
sweepers *Pursuit* (Lieutenant-Commander Romer F. Good), *Requisite* (Lieutenant-
Commander Herbert R. Peirce, Jr.), *Revenge* (Lieutenant-Commander John L. Jackson),
Sage (Lieutenant-Commander Franklyn K. Zinn), *Salute* (Lieutenant John R. Hodges),
Saunter (Lieutenant-Commander James R. Keefer), *Scout* (Lieutenant Edmund G.
Anderson, Jr.), *Scrimmage* (Lieutenant Robert van Winkle), *Sentry* (Lieutenant-
Commander Thomas R. Fonick), *Token* (Lieutenant William T. Hunt), *Tumult* (Lieu-
tenant William K. McDuffie), *Velocity* (Lieutenant George J. Buyse) and the *Zeal*
(Lieutenant-Commander Ernest W. Woodhouse), a total of twenty-six 320-ton motor
minesweepers, the destroyer transport *Sands* (Lieutenant Jerome M. Samuels, Jr.), the
Australian frigate *Gascoyne* (Lieutenant-Commander Neven Robinson Read) and the
Australian harbor defense motor launch HDML 1704 (Lieutenant-Commander Stanley
William Scott Robertson).

*Task Group 77.6 (Lieutenant-Commander Charles Claude Morgan in the destroyer
transport Talbot)*
Alternatively designated the Beach Demolition Group, this formation consisted of seven
UDTs and the destroyer transports *Belknap* (Lieutenant Ralph Childs), *Brooks* (Lieuten-
ant Sidney C. Rasmussen, Jr.), *Clemson* (Lieutenant William Francis Moran), *George
E. Badger* (Lieutenant-Commander Edward M. Higgins), *Goldsborough* (Lieutenant
William J. Meehan III), *Humphreys* (Lieutenant-Commander Owen B. Murphy), *Kane*
(Lieutenant Fran M. Christiansen), *Manley* (Lieutenant Robert T. Newell, Jr.), *Over-
ton* (Lieutenant-Commander Desmond Kiernan O'Connor), *Rathburne* (Lieutenant-
Commander Richard L. Welch) and the *Talbot* (Lieutenant-Commander Charles
Claude Morgan).

Task Group 77.7 (Rear Admiral Robert Ogden Glover)
One RAS formation, under the command of Captain Jefferson Davis Beard, consisting of
the oilers *Ashtabula* (Lieutenant-Commander Walter Barnett, Jr.), *Kishwaukee* (Lieutenant Francis M. Hillman), *Salamonie* (Commander Llewellyn James Johns), *Saranac*
(Commander Harold Rivington Parker), *Schuylkill* (Captain Fred Archibald Hardesty),
Suamico (Lieutenant-Commander Arley Sidney Johnson) and the *Tallulah* (Lieutenant-
Commander William F. Huckaby). This formation, which was numbered Task Unit
77.7.1, was in the company of one formation of five ammunition ships under the com-
mand of Commander Percival V. R. Harris in the *Mazama*, and both were screened
by an escort formation, under Commander Frederick W. Howes in the *Whitehurst*,
that consisted of the destroyer escorts *Bowers* (Commander Frederic William Hawes),
Whitehurst (Lieutenant-Commander Jack C. Horton) and the *Witter* (Lieutenant-
Commander George Herrmann).
Note: The *Ashtabula* survived being torpedoed in Leyte Gulf by a Japanese aircraft on 24
October; she was detached on 27 October and made her way to San Pedro, California,
via Kossol Roads, Humboldt Bay, and Pearl Harbor. She returned to service in February
1945. The formation commander, Captain Beard, was in the *Ashtabula* and transferred
to the *Saranac* on 26 October.

In addition, this task group had under command a number of other formations. These were:

(1) one formation called the Leyte Gulf Unit, under Captain Emory Paul Hylant, that consisted of the tankers *Arethusa* (Lieutenant Regina L. Barrington), *Caribou* (Lieutenant Julian B. Humphrey), *Mink* (Lieutenant William J. Meagher), *Panda* (Lieutenant Nicholas Polk) and the *Porcupine* (Lieutenant Daniel M. Paul), plus the Australian oiler *Bishopdale*.
Note: The Australian records do not contain the name of the *Bishopdale*'s captain.

(2) one formation stationed in the Kossol Roads under Lieutenant-Commander Henry K. Wallace in the oiler *Chepachet*: in company were two unidentified tankers and the destroyer escort *Willmarth* (Lieutenant-Commander James G. Thorburn, Jr.).

(3) the boom defense vessels/net tenders *Indus* (Commander Andreas S. Einmo), *Satinleaf* (Lieutenant Arthur B. Church), *Silverbell* (Lieutenant Harold N. Berg) and the *Teak* (Lieutenant Byron P. Hollett); the landing craft repair ship *Achilles* (Lieutenant Converse O. Smith); the salvage ship *Cable* (Lieutenant-Commander Hertwell Pond); the repair ship *Midas* (Lieutenant Robert A. Young) and the floating dock ARD-19; the water tanker *Severn* (Lieutenant-Commander Owen Rees); the ammunition ship *Murzim* (Lieutenant-Commander DeWitt S. Walton) and the Australian ammunition ships *Poyang* (Lieutenant John Warren Edwards) and *Yunnan* (Lieutenant Thomas Travers Matthew Hehir); and the stores ships *Calamares* (Lieutenant-Commander Lansford Franklin Kengle, Jr.), *Crux* (Commander Charles R. Beyer), *Ganymede* (Lieutenant-Commander Glenn H. Melichar), *Mizar* (Commander Carl H. Christensen), *Octans* (Commander Otto John Stein), *Pollux* (Commander Harry Llewellyn Bixby) and the *Triangulum* (Lieutenant-Commander Charles K. S. Latus), and the Australian stores ship *Merkur*.
Note 1: Morison, p. 423, states that the stores ships *Acubens* and *Arequipa* were with Task Group 77.7, but the *Acubens* did not arrive at Hollandia from New York on her first mission until 25 October and the *Arequipa* did not enter service until January 1945.
Note 2: Morison also gives the *Achilles* with Task Group 77.7 but lists her, p. 417, with Task Group 78.6.
Note 3: The incomplete Australian record does not permit the naming of the captain of the *Merkur*. Lieutenant-Commander Andrew Russell Johnston was with and may have been the senior officer in the ship, but he was in the paymaster branch and probably was not her captain.

TASK FORCE 78 (REAR ADMIRAL DANIEL EDWARD BARBEY IN THE AMPHIBIOUS FORCE FLAGSHIP *BLUE RIDGE*, ALTERNATIVELY DESIGNATED NORTHERN ATTACK FORCE)

Fire Support Unit North (Rear Admiral George Lester Weyler in the battleship Mississippi*)*
Battle Division 4 (Rear Admiral Theodore Davis Ruddock, Jr., in the *West Virginia*): The battleships *Maryland* (Captain Herbert James Ray), *Mississippi* (Captain Hemen Judd Redfield) and the *West Virginia* (Captain Herbert Victor Wiley).
The destroyers *Aulick* (Commander John Douglas Andrew), *Cony* (Commander Allen Willis Moore) and the *Sigourney* (Lieutenant-Commander Fletcher Hale, Jr.).

Task Group 78.1 (Rear Admiral Daniel Edward Barbey in the amphibious command ship Blue Ridge*)*
Alternatively designated the Palo Attack Group, this formation consisted of the *Blue Ridge* (Commander Lewis Richard McDowell), two transport formations under the command of Captain Thomas Baldwin Brittain in the *DuPage*, twelve landing ships from one flotilla under Lieutenant-Commander Danford M. Baker, assorted units and landing

craft and other units under Captain Neill Duncan Brantly, and a screen under Captain Henry Crommelin in the destroyer *John Rodgers*. The transport formations were Transport Division 24 (Captain Brittain) with the attack transports *DuPage* (Captain George M. Wauchope), *Elmore* (Captain Drayton Harrison), *Fuller* (Captain Nathaniel Moore Pigman) and the *Wayne* (Captain Thomas Valentine Cooper), and the attack cargo ship *Aquarius* (Commander Ira Edwin Eskridge), the transport *John Land* (Commander Frederic August Graf) and the LSD *Gunston Hall* (Commander Dale E. Collins), and Transport Division 6 (Captain Harold Davies Baker) with the attack transports *Fayette* (Captain John Campbell Lester), *Leedstown* (Captain Harold Bye) and the *Ormsby* (Captain Leonard Frisco), the attack cargo ship *Titania* (Commander Malcolm Whitfield Callahan), the cargo ship *Hercules* (Commander William H. Turnquist) and the LSD *Carter Hall* (Lieutenant-Commander Cecil Edward Blount) and *Epping Forest* (Commander Lester Martin). Also in company were the fleet tugs *Apache* (Lieutenant Clyde S. Horner) and *Quapaw* (Lieutenant-Commander Northrup H. Castle).
The screen consisted of the destroyers *Harrison* (Commander Walter Vincent Combs, Jr.), *John Rodgers* (Commander James Gilbert Franklin), *McKee* (Commander Russell Bowes Allen) and the *Murray* (Commander Paul Ramseur Anderson).

Task Group 78.2 (Rear Admiral William Morrow Fechteler in the transport Fremont)
Alternatively designated the San Ricardo Attack Group, this formation consisted of the command ship *Fremont* (Captain Clarence Vincent Conlan), two transport formations under the command of Captain Milton Oren Carlson in the attack transport *Harris*, one flotilla of fourteen landing ships under the command of Captain Richard Martin Scruggs, and screen under the command of Captain Albert Edmondson Jarrell in the *Fletcher*. The transports were divided between Transport Division 32 (Captain Milton Oren Carlson) with the attack transports *Harris* (Captain Marion Emerson Murphy), *Barnstable* (Captain Harvey Thomas Walsh), the transport *Herald of the Morning* (Commander Harry Albert Dunn, Jr.), the attack cargo ship *Arneb* (Captain Howard Rutherford Shaw) and the LSD *White Marsh* (Commander George H. Eppleman), and Transport Division 20 (Captain Donald Wood Loomis) with the attack transports *Leonard Wood* (Captain Henry Crawford Perkins), *Pierce* (Captain Francis McKee Adams) and the *James O'Hara* (Captain Elijah Warriner Irish), the transport *La Salle* (Commander Fred C. Fluegel), the attack cargo ship *Electra* (Lieutenant-Commander Dennis S. Holler) and the LSD *Oak Hill* (Commander Carl Arthur Peterson), and nine LSM. The screen consisted of the destroyers *Anderson* (Lieutenant-Commander Ralph Hamilton Benson, Jr.), *Fletcher* (Commander John Lee Foster), *La Vallette* (Commander Wells Thompson) and the *Jenkins* (Commander Philip Daly Gallery).
Note: In addition there were eight landing craft and one tug, the *Sonoma* (Lieutenant Walter R. Wurzler), in attendance. The latter sank off Dio Island after being hit by a crashing Japanese aircraft on 24 October (*DANFS*, VI, pp. 555–556).

Task Group 78.3 (Rear Admiral Arthur Dewey Struble in the destroyer Hughes)
Alternatively designated the Panaon Attack Group, this formation consisted of the Australian landing ships *Kanimbla* (Commander Andrew Veitch Bunyan), *Manoora* (Commander Alan Paterson Cousin) and the *Westralia* (Commander Alfred Victor Knight), assorted landing craft under Captain Charles Dresser Murphey, and the destroyers *Dashiell* (Commander Douglas Lee Lipscomb Cordiner), *Hughes* (Commander Ellis Brooke Rittenhouse), *Ringgold* (Commander Warren Byron Christie), *Schroeder* (Commander Robert McElrath) and the *Sigsbee* (Commander Gordon Paiea Chung-Hoon) plus the British minelayer *Ariadne* (Captain the Lord Ashbourne).

Note: After being involved in the landings on Leyte, the *Ariadne* (which in the official British history is designated an assault troop carrier) along with the destroyers *Caldwell* (Commander George Wendelburg) and *Shaw* (Lieutenant-Commander Victor Bernard Graff), the destroyer escort *Willmarth*, and assorted landing ships and craft, was involved in the occupation of Pegun in the Mapia/St. David Islands, on 15 November; she then returned to Morotai and, on 18 November, landed forces in the Asia Islands.

These groups are some 150 miles to the north of the Vogelkop, Pegun being in 00°50'North 134°16'East, and the Asia group in 01°03'North 131°16'East.

Task Group 78.4 (Rear Admiral Arthur Dewey Struble in the destroyer Hughes)
Alternatively designated the Dinagat Attack Group, this formation consisted of the destroyer transports *Crosby* (Lieutenant George G. Moffatt), *Herbert* (Lieutenant Gerald Sellen Hewitt), *Kilty* (Lieutenant Lloyd George Benson), *Schley* (Lieutenant-Commander Edward T. Farley) and the *Ward* (Lieutenant Richard E. Farwell), the fleet tug *Chickasaw* (Lieutenant Lawrence C. Olsen) and, under the command of Captain Charles Dresser Murphey, assorted patrol and landing craft; escort was provided by the destroyers *Lang* (Commander Harold Payson, Jr.) and *Stack* (Commander Robert Edward Wheeler) and the frigates *Bisbee* (Commander John P. German) and *Gallup* (Commander Clayton M. Opp).

Task Group 78.6 (Captain Samuel Power Jenkins in the transport Crescent City)
Alternatively designated Reinforcement Group 1, this formation, which arrived on station on 22 October, consisted of the attack transports *Callaway* (Captain Donald C. McNeil), *Crescent City* (Captain Lionel Lewis Rowe), *Leon* (Captain Bruce Byron Adell), *Sumter* (Commander James T. O'Pry, Jr.), *Warren* (Captain William A. McHale), *Windsor* (Captain Douglas Castleberry Woodward), the transport *Storm King* (Commander Harry James Hansen), the cargo ship *Jupiter* (Commander John Morgan Bristol) and four unnamed merchant ships, one flotilla of thirty-two landing ships (under the command of Captain Oral Raymond Swigart) and other landing craft, and screen (Captain Edward Alva Solomons in the *Morris*); the destroyers *Howorth* (Commander Edward Stitt Burns), *Morris* (Lieutenant-Commander Rexford Vinal Wheeler, Jr.), *Mustin* (Lieutenant-Commander John Gerard Hughes) and the *Stevens* (Commander William Magnus Rakow) and the frigates *Burlington* (Commander Edgar Vigo Carlson) and *Carson City* (Commander Harold Bateman Roberts).

Task Group 78.7 (Captain John Kenneth Burkholder Ginder in the destroyer Nicholas)
Alternatively designated Reinforcement Group 2, this formation, which arrived on station on 24 October, consisted of a flotilla of thirty-three landing ships (Captain Erskine Austin Seay), twenty-four Liberty ships and other freighters, various support ships and escorts (Captain John Kenneth Burkholder Ginder in the *Nicholas*): The destroyers *Hopewell* (Commander Warner Scott Rodimon), *Nicholas* (Commander Robert Taylor Scott Keith), *O'Bannon* (Commander Richard Wilder Smith) and the *Taylor* (Commander Nicholas John Frederick Frank, Jr.) and the frigates *Muskogee* (Commander Rufus Edward Mroczkowski) and *San Pedro* (Lieutenant Harold L. Sutherland).

Task Group 78.8 (Commander John L. Steinmetz)
Alternatively designated Reinforcement Group 3, this formation, which arrived on station on 29 October, consisted of assorted landing ships and freighters and Destroyer Squadron 5 (Captain William Marchant Cole in the *Flusser*): The destroyers *Drayton* (Commander Richard Starr Craighill), *Flusser* (Commander Theodore Robert Vogeley), *Lamson* (Commander John Vavasour Noel, Jr.), *Mahan* (Commander Earnest

Goodrich Campbell) and the *Smith* (Commander Frank Voris List), and the frigates *El Paso* (Commander Romeo J. Barromey), *Eugene* (Commander Clifford R. MacLean), *Orange* (Commander John Armstrong Dirks) and the *Van Buren* (Commander Charles Breckenridge Arrington).

Task Force 79 (Vice Admiral Theodore Stark Wilkinson in the amphibious force flagship *Mount Olympus*, alternatively designated Southern Attack Force)

Fire Support Unit South (Rear Admiral Jesse Barrett Oldendorf in the heavy cruiser Louisville)

Battle Division 2 (Rear Admiral Theodore Edson Chandler in the *Tennessee*): The battleships *California* (Captain Henry Poynter Burnett), *Pennsylvania* (Captain Charles Franklin Martin) and the *Tennessee* (Captain John Baptist Heffernan).

Cruiser Division 4 (Rear Admiral Jesse Barrett Oldendorf in the *Louisville*): The heavy cruisers *Louisville* (Captain Samuel Hansford Hurt), *Minneapolis* (Captain Harry Browning Slocum) and the *Portland* (Captain Thomas Greenhow Williams Settle).

Cruiser Division 9 (Rear Admiral Walden Lee Ainsworth): The light cruiser *Honolulu* (Captain Harold Raymond Thurber).

Cruiser Division 12 (Rear Admiral Robert Ward Hayler in the *Denver*): The light cruisers *Columbia* (Captain Maurice Edwin Curts) and the *Denver* (Captain Albert McQueen Bledsoe).

Destroyer Squadron 56 (Captain Roland Nesbit Smoot in the *Leutze*): The destroyers *Bennion* (Commander Joshua Winfred Cooper), *Heywood L. Edwards* (Commander Joe Wood Boulware), *Leutze* (Commander Berton Aldrich Robbins, Jr.), *Newcomb* (Commander Lawrence Blanchard Cook) and the *Richard P. Leary* (Commander Frederic Shrom Habecker).

Destroyer Division 112 (Captain Thomas Francis Conley, Jr., in the *Robinson*): The destroyers *Albert W. Grant* (Commander Terrell Andrew Nisewaner), *Bryant* (Commander Paul Laverne High), *Claxton* (Commander Miles Hunter Hubbard), *Halford* (Commander Robert James Hardy), *Robinson* (Commander Elonzo Bowden Grantham, Jr.), *Ross* (Commander Benjamin Coe), *Thorn* and the *Welles*.

Attached to this formation was a salvage group under Commander Henry O. Foss that numbered the fleet tugs *Chowanoc* (Lieutenant Rodney Fred Snipes), *Menoninee* (Lieutenant J. A. Young) and the *Potawatomi* (Lieutenant Charles Henry Stedman), the repair ship *Egeria* (Lieutenant Ansel H. Wilson) and the salvage vessel *Preserver* (Lieutenant Louis Burdett Frank).

Note 1: The units of Cruiser Division 12 and Destroyer Division 112 were with Task Group 78.4 during the assault phase on Dinagat.

Note 2: The *Ross* was mined twice in the early hours of 19 October off western Homonhon Island in the entrance to Leyte Gulf. She was the only major U.S. warship to be mined and was unable to complete repairs locally until 13 December. She was towed to Humboldt Bay and thereafter she made her way to Mare Island navy yard, arriving 2 March 1945; she completed repairs at the end of June. She arrived back at Ulithi on 14 August. See *DANFS*, VI, p. 160.

Note 3: Morison, pp. 420 and 429, gives the *Menominee* as being with both this formation and Task Group 30.8.

Task Group 79.1 (Rear Admiral Richard Lansing Conolly in the amphibious command ship Appalachian)

Alternatively designated Attack Group Able, this formation consisted of the command ships *Mount Olympus* (Captain John Henry Shultz) and *Appalachian* (Captain Charles Richardson Jeffs), and had the following formations and units under command:

Task Group 79.3 (Captain Clifford Geer Richardson in the attack transport Cavalier)

Alternatively designated Transport Group Able, this formation consisted of four transport formations and screen. The transport formations were Transport Division 7 (Captain Clifford Geer Richardson) with the attack transport *Cavalier* (Captain Arthur Graham Hall), *Feland* (Commander George Fry Prestwich) and the *J. Franklin Bell* (Captain Oliver Henderson Ritchie), the transport *Golden City* (Commander Charles Marshall Furlow, Jr.), the attack cargo ship *Thuban* (Commander James C. Campbell) and the LSD *Lindenwald* (Captain William H. Weaver, Jr.); Transport Division 30 (Captain Clinton Alonzo Misson in the *Knox*) with the attack transports *Calvert* (Commander John Ford Warris), *Custer* (Captain Winthrop Eugene Terry), *Knox* (Captain John Huston Brady) and the *Rixey* (Captain Philip Hagenbuch Jenkins), the attack cargo ship *Chara* (Commander John P. Clark) and the LSD *Ashland* (Lieutenant-Commander William A. Caughey); Transport Division 38 (Captain Charles Allen in the *Lamar*) with the attack transports *Alpine* (Commander George Kenneth Gordon Reilly), *Heywood* (Commander Gordon M. Jones) and the *Lamar* (Captain Burntnett Kent Culver), the transports *Monitor* (Captain Karl J. Olsen) and *Starlight* (Commander William O. Britton) and the attack cargo ship *Alshain* (Captain Roland Ernest Krause); and the Transport Division X-Ray (Captain John Arthur Snackenberg) with the attack transports *George Clymer* (Captain John Arthur Snackenberg) and *President Hayes* (Captain Herman Edward Schieke) and the cargo ship *Mercury* (Lieutenant-Commander Nelson D. Salmon). The screen, under the command of Captain William Jefferson Marshall in the *Erben*, consisted of the destroyers *Abbot* (Commander Francis Walford Ingling), *Black* (Commander Edward Reuben King, Jr.), *Braine* (Commander William Wilson Fitts), *Chauncey* (Commander Lester Cameron Conwell), *Erben* (Lieutenant-Commander Morgan Slayton), *Gansevoort* (Lieutenant-Commander John Macauley Steinbeck), *Hale* (Lieutenant-Commander Donald Worrall Wilson) and the *Walker* (Commander Harry Edson Townsend).

Note: The *Rixey* doubled as hospital transport and bore the designation APH-3.

Task Group 79.5

One formation of thirty-one landing ships under the command of Captain Richard Christopher Webb, Jr.

In addition, there were a number of groups assigned to Task Group 79.1 which together numbered thirty-two landing craft and at least eleven other units. In company was the destroyer *Stembel* (Commander William Leonard Tagg) with these groups' commander, Captain Vilhelm Klein Busck; one twelve-strong LCT formation was commanded by Lieutenant Meyer Wassell.

Task Group 79.2 (Rear Admiral Forrest Betton Royal in the amphibious command ship Rocky Mount)

Alternatively designated Attack Group Baker, this formation consisted of the command ship *Rocky Mount* (Captain Stanley Fletcher Patten) with the following formations and units under command:

Task Group 79.4 (Captain Herbert Bain Knowles in the transport Cambria*)*
Alternatively designated Transport Group Baker, this formation consisted of three transport formations, one flotilla of landing ships under Commander Arthur Ainsley Ageton
in the destroyer *Luce* (Commander Hinton Allen Owens), assorted amphibious units
under Commander William K. Rummel, and screen. The transport formations were
Transport Division 10 (Captain George Douglas Morrison in the *Clay*) with the attack
transports *Arthur Middleton* (Captain Severt Andrew Olsen), *Baxter* (Captain Valvin
Robinson Sinclair), *Clay* (Captain Nicholas Bauer van Bergen), *William P. Biddle*
(Captain Robert Wallace Berry), the transport *George F. Elliott* (Commander Walter
Frederick Weidner), the attack cargo ship *Capricornus* (Lieutenant-Commander Benja-
min F. McGuckin) and the LSD *Catskill* (Captain Raymond W. Chambers); Transport
Division 18 (Captain Herbert Bain Knowles in the *Cambria*) with the attack transports
Cambria (Captain Charles Walter Dean), *Frederick Funston* (Commander Charles
Carter Anderson) and the *Monrovia* (Captain John Donald Kelsey), the transport *War
Hawk* (Commander Stanley H. Thompson), the attack cargo ship *Alcyone* (Commander
Hermann Pierce Knickerbocker), and the LSD *Casa Grande* (Lieutenant-Commander
Fred E. Strumm) and *Rushmore* (Commander Elith A. Jansen); and Transport Division
28 (Captain Henry Clinton Flanagan in the *Bolivar*) with the attack transports *Bolivar*
(Captain Robert Paul Waddell), *Doyen* (Commander John Glenn McClaughry) and
the *Sheridan* (Captain Paul Hollister Wiedorn), the transport *Comet* (Lieutenant-
Commander Theodore C. Fonda), the attack cargo ship *Almaack* (Lieutenant-
Commander Clyde O. Hicks), the cargo ship *Auriga* (Commander John G. Hart) and
the LSD *Belle Grove* (Commander Morris Seavey).
The assorted amphibious units included one flotilla of landing craft under the command of Captain Theodore Wesley Rimer with subformations under the command of
Lieutenant-Commander George W. Hannett and Lieutenant Frank R. Giliberty, one
six-strong LSM formation under Lieutenant-Commander John Goodman Blanche, Jr.,
and, with eleven units, one LCT formation under Lieutenant Gordon P. Franklin.
The screen, under the command of Captain Ephraim Rankin McLean, Jr., in the *Pick-
ing*, consisted of the destroyers *Charles J. Badger* (Commander John Henderson Cotten), *Halligan* (Commander Clarence Edward Cortner), *Haraden* (Commander Halle
Charles Allan, Jr.), *Isherwood* (Commander Louis Edward Schmidt, Jr.), *Macdonough*
(Lieutenant-Commander Burton Herbert Shupper), *Picking* (Commander Benedict
Joseph Semmes, Jr.), *Sproston* (Commander Michael Joseph Luosey), *Twiggs* (Com-
mander George Philip, Jr.) and the *Wickes* (Lieutenant-Commander James Barton
Cresap).
In addition, there were a number of formations assigned to Task Group 79.2 which
together numbered six landing ships, thirty landing craft, and ten other units.

Task Group 79.11 (Captain Jesse Grant Coward, Jr., in the destroyer Remey*)*
This formation was tasked to provide escort for landing ships and craft from both Task
Group 79.3 and Task Group 79.4 and consisted of the destroyers *McDermut* (Com-
mander Carter Brooke Jennings), *McGowan* (Commander William Ruffin Cox),
McNair (Commander Montgomery Lientz McCullough), *Melvin* (Commander Barry
Kennedy Atkins), *Mertz* (Commander William S. Eastabrook, Jr.), *Monssen* (Com-
mander Charles Kniese Bergin) and the *Remey* (Commander Reid Puryear Fiala).

Other 7th Fleet Formations

Task Group 70.1 (Commander Selman Stewart Bowling in the torpedo boat tender Oyster Bay)
The MTB tenders *Oyster Bay* (Lieutenant-Commander Walter W. Holroyd), *Wachapreague* (Lieutenant-Commander Harold A. Stewart) and the *Willoughby* (Lieutenant-Commander Archie J. Church), plus a total of thirty-nine motor torpedo boats, which were organized in thirteen three-boat sections under the tactical command of Lieutenant-Commander Robert Leeson, who was in PT-134 in Section 6.
On the night of 24–25 October 1944 the PT boats on station were held between 09°10'North and 10°10'North at the southern entrance to the Surigao Strait. Between Agio Point on Bohol and Sipuca Point on Mindanao were two formations, Section 1 (Lieutenant Weston C. Pullen) with the PT-130, PT-131 and the PT-152, and Section 2 (Lieutenant John A. Cady) with the PT-126, PT-127 and the PT-129. In 09°52'North 125°04'East, off Lamasawa, was Section 3 (Lieutenant David H. Owen) with the PT-146, PT-151 and the PT-190. Off Binis Point, Panaon Island, were two formations, Section 5 (Lieutenant Roman George Mislicky) with the PT-150, PT-194 and the PT-196, and Section 6 (Lieutenant-Commander Robert Leeson) with the PT-132, PT-134 and the PT-137; on the opposite side of the Strait, off Bilas Point which is the northern tip of Mindanao, were three formations, the first, Section 4 (Lieutenant-Commander Theo R. Stansbury) with the PT-191, PT-192 and the PT-195, the second, Section 7 (Lieutenant Joseph H. Moran II) with the PT-324, PT-494 and the PT-497, and the third, Section 8 (Lieutenant-Commander Francis D. Tappan) with the PT-523, PT-524 and the PT-526. Gathered around Tungo Point on western Dinagat were three formations, Section 9 (Lieutenant John H. McElfresh) with the PT-490, PT-491 and the PT-493, Section 10 (Lieutenant Arthur M. Preston) with the PT-489, PT-492 and the PT-495, and Section 11 (Lieutenant Carl Thomas Gleason) with the PT-321, PT-326 and the PT-327, while on the opposite side of the Strait, off Amagusan Point, southeast Leyte, were two formations, Section 12 (Lieutenant George W. M. Hogan, Jr.) with the PT-320, PT-330 and the PT-331 and Section 13 (Lieutenant Howard G. Young) with the PT-323, PT-328 and the PT-329.

Task Group 73.7
The seaplane tenders *Half Moon* (Commander Jack Irving Bandy) and *San Carlos* (Lieutenant-Commander DeLong Mills) with one squadron of twelve PBY-5 Catalina amphibians (Lieutenant-Commander Vadym Victorovich Utgoff).

OTHER FORMATIONS

Task Force 17 (Vice Admiral Charles Andrew Lockwood, Jr., ashore at Pearl Harbor)
The submarines *Atule* (Commander Bernard Ambrose Clarey), *Jallao* (Commander Joseph Bryan Icenhower) and the *Pintado* (Commander John Howard Maurer) all of which sailed from Pearl Harbor on 9 October; the *Haddock* (Commander John Paul Roach), *Halibut* (Commander Ignatius Joseph Galantin) and the *Tuna* (Commander Edward Frank Steffanides, Jr.), the Halibut sailed from Pearl Harbor on 10 October and the other two on 8 October; the *Drum* (Lieutenant-Commander Maurice Herbert Rindskopf), *Icefish* (Commander Richard Ward Peterson) and the *Sawfish* (Commander Alan Boyd Banister) all of which sailed from Pearl Harbor on 9 September; the *Salmon* (Commander Harley Kent Nauman), *Silversides* (Commander John Starr Coye, Jr.) and the *Trigger* (Commander Frederick Joseph Harlfinger, II) all of which sailed from Pearl

Harbor on 24 September; the *Besugo* (Commander Thomas Lincoln Wogan), *Gabilan* (Commander Karl Raymond Wheland) and the *Ronquil* (Commander Henry Stone Monroe), the second of which sailed from Pearl Harbor on 26 September and the last four days later; and the *Barbel* (Commander Robert Allen Keating, Jr.), *Snook* (Commander George Henry Browne) which sailed from Saipan on 25 September, *Sterlet* (Commander Orme Campbell Robbins) which sailed from Midway on 18 September, and the *Tang* (Commander Richard Hetherington O'Kane) which sailed from Pearl Harbor on 24 September.

The groups in this formation operated in general support of those formations committed to the landings in the Philippines.

There is a single reference to the group that included the *Drum, Icefish* and the *Sawfish* as Task Group 17.15 but without any reference to the other groups this designation has not been used.

Task Group 30.2 (Rear Admiral Allan Edward Smith in the heavy cruiser Chester)

Cruiser Division 5 (Rear Admiral Smith in the *Chester*): The heavy cruisers *Chester* (Captain Henry Hartley), *Pensacola* (Captain Allen Prather Mullinnix) and the *Salt Lake City* (Captain Leroy White Busbey, Jr.).

Destroyer Squadron 4 (Captain Harold Page Smith in the *Dunlap*): The destroyers *Cummings* (Lieutenant-Commander William John Collum, Jr.), *Case* (Lieutenant-Commander Robert Soule Willey), *Cassin* (Commander Vincent James Meola), *Downes* (Commander Robert Schley Fahle), *Dunlap* (Lieutenant-Commander Cecil Rice Welte) and the *Fanning* (Commander James Calvin Bentley).

This formation conducted the bombardment of Marcus Island on 9 October and joined Task Group 38.1 on 16 October.

Task Group 30.3 (Rear Admiral Laurence Toombs DuBose in the light cruiser Santa Fe) *with effect from 16 October 1944*

Task Unit 30.3.1 (Rear Admiral DuBose in the *Santa Fe*):

The damaged heavy cruiser *Canberra* and light cruiser *Houston* (both from Task Group 38.1) in the company of the heavy cruiser *Boston*, the light cruisers *Birmingham* and *Santa Fe*, and the destroyers *Boyd, Caperton, Cogswell, Cowell, Grayson, Ingersoll, Stephen Potter* and the *The Sullivans* drawn from Task Groups 38.1, 38.2, and 38.3, and, from Task Group 30.8, the tugs *Munsee* and *Pawnee*.

Task Unit 30.3.2 (Rear Admiral Charles Turner Joy in the *Wichita*):

The light carriers *Cabot* and *Cowpens*, the heavy cruiser *Wichita*, the light cruiser *Mobile*, and the destroyers *Bell, Burns, Charrette, Knapp* and the *Miller* drawn from Task Groups 38.1 and 38.2.

On 18 October the formation turned south, away from Ulithi, in order to avoid a typhoon, and once clear on 20 October, the *Cabot, Miller, Stephen Potter* and *The Sullivans* left in order to rejoin Task Force 38. In their place came Task Group 30.7, which is described in action reports as an anti-submarine group the units of which are not identified, plus two more tugs which were assigned one each to the *Canberra* and *Houston* and which supplemented the *Munsee* and *Pawnee*; these two units, likewise, are not identified. Once Task Group 30.3 joined company, the *Cowpens, Wichita* and the *Grayson* left in order to rejoin their parent formation. The destroyer *Nicholson* is cited as having left with these ships but she is not cited in the action report as having been a member of this group in the first place; her entry in *DANFS*, V, p. 88, is practically worthless and makes no reference to her being part of any formation.

On 24 October the *Boston, Bell, Boyd, Burns, Cowell* and the *Charrette* left in order to rejoin Task Group 38.1, its being noted that they were relieved by the *Farenholt, Grayson, McCalla* and the *Woodworth*. There are three problems herein. First, the action report submitted by Nimitz for October 1944 covering these events make no reference to the *Birmingham* and *Santa Fe* and the destroyers *Boyd, Caperton, Cogswell, Ingersoll* and the *Knapp*, but it seems that the *Santa Fe* was detached on 17 October (*DANFS*, VI, p. 322). The records for the *Caperton, Cogswell* and the *Knapp* (respectively *DANFS*, II, pp. 31 and 139 and IV, p. 667) have references to their returning to Task Group 38.1. but the records for the *Birmingham* and *Ingersoll* make no reference to ever having been away, but, of course, if the *Birmingham* did leave she was back in time—on 23 October—for the loss of the *Princeton* the next day.

Second, Nimitz's action report cites the *Farenholt, Grayson, McCalla* and the *Woodworth* as being with Task Group 38.1 on 24 October, but none of the reports and accounts that give the American order of battle prior to 24 October cite the *Farenholt* as being present with Task Group 38.1. Her entry in *DANFS*, II, p. 392, confirms that she was with Task Group 38.1 but that her "squadron was detached to *rendez-vous*" with Task Group 30.3 and the implication is clearly that this occurred on 24 October. The *DANFS* entries of the other three ships, the *Grayson, McCalla* and the *Woodworth*, make no reference to being in company with the others, the *Farenholt* included, and indeed only the entry of the *Woodworth* (*DANFS*, VIII, pp. 459–460) makes any reference to her joining Task Group 30.3.

Third, this record would suggest that the *Grayson* returned to Task Force 38 on 20 October only to be sent back to Task Group 30.3 three days later. But the *Grayson*'s record (*DANFS*, I, p. 143) makes no reference to such procrastination, noting only that she had on board 194 men from the *Houston*, and that from Ulithi she then proceeded to Saipan.

At best, it would seem that the record of this particular episode is incomplete and confusing.

Task Group 30.3 reached Ulithi on the morning of 27 October.

Task Group 71.1 (Rear Admiral Ralph W. Christie at Fremantle)

The submarines *Angler* (Commander Franklin Grant Hess), *Bluegill* (Commander Eric Lloyd Barr, Jr.), *Bream* (Commander Wreford Goss Chapple), *Dace* (Commander Bladen Dulany Claggett), *Darter* (Commander David Hayward McClintock), *Guitarro* (Commander Enrique D'Hamel Haskins) and the *Raton* (Commander Maurice William Shea).

The *Angler* sailed, presumably from Fremantle, on 18 September; the *Bream* and *Guitarro* sailed from Fremantle on 8 October. The *Dace* sailed from Brisbane on 1 September and refueled at Darwin on 10 September; she and the *Darter* sailed from Mios Woendi on 1 October. The *Raton* sailed, presumably from Fremantle, on 6 October.

The units in this task group operated in general support of those formations committed to the landings in the Philippines.

E. &. O. E.

TASK FORCE 38: FORMATIONS AND UNITS BETWEEN 23 OCTOBER AND 30 NOVEMBER 1944

*(Ships listed by type and alphabetically
and not by division or squadron)*

TASK FORCE 38 ON 23 OCTOBER 1944

Task Group 38.1
The fleet carriers *Hancock*, *Hornet* and the *Wasp*, the light carriers *Cowpens* and *Monterey*, the heavy cruisers *Chester*, *Pensacola* and the *Salt Lake City*, and the destroyers *Bell*, *Boyd*, *Brown*, *Burns*, *Caperton*, *Case*, *Cassin*, *Charrette*, *Cogswell*, *Conner*, *Cowell*, *Cummings*, *Downes*, *Dunlap*, *Fanning*, *Grayson*, *Ingersoll*, *Izard*, *Knapp*, *McCalla* and the *Woodworth*.

Task Group 38.2
The fleet carrier *Intrepid*, the light carriers *Cabot* and *Independence*, the battleships *Iowa* and *New Jersey*, the light cruisers *Biloxi*, *Miami* and the *Vincennes*, and the destroyers *Benham*, *Colahan*, *Cushing*, *Halsey Powell*, *Hickox*, *Hunt*, *Lewis Hancock*, *Marshall*, *Miller*, *Owen*, *Stephen Potter*, *Stockham*, *The Sullivans*, *Tingey*, *Twining*, *Uhlmann*, *Wedderburn* and the *Yarnall*.

Task Group 38.3
The fleet carriers *Essex* and *Lexington*, the light carriers *Langley* and *Princeton*, the battleships *Massachusetts* and *South Dakota*, the light cruisers *Birmingham*, *Mobile*, *Reno* and the *Santa Fe*, and the destroyers *Callaghan*, *Cassin Young*, *Clarence E. Bronson*, *Cotten*, *Dortch*, *Gatling*, *Healy*, *Porterfield* and the *Preston*.

Task Group 38.4
The fleet carriers *Enterprise* and *Franklin*, the light carriers *Belleau Wood* and *San Jacinto*, the battleships *Alabama* and *Washington*, the heavy cruisers *New Orleans* and *Wichita*, the destroyers *Bagley*, *Gridley*, *Helm*, *Irwin*, *Laws*, *Longshaw*, *Maury*, *McCall*, *Morrison*, *Mugford*, *Nicholson*, *Patterson*, *Prichett*, *Ralph Talbot*, *Swanson* and the *Wilkes*.

TASK FORCE 38 ON 24 OCTOBER 1944 (SOURCE: ADM 199.1493, P. 230)

Task Group 38.1
The fleet carriers *Hancock, Hornet* and the *Wasp,* the light carriers *Cowpens* and *Monterey,*
   the heavy cruisers *Boston, Chester, Pensacola* and the *Salt Lake City,* the light cruis-
   ers *Oakland* and *San Diego,* and the destroyers *Brown, Case, Cassin, Conner, Cowell,*
   Cummings, Downes, Dunlap, Fanning, Farenholt, Grayson, Izard, McCalla and the
   Woodworth.

Task Group 38.2
The fleet carrier *Intrepid,* the light carriers *Cabot* and *Independence,* the battleships
   Iowa and *New Jersey,* the light cruisers *Biloxi, Miami* and the *Vincennes,* and the
   destroyers *Colahan, Cushing, Halsey Powell, Hickox, Hunt, Lewis Hancock, Marshall,*
   Miller, Owen, Stockham, The Sullivans, Tingey, Twining, Uhlmann, Wedderburn and
   the *Yarnall.*

Task Group 38.3
The fleet carriers *Essex* and *Lexington,* the light carriers *Langley* and *Princeton,* the battle-
   ships *Massachusetts* and *South Dakota,* the light cruisers *Birmingham, Mobile, Reno*
   and the *Santa Fe,* and the destroyers *Callaghan, Cassin Young, Clarence E. Bronson,*
   Cotten, Dortch, Gatling, Healy, Irwin, Laws, Longshaw, Morrison, Porterfield and the
   Preston. The *Princeton* was sunk and the *Birmingham* and the *Gatling, Irwin* and the
   Morrison were obliged to return to Ulithi this day.

Task Group 38.4
The fleet carriers *Enterprise* and *Franklin,* the light carriers *Belleau Wood* and *San Jacinto,*
   the battleships *Alabama* and *Washington,* the heavy cruisers *New Orleans* and *Wichita,*
   and the destroyers *Bagley, Caperton, Cogswell, Gridley, Helm, Ingersoll, Knapp, Maury,*
   McCall, Mugford, Nicholson, Patterson, Ralph Talbot, Swanson and the *Wilkes.*

TASK FORCE 34

This formation was to be organized thus:

Task Group 34.1
The battleships *Alabama, Iowa, Massachusetts, New Jersey, South Dakota* and the
   Washington.

Task Group 34.2, assigned to starboard
The light cruisers *Biloxi, Miami* and the *Vincennes,* and, from Destroyer Squadron 50,
   the *Miller, Owen, The Sullivans* and the *Tingey* and *Hickox, Hunt, Lewis Hancock* and
   the *Marshall.*

Task Group 34.3, assigned forward
The heavy cruisers *New Orleans* and *Wichita,* and, from Destroyer Squadron 52, the
   Cogswell, Caperton, Ingersoll and the *Knapp.*

Task Group 34.4, assigned to port
The light cruisers *Mobile* and *Santa Fe,* and, from Destroyer Squadron 52, the destroyers
   Clarence E. Bronson, Cotten and the *Dortch,* and the *Bagley, Healy* and the *Patterson.*
Note: the destroyers are listed by formation because of the inconsistencies in the record
for this particular order of battle. See Chapter 5, n. 158.

Task Group 34.5

When formed on 25 October this formation consisted of the battleships *Iowa* and *New Jersey,* the light cruisers *Biloxi, Miami* and the *Vincennes,* and the destroyers *Hickox, Hunt, Lewis Hancock, Marshall, Miller, Owen, The Sullivans* and the *Tingey.*
Source: ADM 199.1494 p. 316.

TASK FORCE 38: FORMATIONS AND UNITS ON AND AFTER 27 OCTOBER 1944

Ships listed by dates and then alphabetically and not by division or squadron.
Source: ADM 199.1493. Operations in the Pacific Ocean Areas during the month of November: 1944. Part IV. Central Pacific. A. Operations of Third Fleet, pp. 286–288.

Task Group 38.1 on 27 October 1944
The fleet carriers *Hancock, Hornet* and the *Wasp,* the light carriers *Cowpens and Monterey,* the heavy cruisers *Boston, Chester, Pensacola* and the *Salt Lake City,* the light cruisers *Oakland* and *San Diego,* and the destroyers *Bell, Boyd, Brown, Burns, Case, Cassin, Charrette, Conner, Cowell, Cummings, Downes, Dunlap, Fanning* and the *Izard.*
27 October: Detached: The fleet carrier *Hancock.*
28 October: Detached: The destroyer *Cowell.*
29 October: Detached: The heavy cruisers *Chester, Pensacola* and the *Salt Lake City,* and the destroyers *Case, Cassin, Cummings, Downes, Dunlap* and the *Fanning.*
30 October: Joined: The destroyers *Blue, De Haven, Maddox, Mansfield* and the *Taussig.*
2 November: Detached: The light cruisers *Oakland* and *San Diego.*
Joined: The battleship *South Dakota,* the heavy cruisers *Louisville* and *Portland,* and the destroyers *Brush, Lyman K. Swenson, Marshall* and the *Miller.*
4 November: Detached: The battleship *South Dakota* and the destroyers *Marshall* and *Miller.*
Joined: The battleships *Alabama* and *Massachusetts.*
5 November: Joined: The destroyer *Spence.*
7 November: Detached: The fleet carrier *Wasp,* the light carrier *Monterey,* the heavy cruiser *Louisville,* the light cruiser *Oakland,* and the destroyers *Boyd* and *Brown.*
Joined: The fleet carrier *Yorktown* and the destroyers *Collett* and *Samuel N. Moore.*
13 November: Joined: The fleet carrier *Wasp* and the destroyers *Boyd* and *Brown.*
16 November: Detached: The fleet carrier *Hornet* and the destroyers *Bell* and *Burns.*
18 November: Detached: The destroyer *Charrette.*
Joined: The light cruiser *Oakland.*
19 November: Detached: The battleship *Alabama.*
20 November: Detached: The light cruiser *Oakland* and the destroyers *Blue, Boyd, Brown* and the *Cowell.*
Joined: The battleship *Alabama,* the light cruiser *Pasadena,* and the destroyers *Dyson, McCall, Thorn* and the *Welles.*
21 November: Detached: The heavy cruisers *Boston* and *Portland* and the destroyers *Conner, Izard* and the *McCall.*
23 November: Joined: The destroyers *Stockham, Wedderburn* and the *Yarnall.*
24 November: Detached: The light cruiser *Pasadena* and the destroyers *Stockham, Wedderburn* and the *Yarnall.*
Joined: The heavy cruisers *Baltimore* and *San Francisco,* the light cruiser *San Juan,* and the destroyer *Blue.*
29 November: Detached: The destroyer *Thorn.*
Joined: The destroyers *Buchanan, Hobby* and the *Thatcher.*

Task Group 38.1 as constituted on 30 November

The fleet carriers *Wasp* and *Yorktown*, the light carrier *Cowpens*, the battleships *Alabama* and *Massachusetts*, the heavy cruisers *Baltimore* and *San Francisco*, the light cruiser *San Juan*, and the destroyers *Blue, Brush, Buchanan, Collett, De Haven, Dyson, Hobby, Lyman K. Swenson, Maddox, Mansfield, Samuel N. Moore, Spence, Taussig, Thatcher* and the *Welles.*

Note: The *San Diego* is not listed as having left Task Group 38.1 but separately she is recorded as having joined Task Group 38.4 on 2 November and must have left Task Group 38.1 the same day. In the fleet report, the *Wasp, Boyd* and the *Brown* are recorded as having rejoined on 18 November, but this was erroneous. The *Wasp* rejoined the formation on 13 November (see Morison, p. 349) and one presumes the *Boyd* and *Brown* were in company. The *Cowell* is listed as a member of the formation on 27 October but also having joined company on 7 November and being detached on 20 November. Her *DANFS* entry, II, p. 199, states that she was with the *Canberra* and *Houston* group before returning to her parent formation, and that she returned to Ulithi 28 October and was then detached and assigned local duties.

Task Group 38.2 on 27 October

The fleet carrier *Intrepid*, the light carriers *Cabot* and *Independence*, the battleships *Alabama, Massachusetts, South Dakota* and the *Washington*, and the destroyers *Colahan, Cushing, Halsey Powell, Stockham, Twining, Uhlmann, Wedderburn* and the *Yarnall.*

27 October: Joined: The fleet carrier *Hancock*, the battleships *Iowa* and *New Jersey*, the light cruisers *Biloxi, Miami* and the *Vincennes*, and the destroyers *Hickox, Hunt, Lewis Hancock, Marshall, Miller, Owen, The Sullivans* and the *Tingey.*

28 October: Detached: The battleships *Alabama, Massachusetts, South Dakota* and the *Washington.*

31 October: Detached: The destroyers *Marshall* and *Miller.*

4 November: Joined: The destroyers *Marshall* and *Miller.*

5 November: Detached: The destroyer *Wedderburn.*

7 November: Detached: The light cruiser *Biloxi* and the destroyers *Colahan, Hickox* and the *Lewis Hancock.*

Joined: The fleet carrier *Wasp*, the heavy cruiser *Louisville*, and the destroyers *Boyd* and *Brown.*

8 November: Detached: The fleet carrier *Wasp* and the destroyers *Boyd* and *Brown.*

9 November: Joined: The light cruiser *Pasadena.*

10 November: Joined: The destroyers *Caperton, Cogswell, Colahan, Hickox, Lewis Hancock* and the *Knapp.*

11 November: Joined: The destroyer *Ralph Talbot.*

12 November: Joined: The destroyer *Halford.*

13 November: Joined: The destroyer *Mugford.*

14 November: Detached: The heavy cruiser *Louisville* and the destroyers *Colahan, Marshall* and the *Uhlmann.*

15 November: Detached: The destroyers *Halford* and *Knapp* and later the *Caperton* and *Cogswell.*

16 November: Detached: The light cruiser *Pasadena* and, separately, the destroyers *Mugford* and *Ralph Talbot.*

Joined: The destroyers *Benham* and *Stephen Potter.*

17 November: Joined: The destroyers *Marshall, Uhlmann* and the *Wedderburn.*

18 November: Detached: The destroyer *Twining.*

20 November: Detached: The destroyers *Benham, Cushing, Halsey Powell* and the *Uhlmann.*

Joined: The destroyers *Boyd, Brown, Cooper* and the *Cowell.*
21 November: Detached: The destroyer *Cooper.*
Joined: The destroyer *Colahan* (also given as 23 November).
23 November: Detached: The destroyers *Stockham, Wedderburn* and the *Yarnall.*
Joined: The destroyers *Capps, David W. Taylor* and the *John D. Henley.*
24 November: Detached: The destroyer *Hunt.*
27 November: Detached: The destroyer *Colahan.*
28 November: Joined: The destroyer *Evans.*
29 November: Joined: The destroyer *Hunt.*
30 November: Detached: The fleet carrier *Intrepid.*
Joined: The fleet carrier *Lexington.*

Task Group 38.2 as constituted on 30 November
The fleet carriers *Hancock* and *Lexington*, the light carriers *Cabot* and *Independence*,
the battleships *Iowa* and New *Jersey*, the light cruisers *Miami* and *Vincennes*, and the
destroyers *Boyd, Brown, Capps, Cowell, David W. Taylor, Evans, Hickox, Hunt, John
D. Henley, Lewis Hancock, Marshall, Miller, Owen, Stephen Potter, The Sullivans* and
the *Tingey.*

Task Group 38.3 on 27 October
The fleet carriers *Essex* and *Lexington*, the light carrier *Langley*, the light cruisers *Mobile,
Reno* and the *Santa Fe*, and the destroyers *Callaghan, Caperton, Cassin Young, Clar-
ence E. Bronson, Cogswell, Cotten, Dortch, Healy, Ingersoll, Knapp, Laws, Longshaw,
Porterfield* and the *Preston.*
28 October: Joined: The battleships *Alabama, Massachusetts* and the *Washington.*
30 October: Joined: The fleet carrier *Ticonderoga* and the destroyers *Gatling* and
Prichett.
3 November: Detached: The light cruiser *Reno* and the destroyers *Caperton* and *Knapp.*
4 November: Detached: The battleships *Alabama* and *Massachusetts* and the destroyer
Cogswell.
Joined: The battleship *South Dakota.*
7 November: Detached: The fleet carrier *Lexington.*
Joined: The battleship *North Carolina*, the light cruiser *Biloxi*, and the destroyers *Benham*
and *Stephen Potter.*
15 November: Detached: The destroyers *Benham* and *Stephen Potter.*
16 November: Joined: The destroyers *Halford* and *Knapp.*
17 November: Detached: The destroyer *Halford.*
18 November: Joined: The destroyers *Caperton* and *Cogswell.*
21 November: Joined: The destroyers *Capps, David W. Taylor* and the *John D. Henley.*
23 November: Detached: The destroyers *Capps, David W. Taylor* and the *John D.
Henley.*

Task Group 38.3 as constituted on 30 November
The fleet carriers *Essex* and *Ticonderoga*, the light carrier *Langley*, the battleships *North
Carolina, South Dakota* and the *Washington*, the light cruisers *Biloxi, Mobile* and the
Santa Fe, and the destroyers *Callaghan, Caperton, Cassin Young, Clarence E. Bronson,
Cogswell, Cotten, Dortch, Gatling, Healy, Ingersoll, Knapp, Laws, Longshaw, Porterfield,
Preston* and the *Prichett.*

APPENDIXES

Task Group 38.4 on 27 October 1944
The fleet carriers *Enterprise* and *Franklin*, the light carriers *Belleau Wood* and *S*
  the heavy cruisers *New Orleans* and *Wichita*, and the destroyers *Bagley*, *Brus*
  Helm, *Lyman K. Swenson*, *Maury*, *McCall*, *Mugford*, *Patterson* and the *Ralp*
28 October: Joined: The battleship *South Dakota*.
31 October: Joined: The destroyers *Marshall* and *Miller*.
2 November: Detached: The battleship *South Dakota* and the destroyers *Marsh*
  Miller.
Joined: The heavy cruiser *Minneapolis*, the light cruiser *San Diego*, and the destr*
  Thorn and *Welles*.
3 November: Joined: The fleet carrier *Yorktown* and the destroyers *Collett*, *Ingrah*
  O'Brien and the *Samuel N. Moore*.
4 November: Joined: The destroyers *Cowell* and *Dyson*.
5 November: Joined: The battleship *North Carolina* and the destroyers *Allen M. Summe*
  Barton, *Cooper*, *Laffey*, *Moale* and the *Walke*.
6 November: Joined: The fleet carrier *Bunker Hill* and the destroyers *Benham* and *Stephen*
  Potter.
7 November: Detached: The fleet carrier *Yorktown*, the battleship *North Carolina*, and the
  destroyers *Benham*, *Collett*, *Cowell*, *Samuel N. Moore* and the *Stephen Potter*.
15 November: Joined: The light carrier *Monterey* and the light cruiser *Oakland*.
16 November: Detached: The fleet carrier *Bunker Hill* and the heavy cruiser
  Minneapolis.
Joined: The fleet carrier *Hornet* and the light cruiser *Pasadena*.
18 November: Detached: The light cruiser *Oakland* and the destroyer *Ingraham*.
19 November: Joined: The battleship *Alabama*.
20 November: Detached: The battleship *Alabama*, the light cruiser *Pasadena*, and the
  destroyers *Cooper*, *Dyson*, *Thorn* and the *Welles*.
Joined: The light cruiser *Oakland* and the destroyers *Blue*, *Cushing*, *Halsey Powell* and
  the *Uhlmann*.
22 November: Joined: The fleet carrier *Lexington*.
24 November: Detached: The destroyer *Blue*.
Joined: The light cruiser *Pasadena* and the destroyers *Stockham*, *Wedderburn* and the
  Yarnall.
25 November: Joined: The destroyers *Franks*, *Haggard*, *Hailey*, *Hazelwood*, *McCord* and
  the *Trathen*.
26 November: Joined: The heavy cruiser *Astoria*.
27 November: Detached: The destroyers *Allen M. Summer*, *Barton*, *Laffey*, *Moale*, *O'Brien*
  and the *Walke*.
Joined: The destroyer *Colahan*.
29 November: Detached: The destroyers *Twining* and *Uhlmann*.
30 November: Detached: The fleet carrier *Lexington*.

Task Group 38.4 as constituted on 30 November
The fleet carrier *Hornet*, the light carrier *Monterey*, the heavy cruisers *Astoria* and *New
  Orleans*, the light cruisers *Oakland*, *Pasadena* and the *San Diego*, and the destroy-
  ers *Benham*, *Colahan*, *Cushing*, *Franks*, *Haggard*, *Hailey*, *Halsey Powell*, *Hazelwood*,
  McCord, *Stockham*, *Trathen*, *Wedderburn* and the *Yarnall*.

E. & O. E.

HALSEY'S RUN TO THE NORTH: THE LAST WORD . . . OR TWO

Halsey's decision to lay bare the exit of the San Bernardino Strait and to go north after Ozawa's carrier force with his three task groups is one that will always attract controversy because, simply, no comment about this decision and its consequences could ever be definitive and final. But perhaps two sets of comments might be in order in these final pages of this book, not least because what is to be put here does not lend itself to inclusion in the text.

In the north, events unfolded according to script: Ozawa's formation played out its decoy role and Mitscher's carriers, in association with the cruisers and destroyers that Halsey detached as he went south, accounted for its four carriers and two of its destroyers. With reference to Halsey's initial decision to go north with his full strength and not to leave a force opposite the San Bernardino Strait, Nimitz, in his comments on the conduct of the battle in his official report,[1] stated (para. 18) that there were three reasons for keeping the battle groups concentrated: to provide a full measure of anti-aircraft support for the carriers, to deal with any crippled enemy units that might be encountered in the mopping-up phase, and to provide against contact by the *Hyuga* and *Ise*. The last of these seems something akin to special pleading, and represents an extraordinary argument. The American carriers were going north precisely to ensure the destruction of Japanese units and there was never any question of such units as the *Hyuga* and *Ise* posing any danger on account of an ability to close with American forces in the face of carrier aircraft from three task groups. It is hard to believe that Nimitz really thought that all six battleships were needed in order to provide against the *Hyuga* and *Ise*.

Nimitz continued:

> 20. . . . sound tactics would have dictated using an overwhelming force instead of a moderately superior force, if the former were available and not needed elsewhere. And here again we must avoid assuming that the need of gunnery forces for a battle with the Japanese Center Force could have been as definitely known on the evening of the 24th as it was proved to be by the events of the morning of the 25th.

Such comments lend themselves to a number of obvious observations. There is no doubting that Nimitz was correct in expressing the view that "sound tactics would have dictated using an overwhelming force instead of a moderately superior force," but the caveat, "if the former were available and not needed elsewhere," is all-important, and the fact was that the battle line was needed elsewhere. The latter might be disputed, but the next part of Nimitz's argument beggars belief. The fact that Kurita's force was coming east, making for the San Bernardino Strait, was known on the evening of 24 October. Japanese intention may not have been "as definitely known" as it was on the following morning, but it could never be, and if Kurita's coming east on the evening of 24 October was not sufficient reason for the battle forces to be held off the Strait, as minimum precaution, then one is at a loss to understand what might have been deemed reason enough. It bears recall that Halsey's own argument—that any success a Japanese force might register would be of small account and could be easily reversed—had as its base the fact that Japanese intention was both clear and recognized, and on the evening of 24 October. There would seem to be no logical basis for Nimitz's argument.

Nimitz then proceeded:

> 21. . . . as things turned out, a smaller force, the Light Surface Striking Force of two heavy and two light cruisers plus destroyers under Rear Admiral DuBose, took care of all cripples overtaken.
> 22. Had the whole of Task Force 34 remained available for the pursuit, instead of turning back at about 1108, it might with safety have pushed ahead faster than did the four cruisers and the destroyers under Rear Admiral DuBose and might thus have rounded up an additional cripple or so, or might even have caught the *Ise* and *Hyuga* which were reported returning at high speed. It is a good subject for argument, however, whether or not the whole of Task Force 34 could have accomplished much more in this pursuit and mop-up than could two of our fast battleships plus the cruisers and destroyers that were actually left north for the purpose.
> 23. The strongest of all arguments in favor of taking the whole of Task Force 38's gunnery strength north, instead of leaving some of it behind to watch for the Japanese Center Force, is that the latter course would have also necessitated leaving some carriers behind to furnish air cover. This would have been a positive and certain drawback, and might have been expected to lessen the damage done to the northern enemy in proportion to the reduction of Task Force 38's carrier strength. How many carriers would have been adequate, and what should have been the relative importance of CAP for Task Force 34 against striking power for Task Force 38 in the existing situation is again a matter for discussion.
> 24. The wisdom of dividing one's forces is always debatable. . . .

One would suggest that these comments invite somewhat jaundiced review. It is hard to see what more could have been done in terms of hunting down Japanese warships by a full battle force than was registered by the force that Halsey assigned to support the carrier formations when he turned back to the south. It is very doubtful that around mid-day and in the early afternoon of 25 October a fully concentrated battle force could have overhauled Ozawa's force and then inflicted upon it losses that would have been greater than were registered during the late afternoon and early evening by the units detached from Task Group 34.5 and reassigned to the carrier formations. In addition, it is difficult to believe that in the late evening a fully concentrated force, or even a force that included the four battleships that were not included in Task Group 34.5, might have been able to close with what remained of Ozawa's force to the north of where the *Hatsutsuki* had been sunk, and such a conclusion would acknowledge Ozawa's turning back to the south.[2] If there had been such a contact then the Japanese might have sacrificed another destroyer or two in order to ensure the escape of the others, but it seems highly unlikely that further and significant losses might have been inflicted on Ozawa's wrecked formation. Perhaps the only safe conclusion that may be drawn from this episode is that what was registered on this day off Cape Engaño was probably the greatest return that could have been exacted by the Americans, there or thereabouts.

Paradoxically, the only real argument in favor of Halsey's keeping his force concentrated was not what might have happened to the north but that any battle force left to guard the Strait would need its carrier cover. As Nimitz noted, the real argument in favor of Halsey's action was not the desirability of keeping the battle force concentrated but in not dividing the carrier force. Nimitz's comments on this particular matter, however, would seem geared to ensure Halsey's exoneration rather than any objective assessment of the situation because it is difficult to see, given the minimal scale of attack to which the carrier formations were exposed on 24 October, that carriers left with a battle force off the San Bernardino Strait really would have represented any real diminution of the overall offensive capability of the American carrier force heading north. The light carriers in Task Force 38 mustered between seven and nine Avengers and Helldivers in air groups that numbered between twenty-six and thirty-four aircraft, and the absence of perhaps two light carriers from a carrier force going north would not have represented any real loss in terms of offensive capability. The argument that Nimitz embraced here would seem to be very dubious, and the unfolding of events would suggest that the division of the carrier force would not have presented any real problem. One would hazard the view that it was Lee who had been correct both in diagnosis and proposed treatment.

There is, however, one other point that arises from Nimitz's twin assertions that leaving a battle force behind "would have . . . necessitated leaving some carriers behind to furnish air cover" and "two of our fast battleships plus the cruisers and destroyers that were actually left north." When Halsey turned back to the south he took all six battleships, and when Task Group 34.5 was formed it had just the *Iowa* and *New Jersey*. The other four battleships, the *Alabama*, *Massachusetts*, *South Dakota* and the *Washington*, were sent to join Task Group 38.2, which was ordered to provide air cover for Task Group 34.5 as it went south. In other words, two carrier groups were left in the north with their screens stripped in order to provide for Task Force 34 as it went south.[3] Thus the very situation that he indicated was unacceptable on 24 October—the division of carrier strength—was not even mentioned by Nimitz in his report, and most certainly was not a subject that commanded critical comment, when this eventuality came to pass on the following day. Moreover, lest the point be overlooked, the battleships were not in company with the cruisers and destroyers during the phase of operations that resulted in the sinking of the *Chiyoda* and *Hatsutsuki*. In other words the battleships were not on hand to support the carriers and were not available for the mopping-up phase. It is very easy to miss the point, but while Nimitz stated that the presence of six battleships might have had a greater effect than the presence of two, there never were two battleships in the north. Why Nimitz should have used such an argument, and particularly the way it was expressed, seems somewhat odd.

It is hard to resist the conclusion that, in setting out these various arguments, Nimitz did not undertake a proper examination of the record, or failed to realize the true unfolding of events, or, quite deliberately, set out an account that was at best selectively misleading and at worst dishonest in its portrayal of events in such a way as to ensure Halsey against criticism and reproach. If the latter explanation is correct then two pleas of mitigation need be addressed. The first would be the shadow cast by the emerging air power controversy, which in a sense provided Halsey, as an "air admiral," with security; the U.S. Navy, as it faced the challenge presented by an Army Air Force intent on being an independent service, could not allow internal divisions to encroach on its position.[4] The second, and indeed the only charitable explanation of Nimitz's conduct, would be a combination of foresight and memory. It would suggest that Nimitz, perhaps anticipating the arguments that were to come after the war, sought to avoid the personalization of issues and thereby possibly avoid any repetition of the Schley-Sampson controversy that had followed in the wake of the Battle of Santiago (July 1898).[5] That battle had been fought when Nimitz was but thirteen years of age, and he had entered a navy determined never to allow itself to be caught again in such an undignified and unedifying (and wholly avoidable) episode.[6] Perhaps Nimitz was guided in this matter by a "circle-the-wagons" mentality.[7]

But if the comments of Nimitz present real problems of understanding and acceptance, these pale alongside the difficulties of comprehension that attend comments on these matters made by Halsey in a letter to King. This letter is to be found in ADM 199.1494 with the report, dated 23 December 1944, entitled "U.S.S. *Lexington*. Action Report of the engagement of enemy fleet units in the Sibuyan Sea on 24 October 1944 and east of Luzon on 25 October 1944." The letter, pp. 176–177, is stated to be from Commander Third Fleet to Commander-in-Chief U.S. Fleet via Commander-in-Chief U.S. Pacific Fleet (i.e., Halsey to King via Nimitz), the subject being defined as

> BATTLE OF THE PHILIPPINES, 24–25 October 1944, Task Group
> THIRTY-EIGHT POINT THREE—Action Report of.

The letter had the serial 00100 and File Number A16–3/(11), and carried the reference:

> 2nd Endorsement on
> CTG 38.3 Secret ltr.,
> Serial 0090 dated
> 2 December 1944.

The letter is dated 8 February 1945.[8] The author cannot recall ever having seen any reference to this letter and its contents—a comment genuinely believed but which no doubt will return to haunt him.

The first paragraph consists of the single word "Forwarded." and the second deals, over sixteen lines, with arrangements for reconnaissance missions. The fourth and final paragraph, on the letter's second page, notes that the question of the effectiveness of torpedoes and bombs was under consideration. The relevant part is the third paragraph, which reads thus:

> The recommendation contained in paragraph three of the basic report is not concurred in [sic]. When an opportunity presents itself to engage a major portion of the enemy fleet every possible weapon should be brought to bear against the enemy. An advanced heavy surface striking force which can attack the enemy during the course of air strikes offers the best opportunity for the complete annihilation of the enemy force. There is no case on record of an enemy force of capital ships having been annihilated by air strikes alone and a doctrine which requires our heavy ships to be held back until they may be employed against cripples will only insure the continued escape of many enemy units.[9]

One would suggest that these observations by Halsey invite four comments, which may close these proceedings. First, "the complete annihilation of the enemy force" is very American, very Mahanian, and, one would suggest, wholly unrealistic. It seems to hark back to the battle of the Philippine Sea and the criticism of Spruance, and it needs to be repeated that the American victory in June 1944 was much greater, more far-ranging, than was recognized at the time; it needs also be noted that this comment can be extended to the series of American victories in the Pacific that were recorded in the course of 1944. But "complete annihilation" in a naval battle is something else.

Second, Halsey might claim that "there is no case on record of an enemy force of capital ships having been annihilated by air strikes alone," but there was: the *Prince of Wales* and *Repulse* on 10 December 1941 in the South China Sea. Admittedly the agency of destruction had been shore-based naval aircraft, and perhaps Force Z really did not measure up to its name in terms of 1944 standards, but Halsey had no excuse for getting this argument wrong. But this would seem of small account when set alongside the claim that "an advanced heavy surface striking force which can attack the enemy during the course of air strikes offers the best opportunity for the complete annihilation of the enemy force." One would suggest, the third comment, that this observation borders on the grotesque,[10] and one is left to wonder what, according to Halsey, was the proper role of carrier aircraft—and what exactly Halsey had been doing for the previous three years. One would have thought that the whole point of carrier air power was to avoid the close-quarter, pell-mell battle, complete with misidentification and friendly fire, and that there could never be any question of committing battleships, cruisers, and destroyers forward in order to seek battle before the issue had been decided. By 1944 the naval battle was decided primarily by carrier air power and not by any other means. Halsey's statement, as the basis for a plan for battle, is astonishing, indeed bizarre, and wholly at variance from the experience of the war to date. There would seem to be no basis for his assertion other than an imagination that bordered on the fantastical. One is left to wonder if this was indeed the battle that he had intended to fight on 24 October, and also how what Nimitz wrote in his report in May squares with Halsey's pronouncement.[11] And, of course, there remains the small matter of how battleships, cruisers, and destroyers were supposed to close a gap of perhaps 200 miles in order to "attack the enemy during the course of air strikes" and how the carriers were supposed to fend for themselves in the meantime.

The fourth and last point would be to wonder why, after such a statement, King and Nimitz did not remove Halsey from command. But, of course, there are no prizes for guessing why that did not happen: Halsey's status as a national hero, Halsey's status as a service hero, the need for naval solidarity in facing the army and MacArthur, the longer-term problem posed by the Army Air Force. But there is a very odd postscript to these proceedings, and that is to be found in Nimitz's own post-war writings on Leyte Gulf. Writing and editing alongside E. B. Potter, Nimitz wrote:

> elements of both the Northern and Center Japanese forces were able to escape because Halsey carried the main American surface strength fruitlessly north and then south throughout most of the crucial hours of the battle, leaving inferior forces to deal with the enemy in two areas.[12]

Leaving aside the fact that one would argue that the escape of elements of both Japanese formations was not "because" of the misemployment of the American battle formations, this comment would seem to be very clear in pointing the finger of blame for sins of omission and commission in Halsey's direction. Nonetheless, it is hard to understand what was meant by the reference to "inferior forces . . . in two areas," and specifically "two areas," but Nimitz went on to state:

> The Battle for Leyte Gulf was the Trafalgar of World War II. Halsey and Kinkaid in 1944, like Nelson in 1805, had finally wiped out the Japanese fleet as an effective fighting force.[13]

In other words, nineteen pages later and nineteen years after the event, Halsey and Kinkaid together recorded an overwhelming victory.[14] In one sense this was true, but the way in which this is portrayed carries the obvious implication of real and very deliberate cooperation between Halsey and Kinkaid as the basis of victory, and this seems somewhat misleading. But this is of small account when set alongside this last observation on the part of Nimitz (and Potter), complete as it is with a revisionist account of history for which this writer is grateful because, evidently, he has stood in need of correction on this matter for all his adult life. He had always been under the obviously mistaken impression that off Cape Trafalgar on 21 October 1805 a British battle force had outfought and defeated a combined French and Spanish fleet.

Finis.

Notes:

1. ADM 199.1493. Operations in the Pacific Ocean Areas. Month of October 1944. Commander-in-Chief U.S. Pacific Fleet and Pacific Ocean Areas. Annex C. Comments.

2. The cruiser-destroyer formation made twenty-five knots as it headed north after the sinking of the *Chiyoda* and hence it is hard to see how a concentrated battle force, with battleships from the *North Carolina* and *South Dakota* classes, could have overhauled the Japanese to the north; the real question mark must be placed against mid-day/early afternoon operations. The problem here was that only the *Iowa* and *New Jersey* were fast battleships and any contact that they made with enemy light forces would have been reported immediately and other Japanese units could have moved clear of the intended battle area—perhaps.

3. At one stage on 25 October the *Intrepid* and the *Cabot* and *Independence* of Task Group 38.2 had just eight destroyers in company. See ADM 199.1494, p. 316.

4. See Thomas B. Buell, *Master of Sea Power: A Biography of Fleet Admiral Ernest J. King*, pp. 468 and 479. I would wish to acknowledge my thanks to Michael Coles for bringing this episode to my attention and pointing to its possible relevance here.

5. One has never seen this argued, and again one is conscious that such a comment leaves one liable to correction, but there seem to be some curious parallels between the battles of Santiago and Leyte Gulf and between Schley and Kinkaid on the one side and Sampson and Halsey on the other, though perhaps one should not labor the point.

6. I would wish to acknowledge my thanks to John Sweetman for reminding me of the origins of the Schley-Sampson dispute and pointing to its possible relevance here.

7. I would wish to acknowledge my thanks to Commander John Kuehn, USN, for this phrase and idea.

8. On the letter's second page there is a penciled note indicating that the letter was received at 1435 on 12 February 1945. One assumes that this was King's office. Interestingly, a marking that states 3rd Endorsement by Nimitz to King is stricken out.

9. The paragraph in Sherman's endorsement to which Halsey objected, and which is to be found in ADM 199.1494, pp. 178ff., reads as follows: "It is considered that the best role of the fast battleships under modern conditions of naval warfare is to remain with the carriers until the air strikes have produced cripples as suitable targets for the battleships and until control of the air has been gained to a point where CAP is not required for the battleships when they are detached." The report bears the serial F-B2-1/A16-3/Rwg.

10. I would wish to acknowledge my thanks to Captain Spencer Johnson for his observation on the draft of this piece; his suggestion that the word "grotesque" be set aside in favor of a more conciliatory term or word was not embraced, but his help and his observations were nonetheless fully appreciated. I would also acknowledge my debt in these matters to Captain Gerard Roncolato and Steven Weingartner.

11. And also with the views expressed in Potter, *Nimitz*, p. 338, that Nimitz "was convinced that Halsey . . . was now . . . forging out ahead of the carrier groups to fight an old-fashioned surface battle with *stragglers and with the cripples left by Mitscher's carrier planes*" (italics added).

12. E. B. Potter and Chester W. Nimitz, *Triumph in the Pacific: The Navy's Struggle against Japan*, p. 132, and Potter, *Sea Power: A Naval History*, p. 795.

13. Potter, *Sea Power: A Naval History*, pp. 813–814.

14. I would wish to acknowledge my thanks to Kenneth Hagen for this comment—which is taken from a paper that is to be published in *From Total War to Total Victory*, ed. Steven Weingartner, by the Cantigny First Division Foundation sometime in 2005—and for the first part of this argument.

NOTES

2. THE OPTION OF DIFFICULTIES

1. One must admit to being somewhat surprised by this fact on the cruiser count. Overall, in the Philippine Sea on the Japanese side were five fleet and four light carriers, five battleships, and eleven heavy and two light cruisers. On the American side were eight fleet and seven light carriers, seven battleships, and eight heavy and thirteen light cruisers, and ninety-seven destroyers. The American totals refer only to the units with Task Force 58 and do not include the escort carriers, battleships, and cruisers with the amphibious, support, and reserve formations.

2. H. P. Willmott, *Grave of a Dozen Schemes: British Naval Planning and the War against Japan, 1943–1945*, p. 110.

3. Forrest C. Pogue, *George C. Marshall: Ordeal and Hope*, p. 255. William Manchester, *American Caesar: Douglas MacArthur, 1880–1964*, p. 283. See also H. P. Willmott, *The Barrier and the Javelin: Japanese and Allied Pacific Strategies, February to June 1942*, p. 165.

4. Willmott, *The Barrier*, pp. 186–187.

5. This, necessarily, is only a summary of events; see also Grace Person Hayes, *The History of the Joint Chiefs of Staff in World War II: The War against Japan*, specifically Chapters XXII ("SEAC and Burma in early 1944"), XXIII ("China's Role in the Pacific Campaign"), and XXVI ("The Recall of General Stilwell"); Charles F. Romanus and Riley Sunderland, *United States Army in World War II: China-Burma-India Theater—Stilwell's Command Problems*, specifically Chapters X ("Facing the Command Problem"), XI ("The China Crisis of 1944"), and XII ("The End of CBI Theater"); and Barbara W. Tuchman, *Sand against the Wind: Stilwell and the American Experience in China, 1911–1945*, specifically Chapter 19 ("The Limits of 'Can Do.' September–November 1944").

6. Hayes, pp. 603–604.

7. E. B. Potter, *Nimitz*, p. 310.

8. Potter, *Nimitz*, pp. 311–315. John Prados, *The Combined Fleet Decoded: The Secret History of American Intelligence and the Japanese Navy in World War II*, p. 586.

9. For a summary of these discussions see Robert Ross Smith, *Triumph in the Philippines*, pp. 3–17. For the final arrangements see Clark G. Reynolds, *The Fast Carriers: The Forging of an Air Navy*, pp. 248–249.

10. Hayes, p. 613.

11. The official American figures for the casualties sustained on Leyte and Samar between 20 October 1944 and 8 May 1945 were 15,584 killed, 11,991 wounded, and 89 missing. M. Hamlin Cannon, *Leyte: The Return to the Philippines*, pp. 367–368.

12. For example, in the whole of the Okinawa campaign American casualties numbered 12,520 killed and missing and 36,631 wounded, and non-battle casualties numbered 26,211 for the U.S. Army and Marine Corps. A total of thirty-six warships were sunk (see Roy E. Appleman et al., *Okinawa: The Last Battle*, p. 473). On average, in any week between 22 June 1941 and 12 May 1945 the Soviet Union lost more dead than did the United States in the whole of the Pacific war.

13. Reynolds, pp. 240–243. Reynolds states that the convoy consisted of eight freighters and three escorts, and that carrier aircraft "sank nine of the ships and . . . cruisers finished off the other two; total sunk, 20,000 tons of Japanese shipping." One's own calculations are that carrier aircraft accounted for three transports of 4,002 tons, four naval merchant-men of 13,677 tons, three army transports of 12,348 tons, and shared with warships in the destruction of the 1,262-ton destroyer escort *Matsu*. Hansgeorg Jentschura, Dieter Jung, and Peter Michel, *Warships of the Imperial Navy, 1869–1945*, p. 152, give the *Matsu* as having been sunk by three American destroyers.

14. Morison, pp. 19–25. The relative slowness with which the Pitoe airfield was brought into service was the result of adverse weather conditions. The number of Japanese killed and captured on Morotai was 117, which was one more than the total number of Americans killed, missing, and wounded. It is estimated that another two hundred Japanese were killed trying to get back to Halmahera when their craft were intercepted by PT boats. On 3 October the Japanese submarine Ro. 41 torpedoed the destroyer escort *Shelton* off Morotai, the American ship subsequently sinking while under tow. The American submarine *Seawolf* was attacked by an aircraft from the escort carrier *Midway* and then by the destroyer escort *Richard M. Rowell*. She was lost with all hands.

15. By the end of October the Japanese positions on Peleliu had been reduced to the Umurbrogol Pocket, which was some 600 yards long and a maximum of 475 yards astride the ridge. Fighting was ended on 27 November, and the last five Japanese surrendered on 1 February 1945. About 13,600 Japanese were killed, with some 400 surrendering. On the American side the 1st Marine Division lost 1,250 killed and 5,275 wounded, the 81st Infantry Division 542 killed and another 2,750 other casualties.

16. By the author's own calculations carrier aircraft accounted for nineteen warships of 10,887 tons, thirteen naval auxiliaries and support ships of 56,677 tons, nineteen army transports of 81,743 tons, and twenty-one merchantmen of 61,434 tons. The units lost to unknown causes in September numbered eight warships of 2,705 tons, one naval support ship of 853 tons, one 6,382-ton army transport, and three merchantmen of 3,483 tons. Of these perhaps five of the warships may have been sunk by carrier aircraft. One should immediately place E.&O.E. against any list supplied by this author.

The problem with any such list is obvious: all sources differ and one has no sure way of knowing which is correct, while one's own calculations have not been afforded any guarantee denied others. One would note that Prados, p. 600, states that 213,250 tons of shipping were sunk during this rampage, Reynolds (p. 251) states that sixty-seven ships of 224,000 tons, and Rohwer and Hummelchen state "150 ships of all sizes are sunk and destroyed," while Morison appears not to have given either an account of the operations of 21–24 September nor any overall statement of Japanese losses.

17. Reynolds, p. 251, gives Japanese losses as 893 aircraft.

18. Harry A. Gailey, *Peleliu 1944*, p. 189.

19. Japanese warship and shipping losses to carrier-based aircraft thus far in the war were as given in Table 2.2 (p. 34).

The clear point was that before September 1944 the carriers had never been in a position to take the war to Japanese merchant shipping, and even in terms of service shipping their achievement was decidedly modest, Truk excepted. Truk provided the carriers with a respectable toll, but between September and November 1944 the carriers more than doubled the number of service and merchant ships they had sunk to date, though given that by this stage of the war the average size of ship sunk was appreciably smaller than previously had been the case, the tonnage increase was less than double.

3. THE SEARCH FOR SOLUTIONS

1. Such advice was given. In the aftermath of the defeat in the Philippine Sea a sign appeared in Naval General Staff headquarters: "Our Imperial Combined Fleet is now powerless. Prepare at once to reform the Cabinet so we can seek peace." This was cited in John Toland, *The Rising Sun: The Decline and Fall of the Japanese Empire 1936–1945*, p. 507, and is quoted in W. D. Dickson, *The Battle of the Philippine Sea*, p. 168, but for the first line of the notice: "Kill Tojo and Shimada!" (i.e., Prime Minister Tojo's closest associate in the *Kaigun*).

2. Rear Admiral Koyanagi Tomiji, "The Battle of Leyte Gulf," in *The Japanese Navy in World War II: In the Words of Former Japanese Naval Officers*, ed. David C. Evans, p. 357. Prados, p. 584.

3. C. Vann Woodward, *The Battle for Leyte Gulf*, p. 21.

4. Koyanagi, p. 357.

5. Prados, p. 581.

6. Prados, p. 588.

7. Yoshimura Akira, *Battleship Musashi: The Making and Sinking of the World's Biggest Warship*, p. 154.

8. H. P. Willmott, *The Second World War in the Far East*, p. 211.

9. These lists and totals make no provision for the *Ioshima* and *Yashojima*, which had been built in Japan for China in the early thirties. Both were captured in late 1938 and given to the Nanking regime by the Japanese; they were requisitioned by the Imperial Navy in 1943. The *Ioshima*, originally the *Ning Hai*, was assigned to escort duties and was lost in September 1944. The *Yashojima*, originally the *P'ing Hai*, was sunk in November 1944.

10. The surviving destroyers were the *Akikaze, Namikaze, Nokaze, Shiokaze* and the *Yukaze* from the *Minekaze* class; the *Hasu, Kuri* and the *Tsuga* from the *Momi* class; the *Asagao* and *Kuretake* from the *Wakatake* class; the *Harukaze, Hatakaze* and the *Kamikaze* from the *Kamikaze* class; and just the *Uzuki* and *Yuzuki* from the *Mutsuki* class.

11. The surviving destroyers were the *Akebono, Uranami* and the *Ushio* from the *Fubuki* class; the *Hibiki* from the *Akatsuki* class; the *Hatsuharu, Hatsushimo* and the *Wakaba* from the *Hatsuharu* class; the *Shigure* from the *Shiratsuyu* class; the *Asagumo, Kasumi, Michishio* and the *Yamagumo* from the *Asashio* class; the *Amatsukaze, Hamakaze, Isokaze, Nowaki, Shiranui, Urakaze* and the *Yukikaze* from the *Kagero* class; the *Akishimo, Asashimo, Fujinami, Hamanami, Hayashimo, Kishinami, Kiyoshimo, Naganami* and the *Okinami* from the *Yugumo* class; and the *Shimakaze*. The six surviving members of the *Akizuki* class were the *Akizuki, Fuyutsuki, Hatsutsuki, Shimotsuki, Suzutsuki* and the *Wakatsuki*.

12. H. P. Willmott, *The Great Crusade: A New Complete History of the Second World War*, pp. 296–299.

13. Woodward, p. 8. Prados, p. 602.

14. Prados, p. 586.

15. A certain care nonetheless needs be exercised in noting these aspects of cooperation between the two services. After the war Yamashita, the army commander in the Philippines, disclaimed knowledge of the *Kaigun's* intentions and complained that the army air formations in the islands were under the orders of Southern Area Army, which had its headquarters in Saigon. See Woodward, pp. 23–24.

16. Willmott, *June 1944*, pp. 228–230. Prados, p. 583.

17. Prados, p. 584.

18. Koyanagi, pp. 335–336.

19. Prados, p. 585.

20. Prados, p. 587.

21. And, it should be noted, air groups which had not received replacement aircraft for the outdated ones presently in service. See Reynolds, p. 219.

22. Vice Admiral Fukudome Shigeru, "The Air Battle off Taiwan," in *The Japanese Navy in World War II: In the Words of Former Japanese Naval Officers*, ed. David C. Evans, pp. 336–337.

23. Woodward, p. 16.

24. Thomas J. Cutler, *The Battle of Leyte Gulf. 23–26 October 1944. The Dramatic Full Story, Based on the Latest Research, of the Greatest Naval Battle in History*, p. 93. Koyanagi, p. 360. Yoshimura, p. 153. Edwin P. Hoyt, *The Battle of Leyte Gulf. The Death Knell of the Japanese Fleet*, pp. 4–5, places this episode after 20 October, but this is at odds with Japanese sources.

25. Prados, p. 587.

26. Prados, p. 588.

27. Toland, p. 539. John Ellis, *One Day in a Very Long War: Wednesday, 25 October 1944*, p. 332. Cutler, p. 66, states that in this exchange the army officers protested that squandering the fleet in an improbable venture in the Philippines would leave the home islands open to invasion, and that Major-General Sato Kenyro reminded the naval officers that the Combined Fleet belonged not only to the navy but the state and that only the existence of the fleet would induce caution on the part of the enemy.

28. Prados, p. 584. Woodward, p. 21. In Andrieu D'Albas, *Death of a Navy: The Fleets of the Mikado in the Second World War, 1941–1945*, p. 164, Toyoda is quoted as having said, "If we were beaten at the Philippines and even if the fleet remained to us, the southern sources of supply would be isolated. When it returned to Japanese waters the fleet could not be refueled: left in the south it could not be supplied with arms and ammunition. It would be pointless therefore, to lose the Philippines and save the fleet."

29. This basic idea, that the destruction of the *Yamato* was sought by the *Kaigun* in April 1945 because the battleships that bore the ancient name of Japan could not be allowed to survive national defeat, has been standard currency for a number of decades. But George Feifer, *The Battle of Okinawa. The Blood and the Bomb*, pp. 3–5, states that the navy did not plan to commit the *Yamato*, or indeed any surface units, to the attack in defense of Okinawa; the special attack forces were to consist of aircraft only. According to Feifer's account, it was the emperor's questioning of the naval chief of staff, Admiral Oikawa Koshiro, at the briefing conducted on 25 March 1945 as to why surface units were not to be committed that represented loss of face relative to the emperor and the recasting of naval plans to include the *Yamato* in a "special attack" formation. The exact definition, on p. 10, states, "It would have been impossible for the Navy not to carry out what His Majesty appeared to have suggested with characteristic Japanese indirectness: that surface

ships must join the sacrifice of the *kamikaze* pilots. Even to admit to him the tiny number of fighting ships left would have been an intolerable loss of face." Interestingly, Feifer suggests, p. 16, that, quite contrary to conventional wisdom, the *Yamato* had sufficient fuel for a return from Okinawa.

30. It may be noted, moreover, that after the air battle for Formosa and the northern Philippines, the Japanese army's view was that reinforcements then fed into the battle would at least allow Japanese air forces to fight for "at least temporary local superiority over the Philippines. This would make possible the safe movement of troop reinforcements and supplies to the Leyte invasion area, thus eliminating the major reason for the original decision to attempt only a delaying action in the central or southern Philippines." See Douglas MacArthur, *Reports of General MacArthur: Japanese Operations in the Southwest Pacific Area*, Volume II, Part II, p. 369. As is so often the case with matters Japanese and the Second World War, it is difficult to determine what was reason, the anticipated and planned, and what was improvised with *ex post facto* rationalization.

31. The losses incurred by the Americans in the Pacific between 24 November 1943 and 24 October 1944 were: on 24 November CVE *Liscome Bay*, 29 November DD *Perkins* as a result of a collision, 26 December DD *Brownson*, .. December SS *Capelin* missing, 12 February 1944 ASR *Macaw* by grounding, 26 February SS *Grayback*, 29 February SS *Trout*, .. February SS *Scorpion* missing, 26 March SS *Tullibee* as a result of an accident, .. April SS *Gudgeon* missing, 1 June SS *Herring*, 14 June SS *Golet*, 4 July SS S-28 missing on exercise, 26 July SS *Robalo* as a result of internal explosion, 13 August SS *Flier*, 24 August SS *Harder* which sunk by a Thai warship, 12 September ADP *Noa* as a result of a collision, 13 September DMS *Perry*, 3 October SS *Seawolf* in error, DE *Shelton*, 17 October DM *Montgomery*, and 24 October CVL *Princeton*, ATO *Sonoma*, SS *Shark*, and the submarines *Darter* by grounding and *Tang* by accident. Overall, therefore, the U.S. Navy lost twenty-six units in this period, of which sixteen were submarines. Of the losses, eight were as a result of accidents and did not involve enemy action, and four were "missing" with cause of loss unknown. Thirteen of the units, including six submarines, were lost as a result of Japanese action or mines. One submarine was sunk by a Thai warship.

32. Professor Tohmatsu Haruo, e-mail to the author, 18 December 2001.

33. H. P. Willmott, *The War with Japan: The Period of Balance, May 1942–October 1943*, pp. 147–148.

34. Ugaki Matome et al., *Fading Victory: The Diary of Admiral Matome Ugaki, 1941–1945*, pp. 478 and 482. (Also given in Rohwer and Hummelchen, p. 309.)

35. As a corrective, it may be of interest to note that in reporting the extent of American carrier success in Huon Gulf in March 1942 when aircraft accounted for one coastal minelayer, one auxiliary minelayer, one armed merchant cruiser, and one transport, Roosevelt, in a letter to Churchill of 18 March, claimed that two heavy cruisers had been sunk, one light cruiser was believed to have been sunk, one destroyer and one minelayer "probably sunk," two more destroyers badly damaged and probably sunk, and another two destroyers "possibly sunk." In addition five transports were either sunk or badly damaged, two patrol boats were possibly sunk, and one seaplane carrier was badly damaged. The Japanese did not have a monopoly on exaggerated claims. See Willmott, *The Barrier*, pp. 61–62.

36. Quoted in Woodward, p. 18, and see p. 19 for a further examination of what is described as "the pathology of fear" and "the epidemic of self-deception."

37. For Kurita's treatment of claims, see James A. Field, Jr., *The Japanese at Leyte Gulf: The Sho Operation*, pp. 29–30. For comments about Toyoda and Fukudome, see Prados, p. 610. It should be noted, however, that the Japanese claims were subsequently revised, and in their final form appear to have been that their actions resulted in either the sinking

of or damage to four American carriers. This was clearly a considerable difference from the claims of 16 October, but it is notable that this revision took place after the battle of Leyte Gulf. See Field, p. 27, fn. 2.

38. Prados, p. 601.

39. Prados, p. 585.

40. Prados, pp. 588, 590. Prados on p. 621 notes that on 18 October Onishi, the commander of the 1st Air Fleet, predicted that the American landings would be made at Tacloban on Leyte.

41. D'Albas, p. 163.

42. MacArthur, p. 381. This was the estimate of the 35th Army after the American landings on Leyte on 20 October 1944.

43. Field, p. 19.

44. Ugaki was to note on 6 August 1945 after news of the attack on Hiroshima had been received that countermeasures had to be prepared immediately and that he wished Japan could have an atomic bomb. See Ugaki, p. 655. It was Ugaki who, as chief of staff of the Combined Fleet, had fixed the war games prior to Midway when the initial results were unfavorable to the Japanese. See Willmott, *The Barrier*, p. 111. His reaction to the games played before Leyte was that if the battle went as well as the games "we shall have a chance to win and also be able to die satisfied even if we do not." See Prados, p. 588.

45. Also detached from Kurita's command at this time (18 October) was the composite 16th Cruiser Division, which mustered the heavy cruiser *Aoba* (which had been at Singapore and scheduled for docking but had been unable to sail to join Kurita's force), the light cruiser *Kinu*, and the destroyer *Uranami*. These units were assigned the protection of transports making their way into the southern Philippines. The destroyers *Wakaba*, *Hatsuharu* and the *Hatsushimo* were likewise detached from Shima's command after they arrived in the Pescadores on the morning of 20 October. These units were sent to Takao to load personnel and equipment of the 2nd Air Fleet for the Philippines. Kurita's force thus consisted of two sections, the first with three battleships, six heavy cruisers, one light cruiser, and nine destroyers, and the second with two battleships, four heavy cruisers, one light cruiser, and six destroyers.

46. Prados, pp. 588–589. Woodward, p. 22. Ozawa's force thus consisted of one fleet carrier, three light fleet carriers, two battleships, three light cruisers, four destroyers, and four destroyer escorts.

47. Prados, p. 630. Prados, pp. 589–590, makes the observation that "had Ozawa's advice all been taken, the battle for Leyte Gulf might have turned out quite differently." Even allowing for the caveat and for the fact that the specific matter under examination here was the attachment of a carrier force to Kurita's command, Nishimura's formation was detached from Kurita's formation because the *Fuso* and *Yamashiro*, being the oldest of Japan's dreadnoughts and the first to have been rebuilt in the early thirties, were considerably slower than the other battleships with Kurita's force. See Field, p. 32, fn. 4.

48. Prados, p. 606. Woodward, pp. 22–23.

49. Prados, pp. 622–623. (MacArthur, p. 371, states that the available strength in the Philippines on 19 October was five naval and three army aircraft.)

50. Woodward, p. 23.

51. Prados, pp. 620–621.

4. PRELIMINARIES

1. Morison, p. 86. Reynolds, p. 258.

2. Kit C. Carter and Robert Mueller, *U.S. Army Air Forces in World War II: Combat Chronology, 1941–1945*, 7 October 1944, p. 468.

3. Task Group 30.2 consisted of the heavy cruisers *Chester, Pensacola* and the *Salt Lake City* and the destroyers *Case, Cassin, Cummings, Downes, Dunlap* and the *Fanning.* Rohwer, p. 308, gives the date of the bombardment as 8 October. Morison, p. 87, gives the date as 9 October. The latter date is given as the date of the bombardment in all the respective entries in *Dictionary of American Naval Fighting Ships* (hereafter *DANFS*), II, pp. 46, 48, 216, 295, 306, and 389, and V, p. 257. The *Salt Lake City's* entry, VI, p. 270, gives the date of 9 September, but this is obviously an error given that she is stated to have sailed for Marcus on 6 October.

Nimitz's report for the month of October 1944 (ADM 199.1493, p. 213) states that the American warships fired 889 8-in. and 1,933 5-in. shells in the course of a bombardment that drew heavy and sustained defensive fire on the part of the Japanese defenders. The Japanese fired to ranges of 18,000 yards and their fire was deemed to have been very accurate, with many near-misses but not a single hit.

After this operation Task Group 30.2 joined Task Group 38.1 on 16 October and remained in company until the return to Ulithi, when its units were detached and subsequently reassigned to bombardment duties in preparation for the assault on Iwo Jima.

The first bombardment thereafter was conducted either side of midnight on 11–12 November by the same formation and ships, less the *Dunlap.* They sailed from Ulithi on 8 November. See ADM 199.1493, p. 288. These bombardments were totally overshadowed by the carrier operations and are seldom afforded as much as a footnote in most accounts of these proceedings.

Before the bombardment of Marcus certain of these ships had been involved in other bombardments, namely those of Matsuwa and Paramushiro in the Kuriles on 13 and 26 June and of Wake on 3 September.

4. Morison, pp. 90–91. Reynolds, p. 260. Rohwer, pp. 308–309, states that the carriers flew 1,936 sorties, but this is obviously a mistake. The author's own accounting of warship and shipping losses is at variance from that given in Morison and used in Reynolds.

5. Morison, p. 94, states that American losses amounted to seventeen fighters and six bombers from the carriers. Prados, p. 609, gives the date for the attack on Formosa by China-based Superfortresses as 13 October, but in fact it was staged on the following day. A potential area of confusion is that Okayama is given in Carter and Mueller, p. 895, as being in Japan. At this time Formosa was part of Japan, a fact easily forgotten in that one makes a distinction between Formosa and the home islands. The author's confusion on this point was resolved as a result of an e-mail to Richard Hallion on 26 January 2002, which was answered most efficiently by Yvonne Kinkaid, Air Force History Support Office, in an e-mail of 28 January 2002.

6. Morison, p. 94. *DANFS*, II, p. 443.

7. *DANFS*, II, p. 24; IV, p. 456. Morison, pp. 94, 98. The *Canberra* was towed to Manus (arrived 27 October) for temporary repairs and then made her way to Boston navy yard for permanent treatment (16 February–17 October). She did not return to service until the end of 1945.

8. *DANFS*, III, p. 376. Morison, p. 102.

9. Morison, p. 94.

10. Prados, p. 590.

11. Prados, pp. 604–605.

12. Prados, pp. 607–608.

13. Morison, pp. 96ff. E. B. Potter, *Admiral Arleigh Burke: A Biography,* p. 191.

14. Kusaka made the decision to implement the air parts of SHO 1 and 2 at 0925. See Prados, pp. 605–606.

15. Prados, p. 606.

16. As per endnote 6.

17. Prados, p. 609. Rohwer, p. 309.

18. Prados, p. 608.

19. Fukudome, p. 351. Field, p. 27, states that there were just thirty-two offensive sorties on 13 October, 419 on 14 October, and 199 on the following day (these figures are also given in Reynolds, p. 260). Field also states that on 14 October the largest single attack, by 225 aircraft, failed to locate its target. These same figures are used by Norman Polmar, *Aircraft Carriers: A Graphic History of Carrier Aviation and Its Influence on World Events,* p. 381.

20. Prados, pp. 609–610. Fukudome, p. 352, states "against the surface units of the enemy carrier task forces, we made 761 sorties in all," it not being clear to what "we" referred. It would appear that he was referring to just the 2nd Air Fleet, and it is worth noting that he states losses to have been 179 aircraft "in these sorties" and that also lost were about 150 aircraft either over or on Formosa. This would seem to be just the 2nd Air Fleet's losses. Toland, p. 537, gives all Japanese losses as more than 500 aircraft in the first three days of operations (i.e., 12–14 October inclusive), as does Reynolds, p. 260. Rohwer, p. 309, states that the Japanese flew 881 offensive sorties between 12 and 15 October.

21. Morison, p. 106. Rohwer, p. 309. The Japanese total was the one admitted at the time and which all but certainly understated losses by a considerable margin.

22. Naval War College analysis. Dickson, pp. 168–169, fn.

23. Woodward, p. 19. Hayashi Saburo, in *Kōgun. The Japanese Army in the Pacific War,* pp. 208–209, gives slightly different figures, stating that these, the final figures, were on 12 October four fleet sunk and one damaged, and eleven other warships damaged; on 13 October three carriers sunk and two damaged, and one other unit sunk and nine damaged; on 14 October again three carriers sunk and two damaged, and two battleships sunk and eight other warships damaged. The Japanese claims for 15 October were one carrier sunk and three damaged and one other warship damaged, and on 16 October one carrier and one battleship damaged. Thus the overall total is that eleven carriers and two battleships were sunk and nine carriers and two battleships were damaged. What is so notable about these claims is the lack of losses except among the most important types. See also Chapter VII, endnote 53.

24. Morison, p. 109.

25. Prados, pp. 608–609.

26. Cannon, p. 85.

27. Apparently the Japanese claims were revised downward to three or four American carriers sunk or damaged, but the revision was not until after the subsequent battle. See Field, p. 27, fn. 2.

28. Fukudome, p. 347. Quoted in part by Toland, pp. 536–537, and in full by Polmar, p. 380.

29. Morison, pp. 100–101.

30. Fukudome, p. 352. Fukudome wrote, "After the war . . . I was told that of the ships in the U.S. Fleet only two cruisers had sustained serious damage. Why on earth had such an exorbitant exaggeration been made in our report? Having been informed of the real damage, I was startled indeed at the great discrepancy. We cannot shrink from the responsibility for having made such a report." Even allowing for the fact that Fukudome admitted culpability, and apparently insisted that elite formations should be credited with one-third of their claims (Prados, p. 610), this does not explain things since the point was that Fukudome here admits having made claims that hardly accorded with what he had witnessed on 12 October. One is left to wonder whether Fukudome fabricated this episode, though why he should have done so is hard to discern.

31. *DANFS*, III, p. 443.

32. Morison, p. 101.

33. According to Fukudome, p. 351, Toyoda "ordered his entire fleet"—i.e., not just Shima's force—"to make an all-out pursuit," and this came after an Imperial General Headquarters release that claimed the destruction of twelve ships—cruisers and above—and the sinking of another twenty-three vessels.

34. Woodward, p. 20. Field, p. 28, states that Shima's formation was ordered to proceed to Amami-o-Shima in the Ryukyus.

35. Morison, p. 104. Field, p. 28, states that at 0900 on 16 October, Japanese reconnaissance aircraft found a force of two large carriers and two battleships 260 miles east of Formosa, and at 1030 "lurking in the distance 430 miles to the eastward, seven carriers, seven battleships and ten cruisers were discovered." It is impossible to reconcile these statements with what the various task groups had under command and with the known position of the American formations, but there is no doubting the essential accuracy of these reports in bringing home to senior Japanese commanders the fact that American carrier formations were more or less intact and on station.

36. Morison, p. 104. *DANFS*, III, p. 376. The *Houston* entry states that she and the *Canberra* arrived at Ulithi on 27 October, and that the *Houston*, after temporary repairs, "proceeded to Manus 20 December and eventually steamed to New York navy yard, arriving 24 March 1945." After extensive rebuilding she sailed 11 October 1945, and thereafter was employed on secondary and training duties. She was decommissioned at Philadelphia navy yard in December 1947 and was stricken in March 1959.

37. Morison, p. 109. Potter, *Nimitz*, p. 328. Toland, pp. 537–538.

38. Toland, p. 538.

39. Cannon, p. 23.

40. Cannon, pp. 26, 31–33. Morison, p. 65, states that 145,000 American troops were to land on Leyte in the first five days of operations, and that these were to be followed by another 55,000.

41. The American formations committed to these operations were X Corps, which had the 1st Cavalry and 24th Infantry Divisions, plus one infantry regiment and two engineer brigades under command; XXIV Corps, which had the 7th and 96th Infantry Divisions under command; a reserve at sea consisting of one regiment and a ranger battalion; plus some 44,600 support and other troops. The strategic reserve consisted of the 32nd Infantry Division at Hollandia and the 77th Infantry Division on Guam. In general terms, the northern force sailed from Hollandia and Manus while the southern force sailed from the Hawaiian islands via Hollandia. Reserve and support formations had been held at Hollandia, Morotai, and Guam.

The shore-based air component was stated to have been some 432 B-24 Liberators and 116 B-25 Mitchells, 286 A-20 Bostons, 375 P-38 Lightnings, 250 P-47 Thunderbolts and 46 P-61 Black Widow night fighters, 111 reconnaissance and photographic units, plus 336 C-47 Dakota transports. The source of these figures is the report of British naval, military, and air force observers with the landing forces which, unnumbered, is to be found in ADM 199.1056.

42. Gerald E. Wheeler, *Kinkaid of the Seventh Fleet: A Biography of Admiral Thomas C. Kinkaid*, pp. 389–390.

43. Morison, p. 118.

44. Morison, p. 94, fn. 10, states that Task Force 38 claimed to have destroyed 655 Japanese aircraft and that the Japanese admitted to having lost 492 aircraft, a total that included one hundred army aircraft of all types. Morison, not untypically, then proceeded to state that the American estimates were probably more or less right, Japanese losses being

stated to have been between 550 and 600 aircraft. Unfortunately for this particular statement, Morison went on to claim that American forces destroyed forty freighters in these
three days, and perhaps thereby provided inadvertent comment on his own objectivity:
twenty-one ships were destroyed. Field, p. 17, gives the total Japanese losses between 11
and 16 October as 807 aircraft and twenty-six ships.

45. Toland, p. 538.

46. Prados, pp. 608–609, states that Japanese submarines were ordered to concentrate
off Formosa in order to pick off damaged American warships, but of the 6th Fleet's fifty-five
submarines only sixteen could be sent into action, and "before any real concentration took
place, MacArthur's Leyte landings began and the subs [sic] went there instead." Hashimoto
Mochitsura, *Sunk: The Story of the Japanese Submarine Fleet, 1942–1945*, states that "the
remnants of our submarine fleet had been ordered to concentrate in the Philippines area
on October 11. In all there were eleven submarines," which are then named (pp. 112–113).
The dates of these two statements cannot be reconciled, but the totals could be and do not
seem mutually exclusive. Interestingly, Hashimoto notes operations on the part of three
named Japanese submarines, and each one of these claimed to have sunk a fleet carrier.

47. Toland, p. 538.

48. Toland, p. 539.

49. Field, p. 36, fn. 6. Quoted in Reynolds, p. 262. Polmar, p. 386, makes the point,
which is often a source of confusion, that the carriers *Junyo* and *Ryuho* and the hybrid-
battleships *Hyuga* and *Ise* were all members of the 4th Carrier Division, the battleships
after 1 May 1944, the *Junyo* after 10 July, and the *Ryuho* after 10 August. (Additional
information: Anthony J. Watts and Brian G. Gordon, *The Imperial Japanese Navy*, pp. 55,
190, and 194.) The other two carriers in commission were the *Amagi* and *Unryu*, and they
formed the 1st Carrier Division.

50. This is derived from René J. Francillon, *Japanese Aircraft of the Pacific War*, pp. 314–
317. Just fifteen Shiun (Violent Cloud/Norm) seaplanes (including prototypes) were built,
and they served only with the *Oyodo*, and the *Oyodo* is not listed as being home to any
other seaplane. These two units, therefore, were E15Ks. The *Oyoda* herself was not properly part of Ozawa's force until 18 October when she was released from dockyard hands.
She had been flagship of the Combined Fleet but with Toyoda going ashore she was
assigned on 5 October for service with the carrier force. See also Field, p. 36.

51. Jentschura, pp. 48, 51, and 57, gives the capacity of the *Zuikaku* as 84 and of the
three light carriers as 30 each for a total of 174 aircraft. Watts, pp. 183, 186, and 189, provide
the totals cited in the text, i.e., 159 operational aircraft and fifteen spares.

52. Prados, p. 621.

53. Prados, p. 622.

54. Prados, p. 620.

55. Prados, p. 622.

56. The *McCawley* was torpedoed by Japanese aircraft off Rendova on 30 June 1943
and was sinking when the *coup de grâce* was administered by six motor torpedo boats in
a case of mistaken identity. There is no doubt, however, that the abandoned *McCawley*
would have sunk in any event. The point, however, is the palpably small number of Allied
warships lost to Japanese air power in this two-year period.

57. Woodward, p. 32. Cannon, pp. 41–42, uses the same total except for the LCTs,
which he states numbered twenty-one, clearly a mistake. Field, p. 26, states that "the
Seventh Fleet . . . comprised a total of 738 vessels (of which) 157 were combatant ships,
420 were amphibious craft, 84 were patrol, minesweeping and hydrographic types, and
73 were service vessels."

5. ADVANCE AND CONTACT

1. Woodward, p. 31.

2. Toland, p. 543. Woodward, p. 32. On the first two days of the assault 103,000 troops were put ashore.

3. George W. Garand and Truman R. Strobridge, *Western Pacific Operations*, History of U.S. Marine Corps Operations in World War II, Volume IV, pp. 310–311. Mary H. Williams, *United States Army in World War II. Chronology, 1941–1945*, pp. 314–318. The main part of the campaign on Leyte was completed by mid-December 1944 with Ormoc taken and secured by the 77th Infantry Division on 22 December. Mopping up began on Leyte with the new year. This task was left to the 8th U.S. Army and was not completed until 8 May 1945.

4. Field, p. 30, Hoyt, *The Battle of Leyte Gulf*, p. 3; and Prados, p. 628, all state that Kurita's force sailed from Lingga Roads at 0100. Woodward, p. 35, gives the time as 0145. Yoshimura, p. 154, gives no time. All, however, give the date as 18 October. Morison, p. 164, states that Kurita's force sailed from Lingga Roads on 22 October.

5. Prados, p. 615.

6. Prados, p. 622.

7. Field, p. 61, states that the 2nd Air Fleet headquarters was moved to Manila on 22 October and that it numbered some 350 aircraft. Field also states that the local 4th Air Army numbered about the same number of aircraft and that Onishi's command had been reduced to about a hundred aircraft. Field also states that only half of the aircraft in these two formations were operational on 24 October. Prados, p. 624, states that some 350 aircraft from Fukudome's command were ordered to the Philippines and that 48 "longer-ranged bombers" were ordered to remain on Formosa. Prados also states that 178 aircraft had reached the Philippines by 1700 on 22 October, and that Onishi's command by that stage had just 24 operational aircraft. The army formation numbered 98 aircraft.

8. Prados, p. 617.

9. Morison, p. 156.

10. Jerome B. Cohen, *Japan's Economy in War and Reconstruction*, p. 142, states that the American carrier raids on Truk (17 February 1944) and Koror in the Palaus (30 March) "sank one-third of the tankers attached to the Combined Fleet." It would seem that these raids accounted for nine oilers, so the summer losses must have accounted for something akin to another third of what had been available.

11. Prados, p. 615. Cohen, p. 194, states that in 1941 half of all Japan's oil needs were carried in foreign oilers.

12. Brunei town, now Bandar Seri Begawan, is in 04°56'North 114°58'East. Ulugan Bay is in 10°04'North 118°47'East and Coron Island (at this time alternatively given as Koron) is in 11°56'North 120°14'East.

13. The *Itsukushima Maru*, *Nichiei Maru*, *Omurosan Maru*, *Ryoei Maru*, *Hakko Maru* and the *Nippo Maru* were each about 10,000 GRT, with a carrying capacity of 13,000 tons of oil. The *Banei Maru* and *Yuho Maru* were 5,266-ton oilers with a maximum load capacity of 7,000 tons. Japanese National Institute of Defense Studies, *Kaigun shogo sakusen (2) Firipin oki kaisen/Navy Sho Operation*, Official War History Series: Volume II. *Battle off the Philippines*, p. 62, indicates that two of these ships were capable of undertaking underway replenishment, and the process of elimination would suggest that these were the sister ships *Banei Maru* and *Yuho Maru*. Because these two oilers carried less fuel than was needed, Kurita's force could not have been refueled when under way and that it had no option but wait for oilers at Brunei Bay.

14. Refueling of Kurita's force was completed at 0500 and it sailed three hours later. The four oilers that arrived on 22 October were not involved in refueling Kurita's force at this time; their only involvement in refueling Kurita's warships was after 28 October. The suggestion that six oilers were involved in refueling Kurita's warships at Brunei Bay at this stage (e.g., Polmar, p. 386) is incorrect.

15. *Kaigun shogo sakusen* (2), pp. 62–63, 71–75.

16. Ibid., pp. 65, 67–68. Notwithstanding this access to the Japanese record, certain inconsistencies remain. Whether the oilers arrived at 1120 (p. 68) or 1700 (p. 67) is not clear. It seems that whatever the time, they arrived before schedule, perhaps because the *Yuho Maru* carried only 6,300 tons of oil and maybe made a knot or two more than expected. Irrespective of the time of arrival, the time taken to refuel the warships—some twelve hours—points to the problems that the Japanese would have had in trying to refuel all ships when under way.

17. Prados, p. 628.

18. Hoyt, *The Battle of Leyte Gulf*, p. 3. Morison, p. 167.

19. Cutler, pp. 91, 95. Hoyt, *The Battle of Leyte Gulf*, p. 37.

20. Cutler, p. 95. Hoyt, *The Battle of Leyte Gulf*, pp. 84–86.

21. This was followed, after dinner, by formation briefings. Ugaki states "that the skippers under my command" were assembled. This would suggest just three officers, namely the captains of the battleships of the 1st Battleship Division. It may be, however, that the reference was to the captains of the ships of the 1st Task Group. See Ugaki, p. 485.

22. Ito Masanori, *The End of the Imperial Navy*, p. 119. Prados, p. 631

23. Hoyt, *The Battle of Leyte Gulf*, p. 5, and Ito, pp. 119–120, give the full text.

24. Prados, p. 657. Watts, pp. 49–51.

25. *Kaigun shogo sakusen* (2), pp. 56–57, 486–490.

26. Prados, p. 629.

27. Prados, p. 613.

28. Reynolds, p. 264, seems to be the only account that makes this point.

29. On 20 October the *Sangamon* was hit by a bomb from a Zeke fighter-bomber that bounced off the main deck into the sea before exploding, causing minimal damage. See *DANFS*, VI, pp. 318. The *Honolulu* was torpedoed on 20 October and sailed from Leyte the next day, arriving at Manus on 29 October. After temporary repairs, she sailed for Norfolk yard on 19 November. She did not re-enter service until October 1945 and was decommissioned in January 1946. See *DANFS*, III, pp. 356–357. The *Australia*, after being hit by a Japanese aircraft that deliberately dived into her, was escorted to Manus by the *Warramunga*: see *Naval Staff History: Second World War—War with Japan*. Volume VI. *The Advance to Japan*, pp. 83, 97. Hoyt, *The Battle of Leyte Gulf*, p. 52, states that the *Australia* and *Warramunga* sailed in the company of the *Honolulu* and the destroyer *Richard P. Leary*, but the latter was involved in the Surigao Strait action, as Hoyt, *The Battle of Leyte Gulf*, notes on p. 220.

30. Morison, p. 106.

31. Morison, p. 125.

32. Morison, p. 150. Woodward, p. 44, states that the order to Task Group 38.1 was given at 2230 on 22 October and that the formation was instructed to attack Yap en route.

33. *DANFS*, III, p. 232, states that the *Hancock* sailed for Ulithi in the company of Task Group 38.1 on 19 October, but this is clearly a mistake. It looks as if a sentence or two somehow managed to get omitted from the fifth paragraph of the *Hancock*'s entry.

34. Reynolds, p. 264.

35. Morison, p. 104.

36. Naval Staff, p. 61.

37. The point of Halsey having parted company with nearly 40 percent of his force is a comment all but unnoted in American histories. Two accounts that do note the fact are Potter, *Nimitz*, p. 331, and Reynolds, p. 264.

38. Woodward, p. 35.

39. Cutler, p. 85. Prados, pp. 644–645.

40. Hoyt, *The Battle of Leyte Gulf*, pp. 28–29.

41. Cutler, pp. 84–85.

42. *DANFS*, III, p. 3. Theodore Roscoe, *United States Destroyer Operations in World War II*, p. 390, indicates that the submarines off the Bungo Strait did provide warning of Japanese fleet movements thus: "The word from (the) *Besugo* and *Skate* told Nimitz that the Japanese Navy was coming out for a fight, and Halsey's Third Fleet prepared to meet the threat from the home empire with appropriate counter-measures. Air search was begun over Surigao and San Bernardino Straits." This does not seem to have any basis in fact.

43. Woodward, pp. 39–40.

44. Prados, p. 654.

45. Woodward, p. 39. *Kaigun shogo sakusen (2)*, p. 73.

46. Field, p. 33. Prados, pp. 654, 656.

47. Prados, pp. 654–656.

48. Prados, p. 660.

49. Field, p. 33. Prados, p. 656.

50. Hoyt, *The Battle of Leyte Gulf*, pp. 85–86. Prados, p. 656.

51. Ito, p. 140. Prados, p. 656.

52. Cutler, p. 96. Ito, p. 117. Prados, p. 635. The seaplanes went to San José airfield, Mindoro.

53. Roscoe, p. 392.

54. Sato Kazumasa, *Reite oki kaisen/The Battle off Leyte*, Volume 1, p. 265. Supplied to the author by Tohmatsu Haruo in letter of 12 October 2003.

55. Ito, p. 165.

56. The cautionary comments about Kurita were included on the advice of Michael Coles in his e-mail of 19 January 2004, for which the author is genuinely grateful.

57. *DANFS*, I, p. 153. Roscoe, p. 391. The position is given in the Admiralty Historical Section, *Battle Summary No. 40. Battle for Leyte Gulf, 23rd–26th October 1944*, p. 22. Jentschura, p. 81. Watts, p. 142. M. J. Whitley, *Cruisers of World War II: An International Encyclopedia*, p. 173.

58. Admiralty, pp. 19–20.

59. The Admiralty paper notes that in her post-action report the *Darter* stated that the Japanese force consisted of three battleships, four heavy cruisers, and three other vessels and that action had been in 09°24'North 117°11'East. The same position is given in Jentschura, p. 84, referring to the torpedoing of the *Takao*. The Admiralty paper states that the *Dace* made a report from 09°29'North 117°20'East. Morison, pp. 169–172. Roscoe, p. 392–394. Woodward, pp. 71–72.

60. Cutler, pp. 101–102. Roscoe, p. 393.

61. Field, p. 37. Ugaki, p. 487. Whitley, *Cruisers*, p. 180, respectively. Woodward, pp. 74–75.

62. Timings depend on whichever source is consulted. For example, Morison gives the time of the *Atago* being torpedoed as 0632 and sinking at 0653. The Japanese Official War History gives the timings as 0633 and 0653. The heavy cruiser *Haguro*'s Combat Report (quoted in Fukuda Yukihiro, *Rengokantai: Saipan Reite kaisenki/The Combined Fleet: The*

Battles of Saipan and Leyte) gives the torpedoing of the *Atago* as 0629 and sinking at 0702. The position of the *Atago* when she sank is given as per Admiralty, p. 21.

63. Field, p. 37.

64. Prados, p. 637.

65. Fukuda, p. 150. The three ships reached Brunei on 26 October, and the *Takao* arrived at Singapore on 12 November. See also Whitney, *Cruisers*, pp. 180–181. Woodward, p. 75.

66. Field, pp. 51–52.

67. Cutler, p. 170. Woodward, p. 70.

68. The narrowness of the Palawan Passage—twenty miles according to Cutler and twenty-five miles in Morison—has been held to be the main consideration in the limited evasive capacity of Japanese ships. Such a distance, the equivalent of the Strait of Dover— does not seem to have inhibited Japanese zigzagging come first light on 23 October. The real restriction was with mean course and the fact that once in the passage the Japanese route was fixed.

69. Morison, pp. 173–174. Roscoe, p. 394.

70. Roscoe, p. 395. *DANFS*, IV, 323.

71. Morison, p. 170.

72. This conclusion was reached independently by the author, but he found that the basic argument was one that had been used by Cutler (p. 107).

73. *DANFS*, II, p. 241.

74. *DANFS*, I, p. 47; III, p. 184. Ellis, p. 330. Hoyt, *The Battle of Leyte Gulf*, p. 83. Woodward, pp. 38–39. Admiralty, pp. 21–22, states that the *Angler*'s initial report, at 2130, was of a contact in the approaches to the Mindoro Strait in 13°00'North 119°30'East with between fifteen and twenty ships, including three battleships. Two subsequent reports, at 0030 and 0330 on 24 October, included two possible carriers with the Japanese formation. The account makes no reference to the *Guitarro*. Nimitz's battle report (ADM 199.1493, p. 229) states that the *Angler*'s contact report was for 12°40'North 118°58'East at 2215 on 23 October.

75. Perhaps it should be noted that the Americans had no fewer than fourteen submarines on patrol west of the main Philippine islands. These were the *Blackfin* northwest of Palawan, the *Gurnard* off Brunei Bay, the *Bergall*, *Darter*, *Dace* and the *Rock* in the Palawan Passage, the *Cobia* in the Sibutu Passage, the *Batfish* in the Sulu Sea off northwest Mindanao, the *Angler* and *Guitarro* initially off Manila, and off northwest Luzon the *Bream*, *Cero*, *Cod* and the *Nautilus*. See Roscoe, p. 391; source stated to be the official report. Hoyt, *The Battle of Leyte Gulf*, p. 59, gives ten of these in his order of battle, plus four British submarines in the Indies.

76. Hoyt, *The Battle of Leyte Gulf*, p. 83.

77. Cutler, p. 150. Admiralty, p. 23. Naval Staff, p. 81. These placed Task Group 38.3 in 15°00'North 123°30'East.

78. Cutler, pp. 115–116. Naval Staff, p. 81.

79. Cutler, p. 115, states that the report was received from the *Darter*, but this obviously is an error. The *Darter* episode is noted on pp. 105–107, but this account makes no reference to the Japanese force being contacted by the *Angler* and *Guitarro*.

80. Woodward, pp. 47–48, states that the individual Helldiver-Hellcat teams were assigned ten-degree sectors, and that Task Group 38.2 had six sectors. Task Group 38.4 had a similar number of sectors, and Task Group 38.3 perhaps two more since its search area was larger than the other two. Apart from Woodward, none of the accounts of the battle (Hoyt, *The Battle of Leyte Gulf*, p. 103, Morison, pp. 174–175, and Reynolds, p. 264) give

details of numbers and search areas while Polmar, p. 387, states that the typical search teams launched by groups "each had eight fighters armed with four 5-inch rockets (in addition to their six machine guns) and six dive bombers armed with two 500-pound bombs." Field (pp. 54 and 66) makes reference to Japanese ships being sighted by American reconnaissance aircraft but there is no reference to the American carriers having staged this effort. Hoyt, *The Battle of Leyte Gulf*, is the only account that states that it was the *Essex* that committed the fighters against airfields in the Manila area.

81. Woodward, pp. 48–49, alone gives the time of first contact. Prados, p. 639, states that the contact was at 0810 but that seems to be when the first report was sent. Nimitz's battle report (ADM 199.1493, p. 230) states that the first contact was made just as Kurita's force changed from cruise to battle formation.

82. Morison, p. 175, states that Halsey gave his orders at 0827, "only five minutes after receiving the contact report."

83. Cutler, p. 121. Morison, p. 175. Woodward, pp. 50–51.

84. Cutler, p. 139, gives this contact as 0820. Hoyt, *The Battle of Leyte Gulf* (p. 129), states that Nishimura's formation was found, some 75 miles east of the Cagayen Islands, "just after 0900." Field, p. 54, gives the time as 0910 and Morison, p. 191, indicates that the attack was conducted at 0918. Given that the American aircraft must have been at the limit of their range and could not have a whole hour gathering before making their attack, it seems that this difference stems from different time zones.

85. D'Albas, p. 171. Woodward, pp. 51–52.

86. *Kaigun shogo sakusen (2)*, pp. 56–57. There were a number of attacks on the *Aoba* and assorted merchantmen in Manila during 24 October, but these were *en passant*.

87. Woodward, pp. 50–51.

88. Her sinking is afforded no more than footnotes, on pp. 134 and 184, in the accounts provided by Field and Morison respectively. Hoyt, *The Battle of Leyte Gulf*, pp. 192–193, notes that the surviving destroyers, the *Hatsuharu* and *Hatsushimo*, were subjected to further attacks during the day and, after the *Hatsushimo* had been damaged, were forced to return to Manila, arriving shortly after midnight.

89. Polmar, p. 387.

90. Morison, p. 177, gives the fifty-to-sixty figure. Woodward, p. 53, states that the first attack numbered about forty aircraft. Prados, p. 624, states that the three missions "added up to about 150 attack sorties."

91. Admiralty, p. 25.

92. Hoyt, *The Battle of Leyte Gulf*, p. 102, states that Japanese aircraft damaged the destroyer *Leutze*, the oiler *Ashtabula*, and LST 552 as well as accounting for the *Princeton*. The *Leutze* suffered eleven casualties when hit in a bombing-strafing run. See *DANFS*, IV, p. 95. The *Ashtabula* is stated to have been hit by a torpedo but incurred no casualties and was not forced out of action. She undertook repairs in San Pedro between 17 December 1944 and 26 January 1945, which would suggest that her damage was most modest. See *DANFS*, I, p. 67. But these units were off Leyte and were not attacked in the course of these efforts off Luzon between 0830 and 0930. Potter, *Burke*, p. 198, states that Sherman's group accounted for seventy-six Japanese aircraft in this phase of the battle.

93. Woodward, p. 56. Morison, p. 178. Harry A. Gailey, *The War in the Pacific: From Pearl Harbor to Tokyo Bay*, p. 357.

94. Hoyt, *The Battle of Leyte Gulf*, pp. 107–108. Woodward, p. 57. Roger Chesneau, *Aircraft Carriers of the World, 1914 to the Present: An Illustrated Encyclopedia*, p. 233. Prados, p. 625. Theodore Taylor, *The Magnificent Mitscher*, p. 257.

95. Hoyt, *The Battle of Leyte Gulf*, pp. 109, 112. Morison, p. 178. Prados, p. 625. Woodward, pp. 57–58. *DANFS*, V, p. 385.

96. Hoyt, *The Battle of Leyte Gulf*, p. 113.

97. The *Irwin* rescued 646 men from the sea. See *DANFS*, III, p. 461. The *Morrison* "picked up approximately four hundred survivors in an hour and a half." See *DANFS*, IV, p. 439. The *Reno* is cited as having rescued survivors, but presumably these were few because she remained with Task Group 38.3 whereas the *Irwin* and *Morrison* proceeded to Ulithi, arriving on 27 October. See *DANFS*, VI, pp. 73–74.

98. Naval Staff, pp. 81–82. Woodward, p. 67.

99. Hoyt, *The Battle of Leyte Gulf*, p. 114.

100. Hoyt, *The Battle of Leyte Gulf*, pp. 115–119. Morison, pp. 179–181. Woodward, pp. 67–69.

101. Hoyt, *The Battle of Leyte Gulf*, pp. 121–122. Woodward, p. 69. Naval Staff, p. 80.

102. *DANFS*, V, p. 385. The *Birmingham* was obliged to return to Mare Island navy yard where her repairs were completed in January 1945. See *DANFS*, I, p. 125. She left the formation in the company of the *Gatling*, *Irwin* and the *Morrison*. See ADM 199.1493, pp. 231 and 251. The same source, p. 256, gives slightly different figures for the *Birmingham*'s casualties and gives those of the *Princeton* as seven killed, 101 missing, and 190 wounded.

103. Morison, p. 182, gives the time of this decision as 1600 but the *Princeton* entry in *DANFS*, V, p. 385, is for 1604. The *Princeton*'s captain left the ship at 1638.

104. Hoyt, *The Battle of Leyte Gulf*, p. 123. Morison, pp. 182–183. Woodward, p. 73.

105. Hoyt, *The Battle of Leyte Gulf*, pp. 123–124. Morison, p. 183. Interestingly, the account of these proceedings in Hoyt's *The Battle of Leyte Gulf* occupies 16.5 pages (pp. 107–124) and Morison affords 6.5 pages (pp. 177–183). Field allows four lines of text and one five-line footnote (p. 62).

The timing and coordinates of her sinking were given at 1750 in 15°12'North 123°35'East. See ADM 199.1494, pp. 6 and 28, with a variation of one minute of longitude.

106. The point made by Cutler, p. 154.

107. Ito, p. 145. Woodward, pp. 129–132. See also Field, p. 47, which gives a detailed account of Ozawa's calculations on 23 October. This states that Ozawa intended to conduct reconnaissance at 0545 (24 October) and if the enemy was encountered there would be a strike mission that morning. If no American force was encountered, Ozawa's formation was to continue southward and conduct a second reconnaissance at 1300 and the appropriate strike if the enemy was found. If Japanese efforts failed to lure the Americans northward, the battleships *Hyuga* and *Ise*, and their escorting screen, might then be sent forward in the hope of forcing some form of night action, but if all these failed to draw American attention away from Leyte, Samar, the San Bernardino Strait, and Kurita, then Ozawa supposedly was ready to proceed to a position off Samar in the hope of undertaking some form of offensive action on the following morning. The gist of this is given in Hoyt, *The Battle of Leyte Gulf*, p. 162. See also Morison, p. 187.

108. Cutler, p. 116.

109. Field, p. 62. This states that Ozawa received a contact report of an American force off northeast Luzon, which was obviously erroneous, and at 0910 a second record of an American force, with four carriers and about ten other ships, north of the Legaspi peninsula. Cutler, p. 154, makes reference only to the 0820 report, noting that it placed the Americans some eighty miles from their true position, but he also states, p. 142, that Ozawa's search aircraft contacted Task Group 38.3 at 0700.

110. Cutler, p. 154. Field, p. 62, states that the Americans were found on a bearing of 210 degrees and at a distance of 180 miles from the Japanese force. Woodward, p. 132,

does not give figures but states that the attack force "was made up of . . . all the Japanese had except for a small and inadequate air cover of twenty fighters which were kept over the fleet."

111. See, for example, Cutler, p. 155, Field, pp. 63, 166, Ito, pp. 146–147, and Prados, p. 650. Presumably the low number of torpedo-bombers in this attack reflected, at least in part, the numbers committed to the reconnaissance missions that morning.

112. Polmar, p. 391, states that Ozawa's carriers were left with just nineteen fighters, five Zeke fighter-bombers, four torpedo-bombers, and one Judy dive-bomber. In fact, the Japanese carriers retained twenty-two fighters, eight Zeke fighter-bombers, fifteen Jill and four Kate torpedo-bombers, and five Judy dive-bombers, which would be the total deduced from the original table of establishment less those committed to this attack. It should be noted, however, that Prados, p. 645, states that on 21 October the carriers lost three aircraft, though one may have crash-landed on the *Zuikaku* just before dusk on 24 October.

113. Details of losses are difficult to determine. Woodward, p. 133, states that some returned to the carriers, and of the remainder "from thirty to forty" which survived the action with the American fighters landed on Luzon. For the description of the action, see pp. 65–66. Field, p. 63, states that thirty reached Luzon and three returned to their carriers. Hoyt, *The Battle of Leyte Gulf*, pp. 165–166, gives no figures but notes that American carrier aircraft must have accounted for at least 150 Japanese aircraft on 24 October. Ito, p. 147, states that the aircraft from the light carriers encountered American fighters "near the target area" and proceeded to Clark Field. Ito claims that the *Zuikaku's* aircraft attacked American warships, damaging one fleet and one light carrier, then flew to Clark Field, and that three aircraft returned to their carriers. Seemingly the only references to Japanese aircraft in action with American warships are Morison, p. 180, which states that six to eight Judys—not that there were eight Judys in this force—attacked the *Essex*, *Lexington* and the *Langley*, and Hoyt, *The Battle of Leyte Gulf*, p. 113, which states that the light cruiser *Reno* "shot down the Japanese planes that were moving in." Woodward, p. 70, states that Sherman's force accounted for 167 Japanese aircraft on 24 October and that five Judys evaded the combat air patrol and attacked the *Essex*, but without result and at the cost of two of their number, and another attacked the *Lexington*. Neither Hoyt nor Woodward states when these episodes took place and it is not clear if these Japanese aircraft were supposed to have come from Ozawa's carriers or Luzon; if they were carrier aircraft, the fact passed unnoticed.

Most of these accounts seem to suggest that the Japanese aircraft either were ordered to make or made for Clark Field, but Admiralty, p. 35, indicates that they were directed to Nichols Field. The source of all information given as definitive in this and the previous note was the e-mail of Dr. Tohmatsu Haruo to the author, 22 January 2002; the total of thirty-nine aircraft making their way to airfields on Luzon is the author's calculation based on the other figures.

114. Cutler, pp. 156–157. Potter, *Burke*, p. 200.

115. Cutler, pp. 154–155. Prados, pp. 646–647. Woodward, p. 132. Hoyt, *The Battle of Leyte Gulf*, pp. 160–161. It appears that the *Zuikaku's* transmitter was not working properly and that her signals were not being received at Combined Fleet headquarters. Presumably, this was the reason she failed to attract American attention.

116. Cutler, p. 146. Field, p. 66. Woodward, p. 85. Hoyt, *The Battle of Leyte Gulf*, p. 146, quoting Ugaki (p. 489), states that she was afforded a single destroyer as escort, but this is misleading. Prados, p. 639, states that she reached Coron Bay the next day and left on 26 October for Brunei, with the *Naganami* as escort. The latter had been previously detached as escort for the *Takao*. The *Myoko*, after temporary repairs at Singapore, was severely

damaged on 13 December when off the Royalist Bank, off southern Indo-China in the South China Sea, by the U.S. submarine *Bergall*. She was towed to Singapore but was never repaired and was surrendered to the British. See Jentschura, p. 83. See also Whitley, *Cruisers*, p. 177, though it needs to be noted that this source wrongly states that the *Myoko* was torpedoed on 25 October.

117. William H. Garzke, Jr., and Robert O. Dulin, Jr., *Battleships: Axis and Neutral Battleships of World War II*, p. 58. Ugaki, pp. 489–490. Field, p. 69, states that the damage inflicted on the *Nagato*—which seems to have been primarily to her radio facilities—reduced her speed, and that of the battle line, to twenty-four knots.

118. Field, p. 69, states that the *Haruna* was hit by a single bomb and that the light cruiser *Yahagi* was damaged by a series of near-misses that temporarily slowed her to twenty-two knots. Woodward, p. 85, states that the *Yamato* was hit by four bombs and the *Nagato* sustained "some damage to her communications system." Hoyt, *The Battle of Leyte Gulf*, pp. 147–148, states that the *Nagato* was hit amidships by two bombs and that the *Haruna* was damaged by near-misses. Garzke, p. 58, states that the *Nagato* was hit by two bombs and that the *Haruna* was damaged by five near-misses.

119. Admiralty, p. 31, names this destroyer as the *Kiyoshimo*, and it notes that she was "reported damaged." It also states that the *Myoko* was forced to return to Singapore but that "with the possible exception of the *Yahagi* no other cruisers were damaged." Naval Staff, p. 82, states that the *Yahagi* and *Kiyoshimo* "also received minor damage."

120. Admiralty, p. 30. Field, p. 63, uses these "guesstimates."

121. Halsey's own comment was that the report "proved to be dangerously optimistic but we had little reason to discredit them [*sic*] at the time." See William F. Halsey and J. Bryan III, *Admiral Halsey's Story*, p. 216. James M. Merrill, *A Sailor's Admiral: A Biography of William F. Halsey*, p. 154. But surely the point was that Mitscher for one retained certain doubts; one suspects that here was filter-up, filter-out.

122. Yoshimura, p. 150.

123. Both formations had six battleships and cruisers in their inner rings. Kurita had seven destroyers and Shima six. There are only two sources that give diagrammatic representation of the Japanese deployment, and they differ with reference to which ships occupied which positions. These sources are Ito, p. 124, and Sato, I, p. 852.

124. These figures, taken from Rohwer, p. 311, give totals of 98 Hellcats, 77 Helldivers, and 76 Avengers, for an overall total of 251 aircraft. The conventional count is Morison's (p. 184) total of 259 aircraft, but individual numbers are incomplete.

125. See, for example, Garzke, pp. 67–73.

126. Admiralty, p. 31, and reference to Interrogation No. 41, pp. 170–172. It should be noted, moreover, that certain of the attacks were fragmented with aircraft from the same formation attacking over quite long periods. There are references, therefore, to the fifth and sixth attacks on the *Musashi* when there were but four, at most three plus two.

127. Garzke, p. 73. It should be noted, however, that this source indicates that the *Musashi* was hit by seventeen bombs but lists eighteen; the last one has been double-recorded (see p. 71).

128. Prados, p. 641.

129. Garzke, pp. 69–70. Yoshimura, pp. 157, 166.

130. Cutler, pp. 146–147. It should also be noted that one of the guns jammed with the result that one turret was silent during the second of the two salvoes that were fired.

131. The *Musashi* was hit in each of the first four attacks, initially by a single torpedo on the starboard beam, then by three torpedoes and two bombs along her port side, then by two torpedoes to port and one to starboard and, in the fourth attack, apparently first

by single torpedo hits on each side and then by three torpedoes to starboard. In human terms the losses incurred in these attacks were considerable. The *Musashi* had aboard personnel from the *Maya* who had been rescued after their ship had been sunk, and these were topside. In addition, of course, there were the many machine-gun positions, none of which could be afforded protection. With American fighters joining attacks with strafing runs, casualties in the *Musashi* were heavy, Yoshimura noting that in the third attack "torrential waves from the explosions crashed over the main decks, sweeping a tide of blood and dismembered bodies before them." With first aid and operating posts full, the fourth attack resulted in a bomb hit near the bow that killed scores of doctors and wounded crewmen in the forward infirmary. See H. P. Willmott, *Battleship*, p. 201.

132. Yoshimura, p. 165.

133. Cutler, p. 148. Garzke, p. 71. Yoshimura, p. 167.

134. Field, p. 69.

135. Yoshimura, p. 167. San José is on the northern coast of east Mindoro. Hoyt, *The Battle of Leyte Gulf*, p. 148 (quoting Ugaki, p. 490), states that the *Musashi* was ordered to Manila in the company of the destroyer *Kiyoshimo*.

136. Garzke, p. 72. Prados, p. 641. Yoshimura, p. 167.

137. Western histories that set out accounts of this episode pass over the numbers and fate of the men from the *Maya* in the *Musashi*.

Yoshimura (p. 157) states that a total of 769 officers and men from the heavy cruiser had been transferred to the battleship. Ugaki, p. 491, states that the *Musashi* transferred the crew of the *Maya* to a destroyer that came alongside, but Yoshimura makes no reference to such an eventuality, though he notes (p. 167) that Kurita did indeed order the destroyer *Shimakaze* to take personnel from the *Maya* off the *Musashi*. According to Fukuda, pp. 165–166, the *Shimakaze* did indeed come alongside the *Musashi* and took off 607 survivors from the *Maya*. She then returned to Kurita's formation and served out the remainder of the battle. This seems extraordinary given the number of men in her during these days. Fukuda states that with the *Hamakaze* and *Kiyoshimo* recovering a total of 1,329 men from the water, the killed and missing numbered 1,179, of whom 117 were from the *Maya*. (Source: e-mail of 3 December 2003 from Tohmatsu Haruo.) Garzke, p. 73, states that a total of 1,023 officers and men were lost, but this figure would seem to relate only to personnel from the *Musashi* and not the *Musashi* and *Maya*.

138. Yoshimura, pp. 168–169.

139. Yoshimura, p. 170. Cutler, p. 154.

140. Yoshimura, p. 176. There seems to be no end of differences in the various accounts of which ships were involved in rescue operations. For example, there are references that the *Hamakaze*, which had been "seriously damaged by near misses," relieved the *Shimakaze* and with the *Kiyoshima* took survivors back to Coron Bay, and there are references that the *Hamakaze* and *Kiyoshimo* took survivors from the *Musashi* to Brunei; Yoshimura asserts that the *Shimakaze* and *Kiyoshima* took survivors to Corregidor.

What happened is that the *Hamakaze*, which indeed had been damaged by near-misses, relieved the *Shimakaze* and she and the *Kiyoshimo* respectively rescued about 850 and 500 survivors from the sunken *Musashi*; they then headed for Coron. The *Kiyoshimo* arrived at 1130 and the *Hamakaze* at 1306 on 25 October. There the two destroyers took on oil from the stricken *Myoko* and then sailed to Corregidor, where the survivors from the *Musashi* were landed. Fukuda, pp. 165–166. Sato, II, p. 40. E-mail of 4 December 2003 from Tohmatsu Haruo.

141. Garzke, p. 74.

142. Admiralty, p. 31.

143. Garzke, pp. 73–74.
144. Garzke, p. 73. Prados, p. 641.
145. Cutler, p. 163. Morison, p. 184.
146. Field, pp. 70–71 for text of Kurita's signal of 1600.
147. Prados, p. 641. Hoyt, *The Battle of Leyte Gulf*, p. 149.
148. Ugaki, p. 490.
149. Prados, p. 641. Wheeler, p. 397.
150. Hoyt, *The Battle of Leyte Gulf*, pp. 153–154. Potter, *Burke*, p. 202. Woodward, pp. 71–72.
151. Admiralty, p. 36.
152. Prados, p. 649.
153. Cutler, p. 150. Morison, p. 187. Potter, *Burke*, p. 201.
154. Halsey, p. 215. Reynolds, p. 266. The author was long convinced that the search to the east was primarily the result of arguments expressed by junior officers on Mitscher's staff, but the only reference to be found concerning this matter is Woodward, pp. 138–139, and reference is to Lieutenants E. Calvert Cheston and Byron R. White.
155. Admiralty, p. 36.
156. Cutler, p. 162. Potter, *Burke*, p. 202. Woodward, pp. 64–66.
157. Morison, p. 198.
158. Cutler, pp. 160–161. Potter, *Burke*, p. 201. Reynolds, p. 266.
159. Cutler, p. 161. Reynolds, p. 266.
160. Merrill, p. 157.
161. This account is taken from Potter's biography of Burke, but the details outlined here are disputed. Woodward, pp. 72–73, states that Mitscher and Burke concluded that one of the Japanese groups consisted of four battleships or heavy cruisers, five (presumably light) cruisers, and six destroyers, and the other of two *Shokaku*-class carriers, one light carrier, one light cruiser, and three destroyers. The inaccuracies of numbers and type need little in the way of elaboration, but when this assessment was sent to Halsey, the latter "concluded that (Ozawa's force) was disposed in two groups, estimated to contain a total of at least seventeen ships and possibly as many as 24 ships." With four battleships and twelve cruisers seemingly identified, the basis of Burke's suggestion seems somewhat nebulous, by the least exacting standard.
162. Hoyt, *The Battle of Leyte Gulf*, p. 179. Potter, *Burke*, p. 204. Woodward, p. 74.
163. Woodward, p. 73.
164. Admiralty, p. 39.
165. Admiralty, p. 37. The formation had seventeen units, namely the four carriers, two battleships, three light cruisers, and eight destroyers and destroyer escorts.
166. Halsey, pp. 216–217. Merrill, p. 155.
167. Admiralty, p. 38. Cutler, pp. 162–163. Hoyt, *The Battle of Leyte Gulf*, pp. 181–182. Woodward, pp. 79–80.
168. Cutler, pp. 164–165, Potter, *Burke*, p. 173. Woodward, p. 30.
169. Cutler, pp. 136–138. Reynolds, p. 267. Woodward, pp. 80–81.
170. Cutler, p. 160. Hoyt, *The Battle of Leyte Gulf*, p. 174. Wheeler, pp. 398–399.
171. A point made, *sotto voce*, in Reynolds, p. 266, but more explicitly three pages later. On p. 269, Reynolds noted the division of the battle force and observed, with reference to the retention of two battleships with Task Group 38.3, Kinkaid's observation that this arrangement "was exactly correct in the circumstances." But the point is that the presence of the *Hyuga* and *Ise* was not known when Halsey gave his warning order.
172. See, for example, Cutler, p. 159.

173. Prados, p. 682. Wheeler, p. 461. Stephen Howarth, *Men of War: Great Naval Leaders of World War II*, p. 240. See Merrill, pp. 171–172, for an alternative view of King's opinion on these matters, but the final comment must be King's own published statement, to be found in Ernest J. King and Walter Muir Whitehill, *Fleet Admiral King. A Naval Record*, p. 371, with its stringent condemnation of Kinkaid.

174. Reynolds, p. 267.

175. Cutler, p. 163.

176. Reynolds, p. 267.

177. Merrill, p. 255.

178. The turn back to the east was at 1714. See Prados, p. 642. Hoyt, *The Battle of Leyte Gulf*, p. 155; Ito, p. 132; and Morison, p. 189, give the time as 1715. Cutler, p. 152, states that at 1715 Kurita decided to reverse course.

179. Prados, p. 642. Cutler, p. 211.

180. Cutler, p. 170.

181. Cutler, p. 211. Morison, p. 189. Wheeler, p. 400.

182. Prados, p. 649.

183. Prados, p. 634.

184. Merrill, p. 160.

185. Morison, p. 245. Woodward, p. 163.

186. Field, p. 91. Merrill, p. 161. Wheeler, p. 400.

187. Cutler, p. 120. Potter, *Burke*, p. 193. Woodward, p. 30.

188. Cutler, p. 121. Howarth, pp. 237–238. Potter, *Burke*, p. 194. It is worth noting that had Halsey's inquiry been answered then he might well never have been able to move to the west. On the previous day, 20 October, the Australian heavy cruiser *Shropshire* snagged a mine in her paravane in the Surigao Strait, but fortunately for the cruiser it failed to explode. See ADM 199.153, pp. 445–448. M/S 0613/45. Report by secretary of Australian naval board, Melbourne, to Admiralty, 1 November 1944. See also Cutler, p. 178, and Hoyt, *The Battle of Leyte Gulf*, p. 43, referring to mines in the Strait.

189. See, for example, Potter, *Nimitz*, p. 331.

190. It is perhaps worth noting one comment from this same source as not untypical of the accounts of these proceedings of dubious worth: "Having been forbidden to go looking for the Japanese fleet and the Japanese fleet being apparently unwilling to come to him, Halsey decided to do the next best thing: send his carrier groups to the nearest anchorage to re-provision and re-arm and get some rest for his men." See Potter, *Nimitz*, p. 331. No comment on these observations is necessary.

191. Merrill, p. 158. Wheeler, p. 404.

192. Jack Sweetman, ed., *Great American Naval Battles*, p. 347. Cutler, pp. 59–60. Potter, *Nimitz*, pp. 325–326. Woodward, p. 28. The full text of this exchange is never given, but in Nimitz's report, "Battle for Leyte Gulf. 24–26 October," which was submitted as Annex A to the report for October 1944, the text is given thus in para. 13: "The Joint Chiefs of Staff gave directions that CincPac furnish necessary fleet support to operations (including Leyte and western Pacific) by forces of the South West Pacific. Forces of Pacific Ocean Areas will cover and support forces of South West Pacific. West Pacific Task Forces (Third Fleet) will destroy enemy naval and air forces in or threatening the Philippines area, and protect the air and sea communications along the central Pacific axis. In case opportunity for destruction of major portions of the enemy fleet offers or can be created, such destruction becomes the primary task (of all POA forces). Necessary measures for detailed co-ordination of operations between the West Pacific Task Forces and forces of the South West Pacific will be arranged by their respective commanders."

Perhaps more interestingly, the next paragraph states that prior to the action, Halsey "indicated by despatch that he considered operating in the China Sea, and that he felt restricted by the necessity for covering the South West Pacific forces (in the Leyte area)." Nimitz indicated to Halsey quite clearly that there could be "no change in the tasks set forth in Operation Plan No. 8–44." Even allowing for the fact that this report was by Nimitz, the use of the word "necessity" does seem significant, as was the use of the term "he felt." It was not a case, it would seem, of "he thought." One makes no further comment.

193. Cutler, p. 237. Halsey, p. 217. Howarth, p. 239.

194. Merrill, p. 156. Potter, *Nimitz*, pp. 325–326.

195. Cutler, p. 170. Morison, p. 193. Potter, *Burke*, p. 204.

196. Admiralty, pp. 33–34.

197. Admiralty, p. 39.

198. Ibid. It is easy to lose sight of the fact that the last contact report was of a Japanese force in 18°10'North 125°30'East as early as 1755. This placed the Japanese force about 240 miles north of the American midnight position. Given the events of next day, one wonders if fuel economy was not a real consideration at this point.

199. Hoyt, *The Battle of Leyte Gulf*, pp. 310–311. Polmar, p. 392. Reynolds, pp. 270–271. It is not exactly clear how many aircraft were launched by the *Independence*, but the reference to one aircraft obviously was the one that renewed contact. The *Independence* had been ordered to fly off five search aircraft. See Halsey, p. 217. Woodward, pp. 135–137, gives the times of contact as 0208 and 0238, and states that two night fighters from the *Enterprise* shot down one Mavis soon after 0140.

200. Cutler, pp. 170–171.

201. Cutler, pp. 207–208.

202. Cutler, pp. 212–213. Howarth, p. 261. Reynolds, pp. 269–270.

203. Merrill, p. 160.

204. Cutler, pp. 210–212. Potter, *Burke*, p. 206. Reynolds, p. 270.

205. Hoyt, *The Battle of Leyte Gulf*, p. 185. Merrill, p. 159. Reynolds, p. 270.

206. Cutler, p. 172. Hoyt, *The Battle of Leyte Gulf*, p. 157. Ugaki, p. 491.

207. Woodward, pp. 83–84.

208. Cutler, p. 206, seems to be the only account that makes this point. Potter, *Burke*, p. 208, does not. It is quite incredible that Halsey should claim to have been concerned lest any carrier force that eluded him by advancing to the west between the American carriers and Luzon should "join the Center Force in its attack on Leyte Gulf." The geography of this is wholly improbable, even by the least exacting of standards.

209. Cutler, pp. 149–151. Hoyt, *The Battle of Leyte Gulf*, pp. 150–151.

210. Prados, p. 641.

211. The precise wording of the Toyoda signal is elusive. Cutler, p. 152; D'Albas, p. 201; Field, p. 72; Hoyt, *The Battle of Leyte Gulf*, p. 155; Ito, p. 132; Morison, p. 189; and Woodward, p. 87, give seven different versions of this signal, and there is confusion in that it is not clear whether the reference is to one force, i.e., Kurita, or all forces, i.e., Kurita and the other naval and air formations.

The translation used in the text was provided by an e-mail of 3 December 2003 by Tohmatsu Haruo. The word-for-word translation is as follows: *Tenyu* assistance of heaven; *Wo* objective indicator; *Kakushin* firm belief, confidence; *Shi* variation of the verb "to be," therefore *Tenyu wo kakushin shi* Trust in divine aid. *Zengun* all forces; *Totsugeki* charge, *Seyo* imperative suffix, therefore *totsugeki seyo* Charge! A free translation might be: "Be assured of Heaven's assistance. All formations: onward/forward to the attack." One would admit that, apart from the "Up, Guards, and at 'em" parallel, this does not readily translate into English.

It should be noted that while this signal states "all forces," it was directed solely to Kurita. One suspects that according to present military vocabulary, *zengun* might translate as "all units."

212. Ito, pp. 132–133.

213. Field, p. 71. Hoyt, *The Battle of Leyte Gulf*, p. 155. Morison, p. 189. Prados, p. 642.

214. Cutler, p. 152. Hoyt, *The Battle of Leyte Gulf*, p. 155. Ugaki, p. 491.

215. Hoyt, *The Battle of Leyte Gulf*, p. 151. Morison, p. 189. Prados gives the time of this signal as 2020. Oddly, 1100 was the same time Halsey and his staff believed Kurita would be in Leyte Gulf if his force turned to the east around midnight—see Reynolds, pp. 267–268—but such a calculation was based on the assumption that Kurita's formation would move at full speed, and in any case ignored the fact that Kurita's formation had already come back onto its original eastward course.

216. Hoyt, *The Battle of Leyte Gulf*, p. 151.

217. Field, pp. 115–116. Woodward, p. 206.

218. Cutler, pp. 255–268. Hoyt, *The Battle of Leyte Gulf*, p. 167. The first *kamikaze* formation was raised on 20 October from within the 201st Air Group, which was based at Mabalacat airfield, which was a part of Clark Field.

219. Prados, p. 642.

220. Morison, p. 208. The time of 0008 was one minute after the moon set. See Prados, p. 661.

221. Two battleships of 69,400 tons, one fleet carrier of 25,675 tons, three light carriers of 33,642 tons, four heavy cruisers of 38,006 tons and one light cruiser of 5,100 tons, five destroyers of 9,402 tons, and one submarine of 2,140 tons.

222. With apologies to the Book of Revelation of St. John the Divine, chapter VI, verse 17.

6. THE GREAT DAY OF WRATH

1. Potter, *Burke*, p. 208. According to this account, Burke dealt with Carney, Halsey's chief of staff, and it was the latter who ordered the search. In E. B. Potter, *Bull Halsey*, p. 331, the exchange was between Burke and Halsey, who ordered the search.

2. Morison, p. 318.

3. Potter, *Burke*, p. 209.

4. Morison, p. 322.

5. Potter, *Burke*, p. 209.

6. See, for example, Field, p. 75, and not the twenty-two as cited in Hoyt, *The Battle of Leyte Gulf*, p. 241.

7. Woodward, p. 87.

8. Field, pp. 76–77.

9. Woodward, p. 88.

10. Morison, pp. 208, 230.

11. Morison, pp. 207–208. Woodward, pp. 99–100.

12. Cutler, p. 184. Prados, p. 661.

13. Morison, p. 209.

14. Field, p. 82.

15. Wheeler, p. 398.

16. Fukuda, p. 216.

17. Ito, p. 133. Woodward, p. 92. Note the comment, "A likely explanation for Nishimura's actions at Surigao Strait was that he felt the weight of responsibility heavily, in the same sense as those who were beginning to flock to join the *kamikaze* corps. It was a cultural trait that valued heroism amid tragedy, what some Western analysts have termed the 'nobility of failure.'" See Prados, p. 658.

18. Ito, p. 134.

19. Cutler, p. 184.

20. Field, p. 83, and Nishimura's 242013 October signal to the effect that his formation would be off Dulag at 0400, ninety minutes before dawn as defined in his original orders.

21. Woodward, p. 94. Cohen, p. 245.

22. Field, p. 86.

23. Morison, p. 203.

24. Cutler, p. 174. Two other destroyer formations, the 48th Destroyer Squadron with eight destroyers and the 49th Destroyer Squadron with nine, had escorted the transports to Leyte. The first formation had already left the area with their charges. See *DANFS*, VIII, p. 61. But the second was still on station (see *DANFS*, VIII, p. 296) and presumably could have been brought forward had Oldendorf considered this necessary.

25. Cutler, p. 175. Presumably this assessment pooled the two Japanese formations making their way to the Surigao Strait. Together these totaled two battleships, three heavy cruisers, one light cruiser, and eight destroyers. In addition, there were two more destroyers at large, the *Hatsuharu* and the *Hatsushimo*, so numbers were close to reality, but just what units were seen and reported is difficult to discern.

26. In this text the American cruiser forces are referred to as the western and eastern formations.

27. This was the formation that had been obliged to detach the *Australia* and *Warramunga*; the other cruiser formation had shed the *Honolulu*.

28. Cutler, p. 175.

29. Morison, p. 223.

30. Thus assigned were the *McNair* and *Mertz*. See *DANFS*, IV, pp. 306 and 339.

31. Woodward, p. 99.

32. Woodward, p. 96.

33. See, for example, Cutler, pp. 182–184.

34. Woodward, p. 99. The 10°North limitation was imposed by Kinkaid. See full text of signal in Hoyt, *The Battle of Leyte Gulf*, p. 174.

35. Cutler, p. 180.

36. Woodward, p. 95.

37. Fire, and plenty of it, are essential characteristics of American fighting, but one notes that on 18 October in response to having been hit by one shell fired by a Japanese artillery piece on Leyte, the destroyer *Goldsborough* fired no fewer than 258 rounds in twenty-five minutes. See Hoyt, *The Battle of Leyte Gulf*, p. 17.

38. Woodward, p. 96.

39. Woodward, p. 96.

40. Woodward, p. 98.

41. See, for example, Cutler, p. 182, and Morison, p. 202. The full text is provided in Hoyt, *The Battle of Leyte Gulf*, p. 191.

42. Cutler, p. 182.

43. Cutler, p. 188. Morison, pp. 208, 210. Woodward, p. 99.

44. Morison, p. 210.

45. Cutler, p. 190. Woodward, p. 104.

46. Morison, p. 214. One finds this claim difficult to sustain given that the range is given as 8,720 yards, whereas almost five minutes later the range from launch to projected target was stated to be 8,200 to 9,300 yards.

47. Cutler, p. 192. Morison, p. 215.

48. Cutler, p. 191. Morison, p. 215.

49. Morison, p. 216.

50. Field, p. 90. Ito, p. 136. Morison, p. 216. Prados, p. 661.

51. Morison, p. 215. Herein is a problem because so many of the early sources, such as D'Albas, Field, and Woodward, and later Breyer and Cutler, state that it was the *Yamashiro* that was hit and fell out of line and that it was the *Fuso* that continued north only to be overwhelmed by fire from the Allied battleships and cruisers. Japanese sources are unequivocal on the matter: it was the *Fuso* that fell out of line and the *Yamashiro* that continued northward.

52. Morison, p. 216.

53. Woodward, p. 121.

54. Field, p. 90. Hoyt, *The Battle of Leyte Gulf,* p. 232. Morison, p. 232. Woodward, p. 122.

55. Cutler, p. 190. Hoyt, *The Battle of Leyte Gulf,* p. 217. Morison, pp. 217, 219.

56. Cutler, p. 193. Morison, p. 218.

57. Hoyt, *The Battle of Leyte Gulf,* p. 218. Morison, p. 219.

58. Morison, p. 220.

59. Woodward, p. 108. Interestingly, Prados, p. 661, makes no mention of this second torpedo hit and seems to imply that the *Michishio* succumbed as a result of one torpedo hit.

60. Cutler, p. 195. Woodward, p. 109.

61. Morison, p. 221.

62. Hoyt, *The Battle of Leyte Gulf,* p. 220. Morison, p. 222.

63. Paul S. Dull, *A Battle History of the Imperial Japanese Navy (1941–1945),* pp. 319–320.

64. A comment courtesy of Edward Drea in a review of a book the title of which has proved elusive.

65. Cutler, p. 197. Morison, p. 227. Woodward, p. 113. It is perhaps worth reference *en passant,* but the *Phoenix* was to be sunk in another war, at another time. As the *General Belgrano* she was sunk on 2 May 1982 in the South Atlantic.

66. Morison, p. 227. Hoyt, *The Battle of Leyte Gulf,* p. 227, states that the *Columbia* alone fired 1,100 rounds. For the cruisers to have used so much ammunition meant an average rate of fire of thirty-four rounds a minute per ship. The heavy cruisers had nine 8-in. guns and the light cruisers twelve 6-in. guns. Prados, p. 661, states that the cruisers, presumably the two sets, fired "about 4,300 shells."

67. Woodward, p. 114. Morison, p. 224, does not give complete salvo figures. Admiralty, p. 57, does.

68. See D'Albas, p. 202, Field, p. 87, Woodward, p. 105, and also Siegfried Breyer, *Battleships and Battle Cruisers, 1905–1970. Historical Development of the Capital Ship,* p. 341, Cutler, p. 199, and M. J. Whitley, *Battleships of World War II: An International Encyclopedia,* p. 193.

69. Exactly as recounted as per Prados, pp. 661–662, and confirmed by the e-mail of Tohmatsu Haruo of 25 October 2002.

70. This is asserted in various histories but nonetheless seems beyond belief. The 0319 explosion was seen in the *Louisville* (see Woodward, p. 109), which must have been thirty miles to the north. How it was not seen in the *Yamashiro* is difficult to discern.

71. Field, p. 87. Ito, p. 136. Morison, p. 217.

72. Ito, p. 137. Woodward, pp. 108–109.

73. Garzke, p. 104.

74. Breyer, pp. 140, 149. Ian Sturton, *All the World's Battleships: 1906 to the Present*, pp. 76, 78. Whitley, *Battleships*, pp. 103, 111. There is slight variation in the number of hits these two battleships sustained, but the basic point is correct. The *Fuso* was broken in two and engulfed by flames as a result of a single torpedo hit.

75. Morison, p. 232.

76. Morison, p. 228.

77. Cutler, p. 199. Morison, p. 228. Woodward, pp. 115–116.

78. Morison, p. 220.

79. Morison, p. 229. Prados, p. 662.

80. Morison, p. 221. When she was first hit and it was realized she might well be sunk, she fired off all her torpedoes in the general direction of the enemy, but there is no evidence to suggest that she hit anything. The *Newcomb* and *Leary* stood by her and she was towed into the Gulf where she underwent sufficient repair to enable her to proceed, via Pearl Harbor, to Mare Island navy yard. She returned to operational duties with the landings in Brunei Bay and at Balikpapan in June and July 1945. See *DANFS*, I, pp. 23–24.

81. Woodward, pp. 114–115.

82. Morison, p. 229.

83. Cutler, p. 197. Dull, p. 320. Morison, p. 222, cites a survivor from the *Yamashiro* who stated that the battleship was hit by four torpedoes, but prior to this time she had been hit by two. One assumes, if this individual was correct, that she was hit twice in this last attack.

84. Morison, p. 229. Woodward, p. 120.

85. Woodward, p. 119.

86. Morison, p. 229.

87. *DANFS*, IV, p. 258.

88. Woodward, p. 113.

89. Field, p. 92. Morison, p. 232, states that the four destroyers were in line abreast of the two heavy cruisers, but the subsequent description of the action that followed does not make sense because they would have been between the *Ashigara* and *Nachi* and the targets to the north and hence in direct line of the torpedoes fired by the cruisers.

90. Cutler, pp. 200–201. Shima had yet to encounter the *Mogami*, so Nishino's rationalization is necessarily flawed. See also Woodward, p. 122. Hoyt, *The Battle of Leyte Gulf*, pp. 238–239, states that the *Shigure* was stopped and making repairs when the *Nachi* was encountered, but that was not the case. The enforced halt came later.

91. Cutler, p. 202. Field, p. 92. Morison, pp. 232–233.

92. Accounts of this collision seem to be perversely varied. Cutler, p. 203, states that the *Nachi* "left a good portion of her port bow aboard (the) *Mogami*." Morison, p. 233, states that the stern of the *Nachi* was badly damaged, thereby implying that the *Mogami* rammed the *Nachi*. Field, p. 92, and Woodward, p. 123, state that the *Nachi* was holed on her port side, while Ito, p. 142, states that the roles were reversed with the *Nachi* putting a hole in the port side of the *Mogami*. Prados, p. 662, states that the *Nachi*'s starboard bow was breached and anchor windlass compartment flooded and the ship's speed was reduced

to eighteen knots. Hoyt, *The Battle of Leyte Gulf*, p. 235, states that the *Mogami*'s bow "crashed into the *Nachi*'s port quarter at an angle of about ten degrees into the anchor windlass room which flooded, and then into the steering room which began to flood."

93. Field, p. 92. Woodward, p. 123. It should be noted, however, that Morison, p. 232, states that the destroyers were recalled at 0425 without their having been given the opportunity to fire their torpedoes.

94. Cutler, p. 203. Morison, p. 233. Woodward, p. 123.

95. Field, p. 91. Woodward, p. 116.

96. Woodward, p. 124.

97. Tohmatsu Haruo, e-mail, 25 October 2002.

98. Woodward, pp. 124–125.

99. Hoyt, *The Battle of Leyte Gulf*, pp. 228–229.

100. Woodward, p. 125.

101. Morison, p. 234.

102. Woodward, p. 126. These units were the *Columbia* and *Denver*, and the *Claxton*, *Cony* and the *Thorn*. Morison, p. 237, states that the *Cony* and *Sigourney* were involved in an exchange of fire with the *Asagumo* before the two light cruisers came on the scene. Prados, p. 663, states that the *Bennion* was involved in this action, and also that the *Asagumo*'s captain, after a day in the water, came ashore on Panaon and was captured by Filipino guerrillas, and her chief engineer was captured the next day on Leyte.

103. Field, p. 92.

104. Hoyt, *The Battle of Leyte Gulf*, p. 236.

105. Field, p. 94, states that originally the *Abukuma* was ordered to proceed to Cagayan. Field, p. 133, then states that the vulnerability of that harbor to attack by American aircraft meant that at 1105 she decided, apparently without orders, to proceed to Dapitan.

106. Cutler, p. 203. Morison, p. 237.

107. Field, p. 94. Woodward, p. 127. Cutler, p. 204, states that she was hit by a bomb that penetrated to her engine room. The *Mogami*, which lost 196 of her crew, was scuttled by torpedo at 1230. See Dull, p. 322.

108. Woodward, p. 127.

109. *DANFS*, VIII, p. 224. Woodward, p. 128.

110. Morison, p. 320.

111. Field, p. 94. At this time the Japanese formations were less the *Kiri* and *Sugi*, which were refueling and which joined later. See Admiralty, p. 84, fn. 4, and Woodward, p. 137.

112. Dull, p. 328.

113. Cutler, pp. 250–251.

114. To summarize, and to anticipate the unfolding of events, these were the fleet carrier *Zuikaku*, the light carriers *Chitose*, *Chiyoda* and the *Zuiho*, the light cruiser *Tama*, and the destroyers *Akitsuki* and *Hatsutsuki*.

115. Woodward, p. 138, is one of the few accounts that gives the composition of the first strike, stated as "approximately sixty fighters, 65 bombers, and 55 torpedo planes."

116. Morison, p. 324, states that Ozawa saw American aircraft at 0653. Reynolds, p. 273, states that the Japanese formations were coming south when their radar detected the American search aircraft, turned around, and put forty miles behind them before they were sighted at 0710. This is possible, but it means that the Japanese must have detected the American aircraft about 0530 and then steamed at full speed, about twenty-seven knots, i.e., ten minutes for a reversal of course and ninety minutes steaming.

117. Field, p. 94. Morison, p. 324.

118. It seems that Japanese surprise was partly the result of not knowing that Halsey had taken his carrier groups north. Their own reconnaissance aircraft, apparently four in number, did not make contact with the American formations. See Field, p. 94. Morison, pp. 324–325, states that the Japanese had between twelve and fifteen fighters as combat air patrol, and that the Hellcats accounted for nine of these; other accounts suggest all were lost. Woodward, p. 140, states that "fifteen to twenty enemy fighters rose to intercept our strike group," but though one Avenger was shot down, the Japanese were quickly dispersed, "leaving our strikes with no air opposition whatever for the rest of the day."

119. Dull, p. 328. Hoyt, *The Battle of Leyte Gulf,* p. 322. Woodward, p. 139. Field, p. 95, states that sixty aircraft attacked the southern group.

120. According to Morison, p. 325. Woodward, p. 140, states that Helldivers from the *Essex* claimed eight hits on the *Chitose* and that Avengers from the same carrier registered two hits on the carrier. He also states that two more bomb hits were recorded by aircraft from the *Lexington.*

121. Field, p. 95. Japanese sources give the time of her sinking at 0856, which is corrected to the time Americans were using. Dull, p. 328, gives the time as 0756, which was the time the Japanese were using.

122. Field, p. 95. Woodward, p. 142.

123. Morison, pp. 324–325.

124. Hoyt, *The Battle of Leyte Gulf,* p. 322. Morison, p. 325. It is not clear whether this damage was inflicted in the first or second attacks. Most accounts indicate that it was sustained at the very start of proceedings, but Field, p. 96, suggests that it was progressive, and that these "finally and unmistakeably broke down" during or immediately after the second attack.

125. Field, p. 96.

126. Morison, p. 325. Woodward, p. 143.

127. Morison, p. 292. Wheeler, p. 400.

128. Morison, p. 292. Halsey, p. 218, states that he replied to Kinkaid's signal "in some bewilderment."

129. Cutler, pp. 226–227. Woodward, pp. 164–165.

130. Prados, p. 668. Woodward, p. 165.

131. Wheeler, p. 400. Woodward, p. 165.

132. Morison, p. 293. Woodward, p. 165, states that the report from the aircraft from the *Kadashan Bay* was "excited and almost unintelligible."

133. Field, p. 100.

134. Wheeler, p. 401. (Morison, p. 292, states that the first reports were received by Kinkaid at 0724 and, p. 293, that Kinkaid signaled Halsey at 0707. Clearly the 0724 timing—which was also given by Woodward, p. 170—was mistaken, but it was not corrected in the supplementary corrections, pp. 144–145.)

135. Woodward, p. 171.

136. Wheeler, p. 401. Woodward, p. 171.

137. Wheeler, p. 401. Woodward, p. 172.

138. Wheeler, p. 402.

139. Woodward, p. 169. This would be the number needed for a single mission by an Avenger formation in a fleet carrier.

140. Woodward, p. 187.

141. Wheeler, p. 401. Morison, p. 285.

142. The point is made—reference the equivalent of five fleet carriers—in Dull, p. 325. The three formations originally each had six escort carriers, but the *Chenango* and

Saginaw Bay were detached from Task Unit 77.4.1. Apparently, on 24 October these two carriers were ordered to transfer their aircraft and crews to other carriers and the group and proceed to Morotai for replacements. See *DANFS*, II, p. 93; VI, p. 231. The suggestion, as per Field, p. 169, that one of the two had been damaged appears to be erroneous.

143. Morison, pp. 286–287. Woodward, p. 187, states that Task Unit 77.4.3 launched sixty-five fighters and forty-four Avengers in the first thirty minutes of action.

144. Commander L. S. Kintberger, quoted by Woodward, p. 182.

145. *DANFS*, III, p. 585.

146. *DANFS*, III, p. 341.

147. *DANFS*, III, p. 556. For the *Johnston* to have fired 200 rounds in five minutes during the advance-to-contact phase would have meant all five guns, including the two rear turrets facing aft, firing eight rounds a minute for five minutes, or her two guns forward of the bridge firing twenty rounds a minute. The second set of figures—thirty rounds fired in forty seconds—would suggest a rate of fire of more than twenty-two rounds a minute.

According to Captain Spencer Johnson, in his e-mail of 8 January 2004, the established rate of fire for the 5-in./38 gun was fifteen rounds per minute, but that if at the right elevation the rate of fire could be as high as twenty-two rounds per minute, and that the gun could sustain a higher rate of fire than the crew could manage. Both might be considered what could be achieved in one trial shoot, but whether a gun crew could sustain such rates of fire over five minutes is dubious indeed.

The range material was cited in Woodward, p. 175.

148. See, for example, Cutler, specifically p. 238, in a chapter entitled "The Charge of the Light Brigade," pp. 219–248. See also the following chapter, "The World Wonders." This book is perhaps the best-written account of Leyte, and one would commend the Prologue (p. xvii).

149. William Shakespeare, *Henry V*, Act IV, Scene III. It seems that Potter, *Nimitz*, p. 339, is the only account that notes that this day is called the feast of Crispian.

150. Prados, p. 669.

151. Ito, p. 151.

152. Cutler, p. 232.

153. Morison, p. 254.

154. Prados, p. 664.

155. Prados, pp. 664–665.

156. Woodward, p. 173. Figures vary depending on source. Koyanagi, according to Morison, p. 248, stated that the American force consisted of one or two battleships, four or five fleet carriers, and "at least" ten heavy cruisers.

157. An *Independence*-class light carrier had a standard displacement of 10,662 tons on dimensions of 660×71.5×12.5 feet. A *Casablanca*-class escort carrier had an 8,200-ton standard displacement on dimensions of 490×65.2×20.75 feet. By comparison, an *Essex*-class fleet carrier had a 27,200-ton standard displacement on dimensions of 820×93×23 feet. See Chesneau, pp. 220, 232, and 238. The differences between light cruisers and destroyers were decidedly small, especially in the Imperial Navy and specifically with reference to the older cruisers, such as the *Yubari*, and the destroyers of 1939 *Akizuki* class and the *Shimakaze*. See Jentschura, pp. 110, 149, 151, and *Conway's All the World's Fighting Ships, 1922–1946*, pp. 187, 195.

158. Morison, p. 298, states that Kurita's staff mistook the *Fletcher*-class destroyers for *Baltimore*-class heavy cruisers and noted that "their profiles are somewhat alike." While conceding this point, the *Baltimore*-class cruiser was almost six times the size of the *Fletcher*-class destroyer. See *Conway's* pp. 120, 130, which give silhouettes which are much more akin than the photographs that appear in *Jane's Fighting Ships, 1943–1944*, pp. 458, 470.

159. Cutler, p. 221.

160. See Dull, p. 323, and the credit of the chart on that page.

161. Cutler, p. 233. Morison, pp. 252–253. According to Field, p. 100, the *Yamato* opened fire when the range was 35,000 yards, or twenty miles, and according to Prados, p. 671, the *Kongo* opened fire one minute later at 26,500 yards.

162. Morison, p. 258. Ugaki, pp. 492–493, states "destroying a ship with two or three salvos, the target was changed to another one. . . . It was about this time that one carrier was sunk, another set on fire, and one cruiser sunk."

163. Cutler, p. 234.

164. Woodward, p. 172. Morison, p. 255, gives the time of the American ships entering the squall as just before 0716.

165. Cutler, pp. 230, 232. Woodward, p. 175.

166. Morison, p. 257. Woodward, p. 175.

167. Cutler, p. 231. Hoyt, *The Battle of Leyte Gulf*, p. 251.

168. Morison, p. 256. Admiralty, p. 73.

169. Prados, p. 675. Dull, p. 326.

170. *DANFS*, III, p. 286. Woodward, p. 176.

171. Cutler, p. 241. According to the *Heermann's* entry as per previous endnote, and also Prados, p. 677.

172. Woodward, pp. 176–177.

173. Morison, p. 259.

174. Morison, pp. 268–269. Admiralty, pp. 68, 73.

175. Morison, p. 269. Woodward, p. 178.

176. The *Roberts* is credited—see Woodward, p. 178—with an attack on an *Aoba*-class heavy cruiser at this stage of proceedings, but there was no *Aoba*-class cruiser in the Japanese order of battle. Presumably what was meant was the *Haguro* or a sister ship.

177. Morison, pp. 263–264.

178. Morison, p. 266.

179. Field, p. 100. Prados, p. 672.

180. Ito, p. 152.

181. Kurita's operations officer recalled, "The smoke was made very quickly, and the use of smoke was skilful." See Prados, p. 677, and Woodward, p. 182.

182. Cutler, p. 234. Woodward, p. 182.

183. Prados, p. 682.

184. Morison, pp. 281–282. Prados, pp. 682–683.

185. Field, p. 106.

186. *DANFS*, II, p. 390–391; III, 585.

187. *DANFS*, III, 660; IV, 355; and VIII, 266.

188. *DANFS*, III, 15. Morison, p. 282.

189. Merrill, p. 163. Halsey, p. 219. In his autobiography Halsey stated that he believed that with eighteen escort carriers Task Group 77.4 would be able to fend for itself. Even in 1947, therefore, he did not know that two carriers had been detached the previous day.

190. Halsey, p. 220. Merrill, p. 163. Potter, *Bull Halsey*, pp. 334–335.

191. Potter, *Bull Halsey*, pp. 177–178, 295–296.

192. Halsey, p. 219. This signal was sent at 0707 and was in clear. See Morison, p. 293.

193. Cutler, p. 237. Halsey, p. 219.

194. Halsey, p. 219. Woodward, pp. 144–145, indicates that at the time when Task Group 38.1 received this signal it was refueling one of its carriers and a cruiser. McCain immediately ordered refueling to end and turned his formation toward the southwest, but

even at thirty knots could not bring the carriers within extreme strike range for an hour, in real terms some two or three hours, and then between two and three hours would be needed for the aircraft to be launched, assume formation, and reach the scene of battle; for aircraft to have reached the area by 1310 would indicate that McCain's formation cut corners. Cutler, p. 260, states that Task Group 38.1 launched its aircraft at a range of 335 miles.

195. Halsey, p. 224.

196. Halsey, pp. 219–220. This signal was sent at 0727. See Morison, pp. 293–294.

197. Halsey, p. 220. This signal was sent at 0725. See Morison, p. 293. Polmar, p. 395, makes the rather surprising statement, "Actually, Kinkaid was in error: his battleships each had just over 21 rounds of armour-piercing ammunition per gun." One would have thought that such a dearth of rounds proved the point.

198. Potter, *Bull Halsey,* p. 335. Halsey, p. 220.

199. Halsey, p. 220. Merrill, p. 165.

200. Hoyt, *The Battle of Leyte Gulf,* p. 185.

201. Halsey, p. 219.

202. Field, p. 95.

203. Morison, p. 325.

204. Field, p. 95. Prados, p. 652. Reynolds, p. 274.

205. Morison, p. 325, states that American aircraft "went in between 0945 and 1000," which presumably is the period of the opening of the attack. Japanese sources suggest that this attack lasted between 1000 and 1030.

206. Field, p. 96. Prados, p. 652.

207. MacArthur, p. 401, fn. 117. Morison, pp. 325–326.

208. Morison, p. 326.

209. Morison, p. 25. This thought was given the time of 0706.

210. Morison, p. 261. Roscoe, p. 427. *DANFS,* III, p. 341. Of her crew, 86 were rescued but 253 were lost.

211. Morison, p. 261. Cutler, pp. 241–242.

212. Chesneau, p. 241. *DANFS,* III, p. 15. Morison, pp. 282–284.

213. Morison, pp. 269–270. Roscoe, pp. 428–429.

214. Morison, p. 273.

215. Cutler, p. 256.

216. Roscoe, pp. 430–431.

217. Cutler, p. 248. Morison, p. 274. *DANFS,* III, p. 556. The latter states that 141 of a crew of 327 officers and men were saved. About fifty were killed in the *Johnston,* forty-five were known to have died on rafts, and the remainder were lost in the water.

218. See, for example, the "official entries" provided by the U.S. Navy. *DANFS,* II, p. 261; III, p. 524; and VI, p. 45.

219. Morison, p. 269. Roscoe, p. 426.

220. Field, p. 101.

221. Woodward, p. 188.

222. Whitley, *Cruisers,* p. 181. Morison, p. 285.

223. Ugaki, p. 494, editorial comment. Field, p. 107.

224. Hoyt, *The Battle of Leyte Gulf,* p. 295. Admiralty, p. 78, implies that the *Chikuma* lost three of her shafts and was reduced to eighteen knots, and explicitly states that she was unable to steer.

225. Field, p. 107. Prados, p. 684. Whitney, p. 181.

226. Hoyt, *The Battle of Leyte Gulf,* pp. 295–296.

227. Ito, p. 152.

228. Morison, pp. 284–285. Most accounts, such as Field, p. 198, and Whitney, p. 181, indicate that the *Fujinami* administered the *coup de grâce* by torpedo.

229. Field, p. 133.

230. Prados, p. 683. Dull, p. 326, states that the order was "Cease action. Come north with me. 20 knots."

231. Ito, p. 156.

232. Cutler, p. 257.

233. Ugaki, p. 497. Morison, p. 299, states that the message was received at 0945, but Ugaki's account is very specific.

234. Field, p. 125, fn. 17.

235. One's own suspicion was that Kurita probably never saw an American escort carrier, but one was reminded, by Cutler, p. 257, that Koyanagi, the chief of staff, claimed to have personally seen an American carrier hit repeatedly, and so one assumes that Kurita must have seen this episode.

236. Ugaki, p. 494.

237. Woodward, pp. 199–200, is perhaps one of the few accounts to note this point, but he does state, p. 198, that the *Hayashimo* had been detached to stand by the *Kumano*. Field, p. 123, also indicates that the *Hayashimo* left Kurita's force in mid-morning.

238. Cutler, p. 234. Morison, p. 280.

239. Cutler, p. 222.

240. Ito, p. 166.

241. Field, pp. 125–126.

242. Prados, p. 685.

243. Prados, p. 685.

244. Fukuda, pp. 333–359. The author expresses his gratitude and indebtedness on this matter to Tohmatsu Haruo and his e-mail of 25 February 2004.

245. Ito, p. 166.

246. Potter, *Nimitz*, p. 337.

247. Morison, p. 329. Reynolds, p. 275, is perhaps the only account to note the passing, or wasting, of the best part of an hour before the order was given.

248. Potter, *Nimitz*, p. 341. Morison, p. 331, states nine destroyers.

249. Potter, *Bull Halsey*, p. 336, and *Nimitz*, p. 341.

250. Woodward, p. 80.

251. Morison, p. 329.

252. Cutler, p. 261.

253. Morison, pp. 329–330.

254. Morison, p. 318–319, 330.

255. Morison, p. 330.

256. Woodward, pp. 217–218. These were first Task Groups 38.3 with 38.4, second Task Group 38.1, third Task Group 34.5, and fourth Task Force 34 with Task Group 38.2.

257. Halsey, pp. 220–221.

258. Potter, *Nimitz*, p. 340, states that Halsey was not accustomed to padding.

259. Potter, *Bull Halsey*, p. 335.

260. Halsey, p. 221.

261. The word "mendacious" is used here in its primary and correct sense, which is the arrangement of facts or evidence in order to confirm a pre-determined argument or conclusion, i.e., what the military term "situating the appreciation."

262. Prados, p. 650.

263. Morison, p. 327. Chesneau, p. 172. Woodward, p. 151.

264. Woodward, pp. 151–152.

265. Dull, p. 330. Morison, p. 327. Sato, II, pp. 299–336. Tohmatsu Haruo, e-mail of 27 January 2004.

266. Woodward, p. 153.

267. Hoyt, *The Battle of Leyte Gulf*, p. 336.

268. Woodward, pp. 153–154.

269. *DANFS*, VIII, p. 290. This is the only entry that does anything other than merely note proceedings. The entries for the *Mobile* and *Santa Fe* (respectively *DANFS*, IV, p. 402; VI, p. 322) are cursory in their dealing with these actions, while that of the *New Orleans* does not mention the action at all and states that she went south with the battle-ships. See *DANFS*, V, p. 68.

270. Woodward, p. 154. This source mistakenly identified the carrier as the *Chitose*. Admiralty, p. 90, gives the time of the *Chiyoda's* sinking as 1655.

271. Field, p. 120.

272. Woodward, p. 156.

273. Field, pp. 120–121. Woodward, p. 156.

274. Morison, p. 331.

275. Roscoe, p. 434.

276. Morison, pp. 331–332. Woodward, p. 158. Admiralty, p. 92, states that the *Hatsutsuki* was "literally punched to pieces" and "sank to the accompaniment of six very heavy underwater explosions." This paper notes that in this action the *New Orleans* and *Wichita* respectively fired 35 and 22 percent of their armor-piercing rounds and that the *Santa Fe* fired 952 6-in., 972 5-in., and 104 5-in. star shells, and the *Mobile* 779 6-in. shells.

277. Woodward, p. 158.

278. Roscoe, pp. 399–400. Field, p. 122, affords the sinking of the *Tama* a one-line footnote; Hoyt, *The Battle of Leyte Gulf*, p. 339, just two lines, in parentheses.

279. Woodward, pp. 160–161.

280. Roscoe, p. 398.

281. Morison, p. 288. Cutler, p. 259.

282. Morison, p. 310.

283. *DANFS*, VI, p. 327. Morison, pp. 300–301. Prados, p. 689.

284. Interestingly, the *Petrof Bay's* entry in *DANFS*, V, p. 279, indicates that four aircraft attempted to make *kamikaze* attacks on the carrier on this day. The entry of the *Sangamon*, *DANFS*, VI, p. 318, makes reference to the attack, and also notes that about noon she suffered a malfunction of her steering gear, generators, and catapult, but it is clear that the two were not connected.

285. *DANFS*, VI, p. 692. Fires in the hangar were promptly extinguished, but the *Suwannee's* rear elevator remained jammed.

286. Morison, p. 302, states that the bomb of this aircraft exploded, causing "considerable damage." The *Kitkun Bay's* entry (*DANFS*, III, p. 660) makes no mention of any damage, noting only one fatality and sixteen wounded. This entry states that the Japanese aircraft was a Zeke and that she shot down a Betty.

287. Morison, pp. 302–303. Polmar, p. 401. David Brown, *Kamikaze*, p. 23, states that the Japanese aircraft, identified as a Zeke, hit but slid along the flight deck and fell over the bows, and that it was its bomb that set off the ship's gasoline system, which in turn set off depth charges, bombs, and torpedoes. The *St. Lo's DANFS* entry unequivocally states that the Japanese aircraft crashed through the flight deck and set off an explosion in the magazine. Brown also states, p. 22, that in the course of this attack the destroyer escort

Richard M. Rowell shot down one Japanese aircraft. The *Rowell* was in the screen of Task Unit 77.4.1 and not Task Unit 77.4.3, and her *DANFS*, VI, p. 98, entry makes no reference to any such episode.

288. *DANFS*, IV, p. 355. Woodward, pp. 210–211.

289. *DANFS*, III, pp. 585–586, 660. Morison, p. 303.

290. Morison, pp. 304–305.

291. Jeffrey G. Barlow, *The U.S. Navy's Fight against the Kamikazes*, p. 399. Naval Staff, p. 98.

292. *DANFS*, II, p. 391; III, p. 586; and VIII, p. 266. Morison, p. 304.

293. *DANFS*, VI, p. 692.

294. The various dates given in the *DANFS* entries are not wholly compatible. The entry for the *Petrof Bay* suggests that the carrier was on station until 28 October, that of the *Sangamon* the next day. The latter is given as being at Manus between 3 and 9 November, the *Santee* between 31 October and 9 November.

295. Raymond O'Connor, *The Japanese Navy in World War II*, p. 125.

296. Inoguchi Rikihei and Nakajima Tadashi, *The Divine Wind: Japan's Kamikaze Force in World War II*, pp. 54–55.

297. Inoguchi, pp. 59–60.

298. Field, p. 123. Dull, p. 326. Ugaki, pp. 495–496.

299. Morison, p. 308.

300. Ugaki, p. 496.

301. Ito, p. 154.

302. Ugaki, p. 496.

303. Ito, pp. 154, 157.

304. Woodward, p. 201.

305. Field, p. 126.

306. Prados, p. 686.

307. Woodward, p. 204.

308. Field, p. 126. Hoyt, *The Battle of Leyte Gulf*, p. 331. Prados, p. 686.

309. Field, p. 127.

310. Woodward, p. 200.

311. Woodward, p. 201.

312. Morison, p. 308.

313. Hoyt, *The Battle of Leyte Gulf*, p. 300.

314. Woodward, p. 204.

315. Morison, p. 309. Forty-eight fighters were dispatched but two were lost on takeoff.

316. Polmar, p. 402. Woodward, p. 212.

317. Woodward, p. 213. Polmar, p. 402, states that ten aircraft were lost in these two attacks.

318. Woodward, p. 214.

319. Field, p. 127. Woodward, p. 214. Morison, p. 310.

320. Woodward, p. 214.

321. Chihaya Masataka and Abe Yasuo, *Profile Warship No. 22: I.J.N. Yukikaze: Destroyer 1939–1970*. See also Jentschura, p. 149.

322. Morison, p. 310.

323. Morison, p. 330.

324. Woodward, p. 220. Roscoe, p. 432, gives slightly different figures. Morison, p. 330, gives the entire action two lines and no detail.

325. It is not clear which destroyers were involved in this action. Woodward gives three and Roscoe gives the units from DesDiv 103, which were the *Miller, Owen, The Sullivans*

and the *Tingey*. While there is no disputing the involvement of the first two, whether the latter two engaged the Japanese unit is not clear. Their respective entries in *DANFS*, VII, pp. 124 and 202, suggest they did not since the episode is afforded minimal coverage, and one suspects that it would have been fully cited had they been in action.

326. Woodward, p. 221.

327. Sato, II, pp. 299–336. Tohmatsu Haruo, e-mail of 27 January 2004.

7. THE NAVAL BATTLE FOR THE PHILIPPINES

1. See, for example, the full title of Cutler's book: *The Battle of Leyte Gulf. 23–26 October 1944. The Dramatic Full Story, Based on the Latest Research, of the Greatest Naval Battle in History.*

2. It should be noted that Morison, p. 306, gives the wrong date for the *Eversole's* sinking. *DANFS*, II, p. 387, Roscoe, pp. 436–437, and Paul H. Silverthorne, *U.S. Warships of World War II*, pp. 174 and 398, give the correct date of 28 October 1944.

3. Naval Staff, p. 102.

4. According to Roscoe, *Submarines*, pp. 402–405, and Naval Staff, p. 113, the *Sealion* fired six bow and three stern torpedoes at the Japanese ships around 0257 on 21 November. She recorded one hit on the *Urakaze*, which blew up immediately, and three hits on the *Kongo*. The latter kept station as the formation increased speed to eighteen knots but then slowed, and with the *Sealion* trying to catch up, she and two destroyers parted company from the other ships. After the *Kongo* was dead in the water, she blew up and sank at 0524. According to Ugaki, p. 520, the *Kongo* was hit by two torpedoes which flooded two of her boiler rooms and reduced her speed to sixteen knots. When her list increased to fifteen degrees to port, she was ordered back to Keelung, in northern Formosa, in the company of the destroyers *Isokaze* and *Hamakaze*, but sank at 0530.

What is easy to miss about this incident is that after the *Kongo* turned back, the *Nagato* and *Yamato* continued in the company of just the *Yahagi* and one destroyer.

The *Kongo* was the only Japanese battleship sunk by a submarine during the war.

5. Most of the material used here is drawn from Jentschura, pp. 176–177, with reference to the probable identity of Japanese submarines, and from Morison, pp. 306–307, 342, and Roscoe, pp. 436–437, with reference to American operations. But see Appendix 11, specifically note 17, with reference to Japanese accounting of these losses.

6. Morison, p. 339.

7. Morison, p. 310.

8. Field, p. 134. Morison, p. 239, states that there were four destroyer-transports, but this seems to be erroneous.

9. Woodward, p. 228. *Kaigun shogo sakusen (2)*, pp. 56–57, 486–490.

10. Prados, pp. 690–691, has been taken as the basis of the information on this episode, but it should be noted that there are a series of differences in accounts that cannot be properly reconciled, perhaps the most obvious being the positions given in Jentschura, pp. 108, 145, and 228, for the sinking of the three ships cited here. For example, the T. 102 is given as having been sunk by aircraft from the *Hancock* in the strait between Panay and Negros. In addition, while Field states there were four landing ships, of which two were sunk, and the Naval Staff, p. 107, fn. 2, states that the claim was that two of three transports had been sunk but in fact none had been, Prados indicates that there were five, of which one was sunk. A careful search of the lists of losses suggests that two landing ships were sunk on this day, but that the second was off Iwo Jima.

11. Inoguchi, pp. 60–61.

12. Morison, p. 305.

13. *DANFS*, VI, p. 692. Polmar, p. 402.

14. Ugaki, p. 499, states that the first attack was conducted by three aircraft at 0800 and that the 0834 attack, conducted by fifty aircraft, was the second attack. D'Albas, p. 204, states that the Japanese ships were attacked by eighty aircraft at 0834. Ito, p. 169, states that this attack consisted of thirty aircraft at 0834. The information used here is drawn primarily from Field, p. 132.

15. Jentschura, p. 112, and Whitney, *Cruisers*, p. 187, state that the *Noshiro* was sunk by aircraft from the *Hornet* and *Wasp*. Admiralty, p. 104, states that according to post-war interrogation the *Noshiro* was hit by two torpedoes in the first attack and by bombs (plural) in the second.

16. Morison, pp. 311–312.

17. Morison, p. 311.

18. Field, pp. 133–134. Morison, p. 238. Hoyt, *The Battle of Leyte Gulf*, p. 327, states that the *Ushio* rescued 283 officers and men from the *Abukuma*. Whitney, *Cruisers*, pp. 162–164, states that the *Abukuma* had a complement of 438 officers and men and was sunk by aircraft from Task Group 77.4, but the latter was certainly not the case. Cutler, pp. 201, 204, twice states that the *Abukuma* was a destroyer.

19. Barlow, p. 402.

20. These were the heavy cruiser *Tone*—ironically she was sunk on 24 July at her moorings in Kure harbor by aircraft from Task Force 38—and the destroyers *Hamakaze* and *Kasumi*.

21. Field, p. 133. M. J. Whitley, *Destroyers of World War II: An International Encyclopedia*, p. 204.

22. Field, p. 134. Whitley, *Destroyers*, p. 202.

23. Ugaki, p. 500.

24. Admiralty, p. 105.

25. The Japanese official history gives the *Yuho Maru* at Miri, but Ugaki, p. 501, states that she was definitely at Brunei because the *Yamato*, down at the bow and with her windlass not in service, fouled the oiler's anchor.

26. Apparently the process was not completed until 0900 on 30 October, which seems rather a long time given the presence of three oilers and the relatively small number of warships that had to take on oil. See Ugaki, p. 502, editorial note.

27. Ugaki, pp. 508, 510.

28. Ugaki, p. 507.

29. Ugaki, pp. 510–511.

30. Ugaki, p. 514.

31. Carter, *U.S. Army Air Forces in World War II*, pp. 500, 504, states that these raids were conducted by Liberators and Mitchells, numbers unspecified, of the Far East Air Force.

32. Ugaki, pp. 517–518. Ugaki's diary entry states that the American force consisted of forty Liberators and fifteen Lightnings.

33. Carter, *U.S. Army Air Forces in World War II*, p. 489. Naval Staff, p. 94, states that this raid took place on 27 October, but this is as erroneous as the statement that the raid was directed against the King George V graving dock. Ugaki, p. 508, indicates that the fleet oiler *Notoro* was damaged in the course of this raid. Jentschura, p. 250, states that the oiler *Notoro*, which was then under repair after suffering severe damage when torpedoed off the Palaus more than thirteen months earlier, was heavily damaged in this attack and was reduced thereafter to the status of storage tanker.

34. Ugaki noted Wang's death in his diary entry of 13 November (p. 516). On 12 November the British Eastern Fleet had three fleet and six escort carriers, two battle-

ships, two heavy and five light carriers, and nineteen destroyers—i.e., the equivalent of an American carrier task group—under command. After the Eastern Fleet was dissolved on 19 November, the East Indies Fleet was raised primarily from its predecessor's escort, coastal, patrol, and amphibious forces. See Willmott, *Grave*, pp. 165–166, 177–178.

35. Naval Staff, p. 99. It could also be added that after landings conducted in such temperatures that various American commanders feared heat stroke among their men (see Charles Bateson, *The War with Japan: A Concise History*, p. 359), and that in the last days of October Leyte was lashed by a typhoon and winds that reached seventy miles per hour. See Department of Military Art and Engineering, U.S. Military Academy, *The War with Japan: Part II—August 1942–December 1944*, p. 84.

36. Morison, pp. 339–340.

37. Prados, pp. 691–692.

38. See, for example, Naval Staff, pp. 107–110.

39. Alan J. Levine, *The Pacific War: Japan versus the Allies*, p. 129.

40. These were the *Akebono* and *Akishimo*, the one survivor being the *Asashimo*: the others were the light cruiser *Kiso* and the destroyers *Hatsuharu* and *Okinami*. Naval Staff, p. 111, states that a total of eighteen transports and freighters of 93,000 tons were sunk in Manila Bay and that as a result Manila was "put out of operation as a port of reinforcement for Leyte for a considerable time." Given this account's skepticism about various claims, this account presents a problem because by the author's own calculation two army and two naval transports, and one merchantman, plus the warships, were sunk inside Manila Bay with two more merchantmen, and a chaser, sunk outside the bay.

41. Prados, p. 691.

42. Morison, pp. 351–352.

43. Taylor, pp. 277–267.

44. Polmar, pp. 404–405. Ugaki, pp. 507–508.

45. Jentschura, pp. 83, 195. ADM 199.1493, p. 281. Naval Staff, p. 106. The latter two sources state that it was claimed that the *Nachi* was hit by nine torpedoes (of the forty-six aimed at her), thirteen 1,000-lb. and six 250-lb. bombs, and sixteen rockets and that the *Nachi* broke into three. Apparently Shima was returning to his flagship from a visit ashore and watched the *Nachi* being sunk. The *Akebono* and escort *Okinawa* were damaged at this same time. The British staff history commented that the claims were obviously exaggerated, and it observed, in fn. 2, that claims of considerable numbers of ships being sunk in Manila Bay on 5 and 6 November were not confirmed in the post-war analyses. Nimitz's report stated that if the claims were correct the episode demonstrated "the ineffectiveness of the fuze settings . . . and inadequacy of . . . our aircraft torpedoes."

46. Morison, p. 354.

47. *DANFS*, III, p. 447.

48. Morison, p. 342. *DANFS*, I, p. 114; II, p. 444. The *Enterprise*, with a full flight deck, was narrowly missed by a crashing Japanese aircraft at this same time. See Polmar, p. 404.

49. *DANFS*, II, p. 125.

50. Morison, p. 344.

51. *DANFS*, I. p. 6. Morison, p. 344. Combining the two sources suggests that the time of the attack was about 1344. The ship lost twenty-three of her crew.

52. Silverstone, pp. 395–398, lists the following ships as sunk: *Abner Read* (1 November 1944), *Reid* (11 December 1944), *Mahan* (7 December 1944), *Colhoun* (6 April 1945), *Mannert L. Abele* (12 April 1945), *Pringle* (16 April 1945), *Little* (3 May 1945), *Luce* (3 May 1945), *Morrison* (4 May 1945), *Drexler* (28 May 1945), *William D. Porter* (10 June 1945), *Twiggs* (16 June 1945) and the *Callaghan* (28 July 1945). Those listed as damaged beyond

repair are the *Evans, Haggard, Hugh W. Hadley, Hutchins, Leutze, Morris, Newcombe, Shaw, Shubrick* and the *Thatcher*.

53. Ugaki, p. 507.

54. Morison, pp. 347–348. Whitley, *Cruisers*, p. 260. Naval Staff, pp. 101–102. The *Reno* was heavily damaged and was prevented from sinking only with great difficulty. She was towed to Ulithi and arrived on 11 November; she then returned to the United States for repairs but did not emerge from the Charleston yard until after the war was over. See *DANFS*, VI, p. 74.

Whatever success the I. 41 enjoyed was short-lived. She was caught east of Samar by aircraft and escorts from the anti-submarine patrol on 18 November and sunk—see Morison, p. 69; *DANFS*, IV, pp. 71–72—and this was six days after the destroyer *Nicholas*, en route to Kossol Roads, the Palaus, from Ulithi, sank the I. 38. See *DANFS*, V, p. 87.

It is perhaps worth noting, if only *en passant*, that two days after the I. 41 was sunk, a Japanese submarine sank an American ship. Interestingly, in light of the relative effectiveness of the *kamikazes* when compared to orthodox air power, the Japanese unit was a midget submarine, one of five launched by the submarines I. 36 and I. 47 off Ulithi. Penetrating into the anchorage, one midget submarine accounted for the oiler *Mississinewa*, while another two were sunk while trying to attack the light cruisers *Biloxi* and *Mobile*. See *DANFS*, IV, p. 387, and Rohwer, p. 314. The *Mississinewa* was the only unit ever sunk by a *kaiten* attack. See Naval Staff, p. 102.

Edwin P. Hoyt, in *The Kamikazes*, pp. 146–147, states that the evaluation of the attack involved some 200 individuals in a single meeting that determined that three carriers and two battleships had been sunk.

55. Polmar, pp. 405–406. ADM 199.1493, pp. 281–283. At the same as the *Wasp* and her escorts proceeded to Guam and Task Group 38.2 made its way back to Ulithi, the *Lexington*, in the company of the destroyers *Hickox, Lewis Hancock* and the *Colohan*, withdrew to Ulithi.

56. Morison, pp. 357, 408–409. Naval Staff, p. 112. Roscoe, pp. 400–401. Ugaki, p. 508. Whitley, *Cruisers*, p. 184. The *Ticonderoga* arrived at Ulithi on 29 October and embarked on her first combat mission on 2 November as a unit in Task Group 38.3. This formation returned to Ulithi after the operations of 13–14 November, arriving 17 November, and sailed again on 22 November; it returned to Ulithi after taking part in the operations of 25 November. See *DANFS*, VII, pp. 182–184.

57. *DANFS*, II, p. 368; III, p. 232.

58. *DANFS*, III, 447. Naval Staff, p. 112. Interestingly, Nimitz's November report (ADM 199.1493, p. 285) states that the *Intrepid*'s casualties numbered fifty-four killed, fifteen missing, thirty-five seriously and fifteen lightly wounded.

59. Morison, p. 359. Seventeen of these aircraft were lost.

60. *DANFS*, II, p. 4.

61. The close air support materialized on 26 November, the bombing raid on 24 November. These seem belated but it had been fighters that had been put into the airfield. These numbered 182 on 25 November and 317 two weeks later. Also at work, obviously, was the weather.

62. This is a line quoted in virtually every history. See, for example, Cannon, p. 92; Cutler, p. 264.

8. TO PAUSE AND CONSIDER

1. Admiralty, p. 106. The aircraft claim, taken from the October 1944 report, ADM 199.1493, p. 201, was that 952 Japanese aircraft were shot down, 60 were destroyed by anti-aircraft fire from the ships and formations of Task Force 38, and 547 were destroyed on the ground. These figures do not include Japanese aircraft destroyed by anti-aircraft fire from the units and formations on Leyte and by aircraft and anti-aircraft fire from the ships and formations of the 7th Fleet. The loss of 239 aircraft from Task Force 38 was admitted.

2. The count is not exact, and the discrepancy is obvious in terms of the loss of the *Princeton*, *Gambier Bay* and the *St. Lo*, but a total of three destroyers, one frigate, two minelayers, and one submarine, plus thirteen transports and one attack cargo ship were either launched or commissioned between 22 and 28 October 1944. Those launched were the attack transports *Okaloosa* (22 October), *Renville* and the *Shelby* (25 October), *Bland* and *Okanogan* (26 October), *Balduck*, *Crenshaw* and the *Grimes*, the destroyer *Duncan* (27 October), and the attack transports *Bosque* and *Rockbridge* and attack cargo ship *Hydrus* (28 October); the units that were commissioned into the U.S. Navy on these days were the high-speed transport *Crosley* and attack transport *Drew* (22 October), the destroyer *Zellars* and high-speed transport *Ringness* (25 October), the submarine *Brill* (26 October), the minelayer *Tolman* (27 October), and the destroyer *Aaron Ward*, frigate *Abilene*, and minelayer *J. William Ditter* (28 October). Put at its simplest, and remembering that the Japanese aim had been to get among the transports, the Japanese could not sink ships as fast as the Americans could build them. No Japanese victory in Leyte Gulf, or even a series of Japanese victories in the Philippines, were ever going to alter this fundamental point.

In the month of October the battleship *Wisconsin*, the light cruisers *Pasadena* and *Wilkes-Barre*, the escort carrier *Tulagi*, eight destroyers, eight destroyer escorts, and four submarines joined the Pacific Fleet.

3. Cutler, p. 264. Woodward, pp. 234–235.

4. Cutler, p. 263, sets out the cowardice argument but does not embrace it.

5. George M. Hall, *The Fifth Star: High Command in an Era of Global War*, p. 112. Potter, *Halsey*, pp. 327, 338. Wheeler, p. 459.

6. Potter, *Halsey*, pp. 405, 441. Wheeler, pp. 459–461.

7. Cutler, p. 292.

8. Stanley L. Falk, *Decision at Leyte*, pp. 209–211, 317, cited in Reynolds, p. 281.

9. Admiralty, p. 63.

10. Admiralty, pp. 65–66.

11. William Shakespeare, *The Merchant of Venice*, Act I, Scene III.

12. Cutler, p. 288. Potter, *Halsey*, p. 340.

13. Hoyt, *The Battle of Leyte Gulf*, p. 127.

14. Potter, *Halsey*, p. 171.

15. Woodward, p. 140.

16. Hanson W. Baldwin, "Leyte Gulf: Kinkaid Vs. Kurita, etc." in *Great Naval Battles of the Twentieth Century*, ed. William H. Honan, p. 277, gives the total as 2,803 killed, but Woodward, pp. 215–216, provides totals of 473 killed, 1,110 missing, and 1,220 wounded. These latter figures are given in Nimitz's battle report (ADM 199.1493, p. 250). These totals are given as the sum of the losses of individual ships from task Units 77.4.3 and 77.4.1, but the totals given do not represent the sum of the losses of individual ships. One's natural assumption would be that the balance of the losses must have been incurred by Task Group 38's air groups and ships, but this cannot be correct because the losses of the *Princeton* and *Birmingham* take all three totals beyond the 473–1,110–1,220 limit. A sec-

ond curious aspect of these figures is why Nimitz's report should have carried the figures for the escort carrier groups from the 7th Fleet. The full figures are as follows:

	Killed	Wounded	Missing
Task Unit 77.4.3			
Fanshaw Bay	4	4	12
Gambier Bay	23	160	97
Kalinin Bay	5	55	—
Kitkun Bay	1	16	—
St. Lo	10	394	104
White Plains	—	13	—
Heermann	5	9	—
Hoel	19	19	234
Johnston	94	40	90
Dennis	6	19	—
Samuel B. Roberts	23	50	66
Task Unit 77.4.1			
Santee	21	29	—
Suwannee	100	106	74
Totals	311	914	877

It is perhaps invidious to name an individual who was killed and not the thousands of others, but one of the dead in the *St. Lo* was perhaps the only U.S. Army fatality in the battle, namely Captain Artemus J. Schnell, an artillery officer. See ADM 199.1494, p. 207.

17. Sixth Army Report, p. 43, quoted in Cannon, p. 92.

18. Woodward, p. 235, makes reference to a Japanese Halsey rather than a Kurita.

19. MacArthur, p. 401, fn. 120, states that Japanese losses, stated to be 271,000 tons, represented 26.1 percent of *Kaigun* losses during the war. Losses in this battle are roughly the same, but by the author's calculation a total of 1,026 Japanese warships of 2,310,734 tons were sunk during the war, E. & O. E.

PRIMARY SOURCES

ADM 199.1493. Admiralty: War History Cases and Papers. Second World War. U.S. operations in Pacific Ocean: Action Reports.
pp. 196–272: Operations in the Pacific Ocean Areas during the month of October 1944. Submitted by Commander-in-Chief U.S. Pacific Fleet and Pacific Ocean Areas. Report dated 31 May 1945. p. 201: Part I. Introduction. p. 201: Part II. Losses. p. 202: Part III. North Pacific. pp. 202–216: Part IV. Central Pacific. p. 217: Part V. South Pacific. pp. 217–221: Part VI. Submarines and anti-submarine activities. pp. 222–224: Part VII. Southwest Pacific. pp. 225–226: Part VIII. Miscellaneous. Annex A. Battle for Leyte Gulf. 24–26 October 1944. pp. 227–235. Part I. Preliminaries. p. 236. Part II. Battle of Surigao Strait, Samar and Cape Engaño. pp. 236–243. Battle of Surigao Strait. pp. 244–250. Battle off Samar. pp. 251–253. Battle off Cape Engaño. p. 254. Summary of Battles for Leyte Gulf. pp. 255–257. Annex B. *Princeton-Birmingham* disaster. pp. 257–263. Annex C. Comments. pp. 264–272. Photographs.
pp. 274–318: Operations in the Pacific Ocean Areas during the month of November 1944. Submitted by Commander-in-Chief U.S. Pacific Fleet and Pacific Ocean Areas. Report dated 1 June 1945. p. 277. Part I. Introduction. pp. 277–278: Part II. Losses. pp. 279–298: Part III. North Pacific. p. 278. Part IV. Central Pacific. pp. 298–303: Part V. Submarines. pp. 303–309: Part VI. Southwest Pacific. p. 310. Part VII. Miscellaneous. pp. 311–315. Annex A. Japanese suicide plane tactics in the Philippines campaign. p. 315. Annex B. Comments. pp. 316–318. Photographs.
Note: The files before p. 176 (which include the monthly reports between February and August 1943 ref. pp. 97–195) and after p. 319 (which include the monthly reports between December 1944 and August 1945 ref. pp. 319–697) were examined but seemingly did not carry material germane to the battle of Leyte Gulf.

ADM 199.1494. Admiralty: War History Cases and Papers. Second World War. U.S. operations in Pacific Ocean: Action Reports.
pp. 1–6: Report of the sinking of U.S.S. *Princeton* on 24 October 1944. Report dated 22 November 1944. pp. 7–109: Battle of the Philippines. U.S. Action Report, including loss of U.S.S. *Princeton*. Report dated 9 December 1944. pp. 110–130: Second Battle of the Philippines. Cruiser-destroyer sweep for crippled enemy warships. Report dated 19 December 1944. pp. 131–157: U.S.S. *Gatling*. Action Report. 24–27 October 1944. Western

Pacific. Report dated 5 December 1944. pp. 158–189: Battle of the Philippines. Action Report. Commander Task Group 38.3. 24–25 October 1944. Report dated 10 December 1944. pp. 190–201: Commander Battle Division 9. Action Report. 24–25 October. Philippines. Report dated 21 December 1944. pp. 202–208: U.S.S. *Santa Fe*. Preliminary Action Report. 18–30 October 1944. Battle of the Philippines. Report dated 5 January 1945. pp. 209–254: U.S.S. *Santa Fe*. Action Report. 18–30 October 1944. Battle of the Philippines. Report dated 9 December 1944. pp. 255–265: Commander Cruiser Division 13. (The *Santa Fe*). Action Report. 25 October 1944. Philippines Area. Report dated 13 December 1944. pp. 266–309: U.S.S. *Lexington*. Action Report of the engagement of enemy fleet within the Sibuyan Sea on 24 October 1944 and east of Luzon on 25 October 1944. Report dated 23 December 1944. pp. 310–317: U.S.S. *Alabama*. Action Report. Mindanao Sea. 24–25 October 1944. Battle of Philippines. Report dated 10 November 1944.

ADM 199.1495. Admiralty: War History Cases and Papers, Second World War. U.S. operations in the Surigao Strait, Philippines: Action Reports.
pp. 1–24: U.S.S. *Boise*. Action against Japanese force in Surigao Strait, 25 October 1944. Report dated 30 October 1944. pp. 25–52: U.S.S. *Pennsylvania*. Action Report. 24–25 October 1944. Surigao Strait. Report dated 18 November 1944. pp. 53–78: U.S.S. *Maryland*. Action Report. 24–25 October 1944. Surigao Strait. Report dated 13 December 1944. pp. 79–139: U.S.S. *Gambier Bay*. Action Report. 20–25 October 1944. Philippine Area. Report dated 27 November 1944. pp. 140–155: U.S.S. *Phoenix*. Action Report. Surigao Strait. Philippine Islands. 25 October 1944. Report dated 26 October 1944. pp. 156–209: U.S.S. *St. Lo*. Action Report. Battle off Samar. 25 October 1944. Report dated 25 November 1944. pp. 210–228: Commander Battle Division 3. Action Report. Battle of Surigao Strait. 24–25 October 1944. Report dated 24 November 1944. pp. 229–237: Task Group 77.3. Leyte. Report dated 3 November 1944. pp. 238–253: U.S.S. *Mississippi*. Battle of Surigao Strait. 25 October 1944. Report dated 21 November 1944. pp. 254–260: U.S.S. *Maryland*. Surigao Strait. Action Report. 24–25 October 1944. ND. pp. 261–275: U.S.S. *Newcomb*. Action Report. 24–25 October 1944. Report dated 31 October 1944. pp. 276–281: U.S.S. *Mississippi*. Battle of Surigao Strait. 25 October 1944. Report dated 5 December 1944. pp. 282–290. Endorsement of U.S.S. *Pennsylvania*'s Action Report. Surigao Strait. Dated 24 November 1944. pp. 291–298: Commander Task Group 77.2. Action Report. Battle of Surigao Strait. 24–25 October 1944. Report dated 6 December 1944. pp. 299–303: Commander Task Unit 77.2.1. U.S.S. *Maryland*. Action Report. Surigao Strait. 24–25 October 1944. Report dated 19 January 1945. pp. 304–322: H.M.A.S. *Shropshire*. Battle Report of Action of 25 October 1944. Surigao Strait. Report dated 4 November 1944. pp. 323–338: U.S.S. *Killen*. Action Report. Surigao Strait. 25 October 1944. Report dated 28 October 1944. pp. 339–355: H.M.A.S. *Shropshire*. Battle Report of Action of 25 October 1944. Surigao Strait. Report dated 4 November 1944. pp. 356–369: U.S.S. *Killen*. Action Report. Surigao Strait. 25 October 1944. Report dated 28 October 1944. pp. 370–379: U.S.S. *St. Lo*. Action Report. War Damage Report. 25 October 1944. Philippines. Report dated 21 November 1944.

ADM 199.1505. Admiralty: War History Cases and Papers, Second World War. U.S. operations in the Philippines: action reports.
pp. 1–35: Operations against shipping in Visayas and strikes against Luzon and Yap by Task Group 38.4 in the period 10–22 November 1944. Report dated 24 November 1944. pp. 36–79: U.S.S. *Enterprise*. Action Report. 10–22 November 1944. Philippines. Report dated 26 November 1944. pp. 80–89: U.S.S. *Iowa*. Action Report. 14–27 November

1944. Philippines Area. Report dated 28 November 1944. pp. 90–99: Report of action against Luzon and Ormoc Bay. Philippines Area. 2–24 November 1944. Report dated 25 November 1944. pp. 100–117: Action Report of Manila strikes, 5–6 November 1944. Report dated 6 December 1944. pp. 118–123: Report of Action. Philippines operations. 14–30 November 1944. Report dated 6 December 1944. pp. 124–141: Action Report. 25 November 1944. Off Luzon. U.S.S. *Essex*. Report dated 24 December 1944. pp. 142–147: Action Report of air strikes in Luzon. 5–6 November 1944. Report dated 8 November 1944. pp. 148–158: Action Reports. Carrier air strikes on Luzon. 25 November 1944. Commander Cruiser Division 13 in the *Santa Fe*. Report dated 28 November 1944. pp. 159–173: Action Report for November 1944. Luzon Area. Commander Battle Division 7 (Task Group 38.2). Report dated 30 November 1944. pp. 174–182: Action Report. Air strikes on Luzon area. 5–6 November 1944. Commander Cruiser Division 13 in the *Santa Fe*. Report dated 21 November 1944. pp. 183–186: Action Report of carrier air operations of Task Groups 38.2 and 38.3 against Luzon. Philippine Islands. 25 November 1944. Report dated 9 December 1944. pp. 187–199: Action Report. 22 November–2 December 1944. Luzon. Report dated 8 December 1944. pp. 200–210: U.S.S. *Washington*. Action Report. 22 November to 2 December 1944. (Philippines Area). Report dated 10 December 1944. pp. 211–223: U.S.S. *Santa Fe*. Action Report. 25 November 1944. Luzon. Report dated 9 December 1944. pp. 224–263: Task Group 38.2. Action Report. 14–27 November 1944. Luzon. Report dated 13 December 1944. pp. 264–281: Task Group 38.3. Action Report. Manila strikes. 13–14 November 1944. Report dated 26 December 1944. pp. 282–285: Action Report. 7–15 November 1944. Visayas and Central Luzon. Report dated 15 November 1944. pp. 286–295: Commander Task Group 38.1. U.S.S. *Yorktown*. Action Report. 11–15 November 1944. Philippines Area. Report dated 20 November 1944. pp. 296–308: Commander Task Group 38.2. Action Report. 5–6 November 1944. Luzon. Report dated 16 November 1944. pp. 309–340: Commander Task Group 38.1. Action Report of Attacks on Luzon airfields. 5–6 November 1944. Report dated 29 November 1944.

The following files were examined, but their contents seemingly did not carry material germane to the battle of Leyte Gulf:
ADM 199.78. Operations in the Pacific area. ADM 199.168. Naval operations in the Far East and surrender of Japanese at Singapore: reports.
ADM 199.461. U.S. actions in the Pacific: reports by U.S. officers. 1942–1944.
ADM 199.903.B. War in the Far East: report. 1945.
ADM 199.918. U.S. naval operations against the Japanese: reports, 1943–1944.
ADM 199.1054. U.S. landings in the Philippines: reports. 1944–1945.
ADM 199.1055. U.S. landings in the Philippines: reports. 1944–1945.
ADM 199.1056. U.S. landings in the Philippines: reports. 1944–1945.
The contents of this file are unnumbered but contain two relevant documents. The first of these is Leyte Operation. Action Report. Commander Amphibious Group 8. This 34-page report is dated 29 November 1944. The second, a 106-page report dated 8 November 1944, is entitled Leyte (Philippines) Operation. British Combined Operations Observers' Report.
ADM 199.1506. Admiralty: War History Cases and Papers, Second World War. American operations in Luzon and Mindoro: Action Reports.
ADM 199.1507. American operations in Luzon, Formosa, Camrahn Bay, etc. Action Reports.
ADM 199.1512. American operations in the Philippines (Lingayen, Luzon), Saigon, etc. Action Reports.

ADM 199.1523. Naval Operations in the Pacific. 1943–1945. This file contains the July 1944 monthly report (pp. 70–118) as well as Commander Task Force 34. U.S.S. *Washington*. Action Report. 26 August–6 October 1944. Western Pacific. Report dated 29 November 1944 (pp. 167–171).

SECONDARY SOURCES

Admiralty Historical Section. ADM 234/365, BR 1736(41)/CB 3081(30). *Battle Summary No. 40. Battle for Leyte Gulf, 23rd–26th October 1944.* London: Naval Staff, 1947.

Appelman, Roy E., et al. *Okinawa: The Last Battle.* United States Army in World War II: The War in the Pacific. Washington, D.C.: Office of the Chief of Military History, Department of the Army, 1948.

Baldwin, Hanson W. "Leyte Gulf: Kinkaid Vs. Kurita, etc." In *Great Naval Battles of the Twentieth Century,* ed. William H. Honan. London: Robson Books, 1993.

Barlow, Jeffrey G. "The U.S. Navy's Fight against the Kamikazes." In *New Interpretations in Naval History: Selected Papers from the Tenth Naval History Symposium Held at the United States Naval Academy, 11–13 September 1991,* ed. Jack Sweetman, pp. 398–418. Annapolis, Md.: U.S. Naval Academy, 1991.

Bateson, Charles. *The War with Japan: A Concise History.* London: Barrie and Rockliff, 1968.

Belote, James H., and William M. Belote. *Titans of the Seas: The Development and Operations of Japanese and American Carrier Task Forces during World War II.* New York: Harper & Row, 1975.

Blair, Clay. *Silent Victory: The U.S. Submarine War against Japan.* Philadelphia: Lippincott, 1975.

Breyer, Siegfried, with Alfred Kurti (translator). *Battleships and Battle Cruisers, 1905–1970: Historical Development of the Capital Ship.* London: Macdonald and Jane's, 1973.

Brown, David. *Kamikaze.* New York: Gallery Books, 1990.

Buell, Thomas B. *Master of Sea Power: A Biography of Fleet Admiral Ernest J. King.* Boston: Little, Brown, 1980.

Cannon, M. Hamlin. *Leyte: The Return to the Philippines.* United States Army in World War II: The War in the Pacific. Washington, D.C.: Office of the Chief of Military History, Department of the Army, 1954.

Carter, Kit C., and Robert Mueller. *U.S. Army Air Forces in World War II: Combat Chronology, 1941–1945.* Washington, D.C.: Office of the Chief of Military History, Department of the Army, 1960.

Carter, Worrell Reed. *Beans, Bullets, and Black Oil: The Story of Fleet Logistics Afloat in the Pacific during World War II.* Washington, D.C.: Department of the Navy, 1952.

Chesneau, Roger. *Aircraft Carriers of the World, 1914 to the Present: An Illustrated Encyclopedia*. London: Arms and Armour Press, 1984.

Chihaya Masataka and Abe Yasuo. *Profile Warship No. 22: I.J.N. Yukikaze: Destroyer 1939–1970*. Windsor: Profile Publications, 1972.

Cohen, Jerome B. *Japan's Economy in War and Reconstruction*. Minneapolis: University of Minnesota Press, 1949.

Conway's All the World's Fighting Ships, 1922–1946. London: Conway Maritime Press, 1980.

Cutler, Thomas J. *The Battle of Leyte Gulf. 23–26 October 1944. The Dramatic Full Story, Based on the Latest Research, of the Greatest Naval Battle in History*. New York: HarperCollins, 1994.

D'Albas, Andrieu, with Anthony Rippon (translator). *Death of a Navy: The Fleets of the Mikado in the Second World War, 1941–1945*. London: Hale, 1957.

Department of Military Art and Engineering, U.S. Military Academy. *The War with Japan: Part II—August 1942–December 1944*. West Point, N.Y.: U.S.M.A., 1945.

Dickson, W. D. *The Battle of the Philippine Sea*. London: Ian Allan, 1975.

Dictionary of American Naval Fighting Ships, Volumes I–VIII. Washington, D.C.: Department of the Navy, 1963–1981.

Drea, Edward J. *MacArthur's ULTRA: Code Breaking and the War against Japan, 1942–1945*. Lawrence: University Press of Kansas, 1992.

Dull, Paul S. *A Battle History of the Imperial Japanese Navy (1941–1945)*. Annapolis, Md.: Naval Institute Press, 1978.

Ellis, John. *One Day in a Very Long War: Wednesday, 25 October 1944*. London: Pimlico, 1999.

Falk, Stanley L. *Decision at Leyte*. New York: Norton, 1966.

Feifer, George. *The Battle of Okinawa: The Blood and the Bomb*. Guilford: The Lyons Press, 2001.

Field, James A., Jr. *The Japanese at Leyte Gulf: The Sho Operation*. Princeton, N.J.: Princeton University Press, 1947.

Francillon, René J. *Japanese Aircraft of the Pacific War*. London: Putnam, 1970.

Fukuda Yukihiro. *Rengokantai: Saipan Reite kaisenki [The Combined Fleet: The Battles of Saipan and Leyte]*. Tokyo: Jiji tsushinsha, 1981.

Fukudome Shigeru, Vice Admiral. "The Air Battle off Taiwan." In *The Japanese Navy in World War II: In the Words of Former Japanese Naval Officers*, ed. David C. Evans, Chapter 10. Annapolis, Md.: Naval Institute Press, 1986.

Gailey, Harry A. *Peleliu 1944*. Annapolis, Md.: Nautical and Aviation Publishing Company of America, 1983.

———. *The War in the Pacific: From Pearl Harbor to Tokyo Bay*. Novato, Calif.: Presidio, 1995.

Garand, George W., and Truman R. Strobridge. *Western Pacific Operations*. History of U.S. Marine Corps Operations in World War II, Volume IV. Washington, D.C.: Historical Branch, U.S. Marine Corps, 1971.

Garzke, William H., Jr., and Robert O. Dulin, Jr. *Battleships: Axis and Neutral Battleships of World War II*. Annapolis: Naval Institute Press, 1985.

Hall, George M. *The Fifth Star: High Command in an Era of Global War*. Westport, Conn.: Praeger, 1994.

Halsey, William F., and J. Bryan III. *Admiral Halsey's Story*. New York: McGraw Hill, 1947.

Hashimoto Mochitsura, with E. H. M. Colegrave (translator). *Sunk: The Story of the Japanese Submarine Fleet, 1942–1945*. London: Cassell, 1954.

Hayashi Saburo, in collaboration with Alvin D. Coox. *Kōgun: The Japanese Army in the Pacific War.* Baltimore: Marine Corps Association, 1959.

Hayes, Grace Person. *The History of the Joint Chiefs of Staff in World War II: The War against Japan.* Annapolis, Md.: Naval Institute Press, 1982.

Holmes, Wilfred J. *Double-Edged Secrets: U.S. Naval Intelligence Operations in the Pacific during World War II.* Annapolis, Md.: Naval Institute Press, 1979.

Howarth, Stephen. *Men of War: Great Naval Leaders of World War II.* New York: St. Martin's Press, 1993.

Hoyt, Edwin P. *The Battle of Leyte Gulf: The Death Knell of the Japanese Fleet.* New York: Weybright and Talley, 1972.

———. *The Kamikazes.* London: Halker, 1984.

Inoguchi Rikihei and Nakajima Tadashi, with Roger Pineau. *The Divine Wind: Japan's Kamikaze Force in World War II.* Annapolis, Md.: Naval Institute Press, 1958.

Ito Masanori, with Andrew Y. Kuroda and Roger Pineau (translators). *The End of the Imperial Navy.* London: Weidenfeld and Nicolson, 1956.

Japanese National Institute of Defence Studies. *Kaigun shogo sakusen (1) and (2): Firipin oki kaisen [Navy Sho Operation, Volumes I and II: Battle off the Philippines].* Official War History Series (Senshi Sosho), Volumes 37 and 56. Tokyo: Asagumo Sinbunsha, 1970; 1972.

Jentschura, Hansgeorg, Dieter Jung, and Peter Michel. *Warships of the Imperial Navy, 1869–1945.* London: Arms and Armour Press, 1977.

Kahn, David. *The Code-Breakers.* New York: Macmillan, 1967.

King, Ernest J., and Walter Muir Whitehill. *Fleet Admiral King: A Naval Record.* London: Eyre and Spottiswoode, 1953.

Koyanagi Tomiji, Rear Admiral. "The Battle of Leyte Gulf." In *The Japanese Navy in World War II: In the Words of Former Japanese Naval Officers,* ed. David C. Evans, Chapter 11. Annapolis, Md.: Naval Institute Press, 1986.

Larrabee, Eric. *Commander-in-Chief: Franklin Delano Roosevelt, His Lieutenants and Their War.* New York: Harper & Row, 1987.

Levine, Alan J. *The Pacific War: Japan versus the Allies.* Westport, Conn.: Praeger, 1995.

MacArthur, Douglas. *Reports of General MacArthur: Japanese Operations in the Southwest Pacific Area.* Volume II, Part II. Washington, D.C.: Department of Defense, 1966.

MacIntyre, Donald G. *Leyte Gulf.* New York: Ballantine, 1973.

Manchester, William. *American Caesar: Douglas MacArthur, 1880–1964.* London: Hutchinson, 1979.

McMurtie, Francis E., ed. *Jane's Fighting Ships 1943–1944.* London: Sampson Low, Marston, 1944.

Merrill, James M. *A Sailor's Admiral: A Biography of William F. Halsey.* New York: Thomas Y. Crowell, 1976.

Morison, Samuel Eliot. *History of United States Naval Operations in World War II, Volume XII: Leyte, June 1944–January 1945.* Boston: Little, Brown, 1958.

Naval Staff. ADM 234/379, BR 1735 (50)(6). *Naval Staff History: Second World War. War with Japan.* Volume VI: *The Advance to Japan.* London: Naval Staff, 1959.

O'Connor, Raymond. *The Japanese Navy in World War II.* Annapolis, Md.: Naval Institute Press, 1969.

Pogue, Forrest C. *George C. Marshall: Ordeal and Hope.* New York: Viking, 1965.

Polmar, Norman. *Aircraft Carriers: A Graphic History of Carrier Aviation and Its Influence on World Events.* London: Macdonald, 1969.

Potter, E. B. *Admiral Arleigh Burke: A Biography.* New York: Random House, 1990.

————. *Bull Halsey*. Annapolis, Md.: Naval Institute Press, 1985.

————. *Nimitz*. Annapolis, Md.: Naval Institute Press, 1976.

Potter, E. B., ed. *Sea Power: A Naval History*. Englewood Cliffs, N. J.: Prentice-Hall, 1960.

Potter, E. B., and Chester W. Nimitz. *Triumph in the Pacific: The Navy's Struggle against Japan*. Englewood Cliffs, N.J.: Prentice-Hall, 1963.

Potter, E. B., and Chester W. Nimitz, eds. *The Great Sea War: The Story of Naval Action in World War II*. London: Harrap, 1961.

Prados, John. *The Combined Fleet Decoded: The Secret History of American Intelligence and the Japanese Navy in World War II*. New York: Random House, 1995.

Reynolds, Clark G. *The Fast Carriers: The Forging of an Air Navy*. Annapolis, Md.: Naval Institute Press, 1992.

Rohwer, J., and G. Hummelchen. *Chronology of the War at Sea, 1939–1945*. The Naval History of World War II. Annapolis, Md.: Naval Institute Press, 1992.

Romanus, Charles F., and Riley Sunderland. *United States Army in World War II: China-Burma-India Theater—Stilwell's Command Problems*. Washington, D.C.: Office of Military History, U.S. Army, 1956.

Roscoe, Theodore. *United States Destroyer Operations in World War II*. Annapolis, Md.: Naval Institute Press, 1953.

————. *United States Submarine Operations in World War II*. Annapolis, Md.: Naval Institute Press, 1979.

Sato Kazumasa. *Reite oki kaisen* [*The Battle off Leyte*]. Volumes I and II. Tokyo: Kojinsha, 1998.

Silverthorne, Paul H. *U.S. Warships of World War II*. London: Ian Allan, 1965.

Smith, Robert Ross. *United States Army in World War II: The War in the Pacific. Triumph in the Philippines*. Washington, D.C.: Office of the Chief of Military History, Department of the Army, 1963.

Smith, S. E., ed. *The United States Navy in World War II*. New York: William Morrow, 1966.

Sturton, Ian, ed. *All the World's Battleships: 1906 to the Present*. London: Conway Maritime Press, 2000.

Sweetman, Jack, ed. *Great American Naval Battles*. Annapolis, Md.: Naval Institute Press, 1998.

Taylor, Theodore. *The Magnificent Mitscher*. Annapolis, Md.: Naval Institute Press, 1991.

Tohmatsu Haruo and H. P. Willmott. *A Gathering Darkness: The Coming of War to the Far East and the Pacific, 1921–1942*. Wilmington, Del.: Scholarly Resources, 2004.

Toland, John. *The Rising Sun: The Decline and Fall of the Japanese Empire 1936–1945*. London: Cassell, 1971.

Tuchman, Barbara W. *Sand against the Wind: Stilwell and the American Experience in China, 1911–1945*. London: Macmillan, 1971.

Ugaki Matome, Chihaya Masataka, trans., and Donald M. Goldstein and Katherine V. Dillon, eds. *Fading Victory: The Diary of Admiral Matome Ugaki, 1941–1945*. Pittsburgh: University of Pittsburgh Press, 1991.

Watts, Anthony J., and Brian G. Gordon. *The Imperial Japanese Navy*. London: Macdonald, 1971.

Wheeler, Gerald E. *Kinkaid of the Seventh Fleet: A Biography of Admiral Thomas C. Kinkaid*. Washington, D.C.: Naval Historical Center, 1995.

Whitley, M. J. *Battleships of World War II: An International Encyclopedia*. London: Arms and Armour Press, 1998.

———. *Cruisers of World War II: An International Encyclopedia*. London: Arms and Armour Press, 1996.

———. *Destroyers of World War II: An International Encyclopedia*. London: Cassell, 2000.

Williams, Mary H., compiler. *Chronology, 1941–1945*. United States Army in World War II: Special Studies. Washington, D.C.: Office of the Chief of Military History, Department of the Army, 1960.

Willmott, H. P. *The Barrier and the Javelin: Japanese and Allied Pacific Strategies, February to June 1942*. Annapolis, Md.: Naval Institute Press, 1983.

———. *Battleship*. London: Cassell, 2002.

———. *Grave of a Dozen Schemes: British Naval Planning and the War against Japan, 1943–1945*. Annapolis, Md.: Naval Institute Press, 1996.

———. *The Great Crusade: A New Complete History of the Second World War*. London: Michael Joseph, 1989.

———. *June 1944*. Annapolis, Md.: Naval Institute Press, 1996.

———. *The Second World War in the Far East*. London: Cassell, 1999.

———. *The War with Japan: The Period of Balance, May 1942–October 1943*. Wilmington, Del.: Scholarly Resources, 2002.

Woodward, C. Vann. *The Battle for Leyte Gulf*. New York: Macmillan, 1947.

Y'Blood, William T. *The Little Giants: U.S. Escort Carriers against Japan*. Annapolis, Md.: Naval Institute Press, 1987.

Yoshimura Akira. *Battleship Musashi: The Making and Sinking of the World's Biggest Warship*. London: Kodansha International, 1999.

INDEX

Formations, formation commanders, ships, and the ships' commanding officers cited but once in the appendixes are not listed separately in this index.

Ships are listed separately at the end of the index and alphabetically by name, not type. Operational formations are cited; administration formations (e.g., warship squadrons and divisions) are not cited even when they appear in text.

Maps and Appendixes are listed separately.

ALLIED WARSHIPS AND AUXILIARIES

JAPANESE WARSHIPS AND AUXILIARIES

H. P. WILLMOTT was educated at the Universities of Liverpool and London and the National Defense University and has been a lecturer at various establishments in Britain and the United States, including Temple University and the University of Memphis, and was a visiting lecturer with the Royal Norwegian Air Force Academy at Trondheim. He has written extensively upon warfare in general and the Second World War in particular. Among his publications are *Empires in the Balance*; *The Barrier and the Javelin*; *The Great Crusade* (a military reinterpretation of the Second World War); *Grave of a Dozen Schemes*; and *When Men Lost Faith in Reason: Reflections on Warfare in the Twentieth Century*. Formerly with reserve airborne forces, currently he is a visiting lecturer with Greenwich Maritime Institute, University of Greenwich, and (2004–2005) holds the Mark W. Clark chair in the Department of History, The Citadel, The Military College of South Carolina.

The process of aging if not exactly maturing has resulted in elevation from the position of *enfant terrible* of British military history to that of *papa terrible*; his last book, *When Men Lost Faith in Reason: Reflections on Warfare in the Twentieth Century*, was to have been subtitled *A Bad-Tempered Reconsideration of Twentieth-Century Warfare*. In any event it is likely to cost him whatever professional reputation he commands. But the book is interesting, and in 2002 he had no fewer than four books published.

He is married with one wife, two children, three dogs, one accountant but no mortgage to support. He misses his dogs when he is in the United States. One medal and no prospects.